AF654542

FOREST RESOURCES AND SUSTAINABLE DEVELOPMENT

By the same author

Planning for Forest Resource and Bio-Diversity Management: Principles, Organization and Methodologies.

About the Author

Kailash Chandra Bebarta, an IFS, presently works in a senior position in the Forest Department, Chattisgarh. Getting Master's Degree in Zoology, he earned Post-Graduate Diploma in Forestry and Business Administration. Also, he has been an Associate of Indian Forest School, Dehradun. Besides many research papers, Mr. Bebarta has to his credit two books, entitled, *Teak: Ecology, Silviculture, Management and Profitability,* and *Planning for Forest Resources and Biodiversity Management.*

FOREST RESOURCES AND SUSTAINABLE DEVELOPMENT

Principles, Perspectives and Practices

KAILASH CHANDRA BEBARTA, IFS

CONCEPT PUBLISHING COMPANY, NEW DELHI-110059

All rights reserved. No part of this work may be reproduced, stored in a retrieval system, or transmitted in any form or by any means electronic, mechanical, photocopying, recording or otherwise, without the prior written permission of the copyright owner and the publisher.

ISBN : 81-8069-132-2 (PB)

First Published 2004

© Kailash Chandra Bebarta (*b*. 1957)

Published and Printed by
Ashok Kumar Mittal
Concept Publishing Company
A/15-16, Commercial Block, Mohan Garden
New Delhi-110059 (INDIA)

Phone : 25351460, 25351794
Fax : 091-11-25357103
Email : publishing@conceptpub.com

Preface

Today humanity stands at a crucial junction in its development. Never before have the earth's resources including forests have been so greatly affected by ours presence. There is now a widespread recognition that no resource is finite and its sustainable development is indispensable for our survival.

Sustainable development of forests has assumed immense priority in the international policy agenda, particularly after United Nation's Conference on Environment and Development (UNCED) in 1992. Now there is a great challenge to reconcile the role of forests in meeting national socio-economic and environmental objectives as well as the global environmental and socio-economic interests of the community of nations.

The forest and scientific communities are handling the onerous task of defining sustainable forest development, formulating an acceptable conceptual framework and establishing approaches and process for the practice of sustainable forest development to meet multiple human needs. This book is an attempt towards finding solutions to such tasks.

Keeping in view the comprehensive nature of the subjects, this book has been divided into three parts. The first part, which includes three chapters, presents a study on environmental problems and global forest resource crisis. The second part which includes three chapters deals with the concept of sustainable development per se and its application in the field of environment and forestry. The third part, which contains four chapters, deals with the concepts and principles of sustainable forest management (SFM). It also presents an outlook on policy and strategies for SFM on a holistic basis.

The chapter 1 has been prepared to highlight the factors and conditions, tangible and intangible that lead to manifestations of global environmental crisis of which deforestation is a critical part. In the beginning, the factors and conditions, which are at the root of the environmental crisis, have been discussed at length. Then the manifestations of such factors and conditions in the form of different environmental problems like global warming, endangered resources, green-house gas emission, industrial air pollution, and the decline of productive ecosystem and living resources have been discussed.

In the past forests were looked upon from local or national context. But over the years, especially after the Rio Summit, forests have provided a global context. The chapter 2 attempts to provide a perspective on widening importance of forests in the world. It also presents an account of distribution of forests in different parts of the globe. The purpose of presenting a short overview on perspective and resource availability is to sensitise the readers about the pace of change in forest resource dynamics in the globe. Information on the extent, condition, types and productivity of forests is also important for efforts to improve forest management worldwide and to assess forests' ability to provide the goods and services to the society. This provides a robust context and necessary backdrop for the discussion on sustainable forest development in the ensuing chapters.

The evolution of human civilisation over the past 8000 years, and especially expansion and intensification of human activities over the past two centuries have brought great changes in the area and character of forests globally. But over the recent years, there has been a clear global trend towards a massive loss of forested area. The current trends are towards acceleration of the loss of primary forest and progressive reduction in the quality of such forests. The chapter 3 attempts to depict the dimension of forest crisis on a global perspective. It also provides an account of reasons, direct and indirect, for the present forest crisis.

'Sustainable Development' is a catchy phrase developed in the penultimate decade of the twentieth century. The term first came into focus in the 'World Conservation Strategy' published by the World Conservation Union (IUCN) in 1980. It gained more prominence with the publication of the Bruntland Report in the year 1987. The principles regarding sustainable development received global acceptability after United Nations Conference on Environment and Development (UNCD) held in Rio de Janeiro in June 1992. It initiated thinking towards natural resource conservation and sustainable development on a global scale. However, the debate on principles of sustainable development and its implication on economic development continues to date. In this context, the chapter 4 on 'sustainable development' has been prepared to bring forth the concepts, basic tenets and widening perspective on sustainable development. An attempt has been made to recapitulate the relevance of Gandhian principles and ethics to the concept of sustainable development.

Sustainable development depends on how mankind uses the

biosphere. Rather, social and economic development of society on the basis of sustainability principles relies on pattern and efficiency of resource use. If resource is used in a sustainable way, then such a development is possible. Otherwise, it is not. To undertake sustainable development approach, it is necessary to understand all encompassing characteristics of natural resources. Therefore, the chapter 5 has been developed to provide the readers a clear perspective on natural resources, especially renewable resources, their limitations, principles governing sustainable development and use of such renewable resources. It also presents a succinct picture of politics of sustainable use.

Sustaining both forests and development simultaneously is a daunting task. However, steps have already been initiated at every level to address this task. The journey from old paradigm of growth to new paradigm of sustainable development, though a protracted one, has already begun. National and international initiatives, measuring to the intensity required, are already afoot. The Earth Summit constituted a watershed in the field of natural resource management. The chapter 6 highlights major initiatives — international and regional, governmental and non-governmental — to promote sustainable forest management. A short account of natural resource use with a historical perspective has been appended in the beginning of this chapter. A detailed discussion about the Earth Summit (1992) has been presented with a specific focus on forest development. The steps taken in international arena in the post-Rio period has also been enumerated at reasonable length so that they provide a distinct perspective on global changes in forest policy, legislation, management and practices.

Forests are the planet's largest and most important terrestrial ecosystem. They have profound influence on the structure and functions of human habitat locally and globally. They constitute the largest reservoir of plants and animals on the land. They sustain much of world's diversity of life embodying stupendous genetic wealth developed over evolutionary time. They provide innumerable goods and services to human society. They provide the means for their livelihoods as well as succor to millions of people who live close to forests. They affect the quality of atmosphere and temperature regime, which in turn regulate global and local climate. They provide spiritual, aesthetic and symbolic value for millions of people.

All these benefits from forests can continue to flow to society, present and future, on a sustained basis. But this is possible if the forest resources are managed on the basis of sustainability principles. Managing forests sustainably necessitates an elaborate management system and practices to maximise the achievement of aforesaid objectives for the benefits of society at large and consolidate them on a sustainable basis. The basic tenets of such an management system and practices are explained in the chapter 7.

There may be certain elements, which will be highly appropriate to a situation in a country and certain elements may not be relevant. Again the degree of relevance of any element to a country is generally determined in the context of that country or locality's need. The chapter 8 provides an overview of such critical elements of sustainable forest management practices.

Sustainable development requires integrating economic viability and human development with the necessity to protect the environment and sustain indefinitely the natural resource base. Considered in this backdrop, sustainable forest management requires integration of environmental, social and economic dimension of forests into the policies and practices for utilising and managing forests, so that economic and social needs are met while leaving forests capable of fulfilling their environmental functions enduring.

Forest management, of late, has become far more complex by the emphasis on aspects of ecological, social and economic sustainability. In order to address this, it is necessary to initiate, among other things, major reforms in policy and legislative environment. What is more important is the fact that supportive environment and conditions are also required to make the policy and legal framework to work in the desired direction. The chapter 9 focuses on critical policy elements along with the conditions, which hold key to success of sustainable forest management.

Success in sustainable forest management depends on strategies too. Strategies translate the policies into actions on the ground. They set the objectives for carrying out activities, which ultimately lead to attainment of the goal. The chapter 10 deals at length with the dynamics of technical aspects of sustainable forest management and strategies required for addressing the management issues. A SFM strategy consists of a broad direction for forest conservation, development, sustainable use, equity based benefit sharing, etc. The purpose of evolving strategies is to determine and communicate a picture of the kind of working, that an organisation visualises. It provides a workable framework for guiding thinking and action at all levels.

The book is written for the readers, students and professionals who are interested in contemporary forest management issues or pursuing studies in natural resources and forestry in a global perspective. It represents an attempt to integrate knowledge and processes relating forests and forest management across a wide array of disciplines and focuses on the underlying environmental, economic and social sciences together so that forestry can be redefined, restudied and reinvented in the backdrop of new paradigm of SD.

I am indebted to my late father, who encouraged me to pursue forestry and it is a choice, which I, inspite of a traumatic phase in my professional career, have never regretted. My colleagues in Indian Forest Service, especially in Madhya Pradesh and Chhattisgarh State where I commenced my career have been generous in sharing their knowledge and experience with me in many occasions. I have benefited greatly from formal and informal interaction with people in other allied disciplines. My greatest debt, however, is to my wife Sushma for encouraging me to undertake the onerous task of writing a book on forest resources and sustainable development with global perspective. Notwithstanding the efforts put in writing this book, the drive to learn and update myself continues unabatedly. Therefore, valuable suggestions from enlightened readers will be gratefully accepted and acknowledged.

Raipur **KAILASH CHANDRA BEBARTA**
5th July, 2003

are interested in contemporary forest management issues or pursuing studies in natural resources and forestry in a global perspective. It represents an attempt to integrate knowledge and processes relating forests and forest management across a wide array of disciplines and focuses on the underlying environmental, economic and social sciences together so that forestry can be redefined, restudied and reinvented in the backdrop of new paradigm of SD.

I am indebted to my late father, who encouraged me to pursue forestry and it is a choice, which I, inspite of a traumatic phase in my professional career, have never regretted. My colleagues in Indian Forest Service, especially in Madhya Pradesh and Chhattisgarh State where I commenced my career have been generous in sharing their knowledge and experience with me on many occasions. I have benefited greatly from formal and informal interaction with people in other allied disciplines. My greatest debt, however, is to my wife Sushma for encouraging me to undertake the onerous task of writing a book on forest resources and sustainable development with global perspective. Notwithstanding the efforts put in writing this book, the drive to learn and update myself continues unabatedly. Therefore, valuable suggestions from enlightened readers will be gratefully accepted and acknowledged.

Raipur
5th May 2005

KAILASH CHANDRA MEBARTA

Contents

Part II: Sustainable Development: Concept, Perspectives and Performance

Part III: Sustainable Forest Management: Principles and Practices

List of Tables

List of Figures

List of Boxes

PART I

GLOBAL ENVIRONMENT AND FOREST RESOURCES: AN OVERVIEW

1

THE ENVIRONMENTAL OUTLOOK

A Global Perspective

Emerging environmental problems worldwide have posed serious challenge to survival of mankind. In the last century, environmental crisis has risen from regional to planetary level. Fears of spreading deserts, shrinkage of forests, shortage of fresh water, accumulation of green house gases and erosion of biological diversity gripped the world. Looking at the increasing incidences of environmental problems like acid rain, deforestation, draught, erratic rain fall pattern in many parts of the world, such fears are not unfounded. What is more disconcerting is the fact that the conditions, responsible for such situations, are building up every day in every parts of the world with increasing intensity.

Environment crisis is the outcome of population explosion and increase in consumption. This apart, technology has also facilitated the process. If this trend goes unchecked, the consequence will be very grave. Therefore, it is high time that we immediately address the crisis and draw a comprehensive strategy to cope with it. Moreover, the root cause of this crisis lies primarily in population explosion, over-consumption, inequality, poverty and technology. These factors initiate a process that leaves a destructive impact on environment directly. Population — the number of people living on this earth; consumption – the amount of resources each person consumes; technology – the element that decides how much space and resources should be used, and how much waste is to be produced to meet consumptive needs. Environmental impact is the result of all these three factors multiplied together. Again the conditions like poverty and inequality accentuate the process of population explosion and unequal consumption; as a result the total environmental impact on society is increased manifold.

This chapter has been prepared to highlight the factors and conditions, tangible and intangible that lead to manifestations of global environmental crisis of which deforestation is a critical part. In the beginning, the factors and conditions, which are at the root of the environmental crisis, have been discussed at length. Then the manifestations of such factors and conditions in the form of different environmental problems like global warming, endangered resources, green house gas emission, industrial air pollution, the decline of productive ecosystem and living resources have been discussed with necessary data support. In the end of this chapter, there is an attempt to focus on the contours of the changing paradigm of development in the world.

Factors and Conditions

Factors are the causes, direct or proximate, of environmental crisis. The government policies, legislation, programmes and lack of strong governance systems, etc. are some of the conditions, which exacerbate the environmental crisis. In as rough estimate, it has been found that 70 per cent of the world's environmental crisis is attributed to population explosion and rest 30 per cent is attributed to other factor like increased consumption of natural resources.

Population

Population growth remains central to many of the global environmental problems. Over the last two centuries, population of the world increased menacingly. In the year 1800 the world population was one billion. It reached two billion in the year 1930 *i.e.*, after a span of 130 years. Then it reached three billion in the year 1960 *i.e.*, after thirty years. Then it took about eleven to fourteen years to add one billion to the world population (See Table 1.1). Now, as the present trend continues, another billion of people will be added to the existing global population in every eleven years. In the year 2025, it is expected that the world population will be about 8.5 billion (See Table 1.2). What is disturbing is the fact that most of the population growth takes place in the third world countries where the resource management is very poor. Apart from this, about 60 per cent of the future increase in population will be in those third world countries. Among all the continents, Africa has the highest projected growth rate, followed by Asia and Latin America.

The linkage between population and environmental degradation was always visible in ancient civilisation, but it was more localized in nature. With the passage of time, industrial growth led to multiplication of per capita consumption of natural resources. Consequently, per capita level of pollution and environmental degradation increased manifold. As that growth continues, air, water, and pollution and depletion of natural resources became more widespread. This cumulatively led to increase in toxic industrial production which impacted adversely on living resources.

Table 1.1: Trend in World Population Growth

Year	*Period for Increase in Years*	*Population Size in Billion*
1800	0	1
1930	130	2
1960	30	3
1974	14	4
1987	13	5
1998	11	6

Table 1.2: Population Indicators

Region	*Population (Million) 1994*	*Population (Million) 2025*	*Average Growth Rate 1990-95*	*Urban Growth Rate (%) 1990-95*	*Fertility Rate 1990-95*
Africa	681.7	1,582.5	2.9	4.6	6.0
Asia	3,233.0	4,900.3	1.8	3.5	3.2
Europe	512.0	541.8	0.3	0.7	1.7
Latin America	457.7	701.6	1.8	2.6	3.1
North America	282.7	360.5	1.1	1.3	2.0
Ocenia	27.5	41.3	1.5	1.6	2.5
USSR (former)	284.5	344.5	0.5	1.1	2.3
Developed Countries	1,237.6	1,403.3	0.5	0.9	1.9
LDCs	4,427	7,069.2	2.0	3.7	3.6
World	5,665.5	8,472.5	1.7	2.7	3.3

Source: UN Population Fund (1994, 55-9).

Now, the world population touched 6 billion mark and world economic activity quadrupled in the last century. The pressure of agricultural and industrial development strained the ecosystem of the planet, which consequently led to the beginning of the phase where carrying capacity of the planets resources like soil, forests, oceans, estuaries and atmosphere are transgressed at an alarmingly rate. Since, population and economic activity still continue their growth, the resources of the planet are under tremendous pressure. The rapidity of changes under way is spelled out justifiably in the following passages from 'Our Common Future': "The planet is passing through a period of drastic growth and fundamental change. Our human world of 5 billion must make room in a finite environment for another human world. The population could stabilize at between 8 billion and 14 billion sometime next century, according to UN Projection ... Economic activity has multiplied to create a $13 trillion world economy, and this could grow five or ten-fold in the coming century".

Consumption of Resources

'Sustainable development' does not antagonize man's consumption of maximum possible resources of earth. The main concern is that the present consumption should not affect the future consumption. This is possible if present consumption is limited to the carrying capacity of the earth. If this is not adhered, then, man's survival will be at risk. In the years 1961 to 1985, population growth was responsible for 72 per cent of environmental change and increase in consumption 28 per cent. In developed countries, the population growth explained 46 per cent and consumption pattern 54 per cent (Simmons, 1997).

Many studies conducted by the United Nations Environment Programme (UNEP) and other agencies have pointed out that the present levels of consumption, especially in industrialized countries, are unsustainable. Besides, the developing countries, particularly, the Asian countries are fast getting on to the consumption bandwagon. However, what is more disturbing is the fact that these countries have adopted policies and actions that promote enhanced consumption of natural resources. Today all developing countries are following the unsustainable consumption trends of the industrialized countries. Country after country is encouraging consumption, both domestic and imported goods, under the garb structural reform programmes.

Although the world economy pumped out nearly $41 trillion of goods and services in 1999, 45 per cent of the income went to the 12 per cent of the world's people who live in western industrial countries. "This wealthy minority is largely responsible for the excessive consumption that drives environmental decline," said co-author Molly O. Sheehan, World Watch Research Associate. For example, per capita paper use in industrial nations is 9 times higher than in developing countries. The number of cars per person is about 100 times higher in North America, Western Europe, and Japan than in India or China, according to Vital Signs.

Therefore, world's environmental crisis primarily revolves around the scale at which natural resources are used and wastes are created. The unsustainable scale of consumption of natural resources has been continuing in developed countries since last century too. What is more disturbing is the increasing consumption trends in developing countries. These trends are mind boggling in comparison to developed countries. With respect to developing countries, there is a desperate attempt to step up the industrialisation and economic development by pursuing policies that accelerate the scale of consumption. A synoptic trend of consumption of certain selected items in developing and developed countries is presented in Tables 1.3 to 1.6. A perusal of the current trends in consumption tells that the future of the planet depends on how we shall grapple these issues in the coming years. There is no gainsaying of the fact that these issues need to be addressed on a priority basis, if our present development and civilisation are to be sustained and the dignity and potential of human life enhanced in the time to come.

Table 1.3: Consumption of Selected Items, North/South

Items	*Share (per cent)*		*ADR North/South*	*EDR North/South*
	North	*South*		
Meat	64	36	6	52
Cereals	48	52	3	6
Round wood	46	54	1	6
Paper, etc.	81	19	14	115
Fertilizer	60	40	5	6
Iron and steel	80	20	13	22
Cars	92	8	24	320
Electricity	81	19	13	46
CO_2	70	30	8	27

Note: The Average Disparity Ratio (ADR) is the ratio of per capita consumption levels in North and South. For example, on an average a person in the North eats six times as much meat as a person in the South. The Extreme Disparity Ratio (EDR) is the ratio between the richest and poorest countries, using the USA and India. Thus on average an American eats 52 times as much meat as an Indian. The eastern European countries are included in the North, and the newly industrialised countries of Asia are included in the South. The ADR is smaller than the real disparities between many European countries and low-income countries of Asia and Africa.

Source: Parikh *et al.* (1991).

Table 1.4: A Comparative View of People's Average Consumption in Developed, Developing Countries and World

Consumption per Person in 1991	*Canada*	*USA*	*India*	*World*
CO_2 (emission in tonnes per yr.)	15.2	19.5	0.81	4.2
Purchasing Power (in $ US)	19,320	22,130	1,150	3,800
Vehicles per 100 persons	46	57	0.2	10
Paper consumption (in kilogram/yr)	247	317	2	44
Fossil energy use (in Gigajoules/yr)	250 (234)	287	5	56
Fresh water withdrawal (in cubic Mt./yr)	1,688	1,868	612	644
Ecological Footprint (ha/person)	**4.3**	**5.1**	**0.4**	**1.8**

Source: Wackernagel Mathis and Ress Willium (1996), *Our Ecological Footprint; reducing human impact on the earth;* New Society Publishers, Canada.

Table 1.5: Consumption of Primary Materials in the World Economy in Year 1980

Consumption	*Region*				
	RDE	*NIE*	*ODE*	*ESU*	*World*
Fish	29.5	12.4	20.2	10.3	72.4
Livestock	116.9	41.6	61.3	42.5	262.3
Oil crops	45.6	25.4	68.1	30.9	170.0
Grains	392.5	160.5	644.8	248.3	1,446.1
Root crops	91.0	69.4	237.0	132.9	530.3
Copper	5.8	0.7	0.6	1.4	8.5
Bauxite	11.7	1.3	1.7	1.9	16.6
Nickel	486.2	30.0	33.5	176.4	726.1
Zinc	3.4	0.5	0.5	1.1	5.5
Lead	2.0	0.2	0.3	0.8	3.3
Iron	261.0	42.5	83.1	149.0	535.6
Petroleum	2,300.8	323.0	398.3	619.4	3,641.5
Gas	1,116.6	90.8	96.7	556.1	1,860.2
Coal	1,179.8	38.1	588.5	907.7	2,714.1
Population	845	505	2,711	377	4,438

Note: RDE = Rich and developed economies.
NIE = Newly industrialising economies.
ODE = Other developing economies.
ESU = Eastern Europe and the former Soviet Union.
Crops and minerals are measured in millions of tonnes, except for nickel, which is in thousands of tonnes. Fuels are in millions of tonnes of coal equivalent.

Source: Ayres, Robert U. (Ed.) (1998); *Eco-restructuring; Implications for sustainable development.* United Nations University. Tokyo. Japan.

Table 1.6: Regional Distribution of Consumption of Primary Materials in the World Economy in Year 1980 (in %)

Consumption	*Region*				
	RDE	*NIE*	*ODE*	*ESU*	*World*
Fish	41	17	28	14	100
Livestock	45	16	23	16	100
Oil crops	27	15	40	18	100
Grains	27	11	45	17	100
Root crops	17	13	45	25	100
Copper	68	8	7	16	100
Bauxite	70	8	10	11	100
Nickel	67	4	5	24	100
Zinc	62	9	9	20	100
Lead	61	6	9	24	100
Iron	49	8	16	28	100
Petroleum	63	9	11	17	100
Gas	60	5	5	30	100
Coal	43	1	22	33	100
Population	19	11	61	8	100

Note: RDE = Rich and developed economies.
NIE = Newly industrialising economies.
ODE = Other developing economies.
ESU = Eastern Europe and the former Soviet Union.
Crops and minerals are measured in millions of tonnes, except for nickel which is in thousands of tonnes. Fuels are in millions of tonnes of coal equivalent.

Source: Ayres, Robert U. (Ed) (1998); *Eco-restructuring; Implications for sustainable development*. United Nations University, Tokyo, Japan.

Fresh water is an important renewable natural resource. Water withdrawal and consumption have increased manifolds in the 20th century. What is more disturbing is the fact that the increase is not evenly distributed. In North and Central America and in Asia the increase in water use is stupendous (See Table 1.7).

Table 1.7: World Annual Water Use (Withdrawal and Consumption in Cubic Kilometer)

World/Continent	*Total Withdrawal in 1980*	*Total Consumtion in 1980*	*Increase in Water Withdrawal (in %) Period 1900-1980*
World	3,320	1,950	2,741
Africa	168	128	126
North and Central America	663	224	594
South America	111	71	96
Asia	1,910	1,380	1,496
Europe	435	127	397
Former USSR	353	NA	NA
Oceania	29	15	28

Source: S.L. Kulshrestha (1993); *World Water Resources and regional vulnerability: Impact of future changes.* Luxembourg: HASA, RR-93-10; WRI (1992) World Resources.1992-93.

If the current consumption patterns continue, the ecosystem that provides us with renewable resources could well collapse long before the world runs out of non-renewable resources. There is thus an urgent need to set up a firm agenda on achieving sustainable consumption in the next few years at a global level. Sustainable consumption—a new paradigm pertains to the use of products and services that respond to the basic needs and ensure a better quality of life. There is also a need to raise the levels of consumption of the world's poor to enable them to achieve a minimum acceptable quality of life. According to World Bank, about three billion people, half of world's population live on an income of less than $2 per day. Therefore, sustainable consumption can be achieved by rational use of natural resources in one hand and minimal emissions of waste and pollutants to the ecosystem in the other. It brings together a number of other key issues, such as meeting the basic needs, enhancing the quality of life, improving resource efficiency, increasing the use of renewable energy sources, reducing environmental burden and reducing health risks.

Poverty and Inequality

Poverty and inequality remains the intractable challenge before the world community today. More than 5.6 billion people in the world live in extreme poverty and almost a third of the world's children are undernourished and half of the global population lacks regular access to the most essential drugs (WHO report, 1999). Likewise, inequality world over is increasing day by day. It has been a mater of life and death for the millions of people since poor pays the price of social and economic inequality in every aspects of life. The inequality between rich and poor with respect to income is increasing over the years. This is distinctly evident from the figures given in Table 1.8.

Table 1.8: Ratio of Income of Richest 20 per cent to Poorest 20 per cent of World Population

Year	*Ratio of income*
1960	30:1
1970	32:1
1980	45:1
1989	59:1
1991	61:1

Source: UNDP (1994) and UNDP (1995).

Off late, there has been greater realisation about harmful impacts of poverty on environment. Poverty has crossed its frontiers from just lack of sufficient income for covering the subsistence needs of a person to turning him into a tool to become a potential threat to humanity itself. In the year 1972 at Stockholm Conference on Development, Indira Gandhi, the then Prime Minister of India highlighted the dreadful impact of poverty on environment and said that 'poverty is the worst polluter'. Mahbub ul Haq, has rightly said, 'poverty is no longer contained within national boundaries. It has become globalised. It travels across boundaries, without a passport, in the form of drugs, diseases, pollution, migration, terrorism and political instability."

Since 1980s the number of poor people has been rising in all developing regions expect East Asia. Today, more than one out of five people around the world are living in conditions of extreme poverty, on little more than US$1.00 per day. That means the richest fifth of the world now has about 85 percent of the world's GNP while the poorest fifth has just 1.4 per cent. (Joshi, S. *Times of India*: 07.11.99)

Global disparities are found not just between rich and poor countries, but also between men and women. "Women make up more than two-thirds of the illiterate population and three-fifths of the poor," said Sheehan, "and they account for only 13 per cent of the representatives in national legislatures." Population growth is most rapid in the world's poorest regions, where women often lack access to family planning and education.

"The disparities between rich and poor are equally striking in the digital world," said Sheehan. "Although Internet access is growing rapidly in the developing world, some 87 per cent of all Internet users live in industrial countries. Fewer than 1 per cent of the people in China, India, or the continent of Africa are online." The poor are left behind in the race to cyberspace. Third World debt hit a new high of $2.5 trillion in 1999, with some of the world's poorest nations devoting 30 per cent of their national budgets to debt servicing. Developing countries are also more vulnerable to environmental change, such as the devastating floods and landslides in Venezuela in December 1999. Worsened by deforestation, this disaster killed more than 30,000 people all over the world.

Manifestations of Environmental Crisis

Global Warming

Global warming brings changes in the climatic system, which result in significant, often adverse, impacts on many ecological systems and socio-economic sectors. It has speeded the melting of two Antarctic ice shelves, which lost nearly 3,000 sq. km of their total area in the year 2000. Researchers at the University of Colorado and the British Atlantic survey in Cambridge say regional warming has increased an annual melt season by up to three weeks over the past two decades, putting the Larsen B and Wilkins shelves on the Antarctic peninsula in 'full retreat'. Larsen B is currently about 7,000 sq. km and Wilkins is nearly twice that size. The scientists from National Aeronautics and Space Administration (NASA) reported that the glacial thinning in southern areas of Greenland is too large to have resulted from increased ice-surface melting or decreased snowfall. Some Greenland regions are shrinking because glaciers are detaching from the main sheet more rapidly than before. Over the years, the glacier in the Iceland has shrunk as much as nine meters in some locations. Increased discharge from the ice sheets leads to rise in sea level. This constitutes one of the greatest threats of human induced climatic change. Insular and coastal population would be the first affected by rises in sea level. The problem could rapidly spill over to inner areas if the volume of water in the oceans increases substantially. Most scientists agree that the rate of recent rise in sea level is two millimeter a year.

According to the Center for Global Change at the University of Alaska, global climate model indicates that global warming induced by the green house effect will be most acute in polar regions. The Center predicts that it will result in changes in the extent of sea ice, increased thawing of permafrost, and melting of polar ice masses, with the possibility of causing profound societal impacts around the globe.

The World Wildlife Fund (WWF) in a recently released statement cautioned that gradual warming of the Arctic due to climate change is seriously endangering the lives of birds in the polar area. According to the study conducted by the said organisation, rising temperatures will cause wooded areas to advance steadily northwards, replacing the current Tundra that hosts millions of birds and many unique species. A loss between 40 to 57 per cent of Tundra by between 2070 and 2099 would mean the destruction of a habitat currently supporting around four to five million geese and 7.5 million waders. The study further added that the very first effects of arctic warming will probably be felt within 10 years, and may well cause the extinction of several species.

Dis-equilibrium in the hydrological cycle is also an offshoot of global warming. The atmosphere contributes carbon dioxide to the oceans, where it mixes with the top layers of seawater. Some mineral ions also become nutrients for vast marine life. The ocean yields sulfur to the atmosphere to the extent of 39 million tonne/year, mostly in the form of dimethyl sulphide (DMS). This is produced by marine phyto-plankton and enters the atmosphere in aerosol form. It then acts as a source of condensation nuclei for water vapour and initiates cloud formation and precipitation downward. Creation of cloudy conditions makes the sea cooler and this leads to decreased production of DMS — a negative feedback effect for further cloud formation. In this way, an equilibrium is being maintained. This apart, ocean also exerts long range controls over precipitation through El Nino phenomenon. This phenomenon is the result of changes in the southern Pacific Ocean that happens every 2-7 years. During the month of December the cold up swelling off the coast of Peru is capped by warmer water, with a temperature ranging up to 5°C above the normal. This has a chain of spillover effect like rise in sea level all around the pacific. This causes lowering of plankton productivity in the Pacific Ocean. At a wider scale, El Nino causes hurricanes, flooding and droughts on different continents in different time. The warming atmosphere has spurred more severe weather events, including the December 1999 storms that caused nearly $10 billion a damage in Central and Western Europe. The El Nino phenomenon has an enormous social and economic cost.

An account of such an economic impact is presented in Table 1.9.

Table 1.9: Impacts of the 1982-83 El Nino Phenomenon

Hazards	*Location*	*Damage in million US $*
Flooding	Bolivia	300
	Ecuador & N. Peru	650
	Cuba	170
	US Gulf	1,270
Hurricanes	Tahiti	50
	Hawaii	230
Drought and Fires	Southern Africa	1,000
	S. India & Sri Lanka	150
	Philippines	450
	Indonesia	500
	Australia	2,500
	S. Peru & W. Bolivia	240
	Mexico, Central America	600
	Total	8,110

Source: NOAA (USA) (1994). *Report to the Nation: El Nino and climate prediction. Washington DC:* University Corporation for Atmospheric Research, p.22.

Greenhouse Gas Emission

Earth's atmosphere constitutes a thin blanket of gases. It protects our planet from ultraviolet radiation and helps in trapping the sun's warmth to keep earth's rivers and oceans from freezing. Now, on account of increase in economic activity, there is increased release of gases into the atmosphere on a scale that threatens to alter both of these atmospheric functions significantly. Apart from this, it degrades the ultraviolet shielding ozone layer and intensifies the heat trapping properties of the atmosphere as a whole.

The total carbon dioxide or other heat trapping 'green house gases' related to atmosphere is around 14.6 billion metric tonnes of carbon equivalent. The most rapidly rising levels are chlorofluroscence carbons, which in the lower atmosphere trap heat but in the stratosphere they are the source of chemicals that degrade the ozone layer (See Tables 1.10 to 1.13). Some chlorofluro-carbons remain in the atmosphere for up to 100 years. Industrial countries with less then 20 per cent of the world's populations are responsible for over 50 per cent of global emissions.

Table 1.10: Atmosphere Concentrations of Selected Greenhouse Gases: 1980-94

Year	*CO_2 (ppm)*	*CFC-11 (ppt)*	*CFC-12 (ppt)*	*N_2O (ppb)*	*CH_4 (ppb)*	*CO (ppb)*
1980	338.5	158	289	299	NA	NA
1981	339.8	166	305	299	NA	71.7
1982	341.0	175	325	301	NA	72.5
1983	342.6	182	341	302	NA	70.2
1984	344.3	190	355	303	NA	73.1
1985	345.7	200	376	304	NA	75.5
1986	347.0	209	394	305	1,600	75.5
1987	348.8	219	411	306	1,611	76.9
1988	351.3	231	433	306	1,619	74.4
1989	352.7	240	452	306	1,641	71.5
1990	354	249	469	307	1,645	69.4
1991	355.5	254	483	307	1,657	67.2
1992	356.3	260	496	308	1,673	68.8
1993	357.0	260	502	308	1,671	NA
1994	358.8	261	509	309	1,666	NA

Note: ppm denotes parts per million, ppb is parts per billion and ppt indicates parts per trillion. N_2O is nitrous oxide; CH_2 is methane and CO is carbon monoxide. NA indicates not available.

Source: World Resources Institute (1994, Table 23.3).

It is axiomatic that degradation of the protective layer of stratospheric ozone will increase the amount of biologically damaging ultraviolet radiation that reaches the surface of the planet. If the present trend of releasing greenhouse gases into the atmosphere continues, the level of such gas will reach the equivalent of thrice the pre-industrial levels of carbon dioxide within fourty years and will double again before the end of the 21st century. At present reckoning even one doubling will raise global temperature a few centigrade. It is widely accepted that temperature would rise an average of 1.5-4.5°C. "The prospective shift in temperature may seem small, but it is nearly comparable to the change between the extreme climate of the last ice age, 18,000 years ago, and today's climate" (Stephen H. Schneider, 1988).

This change is sufficient to alter significantly rainfall patterns and temperature regimes in most part of the world. It will leave unimaginable adverse impacts on agriculture, forestry and overall ecosystems. It is said that even an increase of 2°C in average temperature would render most part of the world inhabitable. If the present patterns of economic activities which constitute the sources of these atmosphere altering gases are not themselves altered, there is a distinct possibility of large scale climate change. If predicted levels of warming takes place, the changes would be rapid compared with most climatic shifts in the geological time scale. The changes may occur more rapidly and drastic than the biome can adjust to new temperature regimes. The occurrences of such changes may be disastrous and it may disrupt the existing ecosystems and accelerate extinction of many plants and animal species.

The major source of greenhouse gas emissions lies with human activities. Use of fossil fuels as a source of energy, and clearing and burning of forest land for agriculture is the primary reason of greenhouse gas emission (See Tables 1.11, 1.12 and 1.13). Use of chlorofluorocarbons for industrial and domestic purpose is another reason for it. The Montreal Protocol on substances that deplete the ozone layer, agreed on 1987, was an important step towards limiting the production and release of the chloroflurocarbons and other chemicals that cause the destruction of ozone. In the late 1989, the Antarctic ozone hole was found to be large enough to cause anxiety at the global level. Again, scientists find that conditions are again ripe for a hole to form in the Arctic as well.

Table 1.11: Major Polluters of Industrial Based CO_2 : 1991

Country	*Rank*	*CO_2 emission (000 metric tons)*	*% of world total*	*Per-capita CO_2 emissions (000 metric tons)*
United States	1	4,931,630	21.8	19.53
USSR	2	3,581,179	15.8	12.31
China	3	2,543,380	11.2	2.2
Japan	4	1,091,147	4.8	8.79
Germany	5	969,630	4.3	12.13
India	6	703,550	3.1	0.81
United Kingdom	7	577,157	2.5	10.00
Iraq	8	520,281	2.3	27.86
Canada	9	410,629	1.8	15.21
Italy	10	402,516	1.8	6.96
France	11	374,113	1.7	6.56
Mexico	12	339,873	1.5	3.92
Poland	13	308,164	1.4	8.06
South Africa	14	278,695	1.2	7.18
South Korea	15	264,547	1.2	6.05
Australia	16	261,818	1.2	15.10
Total		17,558,309	77.4	–
World		22,672,832	100.0	4.21

Source: World Resource Institute (1994, Table 23.1).

Table 1.12: World CO_2 Emissions from Fossil Fuel Consumption and Cement Manufacture

Year	*CO_2 Emissions (millions of Metric tons)*	*Per-capita Emissions (Metric tons)*
1955	7,511	2.71
1960	9,475	3.15
1965	11,556	3.48
1970	14,964	4.03
1975	16,935	4.14
1980	19,390	4.36
1985	19,833	4.10
1990	22,343	4.21
1991	22,673	4.21

Source: World Resource Institute (1994, Table 23.4).

Table 1.13: Major Emitters of Chloroflurocarbons (CFC), 1991

Country	*CFC Emissions (000 Metric tons)*	*Percentage of World Total*
United States	90	22.5
Japan	64	16.0
USSR	44	11.0
Germany	23	5.8
United Kingdom	17	4.3
Italy	17	4.3
France	17	4.3
Spain	11	2.8
China	8	2.0
Canada	8	2.0
Australia	5	1.3
South Africa	5	1.3
Total	309	77.3
World	400	100.0

Source: World Resource Institute (1994, Table 23.2).

Industrial Air Pollution

Industrial pollution has become a great environmental menace in the world (See Box 1.1). Concerns about the impact of air pollution on human health and forests have led many industrial countries to tighten environmental regulation and reduce emission of lead, sulfur dioxide and oxides of nitrogen in recent years. In the coming years, urban air quality will become increasingly crucial to maintenance of normal human health.

BOX 1.1: AIR POLLUTION

- China recorded at least 3 million deaths from toxic urban air between 1994 and 1996.
- The world's cities take up just 2 per cent of the earth's surface, yet account for roughly 78 per cent of carbon emissions from human activities, 76 per cent industrial wood use and 60 per cent of the water tapped for use by people.
- London, now requires roughly 58 times of its land area just to supply its residents with fuel and timber. Meeting the needs of every one in the world in the same way would require at least three more earths.
- Rapid urbanisation in the 20th century has magnified the environmental impacts of cities. In 1990, only 160 million people – one-tenth of the world's population were urbanites. By 2006, half of the world (3.2 billion people) will live in urban areas – a 20-fold increase. Because of inadequate systems and poor planning, cities are disproportionately driving global warming, deforestation and water scarcity.
- Polluted air in 36 Indian cities killed 52,000 people in 1995, a 28 per cent increase from early 1990.

Source: World Watch Institute 1999.

Emission of sulfur dioxide and oxides of nitrogen continues to rise worldwide (See Table 1.14). These pollutants cause economic, environmental and health problems. The oxides of sulfur form particulate that reduces atmospheric visibility, causing enormous inconvenience to human life. Oxide of nitrogen helps to form ozone, a principal constituent of urban smog. Sulfur dioxide and smog, when found concentrated in urban areas, can cause damage and increase the incidences of many respiratory diseases. These pollutants also cause acid rain. Acid precipitation has altered the water quality of many lakes and streams to the point where they can no longer support life. It has also been found to have damaged agricultural and forestry crop in many parts of the globe.

It has been reported that 50 millions hectares of forests in Europe were affected with acid precipitation.

Table 1.14: Sulfur and Nitrogen Oxides Emission for Protocol Countries:1990

Countries	*Sulfur*			*Nitrogen Oxide*		
	Emissions (100 metric tonnes	*Spillins*	*Depositions (% of own emission)*	*Emissions (100 metric tonnes*	*Spillins*	*Depositions (% of own emission)*
Albania	76	172	53.9	4	70	25.0
Austria	256	1,311	44.9	275	677	16.7
Belgium	1,465	404	28.4	615	216	4.4
Bulgaria	4,099	904	61.3	263	276	29.7
Czechoslovakia	7,861	2,573	39.6	1,632	834	13.9
Denmark	419	341	24.1	440	222	4.5
Finland	735	830	52.6	442	443	26.7
France	3,956	1,941	52.1	2,803	1,065	30.8
East Germany	16,030	1,260	36.8	1,127	801	9.1
West Germany	3,239	3,174	44.2	4,615	1,363	19.2
Greece	560	786	67.3	361	180	36.0
Hungary	3,505	1,140	37.5	428	416	14.7
Ireland	333	127	53.5	126	79	14.3
Italy	4,325	1,285	64,4	1,593	708	38.7
Luxembourg	60	26	21.7	38	15	0
Netherlands	574	615	26.8	951	280	5.7
Norway	104	900	57.7	206	718	28.8
Poland	10,529	5,555	49.4	2,244	1,795	22.8
Portugal	359	147	63.0	101	57	30.7
Romania	4,674	2,176	58	442	616	30.5
Spain	3,805	845	80.4	621	389	59.7
Sweden	414	1,413	55.6	568	971	27.6
Switzerland	167	480	50.3	185	304	18.4
Turkey	541	847	83.2	97	339	62.9
USSR	22,309	10,724	92.1	5,043	4,888	88.6
United kingdom	8,189	320	57.4	2,984	232	19.9
Yugoslavia	4,096	2,189	58.7	501	909	32.9

Source: Sandnes (1993, Tables C6, C13).

Pollution in industrialised and populated countries of the world has reached a menacing proportion (See Table 1.14). Recently an area of pollution roughly the size of the United States has been discovered in Indian ocean by an international team of scientist working on the Indian ocean experiment at Scripps Institute of California, San Diego. It has been found that the area of polluted water extends about 10.3 million square kilometer. The area affected by the pollution includes the Arabian Sea, much of the Bay of Bengal and other areas in northern Indian Ocean. On account of the haze constituting pollutant particles called aerosols, there is every possibility of reduction in the ocean surface, which will have a detrimental effect on plant life that depends on photosynthesis.

The Decline of Productive Ecosystem

Life on earth depends on the living soil and aquatic ecosystems of river, lakes, estuaries, and oceans. A catastrophic decline in amphibians is wiping out a rich source for new medicines. Without soil and microbial fauna in the ecosystem, there would have been no food production, no decaying of dead materials and other nutrients. Likewise, without plankton, and algae that form the basis of the aquatic food web, there would have no fish to harvest.

Inspite of all these benefits, the earth's soil resource is degraded, rendered sterile and contaminated with toxic chemicals at a rate that will spell disaster for the ecosystem. According to some estimate, 10 per cent of the land surface of the planet has been transformed by human activities from forest and rangeland into desert. (Paul R. Ehrlich *et al.* 1977); as much as 25 per cent more is at risk. (World Resource, 1986). Crop land is already scarce in most of the developing countries. It is getting scarcer because of expending urban areas and increasing population. Asia is beset with land scarcer problems. In Latin American countries 95 per cent of arable land lies with 10 per cent of the population and so the rest of the population owns 5 per cent of the arable land. Apart from this, most of these people have land on steep slopes which are highly susceptible to erosion. This has resulted into a situation of subsistence farming for most of the farmers in such countries. Likewise, large tracts in Africa are under the influence of draught. If the present rate of expansion of cropland in South America and Africa continues, then the days of unsustainable cropping system are not far away.

The expansion of cropland is severely constrained worldwide by factors like steep slopes, erosion and toxic conditions. These factors affect the agricultural productivity. The loss of agricultural land is estimated at 6 to 7 million hectares per year. Besides, about 1.5 million hectares of arable land is loosing its productivity because of adverse conditions like water logging, salinisation, and alkalisation.

Asia has increased its per capita food production over past decade owing to massive increase in farm inputs like fertilizer, irrigation, pesticides and mechanical equipment. In Africa, the per capita food production declined. However, on global basis, world grain production has continued to rise on per capita basis. Straining the land for higher production further degrades the productive agricultural ecosystem.

The present global average cropland is about 0.28 hectares per capita. Latin America has nearly double the world average, but the land distribution is unequitable and uneven. Asia has only 0.15 hectares per capita. In order to feed the projected population of 8.5 million in the year 2025 and maintain the nutritional level, there is a need to increase the food production by 60 per cent. For this, either the food production should increase or the cropland must expand. The latter option is an impossible proposition, so the former option looks somewhat plausible. However, it is realised that it shall require more inputs of fertilizer, pesticides and irrigation to meet the projected target. Additions of all these inputs shall further erode the productive ecosystem, on which the society depends for its sustenance.

Another area fast emerging as a major challenge is the growing demand of fresh water supply. Fresh water for irrigation is increasingly limited in many regions of the world. Withdrawal of water for industrial and irrigation of cropland is increasing. The environmental impacts of excessive withdrawal of fresh water are amply demonstrated in many instances in the world. The demand for water went up six-fold in the last century. The increasing demand for fresh water is the most pressing concern of the new millennium. Excessive withdrawal of fresh water has the potential to threaten future food production system and deprive people of the basic living standards. This apart, human activities are sending massive quantities of pollutants into aquifers, irreversibly damaging the freshwater supplies that provide drinking water to almost a third of the planet's people. It has been found in many studies that 50 per cent of the drinking water is lost through leaks and 40 per cent of water withdrawn for intensive irrigation goes waste. There is also a huge difference in the quantity of water used by each person in underdeveloped countries and urban areas of industrialised nations. Each member of a family living in an arid area of Africa uses 10-40 liters of water a day per person.

Water pollution has been justifiably described as "a time bomb" by Mr. Andras Szollosi-Nagy, director of UNESCO's division of water sciences. Industry returns most of the water it uses to river and lakes. Water drained off from irrigation usually contains fertilizers and pesticides that pollute groundwater sources. The problem of pollution in our oceans is also emerging intractable day by day. In the coastal areas, the oceans have started showing the bad effects of sea pollution. Many areas in the oceans have begun to witness a substantial decline in fresh catch. The major causes of sea pollution are oil spills, urban sewage silt, dumping of plastic, pesticides, and other organic toxic substances. Coastal tracts which shelter the vast majority of the ocean life face the worst effects of pollution.

Human activity, which witnessed phenomenal increase in its scale over the years, affected the biosphere radically. It increased the rate of soil erosion three times since the pre-historic times. It released toxic substances at 10 times the rate of natural system can assimilate. It also released radioactive materials contaminating soils and accentuating acid precipitation over millions of square kilometer.

Shrinking Bio-diversity

The planet encompasses a vast number of living resources. Out of it, few serves the man for their food and other needs. But, it is the vast diversity of the species, plants as well as animals, which constitutes the biological system on which the life on this earth depends. Now on account of increasing economic activities, diversity of species and its genetic heritage that it represents is increasingly at peril.

Tropical forests of the world constitute the largest repository of diversity of species and its genetic heritage in the earth. Clearing of these forests will have adverse impact on earth's bio-diversity. This apart, tropical forests sequester significant amount of carbon, which would, if released to atmosphere accelerate global warming. Today these tropical ecosystems are under tremendous stress. The phenomenon of deforestation is manifested in the form of loss of trees and habitat, acceleration of soil erosion and most importantly loss of livelihood security for millions in the developed countries. Over the past decades, land conversion and deforestation in developing countries have accelerated alarmingly. An estimate of tropical deforestation has been presented in Table 1.15. In the year 1981, the global loss of tropical forests amounted to 7.5 million hectares and this rose to 20.4 million in the year 1987. The rate of deforestation in the world in the period from 1981 to 1990 was 0.8 per cent (See Fig 1.1). In 1991, the three largest continents beset with deforestation were Latin America, Asia and Africa. Apart from this, deforestation has led to emergence of another problem that is carbon dioxide emission. The fourth column of Table 1.15 indicates the amount of carbon dioxide emissions in thousand of metric tonnes from deforestation in the year 1991. This indicates that tropical deforestation is the second most source of carbon dioxide emission into the atmosphere. This speaks volume of the enormity of the environmental crisis because of deforestation. Expansion of cropland and environmental degradation have accelerated the rate of habitat loss and species extinction to levels not witnessed on earth in the past. It is said that we are losing 100 species per day. (Walter, V. Reid *et al.* 1993).

Table 1.15: Tropical Deforestation Resulting into Carbon Emission: Selected Countries

Country	*Total Forest Area 1990 (000 hectare)*	*Annual Deforestation 1981-1990 (%)*	*Equivalent CO_2 1991 (000 metric tons)*	*% of World Total*
Brazil	561,107	0.6	970,000	28.5
Indonesia	109,549	1.0	330,000	9.7
Zaire	113,275	0.6	280,000	8.2
Bolivia	49,317	1.1	140,000	4.1
Myanmar	28,858	1.2	120,000	3.5
Philippines	7,811	2.9	110,000	3.2
Malaysia	17,583	1.8	110,000	3.2
Columbia	54,084	0.6	100,000	2.9
Peru	67,906	0.4	94,000	2.8
Thailand	12,735	2.9	91,000	2.7
Ecuador	11,962	1.7	68,000	2.0
Mexico	48,586	1.2	50,000	1.5
Gabon	18,235	0.6	47,000	1.4
Sudan	42,976	1.0	38,000	1.1
Laos	13,173	0.9	36,000	1.1
Cambodia	12,163	1.0	34,000	1.0
Zambia	32,301	1.0	33,000	1.0
Vietnam	8,312	1.4	33,000	1.0
Nicaragua	6,013	1.7	32,000	0.9
Total	**1,161,884**	–	**2,706,000**	**79.6**
World	**1,756,299**	**0.8**	**3,400,000**	**100.0**

Source: World Resource Institute (1994, Tables 19.1, 23.2) and Sandler (1997).

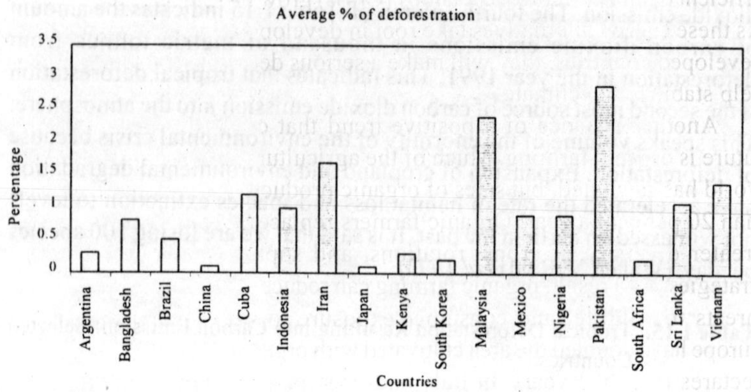

Fig. 1.1: Average Deforestation in Different Countries in Percentage

The quality of living conditions for man in many third world countries is falling drastically. It is said that about one billion people all over the world live in penury and food deprivation. Conditions in urban environment are deteriorating in many developing countries. The causative factors for such degrading environment are untreated sewage, uncontrolled industrial affluents, rapidly growing numbers of automobiles, which pollute air and water and land. Health care system in many developed countries have miserably collapsed and many new health problems, along with the old, have emerged defying solutions. All these factors accelerated the process of deterioration in the biological system on which the survival of humanity depends.

Silver-lining in the Cloud

Population control has become a major development strategy in all most all developing countries. There are many countries in the world where the control measures have been successful in the past. Initiatives have already been taken to eradicate poverty and inequality from developing countries. Such initiatives have borne fruits in many countries.

Vital Signs 2000 highlights several encouraging trends in renewable energy and efficiency technologies. For instance, the year 1999 saw wind power, the world's fastest-growing energy source, surge by 39 per cent, production of solar cells expand by 30 per cent, and sales of energy-efficient compact fluorescent lamps (CFLs) grow by a robust 11 per cent. As these energy alternatives take root in developing countries as well as developed countries, they will make a serious dent in carbon output and help stabilize the climate.

Another instance of a positive trend that could be accelerated in future is organic farming. Much of the agricultural economy around the world has stagnated, but sales of organic products are growing by more than 20 per cent a year. Organic farmers replace agro-chemicals with a greater diversity of crops, rotations, and sophisticated pest control strategies. As a result, organic farming can reduce groundwater pollution, threats to wildlife, and consumer exposure to pesticides. Farmers in Europe have doubled the area cultivated with organic methods to 4 million hectares in only 3 years. In Italy and Austria, the share of agricultural land certified for organic forming reached 10 per cent in 1999.

Another positive trend is declining trend of carbon emissions. Worldwide, climate-altering carbon emissions from fossil fuel burning fell 0.2 per cent in 1999, marking a second consecutive year of decline. However, far more serious reductions are necessary to achieve the 70 per cent cut that many scientists believe is needed to avert dangerous climate change. In this case, consumption in rich countries is required to be scaled down.

Tax reform is one of several policy tools that can accelerate positive environmental change. By levying taxes on fossil fuels and pesticides and other pollutants, governments can simultaneously reduce environmental decay and reduce levies on income and profits. In the last decade, eight Western European countries pioneered "tax shifts," raising taxes on environmentally harmful activities and using the revenue to cut conventional taxes. Although these nations have taken the first modest steps, environmental taxes must be boosted above the 3 per cent of worldwide tax revenue they now generate if they are to halt global environmental decline.

International treaties can help to push reforms forward. The list of international environmental accords now numbers almost 240. Five accords were made in the year 2000 alone, and more than two-thirds of the total were crafted since the 1972 UN Conference on the Environment in Stockholm. The 1987 Montreal Protocol on Ozone Depletion is among the most successful pacts, attempting a reduction in global chlorofluorocarbon (CFC) emissions. However, most of these treaties are neither strong enough nor monitored and enforced sufficiently to reverse ecological decline.

Growth in the satellite remote sensing activity is a potentially beneficial trend for environmental protection efforts. Satellites can collect detailed information about parts of the Earth that are otherwise difficult to access, and can record changes to the environment over large areas and long periods of time. International organizations and national governments can also incorporate satellite monitoring into stepped up efforts to enforce national and international environmental laws.

"As the unfulfilled potential of satellite remote sensing suggests, the solutions for overcoming social inequities and reversing environmental decline will not be merely technical," said Renner. "We need a groundswell of public support to prod governments to use the whole range of tools at their disposal from taxes and laws to new information technologies—to reverse the trends that threaten our future."

Paradigm of Development

The paradigm of development over the past years has been chiefly of accelerating the economic growth rate. In the process of attaining growth, there has been a complete ignorance of considerations pertaining to environmental resource sustainability and equity. As a result, much of the growth has been found to be unsustainable and unevenly distributed.

In the process of development, a lot of degradation of natural resources base has taken place. No doubt, growth of GDP is essential aspect of development process but it is only a means to an end, but not an end itself. Development should be viewed as a process of widening people's choices and enhancing human capability and quality of life. An obsession with the rate of growth could actually run counter to the objectives of development, if it constricts human choice instead of widening of life rather than improving it, as does growth that ignores equity and lowers environmental quality (Pachuri, R.K *et al.* 1998).

There is a lot of debate on appropriateness of development indicators. Initially GDP used to be most favoured and acceptable indicator. Then came the GDP per capita and now Human Development Index or Human Poverty Index has taken over as popularly acceptable indicators. However, these indicators are not the proper matches for indicators of sustainability. The current indicators are all primarily based on consumption of resources, where as the indicator of sustainability accounts for the use of resources or natural capital up to the limit of carrying capacity. Apart from this, they fail to capture the societal aspects, which are crucial for development of the society as a whole *i.e.* from the points of social cohesion, political stability, and the ethics.

Therefore, development requires thinking and actions by several disciplines and by many agencies. There must be a synergy between development related disciplines like health, environment, energy, population control and other developmental processes. Widespread concern about environment is becoming an important political force worldwide. The developing countries are also increasingly waking up to the growing concern for ensuring development without degrading the environment. These initiatives require widespread support if the world's environmental problems are to be successfully confronted and earth is to be sustained as fertile, productive, bountiful planet and the common home of all living things. Therefore, what we need at this juncture is a reconciliation of our development paradigm to emphasise growth with redistributive justice and environmental sustainability. This is what the concept of 'sustainable development' aims at.

2

GLOBAL FOREST RESOURCES IN PERSPECTIVE

Extent, Distribution and Context

Forests have been traditionally looked as a great source of economic values. Over the years, other values of forests have been discovered. This has widened the role of forests in the society. To begin with, the most important function of forests is to contribute to the fundamental ecological process, which keeps the planet in a state of near homeostasis. Forest exerts the greatest influence on the structure and function of the human habitat. They are fundamental to the maintenance of a habitable biosphere. Apart from tangible goods, they provide environmental and social services like conservation of biodiversity, carbon storage and sequestration for mitigation of global climate changes, soil and water conservation, provision of employment and recreational opportunities, enhancement of agricultural production and protection of natural and cultural heritage. Goods and services (See Box 2.1) accrued from the forests are of great significance to the society. In order to maximise the production of goods and services from forests, society interferes into the ecological functioning of the forest ecosystem. This makes the forests vulnerable to many changes, which sometime play disaster with human life. Continuity of forests with its present structure and functions determines the survival of humankind in this earth.

In the past forests were looked upon from local or national context. But over the years, especially after the Rio Summit, forests have provided a global context. This chapter attempts to provide a perspective on widening importance of forests in the world. It also presents an account of distribution of forests in different parts of the globe. The purpose of presenting a short overview on perspective and resource availability is to sensitise the readers about the pace of change in forest resource dynamics in the globe. Information on the extent, condition, types and productivity of forests is also necessary for efforts to improve forest management worldwide and to assess forests' ability to provide the goods and services to the society. This information has been pooled up in this chapter from different sources. This will provide a robust context and necessary backdrop for the discussion on sustainable forest development in the ensuing chapters. In the end, an attempt has been made to depict the changing paradigm of forest development.

Widening Importance of Forests

Bio-diversity

Forest contains at least two-thirds of the earth's terrestrial species. This enormous wealth of species is heavily dependent on primary forests in all regions, although the great diversity occurs in tropics. Plant diversity endures a sufficiently wide range of species to buffer forests and their functions in regulating landscapes from disruption by pests, disease and normal vagaries of climate. The bio-diversity of forests is used as building blocks of selection and breeding of plants and animals to sustain environmental and human uses. This genetic bank strengthens the yield pattern and resistance of domesticated and commercial food crops for material of medicinal, pharmaceutical and industrial value. Until today, we have tapped a fraction of its vast and rich genetic resource base. At the same time, the genetic resource base is under tremendous threat from human activities. It is reported that 10 per cent of world's tree species (more than 8,750 of 80,000 to 1,00,000 species known to science) is threatened with extinction. (WCMC/IUCN/WWF, 1998).

Forests on small island country help to conserve biological diversity. Small island nations, because of their size and physical isolation from others land masses, generally have lower species diversity of plants and animals but a higher percentage of endemism than do continental masses have. For example, in the Dominican Republic, Fiji, Haiti, Jamaica and Mauritius more than 30 per cent of higher plant species are endemic. As regards bird species, Solomon Islands and Fiji have 24 per cent and 20 per cent endemism respectively. State with high level of endemism includes Mauritius (50%) and Fiji (25%). (WRI/UNEP/UNDP/ World Bank, 1996). Many of these plants and animal species are found in forests or dependant on them.

Maintaining Productivity of Land

Forest helps in stabilising the productivity of the land use system. The tree roots slow erosion and consequently help in conserving water. It reduces sedimentation. Forest protects rivers and coastlines, which are the center of fish production. It controls the ground water regime. Forests facilitate rainfall locally. In addition, it protects the landmass from draught. It prevents desertification and natural disaster caused by flood and landslides. It plays a central role in nutrient cycle of elements like nitrogen, phosphorous and potassium as well as calcium, magnesium and iron and trace elements. Trees absorb and store the nutrients, thus preventing them from leeching away.

Regulating Water Supplies

Forests regulate water supplies in the earth. They collect, store, filter and re-circulate it in the earth. On a global and regional level, forests contribute to the integrity and stability of the hydrological cycle and ensures the proper stability of the circulation of water from land to atmosphere and through precipitation, back to the land. The latent heat of evaporation is the major source of energy driving climates globally and forests have a major influence on that part of the global hydrological cycle.

Mountains occupy one-fifth of the world's land surface and are home to one-tenth of the world's population. (Messerli and Ives, 1997). Large areas of the world's mountains and upland areas are covered by forests., These forests have immense value as source of water. Such mountain catchment has critical role in hydrology. Mountains, which have higher levels of precipitation and capture atmospheric water more effectively than lowland areas, are the source of more than half of the world's freshwater and supply all the major rivers and many smaller ones. Forest clad mountains provide critical storage of freshwater as ice and snow, which is latter released to rivers and streams. In semi-arid and arid regions over 90 per cent of rivers flow comes from the mountains. Although the alpine catchment of Rhine River occupies only 11 per cent of the river basin, it supplies 31 per cent of the annual flow and more than 50 per cent of summer flow (Price, 1998).

BOX 2.1: SOME KEY SOCIAL AND ENVIRONMENTAL SERVICES OF FORESTS.

Mitigation of global climate change.
Conservation of soil and water resources.
Enhancement of agricultural systems.
Conservation of biological diversity.
Improvement of urban living conditions.
Protection of natural and cultural heritage.
Generation of employment.
Provision of recreation opportunities.

Ameliorating Climate

The role of forests in ameliorating climate is complex. In one hand, forests cause local precipitation which is a part of the climate and in the other hand, climate determines the nature of vegetation which again influences micro-climate of the area.

The increasing debate notwithstanding, forests have a definite influence on reflectivity of the planetary surface. Removal of forests warms the lower atmosphere and as well as the ground surface, which consequently becomes more reflective. The removal also reduces evaporation and the energy transferred to the atmosphere in the form of latent heat, thereby affecting not only the amount of water and energy transfer, but also the energy content of the atmosphere and its distribution. The magnitude of such disruptions due to depletion of forests are potentially high.

There is another dimension to the role of forests in ameliorating climate. Forests fix carbons and metabolic carbon compounds. They, along with their soil, contain two to three times the amount of carbon currently held in the atmosphere. They, process each year, through the phenomenon of photosynthesis and respiration an amount of carbon equivalent to 15 to 20 per cent of the total. The threat of disruption to this process comes from global warming which, if not contained, shall tilt the balance towards accelerated metabolism, releasing carbon dioxide and methane into the atmosphere. In the backdrop of this ominous possibility, forests vegetation holds immense potentiality to absorb carbon, thereby reducing the accumulation in the atmosphere. But this potentiality of forests is seriously impaired with the increase in deforestation, more particularly in the tropics. The increasing values of forests should singularly convince the mankind to stake steps to protect the remaining primary forests globally and avoiding a further net release of carbon into atmosphere.

Forests can serve as reservoir, sinks and sources of greenhouse gases and thus have a significant role in moderating the net flux of greenhouse gases between the land and the atmosphere. Forests act as reservoir by storing carbon in bio-mass and soils. Evidence suggests that net CO_2 emissions from the world's forests must be close to zero in order to maintain gaseous balance. That is, although forests are an important component of the global C cycle through their regulation of C fluxes and pools, at present they are likely to be contributing little to global warming. This could change in the future for many reasons, including continued clearing and degradation of tropical forests, maturing of mid and high-latitudes forests, and increased incidences of mortality and wildfires in mid- and high-latitude forests as they succumb to climate change. However, with the implementation of sustainable forest management options, it is now possible to conserve and sequester significant amounts of C over the next 50 years or so. Aggressive adoption of management options that conserve and sequester C are necessary not only for sustainable development but also for preventing forests from becoming a significant net source of CO_2 to the atmosphere in the future.

Commercial Products

The production of wood and wood products contributes about US$ 400 billion to the world market. This is about 2 per cent of the total GDP. Wood and wood products having a value of over US$ 100 billion are traded internationally and account for about 3 per cent of world's merchandise trade. Commercial wood production occupies the central economic position in Scandinavian countries, Canada, USA, Indonesia, Malaysia and many Central and South American countries. It creates valuable export revenues for national development and improves their balance of payments in such countries. Now-a-days, a range of non-wood forest products like medicinal products, recreational services have entered into commercial transaction.

Sustainable Livelihoods

A livelihood comprises the capabilities, assets and activities required for a means of living. A livelihood is sustainable when it can cope with and recover from stresses and shocks and maintain or enhance its capabilities and assets both now and in future, while not undermining the natural resource base (Carney, 1998). The assets, which are the building blocks of livelihoods, are not only natural, physical and financial capital, but also social and human capital (kinship and network, nutrition and health). A range of assets is, therefore, needed to achieve sustainable livelihoods. The ability to move out of poverty or food insecurity is critically dependent on access to such an array of assets.

Forests constitute a major source of sustainable livelihoods in the rural sector. They provide employment and income to rural people on a sustained basis. Forestry operations generate employment opportunities in small scale processing and trading activities, which require little financial capital or skill. They provide a wide range of wood and non-wood forest products, which are not reflected in the financial transaction. They, though necessary for living in rural areas, do not reflect in the income profile of economy. But, they play a critical role in the life of poor people living in the villages.

Food Security

Poor people often live precariously with no cushions against adversity. Forests and forestry operations play an important role as a safety net, providing both subsistence and income in time of crop failure, shortfall, unemployment or other emerging hardship. They provide foods, which are most extensively used to help meet dietary shortfall during particular seasons in the year. Energy rich forest foods such as roots, tubers, rhizomes and nuts play an important role in the time of adversity.

Forest contributes to food security of poor community by providing accessibility to food as well as a wide range of foodstuffs to augment their subsistence farming. It contributes to agricultural productivity by maintaining soil fertility, conserving moisture, providing fodder for livelihood. It also protects the watersheds and regulates water flow and quality.

Energy Security

Forests provide energy to a majority of people in the world. Two billion people in developing countries still depend on traditional fuels like fuelwood as their principal source of energy. Bio-mass constitutes about 15 per cent of the world's total energy consumption and represents half of the world wood consumption. Fuelwood is used for 58 per cent of all the energy used in Africa, 15 per cent in Latin America, and 11 per cent in

Asia (WCMC/IUCN/WWF, 1998). Fuelwood, when used sustainably and wisely, offers potentially renewable source of energy for future generation.

Forests have special relevance and significance to women and children. In many developing tropical countries, women and children collect wood, fuelwood, and non-wood forest products and sell these products in the local market. The money received is generally spent by women in purchasing necessary articles for them and their children. Therefore, a forest holds enormous social relevance to development of women and children.

Increased Well-being

Forestry initiatives that supports access to non-wood forest resources, participatory decisions making and equity assist in increasing the well being, especially that of the poor. Forests provide non-material goods that contribute to livelihoods by enhancing social and human capital. The sense of well-being on which development of people depends generally is promoted by numerous factors including sense of involvement and control, access to resources and political enfranchisement. Forest being an open access resource, provides ample opportunity to people for involvement and control which ultimately improves the well-being of people living near forests.

Global Forest Resources: Extent and Distribution

The global forest resource is conspicuous by its extent, complexity, and diversity. Forest occupies about 3,869 million hectares in the world (FRA, 2000). The distribution of forests in different parts of the globe is uneven. This is one of the characteristic peculiarities of global forest resource base. Apart from this, the ecological character and diversity of forest are other significant features of the resource base. These features to a great extent influence the utility of forests in different parts of the globe. On account of the fact that forest ecosystems very greatly in their structure and dynamics, the type and quantum of products and services obtained from such forests differ from one part of the globe to another.

Extent of Forest Resources

The knowledge regarding the extent of global forest resources is limited. During the last three decades, more interests have been generated in the field of forest cover assessment. There are varied and conflicting reports with regard to extent of forests in different parts of world. The estimation of forest area in the last century shows so much contrasts that the total extent of forest varied from 3,000 to over 6,000 million hectares. That means, the estimate of forest area varied from 20 to 45 per cent of the total land surface of the globe. Different persons or organizations have projected different estimates of forest areas or forest cover of the world. An account of the diverse estimate is provided in Table 2.1. The reason for conflicting estimation of forests was primarily attributed to the fact that there was no single definition of forests and woodland in the world. More to it, the terms like closed and open forests, forests and woodland, land under shifting cultivation and agriculture have further increased the confusion. Another reason for such a wide variation might be the method and technology of estimation used. In the background of conflicting and diverse estimation, the most reliable and comprehensible source of data regarding extent of forests and woodland resource is the FRA 2000.

Table 2.1: Estimate of Global Area of Forest and Woodland

Source/year	*Category*	*Area in million hectare*
Zon and Sparhawk (1923)	Forest Area	3,031
FAO (1946/1937)	Forest	3,650
FAO (1963)	Forest land	4,126
Person (1974)	Forest land	4,030
	Closed forest	2,800
Global 2000 (1975)	Closed Forest (2,563)	5,237
Barney (1980)	Open woodlands (1,200)	
World Resource Institute	Closed forest 2,865	
(WRI,1986)	Open Forest 1,282	4,147
	Other Wooded land	1,081
	Total Wooded area	5,228
FAO (1987)	Forests and Woodland	4,087
FAO (1990)	Forest Area	3,442
FAO (1995)	Forest Area	3,454
FRA 2000	Forest Area	3,869

Accepting the statistics given in FAO Production Yearbook (1987), the extent of forests is about 4,087 million hectares. This amounts to 31 per cent of the total land area of the world. Out of the total forests, 2,500 to 3,000 million hectares constitute the closed forests and the rest open forests. Person (1974) is one of the pioneer scientists who estimated the extent of global forest scientifically. The estimated closed forest area was around 2,800 million hectares in the year 1970. The World Resource Institute also estimated the closed forest area to be about 2,865 million hectares.

Forest Resource Assessment (FRA) 2000

The Global Forest Resources Assessment 2000 (FRA 2000), under the aegis of UN Food and Agriculture Organisation, collected and synthesized a vast amount of information on the status and trends in global forest cover, on forest management, and on additional forest–related variables. Some of the major conclusions of FRA are presented below.

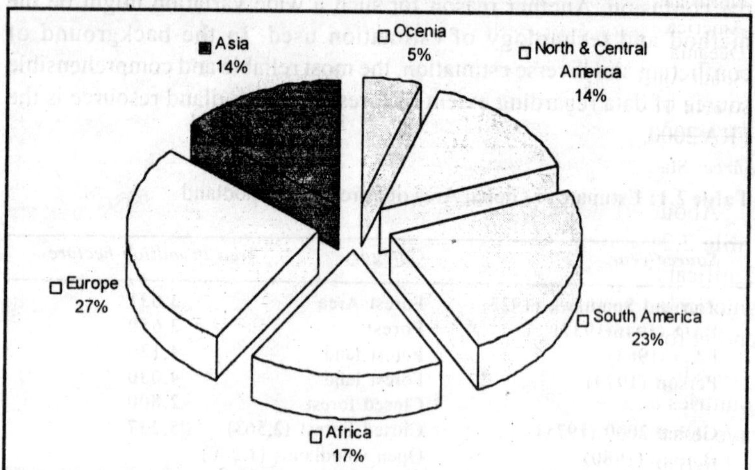

Fig. 2.1: Forest Area in Percentage by Region, year 2000

The world has about 3,869 million hectares of forests, of which 95 per cent are natural and 5 per cent forest plantation. Table 2.2 provides data on the distribution of forests by region. Europe and South America have the largest percentage of the World's forests (27 and 23 per cent, respectively), and Ocenia has the least (5 per cent) (See Fig 2.1). A map showing the location of forests by region is provided in Fig. 2.2. Two-third of World's forests are located in only ten countries: the Russian Federation, Brazil, Canada, the United States, China, Australia, the democratic Republic of Congo, Indonesia and Peru.

Table 2.2: Forest Area by Region, 2000

Region	*Land Area (million) ha)*	*Total Forest (Natural Forests and Forest Plantations*			*Natural Forest (million ha)*	*Forest Planta-tion (million ha)*
		Area (million ha)	*% of land area*	*% of World's forests*		
Africa	2,978	650	22	17	642	8
Asia	3,085	548	18	14	432	116
Europe	2,260	1,039	46	27	1,007	32
North and Central America	2,137	549	26	14	532	18
Oceania	849	198	23	5	194	3
South America	1,755	886	51	23	875	10
World Total	**13,064**	**3,869**	**30**	**100**	**3,682**	**187**

Source: State of World's Forests (2001)

About 30 per cent of the world's land area is under forest (see Table 2.2). The proportion of total land area under forest varies significantly by region and country. About half the land area of South America and Europe is covered by forest but only one-sixth of Asia's land is forested. Africa, North and Central America and Ocenia fall in between, each with about one-fourth of its land covered by forest. Fifty countries and two 'areas' (*e.g.* territories, protectorates) are reported to have less than 10 per cent of their land covered by forest. Twenty countries and two areas have more than 60 per cent of their land under forest.

The largest proportion of the world's forest is in the tropical zone (47 per cent), followed by the boreal (33 per cent), temperate (11 per cent) and sub-tropical (9 per cent) zones. Figure 2.4 shows the location of forests in these four broad ecological zones. The distribution of forests in different ecological zones of the world is presented in Table 2.3. The distribution of forest on the basis of ecological zoning classifications and by region are as follows:

- Tropical and sub-tropical dry forests are concentrated in Africa (containing 36 per cent of the world's total forests), South America (30 per cent) and Asia (21 per cent).
- The majority of tropical rain forests are located in South America (58 per cent), but a large proportion (24 per cent) is also found in

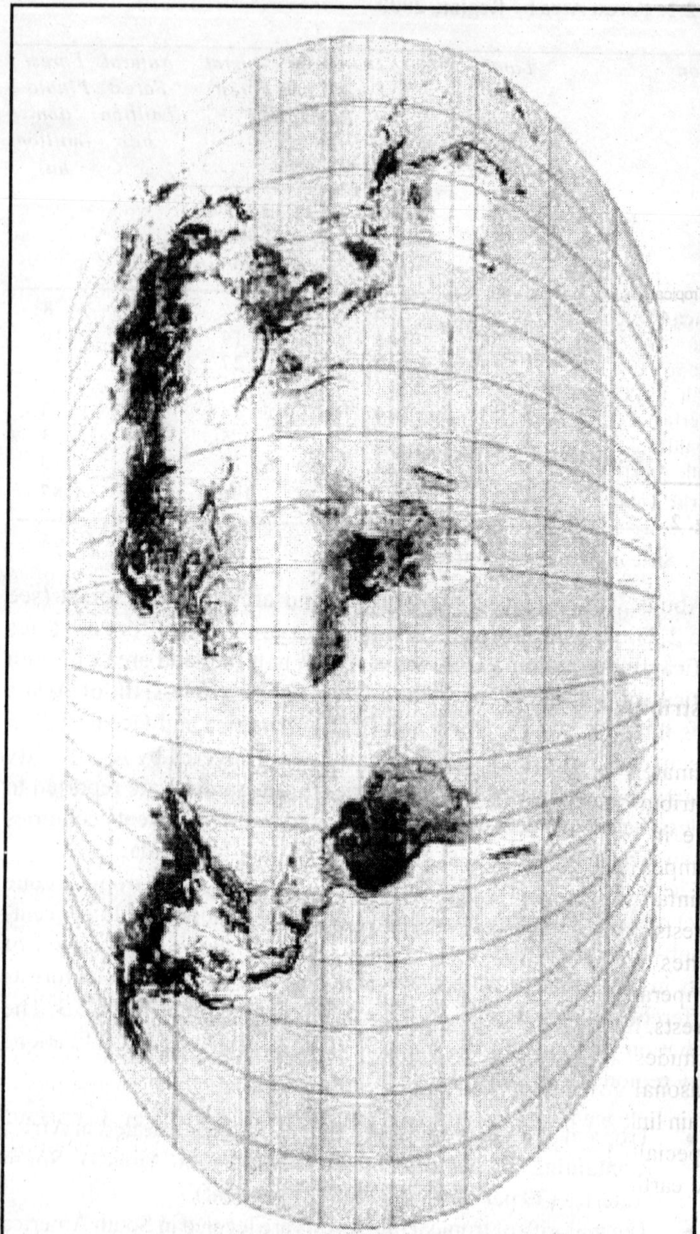

Fig. 2.2: The World's Forest, 2000

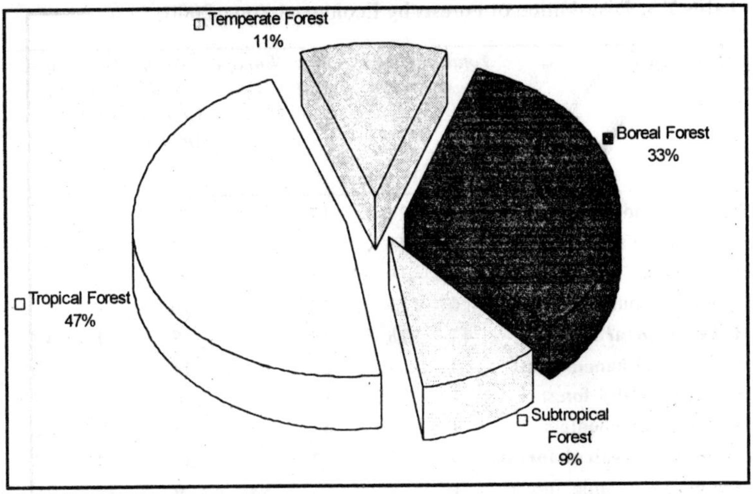

Fig. 2.3: Distribution of Forests by Broad Ecological Zones

Africa; most of the rest is in Asia (17 per cent). Nearly all temperate and boreal forests are found mainly in Europe (40 per cent) and North and Central America (34 per cent).

Distribution of Forests

Climate and geographical location are the factors, which influence the distribution of forests in the globe. Two climatic elements play significant role in distribution of forests. They are temperature and rainfall. Temperature determines the northern latitudinal limits of the forests. Rainfall determines the distribution of low land forests on the mid-latitude forests. Relative absence of rainfall accounts for the desert and steppe zones which separate tropical and temperate forests. Therefore, temperature plays a determining influence on the pole ward expansion of forests. In addition, rainfall acts as the limiting factor in the areas of mid-latitudes. The influence of rainfall on the plant growth depends on its seasonal distribution and amount of evaporation. This phenomenon is again linked with prevailing temperature. Precisely speaking, temperature, especially lower extent and rainfall, determines the forest distribution in the earth.

Table 2.3: Distribution of Forests by Ecological Zone, 2000

Ecological Zone	*Total Forest (%)*	*Africa (%)*	*Asia (%)*	*Europe (%)*	*North and Central America (%)*	*Oceania (%)*	*South America (%)*
Tropical rain forest	28	24	17	-	1	-	58
Tropical moist deciduous	11	40	14	-	9	6	31
Tropical dry	5	39	23	-	6	-	33
Tropical mountain	4	11	29	-	30	-	30
Total tropical forests	**47**	**28**	**19**		**5**	**1**	**47**
Sub-tropical humid forest	4	-	52	-	34	8	6
Sub-tropical dry forest	1	16	11	30	6	22	14
Sub-tropical mountain	3	1	47	13	38	-	1
Total sub-tropical forests	**9**	**2**	**42**	**7**	**37**	**7**	**5**
Temperate oceanic forest	1	-	-	33	9	33	25
Temperate continental forest	7	-	13	40	46	-	-
Temperate mountain	3	-	26	40	29	5	-
Total temperate forests	**11**	**-**	**17**	**39**	**39**	**4**	**2**
Boreal coniferous forest	19	-	2	74	24	-	-
Boreal tundra woodland	3	-	-	19	81	-	-
Boreal mountain	11	-	1	63	36	-	-
Total boreal forests	**33**	**-**	**2**	**65**	**34**	**-**	**-**
Total forests	**100**	**17**	**14**	**27**	**14**	**5**	**23**

Source: State of World's Forests (2001).

Spread of population and habitation has greatly influenced the existence of forests in the world. The forests of the world have been divided into four broad types (See Fig. 2.2 and Table 2.4). They are: (1) The tropical forests, (2) the sub-tropical forests, (3) the temperate forests, and (4) the boreal forests. Much of the forests located in mid-latitude area have since been cleared for establishing human habitation. At present, boreal and tropical forests account for the most of the remaining forests of the world. Tropical forests include evergreen and deciduous forest, open woodland and high altitude vegetation comprising mainly coniferous forests. Sub-tropical and mid-latitude forests have severely shrunk.

The broad forest types of the world and their distribution, along with principal species are as under:

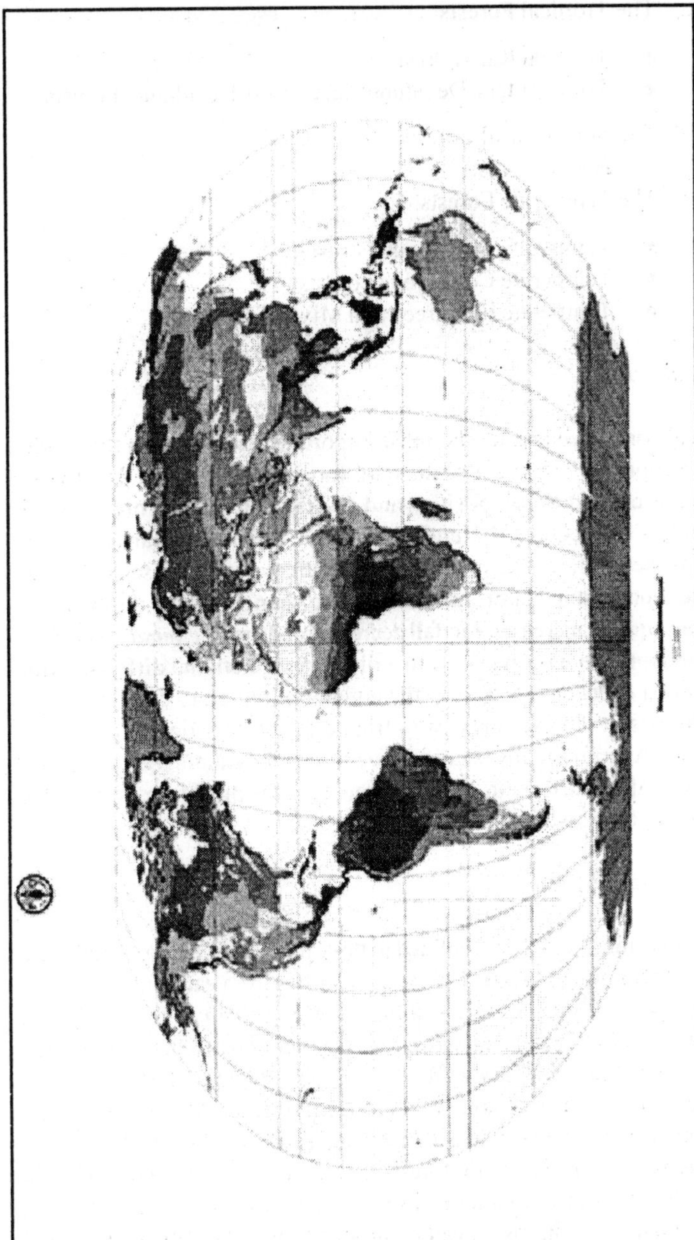

Fig. 2.4: Global Ecological Zones

1. The Tropical Forests:
   - Tropical Rain Forests
   - Tropical Dry Deciduous and Moist Deciduous Forests.
2. The Sub-tropical Forests.
3. The Boreal Forests.
4. The Temperate Forests.
   - Temperate Deciduous Forests
   - Temperate Coniferous Forests
   - Temperate Evergreen and Mixed Forests.

Tropical Forests

Tropical forests constitute the most important forest type in the world. They comprise 47 per cent of the total forests of the world. The forests assume its character, composition and diversity on account of latitudinal gradient of the regions. Latitude plays as a key determinant on which depends the rainfall of an area. With the increase or decrease in distance of a location from equator, rainfall tends to change. As the distance of a site from equator increases, rainfall decreases and the *vice versa*. Therefore, this phenomenon has given rise to a distinct vegetational differentiation from moist evergreen forests in the equatorial region to drier and more open forests in the locations away from equator, merging into savanna grassland. Apart from this, within a spectrum of longitudinal zone, altitude influences the distribution of vegetation, too. Tropical forests have two broad categories, which are as follows:

Tropical Rain Forests

The tropical rain forests are confined to three main areas of South America, Africa and South-East Asia. These forests differ from each other on many counts but the characteristic similarity among them is their splendid diversity. The Brazilian Amazon region contains around 6,000 tree species, many of which are endemic to the region. About hundred of species per hectare occurs in the tree layer of the tropical forests. African forests are rather poor in comparison to South America and South-East Asia.

It is a common site in rain forests to find trees reaching a height of 50 meters. There is also a pattern of distinct stratification in such forests. Moist climatic conditions prevailing in such areas are compatible to rapid plant growth. Individual trees shed their leaves at different times and the forests as a whole present an evergreen look round the year. Because of intense competition for light, barely any sun rays fall on the ground. The fallen leaves, twigs and other tree debris keep on accumulating on the floor of the forests. This leads to formation of thick litters on the ground. Decomposition of the litter takes place very rapidly because of the continuously hot and damp conditions. This boosts the rapid release of nutrients to the ecosystems. The pattern of nutrient cycling and recycling in tropical forests is of critical importance to the ecosystem. It influences the utilisation and management of the forests.

Again within the zone of tropical rain forests, with the increase in altitude, the forests change on account of temperature and rainfall. The rainfall in such areas is higher in comparison with areas of lowland. The composition of such forests is characterised by dominating presence of ferns and mosses. However, with the further increase in height, rainfall decreases and trees are found to be shorter and stunted and eventually they develop into a shrub type of forests.

Tropical Forests

The dry season becomes longer and clearer with the increase in distance from the equator. Therefore, the equatorial forests change to dry type of forests in areas away from the equator. These are semi-evergreen forests in the Northern parts of South America and mountain forests stretching from the north-east India to northern Australia *i.e.* all along the Indo-Malaysian region. In African continent, such type of forests are not well developed. However, the structure, composition and diversity of such forests are similar in comparison with their counterpart in Asia and South America. Teak constitutes one of the dominating species in this type of forests.

A semi-evergreen forests gives way to wet and dry deciduous forests with the increase in length of dry season and decrease in quantum of rainfall. Such types of forests are widespread in Central and South America and Indo-Malaysian region. Again, in Indo-Malaysian region, such types of forests which is less contiguous, constitute teak as the dominant species. Such types of forests are called as dry teak forests. Contrary to this, tropical deciduous forests of South America are more contiguous and provide a distinct identity to their ecological character. Again, in the case of Africa, the spread of deciduous forests is conspicuously discontinuous. African deciduous forests are dotted with large open grasslands. With the decrease in rainfall, a Savannah type of forests

Table 2.4: Distribution of Major Forest Types in the Globe

Forest Types	*Occurrence*	*Main Species*
Boreal Forests	Scandinavian countries *viz.* Sweden, Finland, Norway, North European, Russia	Pinus Sylvestris, Picea abies
	Siberia (Russia)	Larix siberica Abies siberica Picea obovata Pinus cembra
	North America (Canada & Alaska)	Picea glauca Picea mariana Abies balsamea Larix laricina Pinus Banksiana
Temperate Forests Temperate Broad-leaved; Coniferous forests, and the temperate rain forests	Western Europe *viz* Germany, France, Switzerland, Austria, etc.	Fagus silvatica, Fraxinus excelsior, Pinus ponderose Pinus Sylvester's Picea Abies, Abies alba, Larix deciduous Quercus robusta,
	USA (Western part)	Pinus monticola, Thuja plicata, Tsuga hetererophylla, Abies grandis, Pseudotsuga taxifolia,
	USA (North East)	Pinus strobus, Pinus resinosa, Pinus banksiana, oak rickory type wuercus sppecies type, Juglans nigera, Fraxinu american, Acer-beech-birch type.
Sub-Tropical Forests Sub-tropical moist forests	South East China, South West Korea, South Japan	Cinamonus campora, Pinus thunberii, cryptomeria japonica, bamboos (phyllostachys spp. Bambusa spp.)
	South-East USA	Pinus palustris, P. caribea, Pinus taeda P echinata, Quercus borealis
	South Chile	Rotofagus spp. Fitzroya patagonica, Podocarpus spp. Aracaria americana.
	South Africa	Podocarpus spp, Olea spp
	New Zealand	Rotofagus species, Podocarpus spp. Dacrydium cupressium, Agasthis austratis, Aurucaria spp

Forest Types	*Occurrence*	*Main Species*
Sub-tropical forests Subtropical Dry forests	Italy, Spain, Portugal, Greece, Turkey and all other Mediterranean region	Pinus helepensis, P pinea, P. pinaster, P brutia, P. nigra, Quercus ilex, Cedrus exelsa Cuprresus sempervvirens
Tropical forests Tropical Rain forests	The Amazon basin and Guianas in South America	Family dominance of leguminaceae and Swietenia macrophylla, Ochroma peruviane, Octoea rodiaei (green heart), Delbergia nigra, Ceiba pentandra.
	Africa	Family dominance of meliaceae, Khaya ivorensis.
	The Congo Basin, the Cameroon, Nigeria, Ghana, Ivory Coast, Liberia	K. anthothecas, Entrandrophragma utile, E. cyclindricum, E. angolense, E candellei, Terminalia superba, Triplochiton scheroxylon, Chlophor excelsa, Mimusops heckelii, tarrictia utilis, Aukoumea kleineana.
	South East Asia, Papuah New Guinea, Borneo, Indonesia, Malaya, Philippines, Thailand Burma India Sri-Lanka	Family dominance of dipteracarpacea, shorea parvifolia, Dryobalanops aromatia (kapoor) Shorea albida, Eusiderosylon swaderia, (ironwood) Gonystylus bancanus (romin), Dipterocarpus, Shorea, Parasnorea, Hopea, vatica, spp.
Tropical forests	India, Burma, Thailand, Indonesia	Tectona grandis, Shorea robusta, Xylia spp. Terminalia spp. Delbergia spp. Pterocarpus spp. etc.
Moist deciduous forests	West Africa and East Africa	Chloroflora excelse, Terminalia superoa, Aucoumea klaineana.
	South America on either side of the Tropical Rain forests of the Amazon Valley.	Leguminaceae spp., Ceiba pentnadra, Delbergia spp.
Tropical forests	India, Thailand, Indochina, East Africa. Tanzania, Zambia West Thailand	Dry sal and teak forests, dry mixed species forests containing terminalia tomentosa, Anogeisus latifolia, buchnania lanjan, Dendrocalamus strictus.
Dry deciduous forests	Indochina, East Africa. Tanzania, Zambia, West Africa	Tsoberlinia spp, Savannans (west Africa), Chlorospermum spp.

Forest Types	*Occurrence*	*Main Species*
	South America, Brazilian highlands, North Argentina Venezuela, Columbia	Schinopaia spp (Red)

becomes apparent. Trees reach a height of around 20 meters, indicating low productivity. Apart from the phenomenon of recurrent incidences of decreasing rainfall, the soil conditions play as limiting factor to forest growth in such Savannah types of forests. What is significant is the fact that with the increasing incidences of fire in such forests resistant tree species are thriving and density of such fire resistant species are increasing in the population.

Sub-tropical Forests

The sub-tropical forests comprise 9 per cent of total forest of the world. Such forests occur in warm temporal zone in both hemispheres. Although containing a large number of hardwood species, these forests have been heavily exploited in more accessible areas for softwood. Pines are the most important softwoods in this type of forests. A variety of species also occurs in such forests.

The better known species of such forests are oaks and eucalyptus of Australia. Sub-tropical forests of Mediterranean region are poorly stocked containing large number of badly formed and stunted trees. The stocking is low and forest produce poles and fuelwood. Considerable degradation of these forests has taken place as a result of anthropogenic pressure from man and heavy grazing from cattle.

Mediterranean forests are mixed and evergreen in nature. The species found are oak and pine. The Helm oak is the common oak found in such forests. Likewise, among pines, the dominating species are stone, maritime, and Aleppo pines. Much of the drier part of the maritime forests was deforested because of uncontrolled pressure of grazing and agriculture on the forests. Beside the traditional Mediterranean forests, such types occur in some parts of California, South Africa and Australia.

Boreal Forests

The boreal forests constitute another major forests type in the earth. The forests comprise about 33 per cent of the total forest area of the world.

They are distributed in two major zones. The first zone occurs in North America and the second zone in Eurasia. The North American zone stretches from Alaska to Newfoundland and the Eurasian Belt stretches from Atlantic coast of Scandinavia to the pacific coast of Siberia. In both the zones, long and cold winter and short growing season distinctly characterise the climate. The forests in both the zones constitute conifers, mostly of evergreen types.

Apart from the similarities between forests of these two zones, there is much dissimilarity, which stands out distinctly. One of such dissimilarities is species composition. The forests of European zone are much poor in species diversity than its counterparts in Northern American and Siberian region of Asia. In Scandinavian forests, on drier soils, Scots pine dominates, where as on wet areas Norway spruce dominates. The species diversity in Siberian forests increases when one moves towards East Asia. Consequently, density of spruce decreases towards eastern part of Siberia forests. Moreover, spruce is replaced by larch, a deciduous conifer. Larch forests occupy a vast area in Siberia. Again, towards pacific coast firs and spruce becomes gradually dominant.

In eastern Canada, the white spruce is found widespread on areas with well-drained sites. The black spruce occurs on poorly drained soils and is gradually replaced by jack pines. Dominance of single species is the distinctive character of boreal forests. However, few deciduous species like birch and aspen are found. Another characteristic feature of such forests is its very slow rate of decomposition of plant litters. It has been said by Cole (1986) that it takes 350 years to decompose the litter completely where as it takes four years to seven years for tropical forests. (Mather S. Alexander, 1990).

Temperate Forests

Temperate forests constitute an important type of forests. They comprise 11 per cent of the world's forests. These types of forests are mostly found in intermediate latitudes between tropical and boreal forest belt. Such forests differ from other types of forests in its composition, structure, diversity and function. The number of species is considerably higher than the boreal forests. Such forests comprise of a large numbers of sub-types ranging from predominantly coniferous to practically broad-leaved species. The content of softwood in trees found in this type of forests is important as an industrial raw material—especially since many broad-leaved species exhibit poor quality and form. Coniferous forests are found toward the northern parts of former USSR countries. Other important areas are found in mountainous region of Europe, Mexico and in the Himalayas.

The major types of temperate forests are:

- Temperate Deciduous Forests;
- Temperate Coniferous Forests;
- Temperate Rain (Evergreen) and Mixed Forest.

Temperate Deciduous Forests

Temperate mixed and deciduous forests lie south to the boreal forest zone. The change of forests from boreal to deciduous zones is conspicuous. There are many transitional zones all along these boundaries. The deciduous forests of Europe extend from Atlantic to Urals. The principal species of deciduous forests of Europe is oak. The main associate of oak is elm, ash, and beech. Compositional proportion of oak and its associates in such forests alters with changes in edaphic factors like soil, climate, and drainage condition. Beech occurs widely in the Alps and Mediterranean peninsula. In southern part of peninsula of Europe like Northern Spain and Italy, oak remains dominant. Contrary to this, North-American forest belt contains a wide diversity of species. Towards New England, beech and maples are dominant in association with few other broad-leafed species as well as conifers such as hemlock. Further south, forests of oak and chestnut replace the beech maple forest. Again towards west, oak hickory forests dominate in drier types of areas. Similarly, oak dominated deciduous forests occupies a large areas in North China, Korea and South East of CIS countries.

Apart from the aforesaid areas, there are two narrow but distinguishable belts of temperate deciduous forests. One belt is found in Canada. This belt of forests is dominated with balsam, popular and aspen. The second belt is found in Siberia. This belt of forest contains aspen as principal species in association with birch. The areas in these belts are relatively more prone to agricultural use. This is on account of the fact that the climate allows rapid decomposition of plant litters and recycling of nutrients. In the past, large tracts of such forests had been cleared for agricultural use.

Temperate Coniferous Forests

Extensive areas of temperate forests are found in North America. The tract stretching from Minnesota to New England constitutes the so called "Lake forests". White, red pine and eastern hemlock are the principal species in such forests. Towards south and eastern part of lake forests, the composition changes and in such forests loblolly is the predominating species. Other species of pine occupies the coastal tract from New Jersey to Northern Florida and also found westward to Texas. Pure stand of pine is also found on low lying coastal tract. Another patch occurs in Western part of North America. It is called as 'coast forest'. This tract stretching from coastal low land of Alaska to British Columbia is dominated by sitka spruce. Towards south, it is replaced by western hemlock and western cider. Western cider remarkably reaches a height of 60 to 80 meters. More towards south of Oregon, these species give a way to larger coastal redwood. In the coastal tract of British Columbia and Washington and also in drier mountain pockets, forests of Douglas fir occur.

Temperate Rain and Mixed Forests

Temperate rain and mixed forests are also found in some parts of Southern Hemisphere like South America and Tasmănia and New Zealand. The forest composition is different from those of its counterpart in northern hemisphere. In Chile of South America the dominating species is Auracucaria pine. In New Zealand, the dominating species in northern part is Kauri pine and in the rest of the area, pines of podocaarpus species are found along with broad leafed evergreens.

Evergreen forests with broad-leafed species occur in four pockets of both the hemispheres of the globe. In occurs in central China and southern Japan, which are situated in the northern part of the world. In such forests, evergreen oak dominates in association with laurels, magnolias and few conifers. Few pockets of such types of forests are also found in Southeast and Southwest Australia. These forests have dominating species like eucalyptus. Evergreen broad-leafed forests are also found in some parts of New Zealand, which experience a wet climate.

The forest resource base in every region of the globe is highly veritable and complex in its structure, composition and diversity. But the fact remains that, over the years, the forest base is on a downward slide. Initially massive deforestation took place in Europe, especially in

England and Mediterranean forests. The next phase came in North America and Asia. To a great extent, North America recovered from the phase of deforestation; this happened to some countries of Asia, to some extent. The third phase began in the last century in continents like Africa, South and Latin America and Asia. The countries in such continents are still reeling under deforestation till today. Because of myriad factors, including the forces of population, development and agricultural expansion, these forests have still not attained a state of equilibrium.

Conspicuous Features of Forest Distribution

The distribution pattern of closed and open woodland forests and their volume per unit area have the following characteristics:

- The CIS countries (former USSR) constitute the largest block of forests area in the world.
- The forests of Africa are characterized by the conspicuous existence of large stretch of open land.
- The distribution of closed forests is strongly concentrated in few countries. The CIS countries (former USSR), Canada and Brazil account for about half of the total area. The CIS countries alone accounts for over a fifth of the area, nearly a quarter of its growing stock, and 50 to 60 per cent of its coniferous volume. (Sutton, 1975; Barr, 1988).
- In the developing world, South America constitutes the greatest reserve of closed forests. Among South American countries, Brazil comprises the biggest reserve of closed forests.
- Among the countries situated in mid-area latitudes, Japan and Korea constitute the states that have good reserve of forests.
- In the boreal forest belt, Scandinavian countries like Finland and Sweden stand out conspicuously in holding good reserve of forests.
- In equatorial zone, countries like Surinam, French Guinea, Guyana in Latin America, Congo, Gabon and Zaire in Africa and Papua New Guinea constitute dense forest cover.
- Countries situated in arid and semi-arid intermediate latitudes have open forests. Apart from this, Britain, Ireland and few countries of North-West Europe also have forest cover far less than the world average.

Forest Plantation

Forest plantation has emerged as a potential means of expanding the resource base of the world. FRA-2000 provides a picture of the status of forest plantations worldwide. There is an estimated 187 million ha of plantations worldwide, representing 5 per cent of the global forest area. Data on forest plantation area by region is indicated in Table 2.5. Asia has by far the largest forest plantations. Plantations account for over one-fifth of all forests in Asia. About 60 per cent of forest plantations are located in only four countries: China, India, the Russian Federation and the United States. Species in the genera Pinus and Eucalyptus continues to be the most commonly planted trees in forest plantations, accounting for 20 per cent and 10 per cent, respectively, of forest plantation area worldwide.

Table 2.5: Forest Plantation Area by Region, 2000

Region	*Total Forest Area (million ha)*	*Natural Forest Area (million ha)*	*Forest Plantation Area*	*Plantations as % of the Region's (million ha)*	*% of Planta- tion > Total Forest*
Africa	650	642	8	1	4
Asia	548	432	116	21	62
Europe	1,039	1,007	32	3	17
North and Central America	549	532	18	3	9
Oceania	198	194	3	2	2
South America	886	875	10	1	6
World Total	**3,869**	**3,682**	**187**	**5**	**100**

Source: State of World's Forests (2001).

Industrial plantations (*i.e.* those supplying raw material for industry) account for 48 per cent of the global forest plantation estate, while non-industrial plantations (*e.g.* those grown for fuelwood, soil and water conservation and wind protection) account for 26 per cent, and 26 per cent are unspecified. The countries with major industrial plantation areas are China (37 million ha), the United States (16 million ha) and India (12 million ha). These three countries account for 73 per cent of all industrial forest plantations globally in 2000. The countries with a significant proportion of non-industrial plantation areas are India (21 million ha), China (8 million ha), Indonesia and Thailand (4 million ha each), together accounting for 75 per cent of all non-industrial forest plantations in the world (FRA, 2001).

Per Capita Forests

An inverse relationship dominates between forest cover and population density in many countries. Countries with high degree of population density have low degrees of forest cover. The per capita forest area at the global scale is around 0.6 hectare (FAO, 2001). There are, however, large differences among countries. Asia has very little forest area per capita, where as Oceania and South America have a substantial area per person. Only 22 countries have more than 3 hectare of forests per capita and only about 5 per cent of the world's population lives in these countries – mostly in Brazil and Russian Federation. Three quarters of the world's population, in the other hand, lives in countries with less than 0.5 hectare per capita, including most of the densely populated countries in Asia and Europe.

Like per capita forests, average or mean growing stock is also an important indicator of resource potential. Taking the data quoted by Persson (1974) into consideration and combining with population estimate in the year 1985, the world per capita volume of closed forests comes to around 65 and 70 cubic meter. In the broad spectrum of mean volume of closed forests in the world, African forest lies in one end with volume of 45 to 70 cubic meter per hectare and countries of Russian Federation lie in the other extreme end with mean volume of 280 cubic meter her hectare.

Likewise, total wood volume (cubic meter) and above-ground woody biomass (tonnes) in forests are also an important indicator for forest functions and productivity. The total of above ground woody biomass in world forests is 420 billion tonnes, of which more than one-third is located in South America and about 27 per cent is in Brazil alone (Table 2.6). The worldwide average above-ground woody biomass in forests is 109 tonnes per hectare. South America had the highest average biomass per hectare, at 128 tonnes per hectare. The countries with highest standing volume per hectare include many Central American and Central European Countries, the former having high volume tropical rain forests and the latter having temperate forests managed to achieve high stocking levels (FRA, 2000).

Forest Productivity

Forest productivity, conventionally speaking, is the rate of production of timber growth. However, over the years, the definition of forest productivity has changed to cover wider perspectives on forests. Forest is now known to produce goods and services, which are valuable to man. Therefore, in this backdrop of changing concept of multiple use of forests, productivity is now being interpreted as the rate of production of timber and non-timber forest products including bio-diversity and other ecological services in a given ecosystem. However, in the absence of reliable data on the rate of production of goods other than wood and also due to lack of appropriate methodology to compute the forest productivity, only wood products are considered for analyzing the forest productivity in the global scale.

Table 2.6: Distribution of Above-ground Woody Biomass by Region

Region	*Biomass (million tonnes)*	*%*
Africa	70.916	16.8
Asia	45.036	10.7
Europe	61.070	14.5
North and Central America	51.895	12.3
Oceania	12.350	2.9
South America	179.947	42.7
Total World	**421.214**	

Source: State of World's Forests (2001).

The world forest resource base is variable not only in its timber volume and growth rate, but also in its structure and composition. Different types of forest present variable growth and volume standards all over the world. The volume of standing timber varies from 350 cubic meter per hectare in the topical rain forests to 50 cubic meters in Savannah woodland and perhaps 150 cubic meter in temperate forest (Persson, 1974). It is estimated that around 20 to 25 per cent of the photosynthetic matter produced on earth is in the form of wood (Spurrand Vaux, 1976). There is a definite relationship between ecological productivity and forest productivity. But the relationship has not been explored and calibrated.

However, a lot of progress has been made in the area of defining ecological productivity. Ecological productivity has been classified into different categories. The Net Primary Productivity (NPP) is the rate of increment of plant material and is expressed in terms of dry matter per square meter per year. The part of forest represented by wood used as timber, pulp, and fuelwood is said to be equivalent to little more than one-twentieth of the NPP used by man (Diamond, 1987). Different estimates of Net Primary Productivity with respect to different types of forest have been presented in Table 2.7. A cursory look at the table indicates that the tropical rain forest is the most productive forest type and it has the highest biomass. It is a fact that productivity is highest in tropical forests in comparison with non-tropical forests. However, there is a distinction between Total Net Primary Productivity and wood production. It is said that in Russian temperate oak forests, 52 per cent of the plant biomass constitute stems of the trees. In Canadian mature spruce forests, the stem of trees constitutes about 60 to 70 per cent of above ground biomass. However, coming to tropical forest, though the Net Primary Productivity (NPP) is highest, but all plant matter does not contribute to wood production. Apart from this, unlike boreal forests, the timber growth in tropical forests is spread over numerous tree species, few of which are salable and the rest are not usable as wood. Tropical forest constitutes about 60 per cent of the total existing closed forests of the world and it constitutes 70 per cent of the total world timber volume. It therefore, speaks volume about the stupendous significance of tropical forest in the earth.

Table 2.7: Net Primary Productivity

	Area (10^6 km²)	*Net primary Range (g/m²/ year)*	*Productivity Approx (g/m²/year)*	*Total Production (10^9 t)*	*Mean Bio-mass (t/ha)*
Forests	50.0		1,290	64.5	
Tropical rain forest	17.0	1,000-3,500	2,000	34.0	450
Raingreen forest	7.5	600-3,500	1,500	11.3	
Summergreen forest	7.0	400-2,500	1,000	7.0	
Mediterranean forest	1.5	250-1,500	800	1.2	
Warm temperature mixed forest	5.0	1,000-1,500	1,000	5.0	300
Boreal forest	12.0	200-1,500	500	6.0	200
Woodland	7.0	200-100	600	4.2	

Source: Complied from data given by Lieth (1975) and Jones (1979).

The annual increment of growth of tree crop varies with types of forest, ages of crop, and other factors of locality. In managed forests of temperate regions such as Europe, North America and Japan, net annual increment are usually equivalent to between 1 and 6 per cent of the growing stock and usually of the order of a few cubic meters per hectare per annum. In forests of former Soviet Union, Canada and United States, the annual increments per hectare are respectively 1.2, 1.5, and 3.1 cubic meter (Maller,

1990). King (1975) has suggested a global average increment of around 1.1 cubic meters per hectare. If King's suggestion is accepted, then the annual global increment on a forest area of 3,869 million hectares will be about 4,256 million cubic meter per annum. But the present officially recorded outturn from forest is far less than this mark.

However, looking at the productive capacity of the forests, Patterson (1956) tried to measure the potential productivity of different forest zones of the world. He derived a CVP (climate vegetation productivity) index in which data on temperature, rainfall and growing seasons were incorporated. He made an attempt to estimate the potential productivity of the world's forests on the basis of climatic data. The broad estimate pattern with respect to forests of the world is given in Fig 2.5. The estimate did not tally with real production in any country. The reason attributed to this is the unrealistic methodology adopted by Patterson to calculate CVP index. The index did not consider soil and wind as important factors for plant production. However, Petterson helped to project a trend of possibility of wood production on a global as well as regional perspective.

Productivity value of forests is very high in tropical zone. In most of the equatorial zone and humid tropics, the estimated potential productivity in boreal forest is 3 cubic meter per hectare per year. Then it decreases in other zones. The potential productivity in humid temperate forests of Australia, New Zealand, North America and North-West Europe is relatively high. The potential productivity in Western Africa and Asia is very low or near zero.

Forest Decline: The Global Dimension

In the developing countries, where most of the tropical forests are located, the major transition in forests is a rapid reduction in forest area. This is called as deforestation. This is primarily attributed to the process of conversion of forest land to other uses, mostly agricultural purpose. The leading causes of deforestation are the extension of subsistence farming (Africa), estate crops such as rubber and oil palm (Asia), and government backed conversion of forests to other land uses such as large scale ranching (Latin America) (FAO, 1997). Poverty, unemployment, and inequitable land distribution continue to drive forest clearance for subsistence farming in the tropics. Apart from this, a change in the structural integrity of forest is witnessed in many parts of the forests. This change is called as forest degradation or impoverishment of forests. This is taking place because of destructive and unsustainable logging and chronic disturbance including climate change and toxification.

Table 2.8: Extent of Forests and Annual Deforestation

Country	*Land Area (thousand sq.m. 1995)*	*Forest (thousand sq. km. 1995)*	*Annual Deforestation*	
			Sq. km 1990-95	*Average % change 1990-95*
Argentina	2,737	339	894	0.3
Australia	7,682	409	-170	0.0
Bangladesh	130	10	88	0.8
Brazil	8,457	5,511	25,544	0.5
China	9,326	1,633	866	0.1
Cuba	110	18	236	1.2
Egypt	995	0	0	0
Germany	349	107	0	0
India	2,973	650	-72	0
Indonesia	1,812	1,098	10,844	1.0
Iran	1,622	15	284	1.7
Japan	377	251	132	0.1
Kenya	569	13	34	0.3
South Korea	99	76	130	0.2
Malaysia	329	155	4,002	2.4
Mexico	1,909	554	5,080	0.9
Nigeria	911	138	1,214	0.9
Norway	307	81	-180	-0.2
Pakistan	771	17	550	2.9
Russia	16,889	7,635	0	0
South Africa	1,221	85	150	0.2
Sri Lanka	65	18	202	1.1
United Kingdom	242	24	-128	-0.5
United States	9,159	2,125	-5,886	-0.3
Vietnam	325	91	1,352	1.4
Low-income countries	39,294	6,277	38,690	0.6
Middle-income countries	59,884	19,985	74,598	0.4
High-income countries	30,951	6,501	-11,564	-0.2
South Asia	4,781	744	1,316	0.2
World	130,129	32,712	101,724	0.3

Source: World Development Indicators, 1998 (World Bank).

Note:
- '0' indicates data not available.
- In low-income countries, annual per capita income is less than $785.
- In middle-income countries, annual per capita is between $785 and $ 9,635.
- In high-income countries, annual per capita income is more than $9,636.

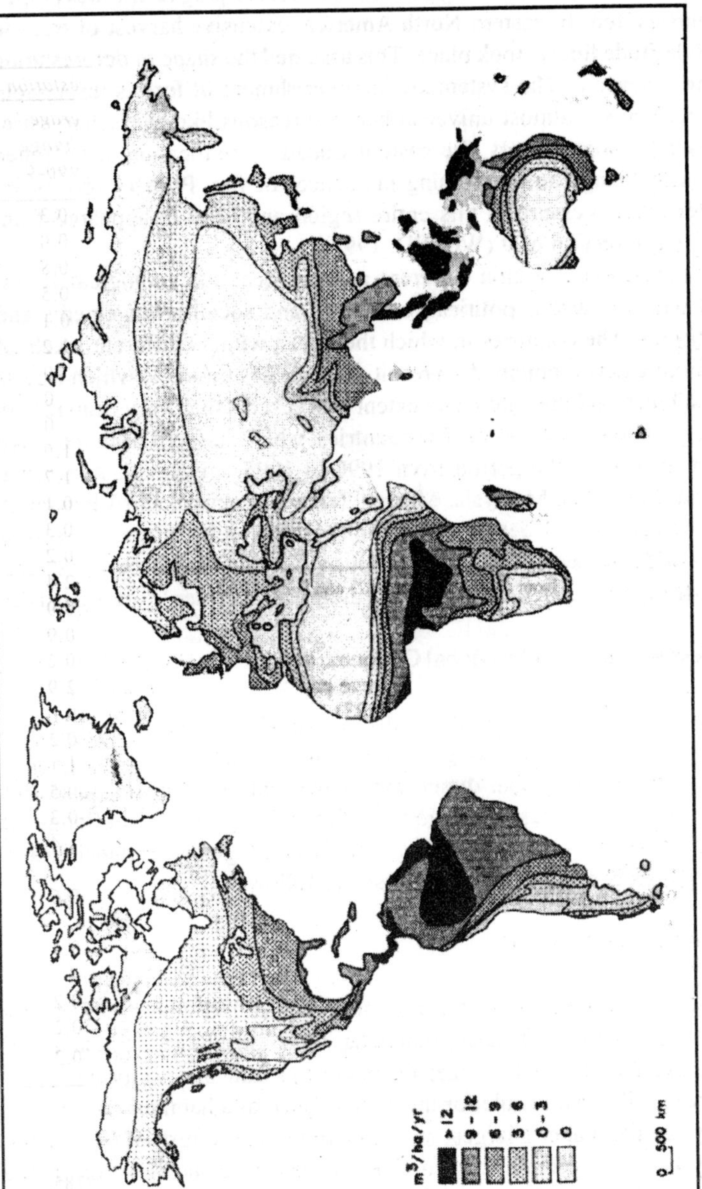

Fig. 2.5: Potential Productivity of Worlds Forests

Deforestation and degradation of forests plague the developed countries, too. In eastern North America, extensive harvest of trees in high latitude forests took place. This assumed the shape of deforestation in any measure. The systematic impoverishment of forests throughout the region was almost universal because reasons like heavy harvest of timber (in some places like eastern Canada), toxification, accelerated climatic change and increasing incidences of fire. Primary forests are under great pressure in this entire region and have disappeared from very large section of it (WCFSD, 1999).

Forest exists within different geographical and ecological zones, and with in various political, economic and social arrangements and traditions. The countries in which they exist witness different levels of economic development. As a result, the precise stresses to which forests are subject, and the nature and extent of forest decline, vary from region to region (WCFSD, 1999). The countries, which suffered from intensive deforestation in the period from 1990 to 1995, are Brazil, Argentina, China, Indonesia, Malaysia, Mexico, Nigeria, Pakistan and Vietnam. A detailed account of deforestation and degradation in different forests of the world is presented in Table 2.8. However, a complete account of threats to different forests of the world is presented in chapter 'Forest Crisis'.

Forest Resources: The Global Context

Forest resources were traditionally managed with national and local perspective. With the passage of time, a new dimension has been added to it. This is the global dimension or the context. Considered in this backdrop, the forest management faces the greatest challenge of reconciling the local and national interests with global responsibilities. The global context can be categorised as follows:

Environmental Context

Despite the emphasis on the economic value, forests are universally significant for their planetary functions. They constitute the fundamental ecological process, which keep the planet in a state of equilibrium. They are primarily responsible for the maintenance of a habitable biosphere. They are the planet's largest and most important terrestrial ecosystem. They have a profound influence on the structure and function of the human habitat locally and globally. Forests are the largest reservoir of plants and animals on land. They symbolise the rich repository of biodiversity of life embodying stupendous genetic information, developed over a long span of evolution. They protect drainage basins and regulate water supplies. They create and conserve soils. They affect productivity of fishery and agriculture. They affect absorption and reflectivity of solar rays and as a consequence affect the temperature regime of earth, which in turn regulate global and local climate. The metabolism of forests affects carbon dioxide, methane and nitrous oxide content of the atmosphere, regulating the quality of the atmosphere and temperature of the earth and its climate. These are the common global services from which all regions and human societies benefit.

Industrial Context

The forests are looked upon as a vital source of industrial wood. This source has also the potentiality of emerging as export earner. There is a wide gap in demand and supply of industrial wood worldwide. Apart from this, the gap is increasing day-by-day. Many developing countries that were formerly net exporters are now net importers. This trend is rising menacingly. In many countries, they export forest products in order to generate the capital required for economic development and to pay the foreign debt. Therefore, the world faces the challenge of meeting increasing demand for a wide range of industrial and non-industrial forest products from a shrinking resource base (Maini, 1991).

Social and Cultural Context

Forests play an intrinsic role in all cultures which have a forest heritage. They occupy a central position in the daily lives of many people, most notably indigenous and rural communities. Others still find the roots of their modern cultural identity in the forests. Now, in the post-Rio Phase, conservation and sustainable development of the forests for the present and future generations have emerged as an ethical issue. This issue has agitated developed as well as developing countries. Sustaining the forests for the future generation raises the ethical issue of inter-generational responsibility of world community. Closely connected with this is the issue of protecting the rights of forest dwellers, indigenous people and communities living in proximity of forests or depending to a great extent, on such resources. Apart from this, the issue of use of indigenous or traditional knowledge for conservation and sustainable development of forest resources, the issue of intellectual property rights, and financial compensation for using these rights are all emerging as important ethical issues related to management of forests. The issue of carbon trading and amount of compensation for aforestation/reforestation are other issues raising their heads in various international fora.

Geopolitical Context

Environmental role of forests extends well beyond their political boundaries. Therefore, forests have geopolitical importance. Management of forests that constitute the watershed to a river system flowing down stream countries raises many issues having deep socio-economic implications. The role of forests in global carbon, oxygen and climatic cycle emphasises their environmental importance, which transcends beyond the political territory of any country. This has emerged as a challenge to the global management of forest resources. Therefore, there is an imperative need on the part of every country to harmonise national interests with international responsibilities.

Sustainable Forest Development: The Changing Paradigm

The concept of sustainable development gained prominence in the year 1980 when International Union for the Conservation of Nature published the World Conservation Strategy (WCS). The World Conservation Strategy had the objective of achieving sustainable development through the conservation of natural resources. The strategy laid emphasis on the fact that development could be sustained only if human activities operate within the realm of resource limitations and carrying capacities of ecosystems. In other words, the Conservation Strategy emphasised the biophysical sustainability of ecosystems. It failed to recognise the fact that development process has political and social overtones which in many cases, act as impediments to conservation. Then the concept of eco-development was introduced in natural resource management. Eco-development focussed on the satisfaction of basic human needs while maintaining ecological health (Sachs, 1979 p. 21). Gradually, the doctrine of eco-development, besides fulfilling the basic human need as the core component, encompassed the aspects like decentralisation, community participation, use of indigenous knowledge, and the adoption of appropriate technology. But the pitfall in eco-development concept was that it limited itself to development at local scale only. However, the basic approach of eco-development with other aspects like enhancing the resource base and intra-generational and inter-generational equity was instrumental in shaping present thinking on sustainable development.

The concept of sustainable development took concrete shape in the report of world commission on Environment and Development in the year 1987. This report, popularly known as the Brundtland Report, defined sustainable development as "development that meets the needs of the present without compromising the ability of future generations to meet their own needs" (WCED, 1987). The June 1992 United Nations Conference on Environment and Development (UNDP) at Rio focussed on sustainable forest development and recognised that problems like poverty, food security, over-consumption of forest products and external indebtedness were linked with forest decline. In addition to it, such problems have reduced the capacity of many countries to manage their forest resources sustainably.

Therefore, the issues, which are going, to dominate the politics and policies of this twenty-first century are: stabilisation of human habitat, population and development, poverty eradication, gender equity, food security and social infrastructure. The most fundamental and urgent among them is the need to stabilise the human habitat where mankind lives. Forest, being an important component of human habitat, assumes significance.

3

FORESTS RESOURCES IN CRISIS

Dimension and Causes

Forests are the planet's largest and most important terrestrial ecosystem. They have a profound influence on the structure and function of human habitat locally as well as globally. They are the largest reservoir of plants and animals. They sustain much of world's diversity of life embodying stupendous genetic information, developed over evolutionary time. They protect drainage basins and regulate water supplies. They create and retain soils. They affect productivity of fishery and agriculture. They provide the means for livelihoods as well as succor to hundred of millions of people who live close to forest boundaries. They affect absorption and reflectivity of sunrays and as a consequence affect the temperature regime, which in turn regulate global and local climate. The metabolism of forests affect carbon dioxide, methane and nitrous oxide content of the atmosphere day by day, regulating the quality of the atmosphere and temperature of the earth and its climate. Benefits from forests go beyond the domain of environmental and material services. They symbolise spiritual and aesthetic value to people.

The evolution of human civilisation over the past 8,000 years, and especially expansion and intensification of human activities over the past two centuries have brought great changes in the area and character of forests globally. But over the recent years, there has been a clear global trend towards a massive loss of forested area. The current trends are towards acceleration of the loss of primary forest and progressive reduction in the quality of such forests. This chapter attempts to depict the dimension of forest crisis on a global perspective. It also provides an account of reasons, direct and indirect, for the present forest crisis.

The world has about 3,870 million ha of forests. This constitutes 30 per cent of the earth's land area. About 95 per cent of total forest areas are natural forests and 5 per cent are forest plantation. Again about 55 per cent of world's forests are located in developing countries, with the remaining 45 per cent in developed countries. The world's forests are equally divided between tropical/sub-tropical forests and temperate/boreal forests. The basic forest data and an account of extent of forests in the globe are presented in Tables 3.1 and 3.2.

Table 3.1: Basic Forest Data, 2001

Item	*Extent*
Forest area	3,870 million hectare
Above-ground woody biomass in forests	420 billion tonnes
Average above ground woody biomass in forests	109 tonnes
Global deforestation rate during 1990s	14.6 million ha per year
Global rate of forest area increase during 1990s	5.2 million ha per year
The net change in forest area during 1990s	–9.4 million ha per year

Source: FAO, 2001. State of World's Forests, 2001.

Forest Decline: The Global Dimension

In the developing countries, where most of the tropical forests are located, the major transition in forests is a rapid reduction in forest area. This is called as deforestation. This is primarily attributed to the process of conversion of forest land to other uses, mostly agricultural purpose. The leading causes of deforestation are the extension of subsistence farming (Africa), estate crops such as rubber and oil palm (Asia), and government backed conversion of forests to other land uses such as large scale ranching (Latin America) (FAO, 1997). Poverty, unemployment, and inequitable land distribution continue to drive forest clearance for subsistence farming in the tropics. Apart from this, a change in the integrity of forest structure is witnessed in many parts of the globe. This change is called as forest degradation or impoverishment of forests. This is taking place because of destructive and unsustainable logging and chronic disturbance including climate change and toxification.

Deforestation and degradation plague the developed countries, too. In eastern North America, extensive harvest of trees in high latitude forests has taken place. This has taken the shape of deforestation. The systematic impoverishment of forests throughout the region is almost universal as a result of chronic disturbance in some places such as eastern Canada, because of toxification, accelerated climatic change, and fire. Primary forests are under great pressure in this entire region and have disparaged from very large section of it (WCFSD, 1999).

Table 3.2: Distribution of Forests in Different Continents

Continent/region	*Land Area (million hectares)*	*Total Forest in million hectares*	*% of World's Forests*
North & Central America	2,137	549	14
South America	1,755	886	23
Africa	2,978	650	17
Asia	3,085	548	14
Europe	2,260	1,039	27
Oceania	849	198	5
World Total	13,064	3,869	**100**

Source: FAO: 2001, State of World's Forests, 2001.

Forest exists within different geographical and ecological zones, and within various political, economic and social arrangements and traditions. The countries in which they exist experience different levels of economic welfare. As a result, the precise stresses to which forests are subjected, and the nature and extent of forest decline, vary from region to region (WCFSD, 1999).

Table 3.3: Estimated Reduction of Forest Areas Since Pre-agricultural Time

Sl.No.	*Category*	*Area million hectares*
1	Total estimated reduction in the forest and wood land:	900
	(*a*) Forest	775
	(*b*) Woodland	125
2	Tropical rain forests	50
3	Boreal Coniferous forests	50
4	Deciduous Forests in Europe and Eastern United States and temperate evergreen forests in Asia and others	800

Source: Adopted from data provided by Mathews (1983).

Dynamics of Forest Decline

Forest decline is a metaphor used for forest loss or deforestation or forest degradation. It is a gradual process taking place in most parts of the globe. Every part of the earth witnessed forest loss at some point of the history. Presently also, every country is facing forest loss, in either in extent (quantity) or quality or both, at different pace. The estimate of forest loss in the world is still based on multifarious sources (See Tables 3.3 to 3.7). Lot of differences in estimation of forest and woodland areas occurs on account of various methods and technologies adopted by different sources. Notwithstanding the differences, such estimation indicates the pace of forest decline on a global scale.

Forest decline has been conspicuously visible in the whole of the second half of the last century. However, for the sake of analysis of forest decline in the world, the period of active deforestation has been divided into three conspicuous overlapping phases. The first phase spreads between year 1975 to 1985. The second phase spreads between year 1980 to 1995. The third phase spreads between year 1990 to 2000. The net deforestation per year in the first phase was 8 million-hectare. It was 13.7 million-hectare in the second phase. It was 9.4 million-hectare in the third phase. The net deforestation in the last phase represents the balance between the global deforestation rate of 14.6 million hectare per year and the rate of forest area increase of 5.2 million hectare per year.

The forest decline in the first phase is alarming. Accepting the data provided by FAO Production Yearbook, the average loss of forest and woodland during the first phase *i.e.* period from 1975 to 1985 remained at about 2 per cent. The net change at this period stood at about 80 million hectares (See Table 3.4). Lanly (1982) has also estimated forest loss in tropical zones. He found that the annual rate of clearance of tropical forests around 1980 was 11.3 million hectares of which 7.5 million were closed forests and the reminder was open woodland. He has also reported that the annual deforestation rate in Africa, Asia and America is 0.77 per cent, 0.67 per cent and 0.6 per cent respectively.

Table 3.4: Net Change in Areas of Forest and Woodland 1975-85

	Area in million hectares	*Change in per cent*
World	–82.9	–1.99
Developed world	–12.9	–0.70
Developing world	–70.0	–3.01
Centrally planned economies	+60.7	+5.55
Latin America	–54.1	–5.21
Africa	–29.0	–3.99
Asia	+13.8	+2.51
Europe	+2.0	+1.29
USSR	+38.0	+4.24

Source: Compiled from data in FAO Production Yearbook. Year 1987.

The spatial pattern of deforestation or change in forest and woodland areas during this first phase *i.e.* period from 1975 to 1985 is presented in Table 3.4. A cursory look at the pattern of forest loss indicates few conspicuous characteristics, which are enumerated below:

- Forest decline or deforestation is witnessed in both developed as well as developing countries.
- The rate of deforestation with respect to extent of forest area in developing countries is alarmingly high *i.e.* about six times higher than the rate witnessed in developed countries.
- The nature of forest decline in developed countries is primarily in terms of quality.
- The biggest change in forest area is taking place in Latin American countries. The loss of forest areas during the said period was about 54 million hectares. It constitutes about one-third of the net global change.
- The major countries suffering from massive depletion in forest cover are Brazil, Columbia, Ecuador, Venezuela, in south America, Ivory Cost, Nigeria, Sudan and Zaire in south Africa and Philippines and Malaysia in south east Asia. These trends of forest decline are still continuing today.
- Countries of former Soviet Union and Eastern Europe, though displayed increase in forest cover or stabilisation, but forest quality of such countries suffers from extensive damage.

BOX 3.1: CAUSES FOR DECLINE IN FOREST QUALITY IN EUROPE

Direct Cause

- draught
- heat
- pests
- a legacy of silvicultural errors.

Indirect Cause

- Air pollution from industrial sources
- Other chronic disturbances.

Sources: European Commission and United Nation Economic Commission for Europe (EC-UN/ECE) 1995.

The pace of forest decline increased in the second phase *i.e.* from period 1980 to 1995. Data published in the State of the World's Forests 1997 (FAO, 1997) provide a picture of the trends in forest cover over a 15-year interval (1980-95). Between 1980 and 1995, the extent of world's forests (including both natural forests and forest plantations) decreased by some 180 million hectares. There was a net increase of 20 million hectares in developed countries, but a net loss of 200 million hectares in developing nations. The estimate of forest cover change in natural forests of developing countries (which is where most of the deforestation is taking place) was an annual loss of 13.7 million hectares per year between 1990 and 1995, compared with 15.5 million hectares per year over the decade 1980-90 (FAO, 1997).

BOX 3.2: FOREST LOSS IN AFRICA: EXTENT AND CAUSE

Extent of Forest Loss in Africa

- Africa during the 1980s alone lost some 40 million hectares of natural forests.
- Nearly three quarters of the original tropical moist forests in west Africa have been lost over the past 50 years.
- Countries like Burundi, Kenya, Madagascar, Nigeria, Rwanda lost more than 90 per cent of their original forest.

Causes of Forest Loss in Africa

- Population expansion.
- Encroachment of forest land (expansion of agriculture).
- Commercial harvesting, mainly in the central and west African tropical humid forest.
- Political instability, especially in the Congo basin.
- Increased fuel wood collection and live stock grazing in open forests of Africa.

Source: FAO, 1997.

Forest Decline During Period from 1990-2000

Forest decline represents the net change in forest area. It indicates the differences between the increase in forest area through both afforestation and the natural expansion of forest (*e.g.* through forest succession on abandoned agricultural lands), and the loss of forest through deforestation. The information regarding average annual change in natural forests and in forest plantations, for both tropical and non-tropical areas during the period 1990-2000, is presented in Table 3.5. These data indicates that the world's natural forests continued to be converted to other land uses at a very high rate during the 1990s. An estimated 16.1 million ha of natural forest worldwide were lost annually during the 1990s (14.6 million ha through deforestation and 1.5 million ha through conversion to forest plantations). Of the 15.2 million ha lost annually in the tropics, 14.2 million ha were converted to other land uses and 1.0 million ha were converted to forest plantations. In non-tropical areas, 0.9 million ha of natural forests were lost per year, of which 0.5 million ha were converted to forest plantations and 0.4 million ha were converted to other land use classes. Against the gross annual loss of 16.1 million ha of natural forests worldwide, there was a gain of 3.6 million ha as a result of the natural expansion of forest, giving a balance of –12.5 million ha as the annual net change of natural forest area globally. Of these 3.6 million ha 2.6 million ha were in non-tropical areas, while 1.0 million ha were in the tropics. Much of the gain in natural forest area was the result of natural forest succession on abandoned agricultural land. Expansion of forest has been occurring for several decades in many industrialised countries, mostly in European countries.

Gains in forest area also occurred through the expansion of forest plantations. The average rate of successful plantation establishment over the decade was 3.1 million ha per year, of which 1.9 million ha were tropical areas and 1.2 million ha were in non-tropical area. The net change in forest area during the 1990s (*i.e.* the sum of changes in natural forests and forest plantations) was estimated –9.4 million ha per year. This represents the balance between the global deforestation rate of 14.6 million ha per year and the rate of forest area increase of 5.2 million ha per year (Table 3.6). Net deforestation rates were highest in Africa and South America. The loss of natural forests in Asia was also high, but was significantly offset (in terms of areas) by forest plantation establishment. This resulted in a more moderate rate of change of total forest area in the region. In contrast, the forest cover in the other regions, which are largely made up of industrialised countries, increased slightly. The countries with the highest net loss of forest areas between 1990 and 2000 were Argentina, Brazil, the democratic republic of the Congo, Indonesia, Myanmar, Mexico, Nigeria, the Sudan, Zambia and Zimbabwe. Those with the highest net gain of forest during this period were China, Belarus, Kazakistan, the Russian Federation and the United States.

Table 3.5: Annual Change in Forest Area, 1990-2000 (*million ha*)

Domain	*Natural Forest*				*Net change*	*Forest Plantations*		*Net change*	*Total forest*
	Loss			*Gain*		*Gain*			*Net change*
	Deforestation	*Conversion to forest plantations*	*Total loss*	*Natural expansion of forest*		*Conversion from natural forest*	*Afforestation*		
Tropical areas	–14.2	–1.0	–15.2	+1.0	–14.2	+1.0	+0.9	+1.9	–12.3
Non-tropical areas	–0.4	–0.5	–0.9	+2.6	+1.7	+0.5	+0.7	+1.2	+2.9
World	–14.6	–1.5	–16.1	+3.6	–12.5	+1.5	+1.6	+3.1	–9.4

Source: FRA (2000).

Table 3.6: Annual Gross and Net Changes in Forest Area, 1990-2000 (million ha)

Domain	*Deforestation*	*Increase in Forest Area**	*Net Change in Forest Area*
Tropics	–14.2	+1.9	–12.3
Non-tropics	–0.4	+3.3	+2.9
World	–14.6	+5.2	–9.4

* Increase in forest area represents the sum of natural expansion of forest and afforestation (see Table 3.5 'annual change in forest area 1990-2000).

Source: FRA (2000).

According to FRA 2000 data, the estimated net loss of forest (*i.e.* the balance of the loss of natural forests and the gain in forest area through afforestation and natural expansion of forest) was lower in the 1990s than in the 1980s. Net annual forest area change was estimated to be –13.0 million ha in 1980-90 period, –11.3 million in the 1990-95 period and –9.4 million ha for the 1990-2000 period.

Forest Decline in Different Continents

Temperate and Boreal Forests

The countries of Commonwealth of Independent States (CIS) contain more than 70 per cent of the world's remaining boreal forests. Presently, the forest is threatened by industrial emissions, by the prospect of massive felling particularly in Siberia and European Russia and by illegal activities and ineffectual government policies. Ecologically fragile boreal forests in parts of the Siberian Permafrost Zone are undergoing severe disturbances from logging, and it is not clear how much they will recover (Shvidenko and Nilsson, 1996) (See Box 3.3).

Europe witnessed a cycle of deforestation and forestation. In 1995, there was no primary forest in Europe and 40 per cent of forest land supports secondary forests. Therefore, deteriorating forest is a major concern. While progressive deforestation is not significant in most of contemporary Europe and forest area may even be increasing at a moderate rate, forest degradation remains a considerable threat. FAO reported that though forest cover in Europe (excluding the former USSR) increased by more than 4 per cent between 1980 and 1994, forest quality worsened (FAO, 1996). While impoverishment in forest condition in Europe has been noted in certain locations, overall forest damage seems to be increasing on a regional level (WCFSD, 1999). Forest damage is severe in some parts of Central and Eastern Europe. All forests of Europe, however, are vulnerable to the ravages of pollution, diseases and climatic disruption (EC-UN/ECE, 1996).

BOX 3.3: FOREST DECLINE IN EUROPEAN AND CIS COUNTRIES

European Countries

- More than one quarter of Europe's trees shows signs of significant leaf-loss.
- A 1997 European Commission and United Nations Economic Commission and United Nations Economic Commission for Europe (EC-UN/ECE) study classified more than halves of Europe's forests as 'damaged'.
- In north-central Europe most notably Poland, the Czech Republic and East Germany at least 1,00,000 hectares of forests died in the last 20 years. (FAO, 1997).
- More than 25 per cent of trees assessed in a survey of forest conditions in Europe were suffering significant defoliation.
- Annual European survey result shows the number of completely healthy trees from 69 per cent in 1988 to 39 per cent in 1995. (EC-UN/ECE. 1996).

CIS Countries

- Forest exploitation is out of control in Siberia and European Russia, at least for the time being.
- About 10,000 square km of forests are estimated to have lost due to air pollution alone.
- Air contamination from nickel smelters of Norlisk has killed 3,500 square km and damaged trees over an additional 1,400 square km of forests.
- The Chernobyl nuclear disaster of 1987 is thought to have contaminated 7 million hectares of forest land and other wooded land in Russia, Belarus and Ukraine.

Forest decline is manifest in North America also (See also Box 3.5). Though net deforestation rates are not significant in temperate North America, they remain high in the sub-tropics of Mexico. In the temperate boreal region, forest degradation is the major concern. The primary forests of Sierra Nevada and other accessible areas are under the spell of degradation or impoverishment. Forests of eastern USA and eastern Canada are facing new challenges. Air pollution including acid rain plays an important role in the decline of various forest species, such as the sugar maple (Acer saccharum) in eastern Canada and the high elevation forests of red spruce (Picea rubens) in the eastern USA (FAO, 1997). In Mexico, there has been a long history of forest loss due to clearing for land for agriculture. This menace continues still today but now new forces of industrialisation over the years have aggravated it more.

Tropical and Sub-tropical Forests

The forests of Asia, the Indian sub-continent, Australia, and the island chain of the southwestern Pacific are under the grip of forest decline. Between 1990 and 1995, tropical forests of Asia and Oceania suffered high rates of deforestation. During this period, tropical Asian forests suffered from deforestation rates averaging 1.1 per cent per year; where as the loss of forests in Oceania was about 0.4 per cent per year. Forested parts of Indonesia, Thailand and Philippines have been reduced to fire prone scrub and grassland in the last decade. Forest decline in Asia and Oceania has occurred mainly through clearing for agriculture (both shifting cultivation and commercial farming) and timber (both harvesting and conversion of biologically diverse forests into plantations) (WCFSD, 1999). High population densities have led to widespread forest degradation from fuelwood and fodder harvesting, cattle grazing, land invasion and shifting cultivation, and timber harvesting for local construction (FAO, 1997). Commercial timber harvesting has been more widespread (measures as a per centage of forest area) and intensive (timber volume removal per hectare) than in any other tropical region. Other activities implicated in the decline include mining, irrigation, hydroelectric projects and urban expansion (FAO, 1997).

African forests have been under great stress since ancient times. During the 1980s alone, Africa lost some 40 million hectares of natural forests. About 50 per cent of the region's potential forest cover have been lost. Primary forests exist on 8 per cent of the potential forest area. Deforestation continues at a high rate, particularly in tropical areas, though deforestation rates are moderate in both the southern and northern reaches of Africa. Over the 1980-95 period, Africa experienced a greater per centage decrease in total forests area—10.5 per cent—than any other region (FAO, 1997).

Nearly three-quarters of the original tropical moist forest in West Africa have been lost over the past 50 years. Several countries like Burundi, Kenya, Madagascar, Nigeria, Rwanda, etc. lost more than 90 per cent of their original forest cover in this short period as population exploded and the demand for agricultural land soared. Much of the West African tropical humid forests, located mainly in lowland areas and accessible to the coast, have undergone substantial commercial harvesting. In many areas, these forests were converted to agricultural fields. Timber harvesting has intensified in some West African countries, and many timber companies are now operating in central Africa, which contains more than 90 per cent of region's remaining forests. Political instability has enabled exploitative use to be made of timber resources in the Congo Basin. Pressures on Africa's extensive open forests are also heavy in many places due to agricultural expansions and increased fuelwood collection and livelihood grazing (FAO, 1997).

The Latin America and the Caribbean region include the large chunk of forests including the primary forests. The Amazon Basin, the largest contiguous area of tropical forests in the world is still the repository of a very high proportion of the world's biotic wealth. This region is under tremendous pressure for forest clearance for the purpose of rehabilitation, agriculture, urban expansion and infrastructure development. The Amazon forests are being fast opened to human settlement to relieve population pressure in South America's mega cities like Rio de Janeiro and Sao Paulo, and to feed the interests of commerce. The Latin America and Caribbean region suffers from some of the highest current –day rates of forest decline. Deforestation rates for the 1990-95 period were high in the whole of tropical areas and very high in central (2.2% per year) and Caribbean region (1.7% per year) (FAO, 1997). The region lost about 9.7 per cent of its forests area between 1980 and 1995 period alone (FAO, 1997). In other words, in the period between 1990 and 1995, the deforestation of that scale caused a loss of about 5.3 million hectares of forests each year.

The loss of forests in Latin America and the Caribbean region is largely due to the direct conversion of forests to non-forest uses, linked to large scale projects to settle and develop the region: clearance for agriculture and stockfarming; construction of roads, dams and other infrastructure; and mining (FAO, 1997). Furthermore, forests decline is driven by inequitable land tenure systems that force large numbers of landless rural people to invade forests in order to survive. Forest decline also arises from fire, pest infestation and extraction of timber and fuelwood

(FAO, 1997). Forest fires are a major contributing factor to forest decline especially in the arid and semi-arid zone. Fires are often lit to clear land for agriculture (FAO, 1997). Fire related deforestation increased sharply in Brazil in recent years. Official estimates indicates that the rate of deforestation in Amazon forest areas, has increased significantly during the period from 1997 to 98, primarily due to the spread of fires during the unusual drought of that period. Satellite data for the Amazon forests region show that there has been an increase of 50 per cent in fire incidences, primarily set by farmers to clear land for cultivation (WCFSD, 1999). What is more disturbing is the fact that, of late, transnational logging corporations who have no concern and commitment for sustainable development are operating in these forest areas, ostensibly with the willingness of some governments who are accepting their operation because of short-term economic opportunity they offer (WCFSD, 1999). Theses logging corporations have been carrying timber extraction operations in such a way that they lead to forest degradation. Despite the series of threat, the region remains the repository of world's biotic wealth.

Root Causes of Forest Crisis

The forests that once covered nearly half of the earth's land surface are being fast replaced with growing urban centres, agricultural fields, degraded forests and land impoverished by degradation and erosion. What is more disconcerting is the fact that much of the remaining forests are being progressively impoverished and increasingly threatened, solely because of rising anthropogenic pressure. The crisis does not lie in the fact that we are losing the forest cover and quality over the years. The crux of the matter lies in the fact that the earth will be deprived of forest functions, which are responsible for maintaining the life supporting system in the biosphere.

A complex set of forces contributes directly or indirectly, to the multiple causes of forest decline. There are certain reasons which are easily seen, like the ways in which forest land is converted to agricultural use or another non-forestry uses. There are certain reasons of forest decline, which are not easily perceptible. These forces originate from the complex and overlapping economic, political and social systems and creates environmentally unsustainable elements in the society. Such elements make the forest use unsustainable. Such forces may originate from international trade agreements or multinational investments or life styles of any region in the world or living conditions or cultural practices in a particular region or

Table 3.7: Land, Forest and Deforestation (period 1990-95)

Country	*Land Area (thousand sq. m, 1995)*	*Land Use (% of Land Area)*			*Forest (thousand sq. km, 1995)*	*Annual Deforestation*	
		Crop land 1995	*Permanent pasture 1994*	*Other land 1994*		*sq. km, 1990-95*	*Average % Change 1990-95*
Argentina	2,737	10	52	38	339	894	0.3
Australia	7,682	6	54	40	409	–170	0.0
Bangladesh	130	67	5	29	10	88	0.8
Brazil	8,457	8	22	71	5,511	25,544	0.5
China	9,326	10	43	47	133	866	0.1
Cuba	110	41	20	39	18	236	1.2
Egypt	995	3	–	–	0	0	0.0
Germany	349	35	15	50	107	0	0.0
India	2,973	57	4	39	650	–72	0.0
Indonesia	1,812	17	7	77	1,098	10,844	1.0
Iran	1,622	11	27	61	15	284	1.7

(*Contd.*)

Table 3.7 (*Contd.*)

Country	*Land Area (thousand sq. m, 1995)*	*Land Use (% of Land Area)*			*Forest (thousand sq. km, 1995)*	*Annual Deforestation*	
		Crop land 1995	*Permanent pasture 1994*	*Other land 1994*		*sq. km, 1990-95*	*Average % Change 1990-95*
Japan	377	12	2	87	251	132	0.1
Kenya	569	8	37	55	13	34	0.3
South Korea	99	20	1	78	76	130	0.2
Malaysia	329	23	1	76	155	4,002	2.4
Mexico	1,909	14	42	45	554	5,080	0.9
Nigeria	911	36	44	20	138	1,214	0.9
Norway	307	3	0	97	81	–180	–0.2
Pakistan	771	28	6	66	17	550	2.9
Russia	16,889	8	5	87	7,635	0	0.0
South Africa	1,221	13	67	21	85	150	0.2
Sri Lanka	65	29	7	64	18	202	1.1
United kingdom	242	25	46	29	24	–128	–0.5

(*Contd.*)

Table 3.7 (*Contd.*)

Country	*Land Area (thousand sq. m, 1995)*	*Land Use (% of Land Area)*			*Forest (thousand sq. km, 1995)*	*Annual Deforestation*	
		Crop land 1995	*Permanent pasture 1994*	*Other land 1994*		*sq. km, 1990-95*	*Average % Change 1990-95*
United states	9,159	21	26	53	2,125	–5,886	–0.3
Vietnam	325	21	1	78	91	1,352	1.4
Averages							
Low-income countries	39,294	13	32	54	6,277	38,690	0.6
Middle-income countries	59,884	10	23	67	19,985	74,598	0.4
High-income countries	30,951	–	24		6,501	–11,564	–0.2
South Asia	4,781	45	10	45	744	1,316	0.2
World	130,129	11	26	62	32,712	101,724	0.3

Source: World Development indicators 1998 (World Bank)

Note:
1. '0' indicates data not available.
2. In low-income countries, annual per capita income is less than $785.
3. In middle-income countries, annual per capita is between $785 and $9,635.
4. In high-income countries, annual per capita income is more than $9,636.

locality. It may also be possible that such forces may influence each other in such a dynamic way that the impact on the forest becomes monstrous. The case in point is the combination of factors like poverty, population and unemployment, which hasten the process of forest decline unimaginingly. To put it briefly, it can be said that interplay of such myriad complex factors determines how people make decisions about using forest lands and products, which lead to decline of forest cover as well as quality worldwide. It is also found that the economic distortions tilt the balance against sustainable use of forest resources. The effect is visible in the forestry sector but the cause originates in some other sector. In other words, the causative factors of deforestation or forest depletion are driven by economic, social and political forces in a broader context of political economy. With the change in intensity of such forces in a specific backdrop of political economy, the result on forest use changes. Therefore, the extent and intensity of forest decline varies from one nation to another. Again, it varies from one region to another in a country because of regional variations. A cursory look at the reasons, direct or indirect, for forest decline indicates the following factors:

- Population growth
- Poverty and unemployment
- Shifting cultivation
- Bio-mass energy consumption pattern
- Land hunger
- Grazing
- Distorted fiscal and development policy
- Market failure
- Management failure
- Fire
- Ethical failure
- Gender inequality
- Governance failure
- Failure in policy and legislative environment
- Subsidies
- Growing divergence between public and private values
- Undervaluation of forest resources
- Other reasons.

Population Growth

Population growth remains central to forest crisis. About 10,000 years ago, the population of the world was probably of the order of four millions.

In 1996, the estimated world population level was 5.83 billion. The overall growth rates remains at 1.38 per cent per annum. At this growth rate, another billion of people will be added to the existing global population in every eleven years. In the year 2025, it is expected that the world population will reach 8.5 billion mark.

The problem of population growth lies in its pattern of distribution. There are many countries where the population is growing slowly or nearly stationary and likewise many countries where population is growing very fast. The region having faster population growth includes Africa (11.5 per cent) and Latin America (8.4 per cent). In total, the industrialised nations have about 22.4 per cent of the world's population and the developing countries 75.6 per cent (Simmons, 1997). The fastest growing parts of the world are mostly the less developed and poorer regions. These are located in South East Asia, Latin America, the Indian continent, the Middle East and Africa. Again in these broad categories, there are countries with very large populations and very high rate of growth, such as India (194 millions, 2.3 per cent per annum), Indonesia (918 million, 2.1 per cent per annum) and Brazil (159 million, 2.3 per cent per annum) (Simmons, 1997).

Africa has the highest set of population growth rates in the world. Within that continent the sub-Sahara region experiences the highest growth rate. It has an average rate of 2.5 per cent per annum and so the doubling time is 28 years.

The UN medium variant projection study has indicated that the world's population will be doubled before the end of 2100. Africa will have the highest growth rates. However, the biggest increase in absolute number will come from Asia. It is estimated that the replacement fertility level (RFL *i.e.* zero growth in terms of natural increases) shall be achieved by around by 2035; this would bring about a stabilization of the world's population by 2100.

Population growth is one of the most important reasons for the present forest crisis. There is a definite inverse relationship between trends of forest areas and population at the global scale. It has been found beyond doubt that in countries with rapidly expanding population, the forest areas are rapidly contracting. Conversely, where the population is stagnating or growing very slowly, the forestland is stagnating or expanding slowly. Allens and Bernes (1985), on the basis of FAO Production Yearbooks, concluded that population growth and change in arable area are associated with deforestation and shown that the relationship is stronger in Asia and Africa than it is in Latin America, where presumably other factors play relatively stronger roles (Allen, *et al*, 1985).

BOX 3.4: SOURCES OF THREAT TO FORESTS AND MANIFESTATION OF LAND DEGRADATION IN ASIA AND OCEANIA

Sources of Threat to Forests

- Clearing for agriculture (both by shifting cultivation and commercial farming).
- Timber harvesting (commercial as well as intensive harvesting).
- Conversion of biologically diverse forests into plantation.
- Fuel wood, fodder collection, cattle grazing, land encroachment and shifting.

Source: FAO, 1997.

Manifestation of Land Degradation Associated with Forest Degradation

- Reduction in agricultural productivity over large areas of productive land.
- High rates of soil erosion.
- Sedimentation of dams, reservoirs and irrigation systems.
- Hill side uplands constituting Nepal, Bhutan, China, India and Pakistan are degraded as a result of wood removal.
- Once forested parts of Indonesia, parts of Thailand and Philippines have been reduced to drought susceptible and fire prone scrub and grass land.

Source: WCFSD, 1999.

Poverty and Unemployment

Poverty and unemployment hasten the process of deforestation. Forest resources and the forest land come very handy to the poor people for their use. They provide employment to the unemployed masses living near the forests. The impact of poverty on forest is visible by many ways, like shifting cultivation, illicit felling, etc.

BOX 3.5: NORTH AMERICA: THE CHALLENGE OF FOREST DEGRADATION

Challenges of Forest Degradation in North America

- North American forests accounts for about 13 per cent of the world's total (457 million hectares) and cover about 75 per cent of their potentially forested area (FAO, 1997).
- Forest degradation is the main challenge in America. However, net deforestation still remains high in sub-tropics of Mexico. In the temperate and boreal region, forest degradation is the main cause of decline.
- Forests of USA and sections of eastern Canada is declining due to air pollution including acid rain. Species falling victim to this menace are sugar maple (Acer saccharum) in eastern Canada and red spruce (Picea rubens) in the high elevation forests of eastern USA (FAO, 1997).
- The rich temperate zone rainforests of Olympic peninsula and Canadian coast, Sitka Spruce forests of south eastern Alaskan archipelago and adjacent Canada (including coastal redwood groves, the giant Douglas fir forests of Sierra Nevada and the Cascades), and the complex of pine forests of California and Mexico are threatened by commercial interests in lumber.
- Alaska Tongrass National Forests—a 7 million-hectare wilderness where some of the trees may be up to one thousand years old, is the largest remaining temperate zone rainforests in the world. The Wilderness is under threat of degradation due to large-scale cutting allowed in a management plan approved by US Forest service (WCFSD, 1999).
- In Mexico, the process of forest degradation still continues due to clearing of forests for agriculture, forces of industrialisation and pollution.

Shifting Cultivation

The menace of shifting cultivation is the manifestation of poverty and population growth. It has been identified as one of the principal causes of deforestation in most of tropical regions of the globe, accounting for 70, 50, and 35 per cent respectively in Africa, Asia and tropical America. About 500 million people and 240 million hectares of closed forests are involved in shifting cultivation, which is increasing at an average rate of 1.25 per cent. More than 5 millions hectares of new forest fallow are created annually (Lanly, 1985). With the further increase in population, the extent of shifting cultivation is expected to increase and the fallow periods are also going to grow shorter, which jointly cause more deforestation in extent and intensity.

The shifting cultivators accelerate the process of forest loss and degradation. Such a degrading process affects the same shifting cultivators in its first place. Shifting cultivators, together with forest dwellers, are the most economically depressed and the politically weakest group, among all interest groups competing for forest resources. What is striking is the fact that such communities with close historical relationships with forests are living in abject poverty and economic insecurity. Forest decline on account of shifting cultivation has grave negative impacts on their ability to survive.

Bio-mass Energy Consumption Pattern

Consumption pattern of bio-mass energy in developing countries has been found to be one of the main factors of forest degradation. The basic survival requirement for an adult is in the region of 2,000-3,000 kcal/ day. But in order to bring certain dignity to life, that is clean water, fuelwood, food, basic medicines and basic education, we need more energy which ranges about 27-37 × 10^3 kcal/day. Out of it, bio-mass energy in most of the developing countries is the principal sources. In some of the countries the per capita traditional fuel consumption ranges above 90 per cent. Per capita energy consumption and per capita traditional fuel consumption in some less industrialised countries are presented in Table 3.8. It is clear from the table that the more underdeveloped a country is, the more per capita consumption of traditional fuel like fuelwood.

India is one such developing country where forest degradation has taken place on account of unsustainable collection of fuel wood. Such unsustainable fuel wood consumption for household energy significantly contributes to pressures on forests. Consumption of wood (timber and fuel wood) in India is considerably (4 to 5 times) higher than what can sustainably be removed from forests. In 1990, the estimated excess (mostly unrecorded) removal of fuelwood from forests was about 250 million cubic meters. This figure has increased to 310 million by 2000. Even though, some fuelwood may come from household plants and non-forest sources, a substantial quantity of fuel wood is obtained by unrecorded over cut, steadily adding to the rate of forest degradation and deforestation (FSI, 1999).

Land Hunger

In developing countries, for want of other options, economically marginalised and displaced communities often invade forestland in order to survive. Subsistence farming in few South East Asian countries like Indonesia and Philippines has played an important role in forest decline. It is said that such conversion in Indonesia has resulted into extensive forest clearance into the tune of about three million hectares.

Table 3.8: Energy Consumption in Some LIEs, 1991

Place	*Per Capita Consumption (GJ)*	*Per Capita Traditional Fuel Consumption (MJ)*	*Percentage of Traditional Fuels, 1992*
World	60	3,702	6
Africa	12	7,275	38
Zambia	20	6,812	26
Nepal	1	10,247	93
El Salvador	10	10,950	43
Brazil	23	13,328	36
Papua New Guinea	8	15,083	65

Source: WRI (1995) World Resource 1994-95. Oxford University Press, 1995, Table 21.2.

Grazing

Overgrazing in forests of the tropical regions is always allowed without considering their carrying capacity. This is basically the principal reason for the forest degradation. The situation is alarming in most of the mountaineous region in the tropical belt of the globe. In all countries of Asia, and Africa the cattle population exerts an enormous pressures on the forests. Managing grazing in forests with in the ambit of carrying capacity is never practicable in any part of the tropical countries.

The case of India is an eye opener for forest policy maker all over world. Presently live stock farming in India is at the level of low productivity. Forests have been an important source of grazing and fodder in the absence of adequate productive pasture land. It is estimated that over half of the livestock population of India, some 270 million, grazes in forests. Additionally, grazers collect an estimated 175 to 200 million tonnes of green fodder annually. This results in over-grazing and over extraction of green fodder, leading to forest degradation through damage to regeneration and compaction of soil. A sample survey by Forest Survey of India (FSI) estimates that impact of grazing affects approximately 78 per cent of India's forests, of which some 18 per cent suffers high incidence and 31 per cent medium incidence (FSI, 1999).

BOX 3.6: SOURCES OF THREAT TO FORESTS OF LATIN AMERICA AND CARIBBEAN ISLANDS

— Increasing population pressures on forests.
— Conversion of forest into non-forest areas.

- Settlement.
- Clearance for agriculture.
- Stock-farming.
- Construction of roads.
- Development of dams and other infrastructure.
- Mining and quarrying.

— Inequitable land tenure system, which encourages land less people to encroach forest land for survival.
— Fire, in arid and semi-arid areas.
— Pest infestation in forests.
— Extraction of timber and fuelwood from forests by timber transnational corporations involved in logging operation.
— Short-term economic opportunities sought by respective government from timber extractions.

Source: FAO, 1997.

Distorted Fiscal and Development Policies

Another important factor responsible for forest loss is related directly or indirectly, to internal fiscal management, or development policies or to export markets in the developed worlds. The case in point is export policies in Latin American and South-East Asian countries where a large chunk of forest earning comes from timber sales and export of meat and its products to developed counties. Large tracts of tropical forests in Latin America have been cleared for cattle ranching to produce cheap beef for North America (Mayers, 1981). Apart from the export policy of some countries, many countries are burdened with huge foreign debts. The need to attempt to service and repay international debts has encouraged many countries to expand exports. This has, in turn, led to more and more land being given over to export crops, and directly or indirectly, led to increased pressures on the forests. These apart, economic adjustment programmes promoted by international institutions have also augmented pressure on forest resources. Many analysts have opined that these programmes have resulted in higher employment and collapse of small business enterprises, which in turn lead to unsustainable use of forest resources, *i.e.* increased clearing of forests for agriculture and/or over harvesting of forest products, particularly fuelwood (as people fall back on it as a house hold energy source). Thus, economic imperatives and developmental policies world over, have contributed to the process of degradation of forests to a great extent.

It is widely believed that there is a complex relationship between policy environment and its effects on forest resources. The relationships between forest and other sectors of the economy are better understood in comparison with the past. However, during the past few years, the policy makers have begun to address to the underlying causes of deforestation and degradation.

Market Failures

Much of the real value of forests is not normally reflected in the calculation which governs investment and management decisions about forest. For example, many non-timber products and services which forests provide do not enter into a commercial or market transaction. It is the failure on the part of institutional, political and economic system to reflect those values in prices that account substantially for the loss of the forest cover. Generally, among the many economic values assigned to forests traditionally the most important is the value of the timber produced. Even then, the full and true costs of producing that timber from a piece of forest are not calculated. The twin effects of this approach undervalue and underprice both timber and forests in the larger sense. Equally important is the fact that today market mechanisms do not value the environmental and ecological services which forests provide to maintain a stable landscape and atmosphere. As result, signals conducive to promotion of tree planting and forest conservation are not emanated from the market. Therefore, the present situation, created out of market failures compounded by distorted government policies increases vulnerability of forests to the fierce of deforestation.

Management Failure

Failures in management practices have also played significant role in forest decline. The most important management failures are high intensity logging, uncontrolled fire incidences, destructive harvesting of wood and non-wood forest produces, legacy of silivicultural errors, etc. The relative importance and intensity of these factors vary from place to place and country to country.

High intensity timber production is a primary reason of forest decline. This is one of the significant factors of degradation in many South-East Asian countries. In Brazilian Amazon, for example, loggers remove around 4 million cubic meters annually—around 0.01 per cent of the area's 50,000 million cubic meters of timber (Westoby, 1989). In South-East Asian countries, timber production and export played a major role in deforestation. It has been found that commercial logging primarily for export and foreign exchange earnings constitutes a significant cause of deforestation at national level in many South American and South-East Asian countries. In fact commercial logging apparently does not look as a prime actor in the forest decline scene. But it accentuates the process of deforestation in three distant ways. One is selection of tree for felling in contravention to sustainability assessment. Second is the large-scale construction of haulage roads inside the forests to extract timber. This damages the forest floor, disturbs the ecosystem and so adversely affects renewability of forest crop. The third is increased accessibility of forest invaders, encroachers or illegal settlers into the forest on account of construction of roads inside forests. Apart from this, increased accessibility into the forests accelerates the process of unsustainable and destructive use of forest by the local communities.

Uncontrolled fire in the forest is also one of the important reasons for forest loss. Lack of control on fire in the forest is a management failure. Likewise, silvicultural errors committed by foresters over the years also constitute important causes of forest loss. Lack of proper study and research with respect to silvicultural management, and impact of non-forest issues on silvicultural practice are some of the reasons of management failure.

Forest Fire

The use of fire is an integral part of land management in both forestry and agriculture. Some forests are ecologically adapted to fire. Prescribed burning is an important component of forest management practices in many tropical countries. However, forest fires have a wide ranging negative environmental impact. The nature and severity of damage depends on the type of forests, availability of fuel and climate factors. In most cases, fire protection is based on traditional systems of fire lines, which is inadequate and ineffective.

There is ample evidence that large proportions of wildfires that occur each year are caused by human intervention. A seven year field study of fire in the Amazon carried out by the Woods Hole Research Center, United States, shows that about half of the wildfires in the region were caused by fires set by farmers and ranchers to clear old cattle pasture and to burn newly cut forests which subsequently burned out of control. Habits of people putting forest on fire have caused a lot of damage to the vegetation in countries of Asia and Africa (See Box 3.7).

BOX 3.7: FOREST FIRE OCCURRENCES IN INDIA

- A Forest Survey of India sample survey conducted in 1995 found that annually fires affect some 53 to 54 per cent of forest in India.
- Out of these about 9 per cent of the area is frequently affected and 44.2 per cent only occasionally.
- State-wise occurrence of fire damage.
  - Assam: 51 per cent
  - Arunachal Pradesh: 93 per cent
  - Bihar: 67 per cent
  - Gujarat: 51 per cent
  - Jammu & Kashmir: 46 per cent
  - Karnataka: 45 per cent
  - Madhya Pradesh:76 per cent
  - Sikkim: 37 per cent
  - Uttar Pradesh: 58 per cent
  - West Bengal: 33 per cent

Source: Forest Survey of India, SFR-1995.

Fire is also a major hazard in many parts of the globe. In Greece, for example, 25,000 to 1,20,000 hectares of forests are damaged or lost each year through fire (Medinos and Tsekourans, 1987). Incendiary habits arising out of disgruntlement amongst the rural population has damaged the Zambia teak forests in southern Africa (Piearce, 1986). Forest fires occur every year in the arid and semi-arid zones of the world. In the year 1997-98 period there occurred widespread wildfires that affected forests throughout the world. Globally both the years 1997 and 1998 were the worst years for forest fires in recent memory. Droughts associated with the EI Nino weather pattern turned moist forests into drier habitats and increased the inflammability of forest vegetation, thus increasing the number, frequency, size, intensity and duration of fires. In 1997, wildfires raged in Indonesia, Papua New Guinea, Australia, and Mongolia, the Russian Federation, Columbia, Peru, Kenya, Rwanda and other parts of Africa. By mid-1998, fires were reported in Indonesia, the Amazon, Mexico and Central America, the United States, Western Canada, Far-Eastern Russia and parts of Europe (FAO, 1999).

Ethical Failure

Failure in ethical standard and erosion in value system play an important role in shaping the society. Generally in a society material consumption assumes an important proportion and conservation gets relegated to a back seat. Therefore, in an explicit way, one can say that some of the important reasons for forest decline have strong ethical roots. The primary issues in the ethical system which are fundamentally responsible for loss of forest, in quality and quantity, are: pattern of consumption, pattern of poverty and inequality, incidences of corrupt and unfair practices in forest management and administration, pattern of concentration and distribution of wealth in the society, level of environmental values in the society, etc. These issues affect the administration of sustainable forest management practices adversely. Besides, such issues have far reaching impact on the social and economic system of the society on which the mechanism for sustainable forest development is built. Therefore, erosion of ethical system in the society affects the process of sustainable development.

Corruption and unfair practices are symptomatic of ethical failure in the society. They are prevalent, inwardly and outwardly, in all levels of forest management practices. They promote large-scale misuse of public resources for personal gains by top level political and bureaucratic functionaries of the state. What is more woeful is the fact that the many top functionaries always make it a point to see that in any forest developmental programme their own interests are maximised at the cost of the organisation and forests. These functionaries are involved in every step of decision-making process in forest management. Over the years, the filth of corruption has trickled down to the lower functionaries of the forest organisations.

Inequality is a deep reflection of ethical failure in the society. It is the result of economic and political systems, which create and contribute to differential concentration of power. Such gross imbalances of power among the interest groups deeply associated with the benefits of forests is an ethical failure. Such a situation in the society discourages people to conserve forests.

Erosion of cultural values is also a part of the ethical failures. It has contributed substantially towards decline of forests. With the onset of materialistic society, people got themselves isolated from the cultural life and attracted towards modern means of income generation and materialistic ways of spending. With the passage of time, the value of forest conservation, which is deeply embedded in traditional life style, got eroded.

Gender Inequality

The gender inequality is well entrenched in social fabric of societies more particularly in developing countries. Women have multiple but disproportionate responsibility in the rural society. Traditionally, they have little ownership or control over the productive assets. This conventional imbalance in the ownership and control over resource *vis-à-vis* gender responsibility places women in a subordinate and disempowered position in comparison to men. It is because women depend upon men and run greater risks of being excluded from their homes and livelihoods. As a result of such gender incongruities men and women do not have commonality of perspectives and perception, priorities and goals with respect of forest and forest products. Therefore, gender inequality in developing countries has played a significant role in hastening the process of unsustainable use of forest resources, which lead to forest degradation in many parts of the earth.

Governance Failure

Governance relates to the systems and process, the legal frameworks and the institutions through which decisions are made in a society, the ways in which these interrelate and their relevance and relationship to the various constituent parts of the nations (WCFCD, 1999). Therefore society should establish a governance system that has pronounced elements of community participation and conflict resolutions. This acts as a incentive to sustainable forest management practices. Absence or erosion of governance system leads to abuse of authority by those who are positioned in the higher echelons of society. As a result, there emerges a social insecurity and inequitable distribution of the benefits from the use of forest resources. The symptoms of social insecurity are reflected in the following dimensions of governance in a society:

- The character of land ownership and land tenure.
- The distribution of the benefits accrued from the exploitation of forest resources.
- The inequality between males and females.
- The displacement of communities and indigenous groups.

When there is erosion of governance in a society, then environment becomes the first casualty. Therefore, evolving right governance structure is a prerequisite for tackling problems related to forest conservation.

Failure in Policy and Legislative Environment

Policy and legislation are powerful instruments of the state. They determine the course of development in society. The government use these instruments to decide the ways and means by which the societies should utilise the forest resource. There is a wide range of policies and environmental laws, which directly contribute to forest decline. Few the elements of the forest policies which run counter to the objectives of sustainable forest development are:

- Regularisation of settlement and encroachment over forest land.
- Subsidies on forest products.
- Uncontrolled dispensation of concession and rights for the use of forest products.
- Price mechanism of forest products.
- Concessional price systems for forest based industries.
- Lack of adequate property or entitled regime with respect to tree and forest products.

Subsidies

Subsidies are powerful tools of social change in developing society. They can accelerate the adoption of aptitudes and practices compatible to sustainable development of natural resources. Subsidies can be particularly beneficial if they are limited in duration and sharply focussed on specific economic, social or environmental goals which cannot be achieved by other means (Earth Council, 1996). Therefore, subsidies can, in effect, play a crucial role in helping development become more sustainable.

However, many of the present subsidies in many countries encourage practices that are economically perverse, trade distorting, ecologically destructive and socially inequitable. It is so because the subsidies are decided without adequate forethought and planning with respect to their social, environmental, and economic consequence. Consequently, the system of subsidy reduces the potential revenues and therefore deprives the society of developmental opportunities, possible from sustainable use of a country's forests. Undercharging of the value of timber and other forest products is a manifestation of indirect subsidy. It also leads to wanton consumption and mindless wastage of the vital resources. In case of western countries, taxpayer's money is spent to subsidise deforestation and other environmentally destructive activities. In countries like Panama and other Latin American countries, deforestation is linked to subsidies for promoting cattle ranching in unproductive forestlands. Also in Latin America, individuals and corporations are encouraged to convert forests into agricultural use because of generous tax incentives and other capital cost concessions. In India also, concessions and privileges for the local communities, without a proper mechanism of distributional justice at the village level, has led to an unsustainable use of forest resources. Apart from this, the revenue forgone because of such unregulated concessions and rights reduces opportunities and choices for development in the rural areas. World Watch Institute (1997) estimates that more than US$500 billion per year of consumer's and tax payer's money is spent by governments to subsidise deforestation and other environmentally destructive activities.

Growing Divergence Between Public and Private Values

Every chunk of forests provides a bunch of private values as well as public values. Government forests also provide a range of benefits mostly in the shape of products to villagers living in the proximity of forests. These benefits are manifestation of private values accrued to poor communities who depend on them. The forest products like timber and other non-timber forest products (NWFP) collected by government symbolise public values. Apart from this, the intrinsic intangible forest products and functions symbolise the public values of the forests. The benefits of such intrinsic public values of the forests accrue to the region or the country where the forest is situated. Unsustainable use of forest leads to decrease in generation of public value as well as private values.

But, when it comes to prioritising the value system, public interests should be permanent and fully secured through appropriate governance and management mechanisms. But, it is difficult to operationalise it. The conflict generally seen in the society has the potentiality to widen the divergence between the public values and private values. A large number of people are directly involved in competing for some part of economic benefits, which forests provide. Consequently, the growing divergence between public and private use of forest benefits, increases and it affects conservation efforts. Few of such conflicts are between:

- Rich and poor.
- Forest dwellers and multinational corporations.
- Politically strong and week groups.
- Cultural needs and economic imperatives.
- Economic needs and environmental functions.
- Private interests and public interests.

Under Valuation of Forest Resources

Forest resources all over the world is delicately susceptible to emerging economic forces. Operation of these forces ranges from local to global levels. Economic distortion in the societies encourages unsustainable use of forest resources worldwide. Such economic forces generally originate in sector other than forestry, but leave an adverse impact on the forest sector.

People use goods and services of forests without understanding the economic value of such benefits. Man derives a large part of the value of forests and does not allow the benefits to go through the process of money economy at all. The forest services which lie beyond the realm of currency economy are bio-diversity, soil and water conservation, climate amelioration, ecological security, cultural and recreation value, etc. In other words, a large chunk of real value of forest resources does not reflect in the national income accounting or GDP. They do not enter the process of market transaction. In traditional forest management practices the main economic value of forest lies in wood and some Non-Wood Forest Produces (NWFP). Again in most of the cases the true cost of wood is not calculated. Rather the market decides the price. This market price is always far below the shadow price of timber or wood. Allowing forest services to remain outside the realm of money economy leads to under valuation of forest resources and products. As a result, consumers get encouraged to use larger quantities of forest products than they would if higher prices reflected their full or true value. This hastens the process of unsustainable use of forests.

The aforesaid discussion speaks volume of the fact that the present day market mechanisms do not value the environmental and ecological services, which forest provides to stabilise and maintain the human habitat. Now the question is why it happens so. It is because market forces do not recognise conservation of forest resources. This is basically attributed to deficiencies in political, economical, social and institutional systems in the society.

Lower returns from forestland constitute another economic force, which acts against conservation of forests. Generally, forests provide lower returns than alternative uses of forestland. A person having a chunk of forests is always discouraged to sustain forests because the other available options of land use have prospect of better monetary yield in comparison with forestry. This is the basic economic reason why no private person wants to sustain an existing chunk of forests. However, the same economic reasons can be used to conserve forests, if a true or real price regime for forest products and services are evolved and suitable market is created.

Other Reasons

Various other factors also play a significant role in deforestation. Such factors are like political instability, war, and incendiary habits of people, urban expansion. The resettlement of Afghan refuges resulted in the destruction of forests in Afghanistan (Allen, 1987). During Vietnam War, an area of around 1.25 million hectares of forests area was sprayed with herbicides and defoliants and more than 4 million hectares were damaged by shells (Lanly, 1982). Urban expansion is another cause for shrinkage of forests all over the world. In the United States, the rate of conversion of forest land to urban uses increased dramatically during the 1970s, and amounted to about 250,000 hectares in 1981 (Miller and Rose, 1985).

Consequence of Forest Crisis

The overall consequence of forest crisis is alarming. At this point of time, it may not be fully possible to visualise the consequence and its ramification on the society, but the spectacle of destruction of life shall be very frightening. An account of social, economic and environmental consequence of forest crisis is presented in Box 3.8. If precautionary actions are not urgently taken, then the dimension of the crisis will assume serious proportion.

Sustaining Forests: How Long?

How long we will be sustaining our precious forest is a million-dollar question. In the absence of completely reliable data on pace of deforestation and future direction of economic growth, the task of estimating the time up to which our forests will be sustained is a daunting one. Many authors have presented their analysis with regard to trends and pace of deforestation that has taken place in the earth since the onset of agricultural period. Mathews (1983) has attempted to compare the present extent of forests and woodland with the 'pre-agricultural' position. He advocated that the estimated reduction in the area of forests and woodland is approximately 900 million hectares. William (1989), another author concluded that a total forest area ranging between 750 to 800 million hectares had been deforested since pre-agricultural time. William and Richards have concluded that an area of about 400 million hectares of forest and woodland may have been cleared between 1860 and 1978 (William, 1989; Richards, 1986). The FAO (2001) indicates that at present a net decrease of 9.4 million hectares per year is taking place on the global scale.

Data published in the State of the World's Forests 2001 (FAO, 2001) provide a picture of the trends in forest cover over a period of two decade (1980-2000). Between 1980 and 1995, the extent of world's forests (including both natural forests and forest plantations) decreased by some 180 million hectares. There was an increase of 20 million hectares ih

BOX 3.8: THE ALARMING CONSEQUENCE OF FOREST CRISIS

Environmental Disruption

• Accelerated forest decline	More forest loss and degradation, at higher loss.
• Species loss	By the year 2020 up to 17 per cent of tropical forest species of Africa, Asia and South America could vanish, reducing resilience.
• Land degradation	Many forest lands suffer from deforestation. Forests are likely to become eroded, depleted of nutrients, and degraded.
• Disruption of water flows	Increased water scarcity, already predicted to be major 21st century issue; threatening billions who rely on water from upland watersheds.
• More forest fires	More carbon emissions, further climate change, more forest decline, more forest fires.

Increased Social Hardship

• More poverty	Reduced opportunities and options for poor households to satisfy basic human needs.
• Fuel scarcity	Over 2 billion people could suffer increased hardship in meeting their fuelwood needs, resulting in lower nutrition and health levels.
• Pressures in marginalised groups	Vulnerable forest dependant groups in society will be more exposed, including many women, children and indigenous peoples.

Increased Economic Hardships

• Squandered capital	Erosion of valuable source of natural capital.
• Fewer employment opportunities	Forest capital erosion reduces the potential for future subsistance and wage employment.
• Reduced commercial potential	Forest capital erosion reduces the potential for future commercial production of wood and non-wood forest products.
• Reduced non-commercial potential	Forest capital erosion reduces the potential for meeting subsistence needs from non-commercial forest products.

Source: *Our Forests; Our Future* (1999).

developed countries, but a loss of 200 million hectares in developing nations. This constituted a net loss of forest at the rate of 13 million hectares per year. In the period 1990-2000, the annual deforestation rate remained at about 16 million hectares. If this pace continues, then the earth shall have only 2,260 million hectares of forests in the end of this century. By this account, the globe shall loose its primary forests after 250 years.

It is significant to know that the deforestation has its genesis in combinations of factors like population growth, poverty, economic growth, consumption pattern, and many such political, social and economic policies and environment. All such causative factors are also expected to continue to dominate the world society in the future also. Therefore, it is very difficult to assume that deforestation will be arrested in the near future. Assuming that the pace of present deforestation continues in future, the estimated 2,800 million hectares of closed forests will disappear in a period of 560 years at a net rate of 5 million hectares. However many writers have concluded that the dense forests will disappear before the close of twenty first century. Lanly (1982) has concluded that tropical rain forests would disappear by the year 2057 (Guppy, 1984). However, it is definitely a inscrutable problem to extrapolate the time when the forest of the world will disappear completely. However, optimists have different logic to the time scale of deforestation. They indicate that at best 70 per cent of the closed forests will remain untouched in spite of all population changes. The main thrust of their argument is that in the course of human history, human pressures has caused a loss of only 15 to 20 per cent of 'original' forests.

Notwithstanding the doomsday scenario, there is enough room for optimism. A lot of initiatives have been taken at all levels. Moreover, the reasons, direct or indirect, responsible for deforestation are being addressed at various level. The transition to sustainable forest development has already begun. The international community has already build up institutions to oversee the process of sustainable forest development. Therefore, now the question is if we want to sustain over forests, we need to help this process.

PART II

SUSTAINABLE DEVELOPMENT : CONCEPT, PERSPECTIVES AND PERFORMANCE

4

SUSTAINABLE DEVELOPMENT:

Concepts and Perspectives

'Sustainable Development' is a catchy phrase developed in the penultimate decade of the twentieth century. The term first came into focus in the 'World Conservation Strategy' published by the World Conservation Union (IUCN) in 1980. It gained more prominence with the publication of the Bruntland Report in the year 1987. The principles regarding sustainable development received global acceptability after United Nations Conference on Environment and Development (UNCED) held in Rio de Janeiro in June 1992. The Earth summit initiated thinking towards natural resource conservation and sustainable development on a global scale.

Now the precept of sustainable development has come to stay for good. Every paradigm of planning developed either on global or national or local perspective takes sustenance from this concept. It is now already an established principle worldwide. However, the debate on principles of sustainable development and its implication on economic development continue to date. In this context, the chapter on 'sustainable development' has been prepared to bring fourth the genesis, basic tenets and widening perspective on sustainable development. In the end, the relevance of Gandhian principles and ethics to sustainable development has been analysed and discussed in the context of present time.

Understanding Development

Development is a commonly used phrase. Linguistically, development is the gradual growth of formation of something; more precisely it is the process in which a person or thing matures, changes or advances to another stage to realise inherent potentials. In the economic and political context, development generally refers to improving the living conditions or material welfare of a given population. It is also defined as a process of expanding human choices, taking into account equity, sustainability and empowerment aspects.

Considered in this perspective, economic growth may not symbolise development or the *vice versa.* In other words, if there occurs an economic growth, it would generally imply economic development but not development. There are innumerable externalities to patterns of economic growth in the form of human or social costs such as increased inequality, health risks, and reduced empowerment. Such externalities have been observed in all most all countries. Now-a-days, there is another word which is in vogue. That is human development. "Human Development" has been defined as a process of enlarging human choices, with an operational focus on equity, sustainability and empowerment (UNDP 1995: 12).

Genesis of the Concept

The concept of development gained prominence in the international agenda only in the post-World War II period. In the context of economic development theory, development became rather narrowly described as consciously, deliberately stimulated growth' (Brenner 1966), with (economic) growth typically defined as non-negative changes in per capita or gross domestic product (*e.g.* Kuznets, 1965; Tinbergen, 1956, 86). The concept of economic growth envisaged accumulation of capital in selected areas of economy like the field of industrialisation, modernisation and urbanisation. This method of development was known as top-down or trickle down process of planning or control. It was expected from this model that benefits of development would spread and multiply at ground level. However, by the end of the 1960's it was realised that the so-called development did not bring the desired change in the standard of living of majority of people living in the poor countries. After this realisation, there emerged another attempt to recast the development model. The concept of redistributive justice or redistribution with growth emerged. Over the time this idea became popular because solution to a host of problems like poverty, unemployment, health care, shelter, nutrition, education, regional disparity, etc appeared to have lied in the concept. It promised to improve the quality of life of common man. But, while pursuing this model, the market forces over-played its role. As a consequence, consumerism took a new height and the culture of material growth of a few section of the society dominated. This resulted into lopsided growth, in one hand and depletion of natural resources in the other.

Then in the seventies, there emerged a concern about environment. Towards this end, the United Nation's Conference on the Human Environment held at Stockholm in 1972 raised the first warning signal about the negative aspects of the prevailing development strategies. Rather, the conference symbolised widespread public demand that government should immediately address the growing environmental crisis. In one way, the conference took initiatives to redefine 'development' and laid a political foundation for the concept of 'sustainable development'. The concept of 'sustainable development' received wide acceptability in the conference. People in the developed countries started acquiring the opinion that the planet is becoming uninhabitable at a faster pace because of increasing negative impacts of industrialisation on the environment and society. This apprehension became more intensified because of the neo-Malthusian prophecies of population explosion in the developing countries. The publication of book/report like 'The Population Bomb' (1970) by Paul Erhlich, and 'The Limits to Growth' (1972) by Donelea Meadows and others, attracted the attention of public in industrialised countries towards doomsday scenarios caused by a shrinking natural resources base, increasing pollution and ever expanding population. This created a climate, which spurred a debate between North and South about the existing paradigm of development and its impact on economic growth. The debate finally led to a confrontation between North and South. The environmental agenda of North clashed with the political and economic priorities and strategies of South. This sharp debate still continues until today.

However, with great difficulty, the conference came out with a 'Stockholm Declaration'. The declaration reflected the acceptance of North's perspective that pollution caused by industrialisation in the North imposed tangible constraints on their own development and the industrialisation process itself. The South's perspective that poverty, not industrialisation was the principal cause of environmental problems in the developing countries for which economic growth would have to provide the principal answer, was accepted. This apart, the South's insistence that national sovereignty should be placed at the center of any discussion or deliberation, before hammering out any international agreement on environmental conservation was also accepted. The Stockholm Declaration established 26 principles of behaviour and responsibility for countries. These principles were intended to constitute the basis for future multilateral agreement on environment and development.

The Earth Summit at Rio de Janeiro, Brazil in the year 1992 marked the beginning of action oriented thinking on 'sustainable development'. It was a landmark in the history of environmental conservation. It initiated thinking towards conservation of natural resources on a global scale. It was a biggest exercise ever made in the history of humanity to save the planet. Notwithstanding many failures, the summit revitalised G77 (a group of developing nations) that languished in the eighties and it marked the beginning of North-South dialogue process. In other words, it initiated a process of international deliberation in the field of natural resource conservation and management. The event opened new vistas for fresh set of negotiation in which North-South axis provided the pivotal line of discourse. It focussed on the linkage between issues of environment and development. It attracted the world's attention on perils of prevailing paradigm of development.

Sustainable Development: The Concept

The concept of 'sustainable development' entails, *inter alia*, societal change. Such changes are most important from the point of society at large. Societal changes may be defined as "alterations in the structure and functioning of society, such as community structure, social institutions, economic relations, attitudes and values, including the concept of nature". These changes may come about spontaneously as well as they may arise from deliberate policies or interventions. Therefore, development is a process of directed change or spontaneous change or an admixture of both.

Change can also be explained from different perspective. It can be defined in terms of quantitative aspects like structural, sectoral or regional characteristics, patters of production and consumption, technology and consumer preferences and their distribution. When structural changes are substantial, then one calls it 'transformation'. Presently the world economy is witnessing a host of such transformations. The most important transformations or changes are globalisation of world economy and emergence of ecological imperatives in the society.

However, the neo-classical economists argue that the economic growth will provide a solution to the present and future environmental problems. Extending their argument further, they assert that rising per capita income will generate an almost ' endogenous' tendency to take environmental consideration into account. Many people in industrialised world today share this view. This approach for exploitation of natural resources in the process of development symbolises frontier mentality (See Table 4.1). The origin of this mentality centers around three erroneous beliefs.

- The world has an unlimited supply of resources for human use.
- Humans are apart from nature.
- Man is born to rule over the nature.

With the passage of time, the economic thinking has undergone a change. There is growing realisation that we are living in a world of limits, whose boundary is shrinking day by day. This has given rise to the concept of carrying capacity. Sustainable development, therefore, became primarily a concept of limited needs. Such limitations in terms of consumptive needs are imposed by society which helps maintain the environment's ability to meet the present and future needs.

'Sustainable development' as a concept is difficult to define and comprehend in its totality. Different people define the concept in different ways. World Commission on Environment and Development (WCED, 1987) has defined sustainable development as "a process of change in which the exploitation of resources, the direction of investment, the orientation of technological development and institutional change are all in harmony and enhance both current and future potential to meet human needs and aspirations". However the phrase 'sustainable development' according to Bruntland Commission (WCED, 1987), implies a form of economic growth as well as technological and institutional change. In that approach, it is assumed that economic growth can be made ecologically viable if appropriate mixes of more environmentally efficient methods of production are achieved and if socio-economic and ecological considerations are integrated appropriately in decision-making process by public and private agents.

Sustainability is an old concept deeply rooted in disciplines such as forestry and economics. The concept of sustained yield is in vogue in forestry since more than 100 years. Likewise, in the discipline of economics, the notion of sustainable income arose some 40 years ago. Sustained growth was regarded as non-negative change in per capita income over time with outside intervention to support it (*e.g.* Brenner 1996; Kuznets 1995; Restow, 1956). However, since the Bruntland report (WECD, 1987), sustainability has come to mean: the capacity to maintain a certain phenomenon (*e.g.* growth) based on the potential of inherent or underlying social, economic as well as ecological processes.

Sustainable development focuses on meeting the basic needs of all deprived people in this world and extending to all, the opportunities to satisfy their aspirations for a better life. The views of proponents of neo-classical theory of development (or frontier society) and sustainable society are presented in Table 4.1.

Table 4.1: Comparison between Frontier and Sustainable Society

Frontier Society	*Sustainable Society*
• The earth has unlimited stock of resources.	• The earth has limited supply of resources.
• Move to another place after having exhausted the resources.	• Recycling and the use of renewable resources will prevent depletion.
• Continued addition to our material wealth will make life better.	• Life's value does not depend on our material wealth.
• The cost of any project is determined by the cost of materials, energy and labour.	• The cost of any project includes external costs such as social and environmental cost along with that of energy, labour and material.
• Man is not a part of nature and born to overcome nature.	• Man is part of nature and should develop symbiotic relationship with nature.
• Environmental problems can be solved through new technologies, new laws and high economic growth.	• Environmental problem can be solved through new technologies and new laws but with increased awareness at personal level.
• Some amount of wastes is bound to be generated in all human activity.	• Waste should be minimised by recycling as far as possible.

The concept of sustainable development caught the attention of the rich as well as poor countries equally and rapidly. Primarily Bruntland's concept received wide acceptability in poor countries. It happened so because of its underlying principles of social justice, equity and ecology. These basic principles were well entrenched in the ancestral culture, wisdom, psyche and value system of the society in developing countries. Apart from this, over the years many dangerous trends and intractable issues emerged in the world. These are:

- Increase in human related activities and their adverse impacts on the available resources of the planet.

- Pace of depletion of natural resources.
- Burgeoning population growth.
- Growing inequalities between rich and poor.

Therefore, the lurking values of ancestral civilisation and culture along with the important global issues laid the foundation for the genesis of a climate where the concept of 'sustainable development' emerged. With the introduction of the said concept, the poor countries felt that few of their basic principles of old civilisation are revived. But the concept revolves around four core elements like (1) responsibility to others, (2) caring for the future, (3) dependence of life on natural environment, (4) love and compassion for living things. Apart from this, it also succeeded to a great extent to draw strong attention from rich countries. It appealed many people who expressed apprehension on continuity of present pace of material development on account of mindless degradation of resources. Besides, it convinced development planners in the west that the concept constitutes the foundation on which the strategy to perpetuate human development can be evolved.

Bruntland has defined 'sustainable development' as development that "meets the needs of the present without compromising the ability of future generations to meet their own needs"(WCED, 1987, p. 8). This is a simplified illustration of the concept. Over the years, the phrase 'sustainable development' is in vogue worldwide with different connotation to different people and to different sectors of economy.

Over the years, the concept evolved to encompass many related elements. But coming to fundamentals of the concept, sustainable development basically encompasses the following essential elements/ objectives.

- There should be a continuous process of development on a sustainable basis.
- The development should aim at 'meeting the needs of the present without compromising the ability of future generation to meet theirs'.
- Maintenance of biophysical productivity in the biosphere.
- Economic efficiency and growth.
- Maintenance of ecological efficiency in the ecosystem.
- Preservation of environmental quality.
- Inter-and intra generational equity.
- Social justice.

- Self-reliance and people' participation.
- Stabilisation of human population.
- Promotion of environmental values and ethics.

Therefore, as things stand today, sustainable development is a process of change in which the exploitation of resources, the direction of investments, the orientation of technological development and institutional change are all compatible and satisfy current human needs and aspirations without jeopardizing the future potential for satisfying these (after WCED, 1987:46).

In order to explain the concept, let us take the example of development of land use system. Land resources are the most vital natural resources of the earth. Sustainable development of such resources throws many challenges. Many environmental problems are directly or indirectly related to poverty and consequent stress on local biophysical system. With the increasing use of productive potential of land and other natural system beyond its replenishing capacity, the resource base for the future generation is fast shrinking. The more we produce to meet the needs of the present, the more we lose the natural resource capital. As a consequence, the prospect of meeting the needs for the future is increasingly reduced. Such a type of growth is at the cost of future. This is not sustainable development. Therefore, the solution for making sustainable land use lies in understanding the biophysical system in its totality. The most important components of the land use system are land, water and vegetation. These are the basic determinants of productivity in the primary sector. Therefore, sustainable land use development requires a planning approach in which ecological integrity is the governing factor and the permissible level of economic activity is the dependable variable. (Narayanan, N.C., 1997)

In spite of the fact that a lot has been done in the field of defining the concept of sustainable development, still there remains many ambiguities and vagueness. More specifically, there are many unanswered questions, which need to be addressed. This becomes clear if we take one example. It is not practically feasible to assess the needs of the future with respect to physical, economic, and more importantly, ecological requirement. In the same vein, it is also not possible to estimate the needs of the present society since the very concept of needs is changing. Besides, in the context of globalised market economy, population explosion, burgeoning poverty, growth imperative and shifting political priorities, it is difficult to develop sustainable development models.

Sustainable development, however, if adopted will take care of the present as well as the future. In some fronts, it may be possible that the needs of the present may be met decreasingly, but the needs of the future are ascertained. Therefore sustainable development is intractable, if not impracticable concept to apply. According to David Reid, 'development, if it is to be sustainable, is faced with a rather tall order – to work within constraints it has so far failed to observe, to achieve goals it has so far failed to meet.

Fusion of Many Systems

Sustainable development entails a cyclical relationship of nature with man. It is a relationship that moves from and returns to nature, but it does not transcend the threshold capacity of the nature to transact, without impairing the productive system. This ensures the continuance of socio-economic development in the long run. Therefore, considered from this perspective, sustainable development symbolises a harmonised blend of many systems in a society. Such systems are as follows:

- A political system that secures effective citizen' participation in decision-making process.
- An economic system that is able to generate surpluses and technical knowledge on a self reliant and sustained basis.
- A social system that provides solutions for the tensions arising from a disharmonious development.
- A production system that respects the obligation to preserve the ecological base for development.
- A technological system that searches continuously for new solutions to the problems.

Environmental Space and Sustainability

There is a definite relationship between environment space and sustainability. This can be easily be illustrated by taking natural resource use pattern in the society. Nature provides society with an environmental space (*e.g.* Opschoor, 1992) for economic utilisation. If economic activities generate claims on the environment that exceed the limits of this environmental space, the biosphere's (future) capacity to satisfy human needs is adversely affected. Sustainability implies that any current level of consumption or use of natural resources should not impair the functioning of the system to the extent that the future generation of welfare per capita would be jeopardised.

Sustainable development is an integrated and dynamic concept encompassing social, environmental and economic sustainability. Economic sustainability focuses on the maintenance of a set of factors of production large enough to ensure future non-negative changes in income or welfare per capita through the economic process of extraction, production and consumption; environmental sustainability implies concern for the maintenance of a life supporting environment essential for production and the continued existence of humanity or life in general (See e.g. Gooland, 1995).

Underlying Principles

Sustainable development is a complex process. It involves multidisciplinary sectors in the economy. 'Laws of nature' influence it. However, over the years, with the increase in man's power to alter the environment, the complex and quantitative relations among different 'laws of nature' have been understood better and measures to manipulate them have been developed. To keep these laws at harmony to each other, certain social and economic principles have been evolved to act with 'laws of nature' and promote harmony among them. Few of the important principles that govern the use and development of natural resources are enumerated below:

- The concept of ecosystem and the homeostasis.
- Liebeg's law of limiting factors.
- The Principle of Carrying Capacity.
- The Precautionary Principle.
- Principle of Conservation .
- Principle of eco-development.
- Polluter Pays Principles (PPP).

Maintaining Generational Equity

Every economic action on the part of individual or nation by using natural resource creates a cost or benefit for another. Market price fails to take into accounts the cost or benefits of such action. Harms created by a mountaineous country by not taking proper watershed conservation measures lead to recurrent flood in the downstream countries. This damage is not reflected in the price of the agricultural products. Rather the forces of demand and supply determine the price. Likewise, cost of maintaining the watershed that constitutes the catchment of river does not reflect in the irrigation price or power tariff in the downstream areas where the irrigation potential or electricity has been generated. Rather, the forces of demand and supply determine the cost of irrigation and electricity. Such elements of interdependency among two or more individuals or nations not taken into account by a market transaction are called externality. This type of dependency with in a generation is intra-generational externality.

Managing intra-generational externality is a great challenge. Again, the challenge gets compounded with the emergence of the issue of inter-generational externality. Inter-generational externality symbolises a state of interdependence among two or more generations. Any decision today not only affects the present but also the future activities. That means many decisions taken today have an implication for the present as well the future. Our destructive harvesting practices impair the habitat's capacity to carry the present biological activity, sustainability and consequently it limits the option for future. Disruption of ecosystem in such a way impairs the interests of the present generation as well as the interest of the future generation.

Many of the environmental problems involve intra-generational and intergenerational implication. Environmental externalities created out of human activity, pose problems for the present generation as well as for the future. Some of the environmental problems having inter-generational significance are:

- Depletion of ozone layer.
- Deforestation.
- Loss of biodiversity.
- Disruption of watershed.
- Building-up of green house gases.
- Land degradation and soil erosion.

Sustainable development of natural resources necessitates proper management of environmental externalities. Such externalities may be of intra-generational or inter-generational in nature. Managing inter-generational externalities is itself a great task. But, managing inter-generational externalities, along with intra-generational problems throws a great challenge to the humanity. A list of intra-generational and inter-generational environmental problems is presented in Table 4.2.

Table 4.2: List of Environmental Problems with Generational Implication

Generation	*Local/National/Regional*	*Global*
Intra-generational	• Tropical deforestation • Soil erosion • Desertification • Acid rain • Forest fire	• Tropical deforestation • Loss of habitat for wild-life • Loss of bio-diversity
Inter-generational	• Tropical deforestation • Ocean pollution • Acid rain • Desertification • Soil salinization	• Loss of bio-diversity • Ozone depletion • Global warming

For managing inter-generational problems, we need action at three levels. One is local level, second is national level, and the third is global level. Apart from this, it requires efficient allocation of resources and equitable distribution of benefits, especially economic goods. Normally, while addressing an environmental problem the interests of the present generations are taken into consideration. Such decisions leave a cost on the future generation. We can take the example of biodiversity—rival benefits accrued from forests. It is important that in such a case of rival benefits, sharing of biodiversity between two and more generations is possible if it is done on the basis of equity. Equity also helps to sustain the flow of non-rival products. Therefore, like biodiversity many goods and services of forests should be managed in such a fashion that it leads to sustainable growth or development. By sustainable growth, we mean a growth which does not limit the options still available to the future.

Management of environmental problems with high intra-generational and inter-generational implications is a challenge. Rich countries have a capacity to forgo certain benefits. But they do not forgo any benefits. It is because; they fear that such a course of action shall slow down their process of economic growth. Contrast to this, developing countries with the increasing poverty and population growth in one hand and limited economic opportunity in the other, cannot afford to forgo any benefits. They always concentrate on current growth and benefits, which generally accrue at the cost of future growth. Notwithstanding uncompromising stance taken by both developed and developing countries, it is still not impossible to find out solutions to such problems.

Operationalising Sustainable Development

Sustainable development is people oriented. It aims at improving the quality of human life. It draws sustenance from ethos of conservation. It is conditioned by the need to respect nature's capacity to provide resources and to maintain life-supporting services. Therefore, considered from these perspectives, sustainable development means improving the quality of human life without impairing the natural capital of the ecosystem.

Sustainable development aims to maintain a balance between needs of survival and well being in one hand and capacity of the ecosystem to meet those needs in the other. Maintaining such a balance necessitates observation of certain level of discipline and behaviour at the level of human society. These elements of discipline and behaviour can be classified into three broad categories or components. They can also be visualised as distinct dimensions of sustainable management. Therefore, operational definition of sustainable development embraces three basic components or dimensions – the economic, the social, and the environmental. They constitute the foundation of sustainable development. These components are interconnected and complementary to each other. Any programme of sustainable development requires promoting all these three components on a synergistic and sustainable basis.

Three Dimensions of Sustainability

The Economic Dimension

Economic sustainability comprises identifying, assessing, evolving management plan and investment planning programme for maintaining the resources or making an improvement over the resources by bringing suitable changes in the policy and fiscal environment. This approach requires long-term view, which needs to be incorporated into the developmental programming.

The economic dimension of sustainability consists of the following aspects:

- Pursuing long-term policy of sustainable economic growth that generates an increase in true income without any impoverishment, either short-term or long-term.
- Generating an optimal flow of increase while maintaining their basic stock of man-made, human and natural capital.
- Identifying man-made and natural capitals, which are substitutable and complementary.
- Increasing the productive capacity of the capital without jeopardising the intrinsic strength of any of them.
- Reducing the consumption of natural resources in industrial countries and promoting use of such resources more efficiently.
- Internalising all costs, including the social and environmental costs associated with the production and disposal of goods, which promote the implementation of the full-cost principle.

Strategy for Promoting Economic Discipline and Behaviours

Strategy for promoting economic discipline and behaviour is based on the following aspects:

- *Sound macro-economic management*: Sound macro-economic management by pursuing prudent fiscal policies and maintaining the international balance of payments in the long-term.
- *Poverty alleviation*: Poverty alleviation by promoting labour intensive economic policies to maximise employment generation for the poor, down trodden and vulnerable section of the society.
- *Increasing agricultural production*: Increasing agricultural production by correcting policy bias against agricultural sector, strengthening food security, promoting public investment for improving infrastructure development in agriculture and related field.
- *Maximising the role of state*: Maximising the role of state as the promoter and facilitator of economic development in the society.
- *Strengthening the functions of the government*: Strengthening the administrative, regulatory and standard setting functions of

government in areas where management of public goods, protection of public interests and welfare of majority of people assume paramount importance.

- *Internalising the social and environmental costs*: Internalising the social and environmental costs by eliminating distortions in existing pricing structures and by including environmental and social costs in the price structure of goods for the purpose of promoting efficient and rational use of resources.

Social Dimension

Social sustainability comprises legal, political, societal, administrative and institutional aspects and processes, which engage the society in harvesting and use of the resources for attaining development. Evolving appropriate institution and creating compatible socio-political climate at different levels for implementing ecologically and economically sustainable model is a prerequisite for sustainable development of natural resource.

Social dimension of sustainable development revolves around two aspects. One is social equity and the other is interdependence in community. Fulfillment of both aspects leads to development. Social equity means ensuring that all people have access to resources and opportunities to make productive contribution to society. Interdependence implies the fact that standard of living of people is intimately linked to each other and to available environmental resources. Furtherance of interdependence of people leads to multiplication of economic opportunities, which ultimately drive the society towards faster development. In order to make development sustainable on a long-term basis, it is necessary to ensure that resource and opportunity are shared in such a way that all people should have access to minimum standards of security, human rights and social benefits such as food, shelter, education, health care etc. To sum up, social dimension essentially consists of the following elements:

- Active participation of people in developmental process.
- Empowerment of peoples especially the women, weaker and marginalised section.
- Accountability of government to public in making social policy.
- Duties of citizen in maintaining the natural capital.
- Responsibility of government in improving the capacity of the community to shape and manage their own lives.

Strategy for Promoting Social Discipline and Behaviour

Strategy for promoting social discipline and behaviour is based on the following aspects:

- *Distributional equity*: Institutional mechanisms for redistributing resources and productive assets to ensure maximum participation of community, especially poor, in income generating activities and their access to productive resources.
- *Social services*: Providing basic amenities like shelter, education, health, clean water, sanitation, communication, health care, etc. Ensuring equal access to legal remedy, credit, and financial services and employment opportunities.
- *Gender equity*: Providing equal opportunity for women in income generating activities, education, and health care. Providing equal legal status for women ensures rights to property ownership and access to credit.
- *Population stabilisation*: Stabilising the population at such a level that anthropogenic pressure on the natural capital does not transcend the carrying capacity of the ecosystem.
- *Political participation and accountability*: Establishing transparent and accessible mechanisms by which governments are held accountable to the public on all developmental matters. Establishing the process of consultation and participation of all sections in planning and management of development projects.

Environmental Dimension

The environmental dimension of sustainable development symbolises the aspects of maintaining the long-term integrity of the natural capital as well as planet's life support systems. Meeting this objective necessities constant care and investment in the biosphere management. Therefore, environmental sustainability requires use of environmental goods and services in such a way that it does not impair the structural and functional integrity of the ecosystem. Application of 'precautionary principles' and 'polluter pays principles' should become the integral part of all developmental and management programme. This will ensure minimising negative developmental increment on our environment.

To operationalise the components of environmental or ecological sustainability we require (1) identifying, assessing and evolving management plan on the basis of carrying capacity of the ecosystem from which the resource is proposed to be harvested, (2) planning for maintaining the ecosystem without impairing the replenishment capacity, and (3) implementing and controlling the plan with the focussed objectives of sustainability.

Strategy for Promoting Environmental Sustainability

Strategy for promoting environmental sustainability is based on the following aspects:

- *Sustainable Resource Use*: Limiting consumption of renewable natural resources to regenerative rates. Ensuring non-renewable resource consumption at a rate that does not exceed the pace of substitute development.
- *Sink Function*: Decreasing the discharge of pollutants and contaminants. Ensuring emission of toxic wastes to the level where it does not exceed the ecosystem's capacity to assimilate.
- *Natural Capital*: Establishing regulatory and market based mechanisms to ensure that the total stock of natural capital remains constant over time.
- *National Policy*: Establishing national policy to augment the quality and quantity of natural capital for prudent and holistic management of natural resources.
- *Precautionary Principle*: Refraining from pursuing activities whose negative effect impair the ecosystem functions.
- *International Framework*: Establishing clear, enforceable, legal and regulatory regime and standard for government and private sector in order to ensure and promote management of natural resources on ecosystem principles.

While formulating any broad strategy for implementing sustainable development, all the three components or dimensions should converge in such a way that it facilitates to generate a steady flow of products and income, ensure social equity, pursue a population control strategy, maintain natural capital and protect life-support system of the biosphere.

Measuring Sustainability

Unless we measure and evaluate our efforts towards sustainable management on a periodic basis, it is not possible to achieve the broad objectives of sustainable development. In order to put sustainability into practice, it is necessary to evolve some measuring thresholds or indicators or standards. Now the question is what could be such standards. The means of measuring sustainability can be based on the following parameters:

- The extent of natural capital.
- The rate of consumption of natural capital.
- The rate of harvest of natural resources.
- The pattern of harvest and their impact on the natural capital.
- The progress in our attempt to reduce the consumption of natural resources.
- Environmentally adjusted domestic product and income.
- Human development index.

To begin with, sustainability requires to be measured in quantitative terms only. It can be done by adopting two approaches: (a) the inclusion of natural resource capital into national accounts; and (b) the development of indicators or set of indicators to assess the sustainability of the development path.

Over the years the concept of natural resource accounting has emerged as a viable solution to integrate environmental and economic data and analytical variables (Bartelmus, 1994). UNCED in its agenda 21, requested that all member states of United Nations to establish integrated environmental and economic accounting as a complement to traditional accounting practices for the foreseeable future (United Nation, 1993).

The statistical division of the United Nations (UNSTAT) has developed methodologies for a system of Integrated Environmental and Economic Accounting (IEEA) in an United Nations System of National Accounts Handbook (United Nations, 1993). The IEEA system has the following objectives:

- *Segregation and elaboration*: Segregation and elaboration of all environment related flows and stocks of traditional accounts. This enables identification of that part of the GDP which reflects the cost necessary to compensate for the negative impacts of economic growth, or the environmentally defensive expenditures.

- *Linkages of physical resource accounts with monetary and environmental accounts and balance sheets*. Physical resource accounts cover the total stocks or reserves of natural resources and changes therein, even if those resources are not yet affected by the economic system.
- *Assessment of environmental costs and benefits*: The system of Integrated Environmental and Economic Accounting seeks to expand and complement the existing System of National Accounts (SNA) with regard to cost of the use (depletion) of natural resources in production and final demand, and the changes in environmental quality, resulting from pollution and other impacts of production, consumption and natural events, on the one hand, and environmental protection and enhancement, on the other.
- *Accounting for the maintenance of tangible wealth*: The concept of capital is to cover not only human-made but also natural capital. Capital formation is changed into a broader concept of capital accumulation allowing for the use/consumption and discovery of environmental assets.
- *Elaboration and measurement of indicators of environmentally adjusted product and income*: The consideration of the costs of depletion of natural resources and changes in environmental quality permits the calculation of an environmentally adjusted net domestic product (NDP).

The UN Handbook on IEEA applies three categories of monetary valuation to environmental assets and their changes. They are: (1) a market valuation approach with rearrangements for environmental changes in asset accounts of the conventional System of National Accounts (SNA), (2) a maintenance valuation approach which estimates the costs needed to preserve the environmental assets intact during the accounting time interval, and (3) an approach which combines the market valuation method with a contingent valuation approach to assess environmental costs of environmental degradation.

In the case of renewable resources like forests, the second approach is generally adopted. We can safely estimate the quantum of standing growing stock, which is synonymous with natural capital in a forest ecosystem. Likewise, we can determine natural and artificial regeneration, which shall indicate the rate of renewability. Again the sustained yield of wood and non-wood forest products shall indicate the rate at which resources should be harvested or rate of sustainable production from forests. Then the cost of maintenance can be estimated. This analysis shall indicate the ecological sustainability of the existing forest production system. In other words, we can know weather the forest resources are being used in a sustainable manner or unsustainable fashion. Likewise, in an agricultural ecosystem, the fertility and conservation of soil are the key indicators and declining crop yields symbolise the decreasing fertility of the land use system. Apart from the productive functions, the ecosystem provides the life support services to the planet. With increased incidences of production from the ecosystem beyond its rejuvenating capacity, its potentialities for generating life support services are severely impaired. Such indicators with respect to different ecosystems can be identified and monitored. Few of such broad indicators for monitoring a forest ecosystem are rate of depletion of biodiversity, absorption of carbon dioxide, average temperature, incidence of radiation, rate of soil erosion etc.

National resource accounting led to the development of one indicator. That is EDP or Environmentally Adjusted Net Domestic Product. This is an attempt to replace the universally used NDP (Net Domestic Product) as an indicator of development. This reflects the levels of development as well as elements of sustainability in the developmental approach. Several attempts at developing indicators or sets of indicators comprising of two or three variables, which reflect different dimensions of sustainability, have been made. However, the process of evolving many such variables or indicators is still on. Presently few such indicators reflecting multidimensional aspects of development or change have been developed. The basic elements required for measuring multidimensional aspects of sustainability are:

- Consumption of economic aggregates in per capita terms.
- Definition of an over all human development index.
- An assessment of the carrying capacity of land for human populations (Bartelemus, 1994).
- Criteria of human progress and economic welfare.

However, two development indices are worth considering from the point of sustainable development. The Human Development Index (HDI) of the United Nations Development Programme (UNDP) is a measure of human progress. This is determined by combining national income with two other indicators like adult literacy and life expectancy.

However, sustainability issues can be integrated into the concept of carrying capacity, which stands central to the measurement of sustainability. The total number of people that can be sustained by a given region can be termed as its carrying capacity. This capacity also depends on the desirable quality of life of the people. As Hardin (1991) said, the higher the standard of living, the fewer the number of people who can enjoy it.

The Daly-Cobb Index of sustainable economic welfare (Daly and Cobb, 1994) is based on casual relationship between livelihood, quality of life and sustainable development with the framework of carrying capacity. It develops an unified index based on a set of variables representing the three aspects of economy, ecology and equity and ranks the.various regions against the overall index as well as against specific aspects such as equity.

The process of defining human progress and welfare and identifying appropriate indicators for measuring sustainability is a protracted exercise. It may take many years to complete. Till date, only a beginning has been done. Owing to complexity of natural ecosystems, it is definitely a daunting task to identify appropriate indicators for different ecosystems. Lack of comprehensive data on aspects of natural resource management compounds the problem. The rate of destruction of natural resource system is faster than the pace at which we are swinging into action to evolve sustainable development programme. Some of the impacts of human activity on bio-physical systems may have passed a threshold, which may mean unpredictable and possibly catastrophic change before the global system finds a new balance (Ehrlich,1989). It may also happen that there are many ecosystems, which are used below the threshold limit, but today in the context of increasing resource use and population growth, we do not know how to conserve it. Nor we know whether the present society based on increasing consumption of natural resources, will be able to accept socio-political constraints necessary to curb the unsustainable practices.

Operating within the Boundaries of Carrying Capacity

Sustainability operates at multiple levels. It begins with international level and ends at local level. If sustainability is to be attained then the total impacts of global economic activity must not exhaust the natural resources or upset irretrievably the balance on which the life support system depends. A nation should not consume its natural capital faster than it can regenerate. It should maintain its development and protect its own natural resources by drawing on the surplus natural capital of other nations. A national economy can be said to be sustainable if its activities do not reduce environmental capacities with in its own countries and also do not cause their reduction elsewhere. This principle can also be applied to sub-national levels.

Development requires use of natural resources. Sustainable development necessitates sustainable use of resources. But most of the developmental models are based on unsustainable use of natural resources. Besides, many of the rates of consumption of natural resources are simply unsustainable in many countries. Therefore, sustainable development immediately requires examination of all existing development models and drastic reduction of rate of consumption of resources. This will decrease the ecological impacts of economic activity to the level at which they can be limited to the replenishment level of the system. Adjusting the economic activity by reducing its dimension and intensity may pose lot many constraints. But removing these constraints should constitute the principal strategy for operationalising a sustainable economy. In order to make it sustainable the present pattern of development should fall in line with carrying capacity of the bio-physical system.

There are many ways of bringing the total impacts with in the limits of carrying capacity. Those ways are:

1. *Extending the ecological boundary or improving the carrying capacity*: Extending the ecological boundary involves increasing the dimension of natural capital. This will, as a consequence, increase the capacity of the ecosystem to produce more yield as well as to absorb the negative impacts of the expending economy. In other words, expending the ecological boundary will increase the 'environmental space'. Now the question is whether this proposition falls is in the domain of possibility or not. Given the pace of scientific and technological development in the field of biotechnology, this appears fairly possible.
2. *Reducing the economy's consumption of natural resources and prohibiting the use of natural capital*: There are different approaches to achieve this. First, the scale of economy needs to be drastically reduced to stop economy's consumption of natural capital. Then the sustainable yield should be decreased in order

to improve the natural capital. This will ensure increasing sustainable yield in future. But, as a fall out of this approach per capita availability of resources will be decreased for a short-term time scale. In spite of this, the level of consumption can be maintained, if the economy uses the natural resources more efficiently.

However, the major constraints to achieve the goal of operating within the boundary of carrying capacity will be the burgeoning population in developing countries and increasing trend of consumption of natural resources, especially in the developed countries. If we consider the current rate of consumption of natural resources in developing as well as developed countries, it clearly comes out that consumption exceeds the present carrying capacity of their natural production systems. Moreover, the developed countries, in order to keep the harvest from their own natural production system at a sustainable level import natural resources from developing countries where unsustainable international trade leads to exploitation of resources beyond its carrying capacity. In the opinion of Ehrlichs, we live in a "a world where US consumption is so profligate that the birth of an average American baby is hundreds of times more of a disaster for the earth's life support system than the birth of a baby in a desperately poor nation" (Ehrlich and Ehrlich, 1990 p. 10).

Improving Ecological Efficiency

The sustainable development model should be based on the changes that have a bearing on ecological efficiency. The first and foremost change should be that the consumption of natural resources be reduced to the level of need only. It is because of the fact that the present rates of consumption in many parts of the globe are based on wants and so they are very high and simply unsustainable.

Notwithstanding the issue of increasing rate of consumption of natural resources, improvement in ecological efficiency of the productive system is indispensable. The main components of any programme to improve ecological efficiency encompasses (1) need and simplicity based life style, (2) reducing per capita consumption of natural resources, (3) increasing the efficiency of harvesting and use of natural resource, (4) increasing the natural capital. Towards this end, the following examples may work.

- Changing to a system, which uses less natural resources.

- Adopting the indigenous products, which, in turn saves energy in transportation as well as encourages sustainable use of resources at local level.
- Changing to more energy efficient system of production.
- Switching to a system, which generates minimum quantity of wastes and maximum quantum of welfare goods.
- Evolving and adopting technologies, which processes and decreases the negative impacts of development. Recycling of wastes is one such technology.

Relevance of ecological efficiency in this age of rapid economic growth is no doubt an accepted fact. But, to what extent we can bring ecological efficiency is a moot point. It is definitely a matter to ponder whether we can bring economic efficiency to a level where economic growth remains not only stable but also compatible to the attempt to reduce the environmental impact. There are many obstacles on the way to achieving ecologically efficient practices and technologies. It is not clear weather we can be able to translate the concept of sustainable development into a programme of practice, given the mind set of people, and current extent of unsustainable practices and the time required to bring development in the field of ecological efficiency.

Environmental Ethics

Ethics holds the key to sustainable development in a society. It is understood as the pursuit of goodness in a way which transcends individual interests and human imperfections (Pitt, 1988). It influences the behaviour of society towards use of environmental resources. It shapes the responses of people towards the sustainable use of natural resources. It influences the government's policy and programmes for sustainable development. Ethics and self-discipline in resource use is an over-riding criterion of development. In order to practice ethics it is pertinent to analyze certain concepts relating to ethics.

Within the core concept of ethics, there are a number of components which can be called as ethical norms (Simmons, 1997). Such ethical norms are: rights, justices and values. Rights are those conditions and actions which the holders of rights are ought to have access to it if they chose. Justice is based on the idea of fairness, in terms of equality of treatment, either in opportunities or outcomes. Values are based on cultural and aesthetic preferences. Based on such norms, ethical system is developed. Components and sub-components of system are presented in Table 4.3.

Table 4.3: Components of Environmental Ethics

Components	*Sub-components*
Equality	Opportunity
	Accessibility
	Distribution
Rights	Individual
	Community
Justice	Inter-generational
	Intra-generational
	International, regional and local
Values	Socio-economic
	Religion
	Cultural/Aesthetic
	Economic
	Cognitive

Establishing environmental norms in a society is a time taking process. Certain norms in the society are already built up in the society. There are certain norms, which get established because of promulgation of laws. There are again certain norms, which gradually emerge as a response to a specific situation. For example, with the decreasing forest resources, the value system attached to forests improves. But it depends on many other factors. Therefore, establishing ethical norms appropriate to the needs of sustainable development is a difficult task. Success of sustainable development depends upon a compatible and sound ethical system in the society.

Therefore, in order to promote sustainable development, we need to attend to our ethics. Some of the most important reasons for decline of forest have ethical roots: excessive concentration of wealth and power, both within countries and internationally; governance failures, pattern of consumption of natural resources; pattern of corruption and cultural discrimination which can be detrimental to the sustainability of forests. Therefore, we need to bring over ethics in line with requirements of sustainable development; equality, rights, justice, values and sustainability.

Relevance of Gandhian Legacy

Mahatma Gandhi, a world leader in the last century, tried successfully to integrate the traditional ethical principles with the modern political thinking. Such ethical principles, which have stupendous relevance to sustainable development are civil liberties, equality, concern for poor, religious tolerance, simple living and respect for all living things. (See also Box 4.1). Martin Luther King (Jr.) said, "If humanity is to progress, Gandhi is inescapable. He lived, thought and acted, inspired by the vision of a humanity evolving towards a world of peace and harmony. We may ignore him at our own risk." He is popularly perceived as a great synthesiser within the framework of traditional values.

Mahatma Gandhi's entire life and work is an environmental legacy for all humanity. This was not because he wrote a big treatise on environment. This was because he was a practitioner of sustainable development in the real sense of the word. In brief, his whole life was his message and a lesson on environment and development for Indians and world at large to follow (Khosho,1995).

BOX 4.1: SELECTED QUOTES OF GANDHI ON ENVIRONMENT AND DEVELOPMENT

Selected Quotes of Gandhi

Nature and Biodiversity

- We cannot have ecological movement designed to prevent violence against Nature, unless the principle of non-violence becomes central to the ethics of human culture.
- Man has no power to create life, therefore he has no right to destroy life.
- A society can be judged by the way it treats its animals.
- In nature there is fundamental unity running through all the diversity we see about us.
- I need no inspiration other than Nature's. She has never failed me as yet. She mystifies me, bewilders me, to ecstasies.
- It is arrogant assumption to say that human beings are lords and masters of the lower creatures. On the contrary, being endowed with greater things in life, they are the trustees of the lower animal kingdom.

Resource Use, Exploitation, and Environmental Ethics

- Man's aim in life is not therefore, to add from day-to-day to his material possessions.
- The incessant search for material comforts and their multiplication is an evil. I make bold to say that the Europeans will have to re-model their outlook, if they are not to perish under the weight of the comforts to which they are becoming slaves.
- A time is coming when those who are in mad rush today of multiplying their wants, will retrace their steps and say; what have we done. The main purpose of life is to live rightly, think rightly, act rightly.
- A certain degree of physical harmony and comfort is necessary, but above a certain level it becomes hindrance instead of help. Therefore the ideal of creating an unlimited number of wants and satisfying them seems to be a delusion and a snare
- Man falls from the pursuit of the ideal of plain living and high thinking the moment he wants to multiply his daily wants. Man's happiness really lies in contentment.
- The earth provides enough to satisfy every man's needs but not every man's greed.
- The rich have a superfluous store of things which they do not need and which are, therefore, neglected and wasted; while millions starve and are frozen to death for want of them. If each retained possession only of what he needed, non would be in want and all would live in contentment.

Source: Gandhi M.K. 1936 and Khoshoo, 1995.

The core of Gandhian legacy rests with few cardinal principles like truth, equality, social justice, non-violence, simple living and reverence for nature. Gandhi believed and proved that practising these principles should bring triumph to man and mankind. He emphasised on harmonising various segments of God's creation and believed that this would nurture the essential goodness in each one, both the visible and invisible threads uniting the entire humanity in a single entity. This sounds utopian but it is the reality. By the meaning of non-violence, he meant and practised compassion for all living things.

Increasing consumption of resources, a menace in the emerging society, received Mahatma's attention. Gandhi warned humanity of this dangerous situation as early as 1909 when he pointed out in the seminal work 'Hind Swaraj' that unprincipled growth will land humanity on the brink of disaster. Principles like 'give and take', 'live and let live' and 'love and to be loved' are the cornerstone of his philosophy. He advocated a holistic vision of life and emphasised equality and justice for all the people in the earth. He stressed on the simple truth that each individual is unique and we should respect his individuality.

Gandhi cautioned humanity against ecological devastation and other human misery that might arise unless modern civilisation takes care of nature and man tries to live in harmony with nature and reduce his wants. He exhorted that unlimited consumerist tendencies and indifference to social values would not help humanity to progress towards peace and prosperity.

Gandhi advocated practice of simple living and high thinking and discovered the strength of people's power of participation. The power and practice of simple living have stupendous relevance to present concept of sustained development. Simple living ensures minimum and judicious consumption of natural resources. Gandhi demonstrated that the life of a leader should also be open and capable enough to influence the masses so that they will also emulate the leader unreservedly. He did what he preached. Gandhi discovered the strength in people's participation in any action. He lunched his first '*Satyagraha*' movement and witnessed wilful and mass participation of people in large numbers. He proved that people would respond to any genuine call for social action provided that they are totally convinced that the issues identified have relevance to their welfare. He said that one who leads the movement should be an object of love, respect and dedication. The Salt Satygraha, and the Non-Cooperation Movement during the Indian freedom movement proved the power of participation in realising political and social aim.

Gandhi offered a package of alternatives to humanity. He offered a blue print for a holistic vision. Such a vision has wide applicability in the contemporary situation also. Some of the important features of the said vision are as follows:

- Insistence on non-violence rather than violence.
- Persuasion and reconciliation to end hostilities.
- Trusteeships to end economic injustice.
- Development of the depressed sections by abolishing factors that perpetuate social iniquities.

- Ending man's tyranny on nature by respecting nature as the protector of human race.
- Limiting one's wants.

Gandhi convincingly demonstrated through his ashram experiments the use of alternative source of energy, appropriate technology in harmony with nature, simple living, etc. He showed to humanity that these are workable and sustainable alternatives. The only thing, he said, is that we must have the courage to accept and work towards it. It requires self-control and collective disciplines of various kinds. Gandhian views and approaches over the years have been found effective in bringing social reforms.

One important thing that stands conspicuously in Gandhi's teachings and strategies is the adoption of pure means. Gandhi attached immense significance to pure means to attain lasting ends. Gandhi's attempt to make politics value based was part of a New World vision. He emphasised that politics bereft of spiritual and ethical considerations will not sustain humanity.

Gandhi had different approaches to social change. Some of the approaches are accepted now. He thought that social change depends on:

- Acceptance of non-violence as an end and means, in all individual and social actions.
- Endorsement of Ruskin's maxim that 'good of the individual is contained in the good of all' or the doctrine of universal welfare, or Sarvodaya.
- Emphasis on moral approach to civilisation and development.

Unregulated consumption of natural resources is one of the important reasons for the environmental crisis. It has been established beyond doubt that developed countries consisting of about one-fifth of the world's population consumes twenty times more goods and services than that of the rest of the world does. Apart from this, there is a competition among rich as well as poor countries to acquire more wealth in order to satisfy their growing demands. One can imagine what will happen to this earth. when each and every man in developing countries aspires to consume the equal quantum of natural resources as that of developing countries. Gandhiji, therefore, advocated simplicity in our life-style and a change in the standard of values. According to him, "The idea of creating an unlimited number of wants and satisfying them seems a delusion and a snare. The satisfaction of man's physical needs, even the intellectual needs of one's narrow self, must meet at a certain point a dead stop, before it generates into physical and intellectual voluptuousness (Gandhi, 1936)".

Industrial revolution, which initiated a drive for material development, had led large-scale exploitation of nature. In this context, Gandhi said that no civilisation is worthwhile unless it saves nature and provides full opportunity for the fullest development of human beings. He, therefore, says, "nature produces enough for our wants from day-to-day and if everybody takes enough for himself and nothing more, there would be no pauperism in this world, there would be no man dying of starvation in this world." To explain it more lucidly, he said that, "The Earth provides enough to satisfy every one's needs but not for anybody's greed".

Gandhi showed how pride, greed and lust lead to emergence of consumptive behaviours in man. He always emphasised on relinquishment of pride, greed and lust. Gandhi warned that greed would lead to acquisitive temperament. He was always against the elements of possession. He always laid emphasis on real need. He cautioned against multiplying our wants. He exhorted rich to shun the tendency to acquire more and more without needing them, while millions are starved to death for want of sustenance. As a result of such a tendency the rich crave for more and the poor is deprived of the basic necessities of life. About consumerism, he said that it is a reflection of lust. It is the lust, which creates chasm between haves and have-nots and ultimately leads to social tension.

Gandhi advocated harmonised social relation among different groups and pattern of development in the society. Gandhi believed in trusteeship. Every person should use his wealth to the point he reasonably requires for his personal needs and act as trustee of the remaining to be used for the society. By this analysis, Gandhiji tried to make a distinction between legal and mere ownership. Some wealth may legally belong to the owners, but morally all wealth belongs to the whole society.

Strategy of Development

Gandhian strategy of development lays emphasis on two aspects. One is individual response to development and second is pattern of economic development. Individual response to development is aimed at individual behaviour.

Gandhiji's concept of development is pervasive and holistic. It becomes relevant to consider few of the elements, which are significant from the point of societal change. Theses are as follows:

- He emphasised on austerity in consumption.
- He exhorted to choose technology, which does not create ecological imbalance.
- He said that production and consumption should be as proximate as possible. This facilitates proper use of local resources. This also achieves self-sufficiency in villages. Reasonable self-sufficiency should be the integral part of the economic system.
- He laid stress on decentralised mechanism operating on the principle of participatory democracy and management.
- He laid emphasis on improving the moral values of the society.
- He fought for promoting values, which encourage consumption standard in consonance with ecological parameters.
- He said that the production pattern should be non-degrading and non-destructive of environment.
- He said that the thrust of development lies on a volume of output that commands maximum social value rather than market value.

Gandhiji also stressed on equalitarian and non-exploitative society that ensures the basic needs of the community and empowers all the sections of the society to raise to the level of conscious, critical and creative participation in the organisation and management of the community. Gandhiji made it abundantly clear that economic growth alone cannot bring benefits to all the sections of the community. He stressed on moral character of the nation. Therefore, the principle and ethical elements propounded by Gandhiji, if practised in a wide scale, shall go a long way in establishing a society based on the principles of sustainable development.

Obstacles to Sustainable Development

Votaries of frontier society believe that the world has an unlimited supply of resources for human use. They also think that the problems of 'nature' can be over come with the help of science and technology. It is a fact that science and technology have created enormous possibility for faster economic growth by inventing new methods of exploitation of natural resources. Over the years, man started thinking that development depends on man's ability to use technology to control natural process and manage resources to satisfy human needs. Such thinking have taken deep roots in the minds of the people in the society. In other words, such thinking has taken the shape of values that pervade into all walks of life and perpetuate attitudes that lead to unsustainable use of natural resources. Therefore, the first obstacle to sustainable development is the existing mindset of people.

Increased wants of people led to increased production in the economy. This resulted into generation of more disposable income that stimulated the demand for material goods. This again spurred the production. These factors constituted a vicious cycle of increasing wants, rising demand and enhancing production with increased use of natural resources. Therefore, man's attempt to use the resources beyond the limit of bare needs does constitute an obstacle to sustained development.

Consumption of resources beyond its carrying capacity has a ecological cost which is not immediately visible in the society. The ecological cost is generally overshadowed by marketing blitz of the commodity. The producer of the good neither intends to educate the consumer about the environmental cost. The consumer is also not so economically sound nor socially so sensitised about enormous ecological cost associated with the goods produced from resources extracted unsustainably. Therefore, the fact that the environmental costs of any goods and products which do not reflect in the market price is one of the impediments of sustainable development.

The uncertainties and constraints are so enormous that they defy any easy solutions. But, what is heartening is the fact that a lot of change have taken place in the mindset of people, leaders, development planners and economists. However, lot have to be done.

Conclusion

Sustainable development exerts its influence over the conventional development thinking and process. In other words, it has, to a great extent, altered the paradigm of conventional development. It introduced the concept of social costs of adverse environmental impacts into the process of project planning and management.

Most importantly, there has been an increased concern for preserving the natural resource base. This is evident in the fact that externalities are being included in social costs to a great degree than before. This has been corroborated in the policies of funding agencies for sustainable development in many countries.

There is also great effort to evaluate the environmental impact in terms of money. However, natural resource accounting has not taken deep roots in development planning. But, over the years recognition is being given to certain types of resource degradation as a social cost and efforts are made to internalise it. The case in point is the growing concern about the idea of a tax on carbon dioxide emissions as a means of reducing green house gases. The use of fees or tariffs or taxes on certain type of pollution and marketable emission to internalise environmental costs has been accepted by economists generally. The acceptance of stringent tax regime on the consumption of polluting commodities is another example which speaks volume about the change in mindset of people, leaders and economists.

Now, there is a wider acceptance of the doctrine of progress which includes criteria like (1) elimination of poverty, (2) expansion of health and education, (3) opening of economic opportunities for the people in the developing countries. The criteria of progress are changing and gradually moving closer towards sustainable development.

Notwithstanding all such changes in our thinking and practices, there are many things which remain to be done. It is a fact that many initiatives have been taken to sensitise the thinking about development, but ethical concern for the welfare of generation, both inter and intra, is still out of domain of economic development doctrine. To date, a lot of debate are still going on, about the merits and constraints of sustainable development. But now, with the dawn of new century, consensus about the appropriateness of the new paradigm – sustained development is fast building up.

5

NATURAL RESOURCES AND THEIR SUSTAINABLE USE

The social and economic development of the society largely depends on resources and their pattern and efficiency of use. Man depends on earth for all sort of resources. Resources have been commonly identified as agents or factors of production used in an economy to produce and distribute goods and services. In common parlance, resource means anything, which has a value, tangible or intangible. Resources are conventionally classified as land, water, labour and capital. Land resources encompass soil, and other natural resources under the ground like minerals, fossil fuels and hydrological and biotic component of the ecosphere. The living resources of earth are housed in as 'biosphere'. The biosphere is itself an amalgamation of complex interrelated ecosystems existing in the earth.

Biosphere symbolises an integrated web of ecosystems. It provides resources to humanity in the form of 'goods' and 'services'. Such living resources are called as primary resources because of the fact that they primarily constitute the building block of the society. What is more significant is the fact that biosphere, having a web of inter related ecosystems, acts as source of services which are of immense use to mankind. Mainly there are two kinds of services the ecosystems of the biosphere provide to mankind. One is the life supporting services of the ecosystem. This is the service by which the ecosystem is perpetuated indefinitely. Some of the important services under this category are maintenance of gaseous balance, regulation of earth's temperature, maintenance of weather pattern all over the globe and soil and water conservation. These services are basic to earth's biosphere. The second is cleansing services of the ecosystem. This is the service by which wastes created by the economic system adopted by man are cleansed to a great extent. However, functioning of the ecosystem depends, to a critical extent, upon non-renewable resources like minerals in rocks and soil. Therefore, the biosphere provides, in one hand, all primary goods and services necessary for the economic activities in the society, and in the other, life supporting services for perpetuation of the very biological productive system itself.

Sustainable development depends on how mankind uses the biosphere. Rather, social and economic development of society relies on pattern and efficiency of resource use. If resource is used in a sustainable way, then such a development is possible. Otherwise, it is not. To undertake sustainable development approach, it is necessary to comprehend all encompassing characteristics of natural resources. Therefore, this chapter aims at providing the readers a clear perspective on natural resources, especially renewable resources, their limitations, principles governing development and sustainable use of such renewable resources. It also presents a succinct picture of politics of sustainable use in the world.

Natural Resource

Natural resource is a term generally used to indicate resources like land, air, water, and forests. They constitute the physical basis of human life. Environmental resources are parts of nature that humankind considers to be useful or valuable. What is 'nature' can be debated endlessly, but for the sake of present discussion, it is simply the physical environment which includes, mainly air, sea, land, plants and animals. 'Useful' here relates to the production of material benefits, such as food, timber, while valuable means 'able to produce valued experiences' (Holmes Rolston, 1988: 272). He has listed about 14 different types of value associated with nature, ranging from economic and life-supporting value to religious and character-building value. Therefore, environmental resources can be defined as those parts of nature that can provide the goods and services sought by humans—including services such as opportunities for recreation, the appreciation of scenic beauty, or the disposals of wastes. (Mather, A.S., 1990).

Environmentally, resources can be grouped under three categories on the basis of their functions they form in the society. These three major groups of environmental resources are as follows:

- The first group consists of raw materials and energy sources used by humans, usually as inputs into the economic system. These have been traditionally termed as natural resources. Use of such resources as raw material leads to production of goods and services. Examples of such resources like mineral ores, oil, coal, etc.

- The second group comprises parts of the environment that can provide services rather than material goods. The examples of such resources are recreation and wildlife tourism.
- The third group consists of essential life support system for humans, including oxygen to breath and water to drink as well as material goods such as food, timber. It provides the sump in which the wastes products generated from the human activities are assimilated.

Natural resources always attract humankind's attention. Man depends on natural resources for its entire requirement. It has developed technologies and methods to exploit natural resources. A comprehensive picture of exploitation of natural resources in a historical perspective is presented in the ensuing chapter "transition to sustainability".

Defining 'Resource'

'Resource' is the most elusive term. There are many types of meaning. In one hand resources can be 'stock resources', like coal or iron or 'flow resources' like air, forests. Dictionary meaning of resource is given in Table 5.1. Erich Zimmerman (1951:7) gave a different view about natural resources. He took the functional view of resources. He described that resource does not refer to a thing or a substance but to a function which a thing or a substance may perform. By this he meant that 'resources are not, they become.' In other words, he meant that any part of nature could become a resource when people perceive it as having utility or value.

Changing perceptions, technology and economy create resources. Likewise, resources are destroyed or their value or utility reduced, in the same way it is created. A more common form of resource destruction involves degradation of resources. Degradation takes place when the use of the resource goes beyond its carrying capacity. But if resource is used within its threshold limit, then it does not degrade. Therefore, use of resource can be managed in such a way that productivity of the natural system does not reduce. Intensive agricultural practices can lead to soil erosion, which in turn leads to decline in land productivity and crop yield. Likewise, in case of a forest, when resources are removed at a faster rate than it is replenished by biological processes, then degradation sets in. The degradation process generally encompasses a series of stages.

A change in technology or increased demand may lead to renewed pressure on the resources, and it initiates a cascade of negative changes leading to final exclusion of the resource from the earth.

Table 5.1: Selected Dictionary Meanings of 'Resource' and Resources'

1. 'Means of supplying a want; stock that can be drawn on; country's collective means for support and defense; expedient device; skill in devising expedients, practical ingenuity, wick wit'.
2. 'Available means; something to which one has recourse in difficulty; capability or skill in meeting a situation.'
3. 'Source or possibility of help; and expedient means of support'.
4. 'Source or possibility of help; cleverness in finding a way round difficulties'.
5. 'That to which one resorts, or on which one depends, for supply or support; funds, wealth, riches, available means.'

Types of Resources

Resources have been categorised into two broad types on the basis of their renewability or lack of renewability. These types are as follows:

1. Non-renewable Resources

Non-renewable resources are those resources, which do not have the potential to renew. Such non-renewable resources are also called as exhaustible resources. They are those resources, which have taken millions of years to form. They are fixed in supply in terms of human scale. Once these resources are used or consumed they get depleted out of the total limited reserve. These resources encompass all the elemental minerals, apart from the energy resources like coal, petrol, natural gas, and other minerals. These resources have been formed by biological and organic process millions of years ago.

Non-renewable resources displays variegated characteristics. Since the stock is limited and renewability is not possible, there is a limit to the quantity, which can be exploited by the society. But, in most cases this limit remains beyond the realm of human assessment. In the context of developing science and technology, human endeavour to discover new reserves of resources continues unabatedly. However the quantity of such reserves is fixed with respect to time. So the quantum of supply of such resources cannot be drastically increased. Another point with regard to its characteristics is the fact that such resources once consumed or used lose its utility forever. Therefore there is an element of irretrievebility in its usage also. The generational implication of such characteristics for the economy and social development is that the consumption rate of such exhaustible resources affects their future availability. In other words, the more we use, the more we deprive the future generation of such resources.

2. *Renewable Resources*

Renewable resources are those resources which have the capability for renewal. However, the distinction between non-renewable or exhaustible resources is not altogether watertight. Renewable resources can be exhausted, destroyed or depleted like exhaustible resources. Tropical forests are a case in point. The distinction generally adopted between renewable and non-renewable resources is based on the rate of formation or replenishment. Fossil fuels are created by their organic and geological process and this process still continues today. But the rate of formation is so slow that it is negligible in comparison with the time span considered for our analysis. In contrast to this, forests which regenerate or have the capacity to regenerate well within a finite period of time are aptly classified as the renewable resources.

Characteristics of Renewable Resources

The renewable resources have the following characteristics:

Renewability

This is a critical concept which characterises the nature of renewable resources. As we discussed, all renewable resources are renewable in nature but their ability to renew themselves is off course dependent on the systems that supply moisture and nutrients and maintain the media of air and soil in which they grow. Apart from this, they also depend upon ecological efficiency and resilience of the ecosystem in which other renewable resources play a critical role.

Irreversibility

This is the second critical concept that characterises nature of renewable resources. If the forest ecosystem is used beyond its carrying capacity, then irreversible changes take place in the structure and function of the ecosystem. Consequently, such changes finally drive the ecosystem to a different state with the loss or extinction of species. Economically, irreversibility leads to uncertainty in resource allocation in an ecosystem. As a result, it affects efficiency and productivity of the ecosystem.

Time Gap between Exploitation and Regeneration

This is the third critical concept that characterises the renewable resources. There is always a time gap between exploitation and regeneration of renewable resources. The resources are exhausted or depleted if the rate of exploitation is more than the rate of regeneration.

Therefore, due the aforesaid characteristics, it is imperative to manage the renewable resources in accordance with the ecological principles. Otherwise, they will affect the production of goods and services in the ecosystem on which man depends for its existence.

Natural Capital vs Man-made Capital

Sustainable development economists focus on the limited capacity of environment to absorb wastes created by economic activity. There are limits to the ability of the ecosystem to assimilate solid wastes, toxic materials that are by-products of industrial and agricultural productions, and gases that foul our cities and collect in the atmosphere, without impairing the capacity of the land, air, water to sustain life as well as economic activity. Therefore, an important function of our economic system should be to reduce these wastes and to change their character so that assimilation limits are not exceeded.

Apart from this, sustainable development economists regard natural resources as natural capital, which is limited in supply than man-made capital. Capital, broadly, means 'a stock of something that yields a flow of useful goods and services'. Besides, capital is generally construed as man-made *i.e.* human made means of production. Whereas, the nature made capital like forests, water, land, air in contrast to man-made capital can be called as natural capital. Natural capital functions as a stock that yields a flow of goods and services necessary for the survival of man. It consists of physical and living stocks complementary to man-made capital. It can be inherited and also be passed on to the next generation. A part of the natural capital can be generated as sustainable increment and it can be marketed. This is how raw materials from the stock of natural capital are supplied to engines of production *i.e.* man-made capital. The food crop or forest harvests are the symbols of cultivated natural crop.

As already said, such natural resources, like other resources, have definite value. The nature of value may be social, economic, cultural, or ecological. All such natural resources, which act as 'natural capital', provide goods and services to humanity in the form of 'increment'. Such incremental benefits can continue indefinitely if the quantum of said 'natural capital' is kept constant. If the natural capital is reduced or depleted because of any activity beyond the carrying capacity of the system, then the flow of goods and services, including the life supporting services from the nature keeps on decreasing and finally it may come to naught. Therefore, the moment we begin to lose a part of the capital, the flow of benefits we receive in the form of incremental value starts decreasing. This leaves an impact of immense consequence to man and its society. The productive and life-supporting system of the biosphere is severely affected leading to a situation where the present rate of economic activity in the society will be unsustainable. Giving a word of caution, David Reid (1999) said, "We can deplete such capital (Natural) for short-term gains, but this reduces the level of future income. It may be very difficult to make good any depletion of capital and in extreme case, of course, squandering capital leads to permanent impoverishment". However, if the 'natural capital is remained intact and the life-supporting system is maintained efficiently, we can continue to receive flows of benefits in the form of goods and services indefinitely and thereby the necessary economic activity in the society can be continued on a sustained basis. With the increase in flow of economic activity, there is an expansion of man-made capital in the society.

Notwithstanding ecological overtones, there is a critical economic relationship between man-made capital and natural capital. Economic rationale necessitates maximisation of productivity of the scarcest goods (limiting factor) and increase of their supplies to the society. That means, economic policy should be designed so as to increase the productivity and amount of natural capital rather than the productivity and accumulation of man-made capital. It is because natural capital acts as a limiting factor and once management of natural capital is successfully addressed, then formation of man-made capital will follow. Herman E. Daly (1994) in his book ' Future of Forests' said, "Productivity of man-made capital is more and more limited by decreasing supply of complementary natural capital. In the past, when the scale of the human presence in the biosphere was low, man-made capital played the limiting role. The switch from man-made to natural capital as the limiting factor is thus a function of the increasing scale and impact of the human presence." The complementarity of man-made and natural capital is elucidated in Table 5.2.

Table 5.2: Complementarity of Man-made Capital and Natural Capital

Man-made Capital	*Natural Capital*	*Steps to Improve Natural Capital*
Hydroelectricity	Mountain range and forests in the catchment areas	Watershed conservation
Agricultural production system	Climate, soil and watershed areas	Sustainable agriculture
Dam	Mountain range and forests in the catchment areas	Watershed conservation
Irrigation infrastructure	Water resources	Watershed conservation
Paper mills/sawmills and wood industry	Forests	Sustainable forest management
Beach resort and hill resort tourism	Coastal and hill station ecosystem	Sustainable development of natural resources
Animal husbandry	Grassland and forests	Silvipastural development
Agro-industry	Agricultural ecosystem	Sustainable agriculture
Pisci-culture	Fish population and aquatic ecosystem	Conservation of aquatic ecosystem

Reconstructing Natural Capital

Rather than symbolising economic growth, development must evolve into a reconstruction of natural capital. Unlike the post-World War phase, when there was tremendous emphasis on man-made capital, it is now the need of the hour to develop natural capital, particularly in those areas where it has been destroyed by the activities of 'so called development'. This will mark the beginning of a new era of natural capital worldwide. This era should initiate the process of (1) augmenting and conserving the remaining natural resources, (2) their sustainable use, (3) reducing our own level of exploitation of resources, and (4) increasing the end use efficiency. Once these elements are integrated into a well-knit programme of action for reconstruction, it will herald a new beginning in our journey towards sustainable development.

Therefore, the present challenge revolves around how to reconstruct natural capital and develop its sustainable use. There are only very few choices, which are as follows:

- By undertaking suitable conservation measures.
- By controlling wants of people; *i.e.* confining the resource use to the limits of needs only.
- By shifting investment from man-made capital to natural capital.
- By developing and employing appropriate technology to increase the productivity of natural capital and their efficient use.
- By developing technological, social, political and economic framework for efficient use.
- By developing pricing system of natural capital in such a way that it reflects the concern for becoming scarce. If this is done, then it will facilitate efficient end use of natural resources in the society. This can be done by internalising the cost of managing natural resources into the production and pricing system.

Reconstruction of natural capital is an uphill task. It requires formulation of a broad strategy. The strategy must emphasise on three things. One is increasing the net worth of natural capital. The second is increasing the product out-put of natural capital. The third is increasing the efficiency of end use of natural capital. All put under one umbrella, then it can be captioned as ' Natural Capital Reconstruction Strategy' (See also Fig. 5.1).

Natural resource economists argue that the depletion and degradation of natural capital in the course of economic activity should be treated as social costs analogous to the depreciation of man-made capital. Therefore, capital depreciation of natural resource should be treated as a social cost in economic policies and programmes. Going a step further, some sustainable development economists have suggested that in allocating natural resources among different uses, it is necessary to choose the use that maximizes the net present social value of resources. There is a feeling in some quarter that certain characteristics of natural capital like irreversibility should not be lost sight of. It is because this characteristic has been useful in understanding the impact of over-use on renewable resources.

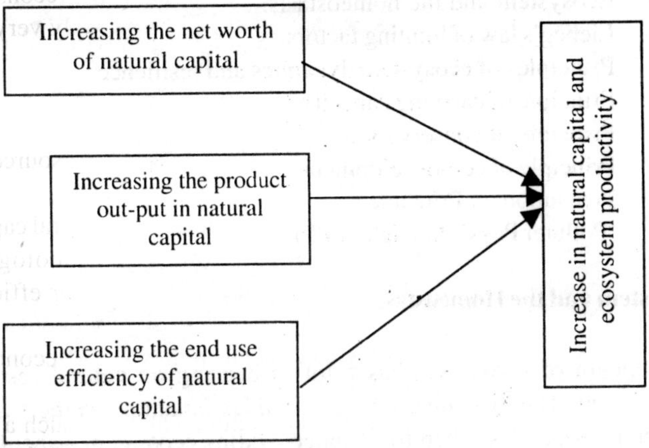

Fig. 5.1: Natural Capital Reconstruction Strategy

The concept of capital depreciation is being followed in some quarters to compensate the loss of natural capital. Many natural economists have pointed the folly in such argument. Daly (1991, p.18) says that the possibility of substitution of man-made capital for natural capital is very limited, but that since man-made capital requires natural resources, there is more complementarity than substitutability between the man-made capital and natural capital. Apart from Mr. Dally, there are many economists, now believe that there is only complementarity rather than substitutability, between these twos. This concept is being widely accepted worldwide.

Underlying Principles of Sustainability

Sustainable development is a complex process involving multidisciplinary sectors in the economy. It is influenced by 'laws of nature' as well as the human behaviour. However, over the years, with the increase in population and man's power to alter the environment, the behaviour of man towards natural resources and quantitative relations among different 'laws of nature' have changed drastically. Therefore, to keep these laws in harmony, it becomes necessary to evolve certain social and economic principles which when allowed to act with 'laws of nature' help to promote environmental sustainability. Few of the important ecological and general principles are enumerated below:

- Ecosystem and the homeostasis.
- Liebeg's law of limiting factors.
- Principles of ecosystem dynamics and resilience.
- Principle of carrying capacity
- Principle of conservation
- Principle of eco-development.
- Precautionary Principle
- 'Polluter Pays' Principle (PPP)

Ecosystem and the Homeostasis

The concept of ecosystem has a lot of bearing on natural resource management. The biosphere where man lives functions on the basis of ecosystem principles. Therefore, understanding ecosystem principles is key to managing natural resources sustainably.

All living resources are found in the ecosystem. Eugene P. Odum defines ecosystem in the following way:

'Living organisms and their non-living (abiotic) environment are inseparably interrelated and interact upon each other. Any unit that includes all of the organism (*i.e.* the community) in a given area interacting with the physical environment so that a flow of energy leads to clearly defined trophic structures, biotic diversity, and material cycles (*i.e.* exchange of materials between living and non-living parts) within the system is an ecological system or ecosystem'

Structurally, the ecosystem encompasses five components like: (1) Inorganic substances, (2) Organic compounds, (3) Climate regime, (4) Green plants or producers, (5) Micro and macro consumers and decomposers.

Functionally, the ecosystem constitutes the six critical components. They are: (1) Energy flows, (2) Food chains, (3) Diversity pattern in time and space, (4) Nutrient cycles, (5) Development and evolution, and (6) Control. The concept of ecosystem approach emphasises on managing the mutual relationship and interdependence among structural and functional components of the ecosystem.

Managing ecosystem with the objectives of providing social, cultural, political and economic benefits on a sustainable basis is a challenge to humanity. It must be consistent with the necessities of ecology as well as development. It should apply all inter-disciplinary principles with the sole aim of developing the ecosystem resources and the people who depend on it for their survival. However, ecosystem management, from the point of ecology, aims at: (1) sustainable rate of harvest of renewable resources, (2) determining their impact on environments, (3) maintaining the physical and functional component, along with the productive efficiency of the system.

The important ecological aspects behind ecosystem management are limiting factors, homeostasis, dynamism, resilience and carrying capacity. There are two laws, which explain the organism's response to these environmental changes. They are: (1) the law of minimum, and (2) the law of tolerance. These two laws, popularly known as 'laws of limiting factors', have been dealt in the next category of principle.

Ecosystem is a dynamic system. All the components of the ecosystems are operationally inseparable. They interact with each other on a continuous basis to form a functional unit. This leads into emergence of a vital process of production, consumption and decomposition in a functional unit. There is inherent functional and structural harmony among all the components in the ecosystem. Apart from harmony, ecosystem has the capacity for self-maintenance and self-regulation. In other words, the ecosystem has an inbuilt system of internal control.

It is always difficult to assess the true impacts of economic activity on the ecosystem. Therefore, it is incumbent on our part that we should avoid risks or reject policies and practices that has the potentialities of imparting negative impacts or fallout on our ecosystems. This premise has led to an emergence of another concept like 'Precautionary Principle'. This principle has been dealt separately.

Liebeg's Laws of Limiting Factors

In an ecosystem, various environmental factors like light, temperature, humidity, wind speed, availability of food and nutrients play an important role in its functioning. These factors also keep on changing quantitatively as well as qualitatively. These changes affect the well being and survival of the organism in an ecosystem as they can thrive only if all factors essential for life are available. The essential factors, which become scarce, act as limiting factors for the organism's growth and survival.

There are two laws, which explain the organism's response to these environmental changes. They are:

- *The Law of Minimum*: This law states that the growth and well being of an organism is ultimately regulated by that essential resources that is in its lowest supply relative to what is required. The most deficient resource is, therefore, called the limiting factor.
- *The Law of Tolerance*: This law states that for each physical factors in the environment, a minimum and maximum limit exists. This limit is called tolerance limit, beyond which the organism does not thrive or survive. In other words, either too little or too much of required factor like food, energy, heat, vitamins, minerals, water or oxygen threatens the survival of organisms and even the entire species.

Principle of Ecosystem Dynamics and Resilience

Ecosystem is a dynamic system. It has many components which are operationally inseparable. They interact with each other on a continuous basis to form a functional unit. This gives rise to a vital process of production, consumption and decomposition in a functional unit. There is inherent functional and structural harmony among all the components in the ecosystem.

Apart from harmony, each ecosystem has the capacity for self-maintenance and self-regulation. In other words, the ecosystem has an inbuilt system of internal control. But, with the rise in demand for more goods and services from the ecosystem, the degree of human intervention in the resource use system has increased manifold. In many instances the interventions have lead to disruption of the natural control system. But, every biological system, to a great extent, resists such interventional changes and tries to remain in a state of equilibrium or homeostasis. Homeostasis means inherent capacity of a system to revert back to its normal state after a period of perturbation.

A homeostatic mechanism exists at different levels of biological organisation. Besides, there is equilibrium between living and non-living components of the environment also. This homeostatic mechanism has the propensity to resist any change to a great extent. This mechanism at structural and functional levels of ecosystem symbolises the principle of 'balance of nature'. But over the years, it has been found by the ecologists that instead of 'balance of nature', there is 'flux of nature' in the ecosystem functioning. The new concept of 'flux of nature' indicates that the equilibrium is not static but dynamic. That means the ecosystem allows a number of changes to interact with and evolves itself into a dynamic system. However, if certain thresholds are not maintained, the homeostatic mechanism or dynamic equilibrium system collapses. Violent interventions of man into the nature's system of production, consumption and decomposition lead to transgression of all such thresholds.

The thresholds, which are required to be maintained in ecosystem management practices, are the physiological limits under which organisms can continue to survive and function without stress. Within such limits, the biological processes do permit some degree of adaptations in response to marginal random disturbances, induced anthropologically or otherwise. The time required for such adaptation responses is critical: if a naturally (literally) determined time-lag is not allowed, the outcome is an unsustainable continued perturbation of the ecosystem leading to non-linearities, irreversibilities and consequent surprises (Rao, 2000).

The capacity of the living community to recover from any kind of disturbance is known as resilience. In nature, the physical environment poses continuous challenges to the life forms with disturbance of various kinds. Apart from the natural disturbance, the human factor also inflicts perturbations and major disruptions in the communities. The recovery of the communities to its original structural and functional state after a span of time reflects the community's resilience, *i.e.* inherent tendency and capacity of the community to attain a dynamic equilibrium. The degree of resilience differs from communities to communities and ecosystem to ecosystem.

Principle of Carrying Capacity

Carrying capacity is the threshold limit of any human activity beyond which physical capacity of the ecosystem is diminished and ecological capacity is degraded. The concept of carrying capacity has tremendous relevance to sustainability of resources. It is traditionally an ecological concept. It was basically developed to explain characteristic population growth forms in an ecosystem. It aims at explaining the upper limit of resource utilisation in an ecosystem. It is significant for scientific planning and management of natural resource use.

Over the years, the concept has emerged as an effective tool for natural resource management. The concept has tremendous application value. But difficulties in measuring the thresholds have restricted the concept to its use as only a planning tool. A blend of factors determining physical and ecological capacity, along with existing social realities, helps to determine the optimum carrying capacity for any resource.

In human environment, carrying capacity is primarily influenced by the following factors:

- Lifestyle prevalent in the society.
- Level of science and technology.
- Institutional innovations in the society.
- Increasing hopes and aspirations of the people for better standard of life.

In any ecosystem, the carrying capacity depends on the available resources, degree of human interventions and the ability of the system to cope with it. The conceptual model of carrying capacity comprises:

- *Supportive capacity*: This symbolises the ability of the ecosystem to allow withdrawal of resources like raw materials, water, etc without causing permanent damage to the environment.
- *Assimilative capacity*: This symbolises the ability to absorb certain amount of wastes without ill effects or without affecting the inbuilt assimilative capacity.

In the context of above cited perspective, carrying capacity of a region can be explained in terms of the number of persons that can be supported by a unit area of land while producing raw material and assimilating the wastes. The linkages of carrying capacity to different developmental activities are explicated in Fig 5.2. The human population has shown manifold increase, which necessitated an ever-increasing demand on resources. The propensities of the societies to over-consume the natural resources lead to depletion of the natural capital *i.e.* the base of productive resources itself. This phenomenon is synonymous with ecological equivalent of deficit financing. Likewise, the assimilative capacity can absorb wastes, to some extent but cannot regenerate the land productivity or recover the ecosystem functioning, or replenish the water regimes or restore the lost biodiversity beyond a limit. However the carrying capacity is subject to change. The expansion of ecological boundaries of carrying capacity is possible in consequence to natural evolutionary forces transforming both physical resources and composition of life forms into an efficient structural and functional ecosystem. But the pace of evolutionary process is so slow and the forces acting on the ecosystem are so negative that it is unthinkable to expect a positive change in the carrying capacity of the system. Nevertheless, a progressive change in the carrying capacity can occur as a consequence to changes in human society due to either introduction of new eco-friendly technology, institutional innovations, resource need management, government policy or factors such as minimum per capita income and resource requirement. This apart, introduction of ethical and environmental standards into the society can bring changes in mindset of people towards environmental conservation.

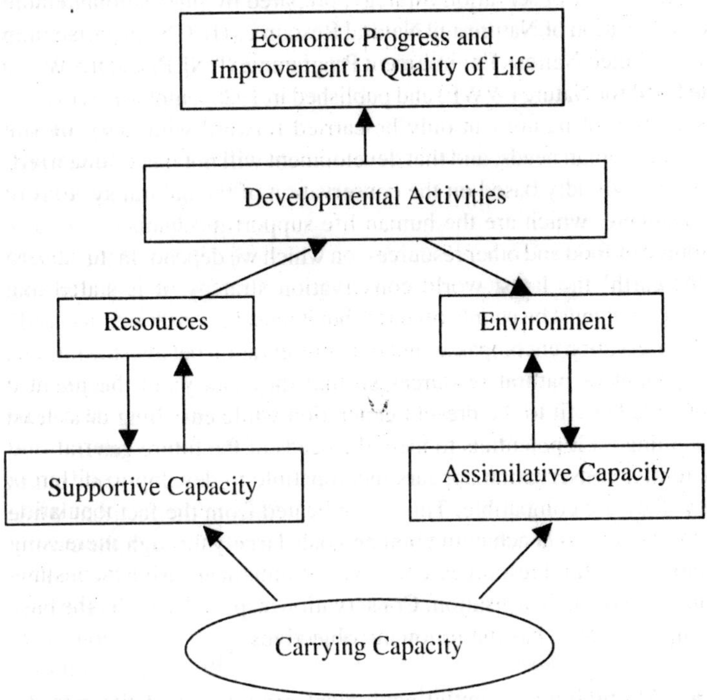

Fig. 5.2: Linkages between Carrying Capacity and Economic Progress

Principles of Conservation

Conservation is a broad concept, which involves not only the scientific but ethical, moral, economic, social and political aspects as well. It deals with judicious development and manner of use of natural resources of all kinds. A generalized definition of conservation is "the maximisation over time of the net social benefits in goods and services from resources". However, more precisely, conservation may be defined as the achievement of the highest sustainable quality of living for mankind by the rational utilisation of environment, protection of nature to enrich the life of man and control or elimination of environmental pollution in its manifestations. It advocates practices that will perpetuate the resources of earth on which man depends. In other words, conservation involves perpetuation of the natural environment of man including the infinite resources of air, water, soil, and life forms.

The world Conservation Strategy, prepared by International Union for Conservation of Nature and Natural Resources (IUCN) in partnership with the United Nations Environment Programme (UNEP) and the World Wide Fund for Nature (WWF) and published in 1980, emphasises that the conservation of nature can only be carried forward with development that meets human needs, and that development will not meet those needs unless it is soundly based on the conservation of the natural systems of the biosphere, which are the human life support mechanism, and also the source of food and other resources, on which we depend. In the 'caring for the earth' the latest world conservation strategy, it is stated that 'development must be people oriented, but it must be conservation based'.

Conservation encompasses not only preservation but also the rational management of natural resources so that they can yield the greatest sustainable benefit to the present generation while enriching or at least maintaining their potentials to meet the needs of the future generations. Apparently, conservation appears incompatible to development, but in reality, they are compatible. This is vindicated from the fact that while development aims at achieving human goals largely through the current utilisation of natural resources, conservation aims at ensuring the endless continuance of such utilisation. Conservation, especially with reference to living resources, has the following objectives:

- Maintaining essential ecological processes and life support systems.
- Preserving bio-diversity, especially genetic diversity.

Conservation aims at (1) ensuring the preservation of environment in its normal state, (2) ensuring a continuous yield of goods and services by establishing a balanced cycle of harvest and renewal, and (3) sustainable utilisation of goods and services. It is achieved through different means of conservation measures. Some of the conservation measures are illustrated below:

- *Rational use of resources.* Preservation serves an ecological purpose by maintaining the function of the total environment. But, not withstanding preservation, rational use implies the direct use of resources for their utility or product value. Thus harvesting a forest crop can be considered a legitimate component of rational use of natural resources, if they are carried out in such a way that the resource is perpetuated and not endangered.
- *Sustained yield*: The concept implies that in any biological production system, the yield should not be more than the increment.
- *Restoration*: The concept implies correction of past careless activities that have impaired the productivity of the resource base. The process of restoration is possible, only so long as species are protected and genetic diversity of life is maintained. When species become extinct, the restoration of past conditions become impossible.
- *Protection*: It implies protection of natural resources from commercial exploitation to prolong generation of goods and services from the resource base.
- *Reutilisation*: It implies a process of recycling and reuse of waste materials in order to minimise pressure on the resource base as well as to maximise the material benefits.
- *Substitution*: It is a concept, which encompasses two aspects. One is use of a common resource instead of a rare one when it can be used for the same purpose. Secondly, the use of a renewable rather than a non-renewable resource when condition permits.
- *Allocation*: It implies a strategy of use to derive the maximum social benefits. For many produces and their products, the market decides the pattern of use, but in a matter of immense public importance, general welfare may dictate the use to which the resource is put.
- *Integration*: The concept of integration aims at maximisation, over a period of time, of the sum of goods and services that can be produced from a complex resource base or system. This is in

lieu of maximisation of certain benefits from a single resource at the expense of other benefits or other resources. Integration in a complex resource system is key to synergy and optimum performance of the system as a whole.

Principles of Eco-development

The principle of eco-development emphasises strengthening of the ecosystem as well as ensuring an accelerated rate of socio-economic development in the society. The essential feature of eco-development is its sustainability. Eco-development is a process of change, in which exploitation of resources, the direction of investment, the orientation of technological development and institutional changes stand in harmony to each other and enhance both current and future potentials to meet human needs and aspirations.

Eco-development strategy necessitates a pragmatic scheme of prioritisation of resource use. The basis of prioritisation should be the degree of expendability of the resource. From the perspective of eco-development, natural resources are classified into four types on the basis of renewability, exhaustibility and cyclicality. This is a four-way classification system instead of traditional two-way classification. These four classes of natural resources may be arranged vertically from higher to lower in terms of their degree of expendability. The different classes of natural resources are as follows:

(1) Inexhaustible resources *e.g.* solar energy.
(2) Cyclic resources *e.g.* water in the hydrological cycle.
(3) Renewable resources *e.g.* natural vegetation.
(4) Non-renewable resources *e.g.* fossil fuels.

A rational resource use policy in the context of eco-development should be based on the principle that moves on to a lower order in the scale only after exploring the possibility of utilising the natural resources in the higher order.

Eco-development approach, which has many shortcomings, emerged after the concept of biophysical sustainability failed. It focussed on the satisfaction of basic human needs while maintaining ecological health (Sachs, 1979; Glaeser and Vyasulu, 1984). In contrast to the biophysical sustainable approach, eco-development concentrated on need fulfillment at the local level. It remained marginal to the development debate as it limited itself to development at the local scale and neglected larger issues of national economic management (Adams, 1990). However the 'basic need approach' of eco-development remains instrumental in shaping present thinking on sustainable development.

Precautionary Principle (PP)

The precautionary principle states that, while embarking on developmental process, we should avoid risks or reject policies and practices that could have unsustainable outcome or negative impacts on the ecosystem. In other words, it advises to take sufficient precaution in any initiative in the field of natural resource management. Putting it in another way, it offers a way of living with uncertainties about limits and impacts of economic activity or new technologies on ecosystem. It is an important tool for environmental governance.

Montreal Protocol (1996) is considered as historic because of adaptation of this principle. It suggested governments to adopt sufficient measures for environmental protection well before full scientific knowledge about the threat has been acquired. Sustainable development cannot afford to ignore developmental policies that are based on incomplete and uncertain information. In addition to these features, system uncertainties or socio-economic changes or stochastic features of bio-geographical phenomenon warrant a cautious approach, largely expressed as 'Precautionary Principle'. The principle is based on the premise that uncertainty should be interpreted towards a measure of safeguard. It is like a 'better safe than sorry' approach. Agenda 21, Principle 15 of the Rio Declaration of the Earth's Summit (1992) states: 'in order to protect the environment, the precautionary approach shall be widely applied by states according to their capabilities'. Two key elements of the principle are as follows:

- A threshold of perceived threat against which advance action would be deemed justifiable; and
- A burden of proof on the activity contributor or entrepreneur to show that a proposed action will not cause actual harm.

Polluter Pays Principle (PPP)

Polluter Pays Principle (PPP) is another important economic instrument, which is required to be applied for operationalisation of the concept of sustainable development. It represents property rights on the environmental assets to convince producer of pollution to pay the difference between the social cost and private costs of provision goods and services.

Polluter Pays Principle has its application in the field of natural resource management and this was institutionally advocated by the OECD (1975) for adoption in its member countries, which are typically industrial economies. The principle focuses on two things:

- Allocating costs of pollution prevention and control measures to encourage rational use of scarce environmental resources and to avoid distortions in trade and investment.
- Reflecting the costs of these measures in the costs of goods and services, whose extraction or production or consumption cause pollution. This is internalisation of environmental costs.

Sustainability of Ecosystem Processes and Function

The biosphere is a repository of resources. It has the unique capacity to support the living resources which are though renewable but depletable. Apart from this, it has a capacity not only to assimilate wastes generated because of burgeoning economic activities world over but also to recycle the flow resources such as fresh air and clean water. The most important function of the biosphere is its life supporting services. Ecological sustainability pertains to sustainable continuance of ecosystem processes and functions of the biosphere. All the ecological principles must be adhered to, if the ecological sustainability is to be achieved. The ecological limits of resource will be determined by the recovery – both regenerative rate of renewable resources and the recovery rate of the assimilative capacities of sinks of biosphere. Sinks extend beyond the boundaries of many countries. In other words, sustainability of ecosystem functions operates at every level like local, regional, national and global. Therefore, action for achieving sustainability requires initiative at every level. Thus, as Michel Jocob (1991) points out: "A national economy can only be described as 'sustainable' if it's activities not only do not reduce environmental capacities with in its own border, but do not cause their reduction elsewhere".

Perspectives on Sustainable Use

Sustainable use means the use of components of biological resource system in a way and at a rate that does not lead to the long-term decline of the system, thereby maintaining its potential to meet the needs and aspiration of present and future generation. The basic objective behind sustainable use is to ensure that succeeding generations have the same degree of access as we have today. The quantum of benefits from such resources should also be continued to the next generation. In order to achieve this avowed objectives, it is imperative to follow certain principles. The most important principle of sustainable use of resource system is that at best we may use the "increment" and not the capital. In other words, we should utilise the goods and services from the natural resource system at a rate preferably lower than, or utmost equal to, the rate at which the system regenerates. The second principle is that before we decide to use the increment, it is necessary to calculate the quantum of increment correctly. This is the sustainable rate of harvest. Sometime the harvest is annual increment or sometime it is an accumulation of increments over a period. If the sustainable harvest rate is not calculated correctly, the determined rate of harvest transcends the rate of renewability. In such situation it will affect the very survival of the ecosystem, notwithstanding productivity. In a forest ecosystem, removal of sustained yield must confirm the renewability of the crop, otherwise the harvest is not sustained. Continuance of timber yield on a sustained basis necessitates maintenance of growing stock, continuity of regeneration, and survival of biotic and abiotic components and preservation of life supporting services like suitable hydrological and gaseous cycle.

Sometime one ponders weather it is possible to exceed sustainable rates of use or not. In fact it is not impossible to use the resources beyond the sustainable limit for a relatively short period over a comparatively small areas. But this practice is fraught with risks and uncertainties. There is a critical point in the growing stock. The population in any ecosystem at any period of time should not go below this critical point. If human society manages to recover the declining growing stock before it reaches the critical minimum below which survival or regeneration is impossible, then it will entail no loss and this augurs well for the sustainable use. But till the complete recovery is attained, it will be indispensable on the part of human society to do away with the said resource or use very little which is much lower to the rate of regeneration. Besides, during the period of using any alternative resource, it is important to ensure that the rate of consumption or use of the alternative resources is lower than its recovery rate. In the words of David Reid, "A sustainable policy on non-renewable resources does not require a complete ban on their consumption, but involves wise economic use, so we leave as large stocks as possible for future generation".

Therefore, the basic elements of environmental sustainability with relation to natural resources are based on the ecological principles. Again, these principles are succinctly enunciated below:

- The stock of the natural capital should not diminish and it should be conserved in sufficient abundance.
- Rate of exploitation or use of natural resources should be linked with the rate of regeneration.
- Demand should be linked with the rate of sustainable use.
- The price of the product should reflect the economic price encompassing the environmental costs.
- There is need to identify or develop substitutes for the natural resources.
- The rate of discharge of wastes must not exceed the rate at which these flows can be assimilated without impacting ecosystem negatively.

The most pertinent point is the fact that how to establish practices compatible to sustainable use of non-renewable natural resources. The priority requirements to promote sustainable utilisation have been enumerated by World Conservation Strategy (IUCN, 1980). Few of the important requirements (as mentioned in different paragraphs of the IUCN document) are as follows.

- Determine the productive capacities of exploited species and ecosystems and ensure the utilisation does not exceed those capacities (para 7.1).
- Adopt conservation management objectives for the utilisation of species and ecosystems (para 7.2).
- Ensure that access to a resource does not exceed the resource's capacity to sustain exploitation (para 7.3).
- Reduce excessive yields to sustainable levels (para 7.4).
- Reduce incidental take as much as possible (para 7.5).
- Equip subsistence communities to utilise resource sustainably (para 7.6).
- Maintain the habitats of resource species (para 7.7).

- Regulate international trade in wild animals and plants (para 7.8).
- Allocate timber concessions with care and manage them to high standards (para 7.9).
- Limit firewood consumption to sustainable levels (para 7.10).
- Regulate the stocking of grazing lands to maintain the long-term productivity of plants and animals (para 7.11).
- Utilise indigenous wild herbivores, alone or with livestock, where domestic stock alone would degrade the environment (para 7.12).

Obstacles to Sustainable Development

There are many obstacles in the process of translating the concept of sustainable development to a definite programme of actions and practices. The most important one is the mindset of man towards use of natural resources. It is still a common thing that people from developed as well as developing nations, think that natural resources, in spite of their uncontrolled use, are infinite and inexhaustible. The second obstacle is the psyche of man that he is born to conquer on nature and its forces. The third is the perception of majority people that conservation of natural resources comes at the cost of economic development or the *vice versa.* These three important obstacles have prevented man to accept the concept and principles of sustainable development. Apart from this, there are many hurdles on the road to sustainability. These hurdles are the demand for natural resources on account of increasing economic activities, population explosion and rising inequality and poverty in the world. The fact that the rate of exploitation has transgressed the rate of recovery or regeneration also constitutes a potential hurdle. These hurdles come in the form of pressures on decreasing renewable natural resources. Consequent to this, the natural resources or the natural capital is decreasing at an alarming rate. What is more significant is the fact that the per capita consumption of natural resources is increasing in the developed world and people there are emitting more wastes than the natural ecosystem is capable of assimilating. Apart from this, unsustainable economic activities in both developed and developing world destroy the life supporting system of the earth. As a result, the natural capital of the world is shrinking at an alarming rate.

The present pattern of economic system encourages use of natural resources beyond sustainable limit. Market forces decide the use of resources and there lies the present imbroglio. If we want to establish the practice of sustainable use of natural resources, then the rate of renewability or recovery must decides the rate of use.

Improving Ecological Processes and Efficiency

Not withstanding the issue of addressing the obstacles to sustainable development, improvement in ecological processes and efficiency of the productive system is indispensable. The main components of any such programme encompass (1) establishing a need and simplicity based life style in the society, (2) reducing per capita consumption of natural resources, (3) increasing the efficiency of harvesting and use of natural resource, (4) expanding the natural capital base. Towards this end, the following measures are urgently required to be taken up:

- Changing to a system, which uses less natural resources.
- Adopting the indigenous products and saving energy in transportation.
- Encouraging sustainable use of resources at local level.
- Changing to more energy efficient system of production.
- Switching to a system, which generates minimum quantity of wastes and maximum quantum of welfare goods.
- Evolving and adopting technologies, which process and decrease the negative impacts of development. Recycling of wastes is one such technology.

The World Conservation Strategy (IUCN, 1980) has enumerated the priority requirements for improving the ecological processes. Few important requirements are: (1) reserve good cropland for crops, (2) manage cropland to high, ecologically sound standards, (3) ensure that the principal management goal for watershed forests and pastures is protection of the watershed, (4) ensure that the principal management goal for coastal wetlands is the maintenance of the processes on which the fisheries depend, and (5) control the discharge of pollutants.

Relevance of ecological efficiency in this age of rapid economic growth is no doubt an accepted fact. But, to what extent we can bring ecological efficiency is a moot point. It is definitely a matter to ponder whether we can bring economic efficiency to a level that economic growth which has always meant increased consumption of natural resources shall support. It is not clear weather we are able to translate the concept of sustainable development into a definite programme of action and practice, given the mindset of people, and current extent of unsustainable practices and the time required to bring development in the field of ecological efficiency. But we need to remain optimistic and keep on making serious efforts towards establishing sustainable development.

The Politics of Resource Use: A Global Perspective

The relation of man and development with environment over the years has assumed immense proportions. However, a plurality of perspectives on the question of such relations exists in the socio-political landscape. Various political perspectives on development and environment over the years represent a curious mix of convergence and divergence of viewpoints. This has been attributed to many factors like increasing human knowledge on the relation between man and environment, rising expectation of man on the front of material consumption and policies and programmes adopted in different countries.

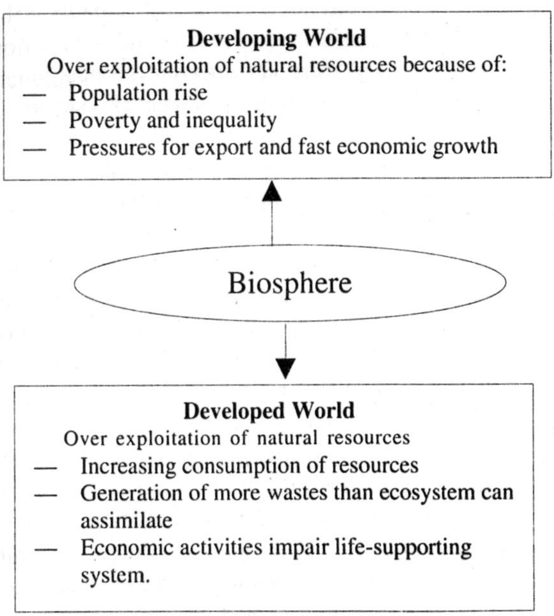

Fig. 5.3: Man-Biosphere Relationship

Till 1950, the dominant thinking was that the environment could be taken for granted. Man utilised them indiscriminately without thinking about the possible consequence. Natural resources were understood to be inexhaustible. The concept that natural resources are meant to be indiscriminately used for the material development of mankind gained currency. This perspective pervaded much of the thinking on economic development in the industrialised countries. This trend continued till the sixties. In the seventies, the concept started changing. There emerged a slow realisation towards the grave consequence of depletion of natural resources and degradation of ecosystems.

Now, the need of conservation of natural resources has emerged as not just a virtue but a bare requisite for human survival. The developed nations, because of their economic and political superiority, have appropriated a much greater share of the natural resources of the earth. It is estimated, for instance, that about 27 per cent of the world population living in developed countries enjoys about 75 per cent of the world's wealth and resources. This process has inevitably led to conditions, which create a severe environmental stress. The on-going debate between developing countries around the subject of accountability for the present state of affairs in environmental degradation still remains unresolved (see also Fig. 5.3). Apart from this sharp global debate on accountability, even within the nation states, there are different groups and classes, which have uneven accessibility to natural resources. This situation within a nation sharpens the existing social conflict in the society. Therefore, the issues like question of man's relationship with environment, responsibility for their degradation, competition between different nations *vis-à-vis* resources, consequences of such activities on environment, the conflict between different social groups and strata regarding access to natural resources and utilisation of natural resources by different countries at different scale have entered into the domain of international politics. Again the situation of conflict over the sharing of resources and responsibility for their degradation has assumed intense political overtones transcending national boundaries. Therefore, all such environmental conflicts necessitate an urgent political resolution.

Considered in this backdrop, the global debate on sharing and distribution of natural resource distribution and owning accountability for degradation of environment is being sharpened over the years. The politics on environment began in 1960s onwards after realisation that man's physical and biological environment has been undergoing rapid changes. It was also felt that these changes on account of human activities, if unchecked, are capable of bringing about immense suffering and destruction to the society. Three developments have become crucial in this respect. They are as follows:

- High consumption standard in the developed countries.
- Accelerated technological development overlooks environmental protection measures all over the world, particularly in the developed countries.
- Unprecedented rise in the population especially in the developing countries.

It is widely believed that these aforesaid factors are interrelated to each other and juxtaposed in such a manner that they contribute to the depletion of earth's resources and environmental degradation This concern about degradation of environmental resources has led to emergence of global environmental movement. The politics of environment draws sustenance from this.

The environmental movement evolved on a phased manner. In the first phase, the initiative in this direction has been taken by the developed countries, mainly the United States of America. However, the first phase starting roughly in the 1970s, was more localised in nature. The environmental issues of local importance only highlighted with little concern for their larger implication. This first phase evolved into a more wide second phase encompassing co-ordinated concern for the environment and integrating local issues with global context. In this phase, the universality of the environmental issues was conspicuously emphasised. Some of the global environmental issues, which remain in the forefront of world today, are as follows:

- Global warming
- Destruction of planet's ozone layer.
- Loss of tropical rain forests and bio-diversity.
- Acid rains.
- Ocean, land and atmospheric pollution.

The politics of environment in the second phase displayed a more global concern for environmental degradation. It is now well established that the ecological ills may have local roots but they create an intricate chain of effects which link different ecosystems and natural orders. Therefore, environmental degradation, besides having local concern, has assumed universality in its perspective and placed itself in the global agenda for the first time.

The spectrum of politics on environment in a global context represents a combination of consensus and divergent views. Broadly speaking, at the global level, one finds two distinct position and accompanying concerns. Both the perspectives betray extreme positions. However, both the positions have some positive elements. The first position originated in the third world countries or the developing countries. It symbolises some of the apprehensions of these countries on the environmental initiatives of the west. This position looks upon the concern of the west as the conspiracy to prevent the developing countries from improving their economies, by raising the bogey of environment. In other words, the logic in this position is that western countries have developed their economies by going through a process of rapid industrialisation. They did it by indiscriminately exploiting the earth's resources to the maximum with the help of modern technology. Having developed their economy and ensured better living standard for their people, their priority now shifted to environmental conservation.

Such voices were raised at the United Nation's Conference on the Human Environment held in 1972 in Stockholm. Many delegates from the developing countries argued that solution to the environmental problem lies with economic development. The delegates from Brazil declared that smoke is a sign of progress and not a sign of environmental degradation as assumed by the west. The Indian delegate led by the then Prime Minister Indira Gandhi declared: 'Poverty is the worst polluter of the environment' Putting it succinctly, the general impression of the developing nation is that the developed nations was trying to overstretch the environmental concern to an extent unacceptable to the rest of the world and that to at the expense of the poor countries.

The first position holds the west responsible for many of these ills. The major environmental problems in the third world countries are those related to over exploitation of natural resources. This process of utilisation and appropriation of natural resources available in the developing countries for the development of the developed countries is still continuing. The food needs and consumption patterns of the west have also deprived the third world countries of their resources. Developed countries still enjoy the required political and economic clout to exert pressure on developing countries to continue the process of exploitation of natural resources.

The second position originates in the developed countries. It presents the argument that poor countries are mainly responsible for the degradation of the environment. This perspective of the west considers the ever increasing population responsible for environmental degradation. The position lays the argument that the growing population in the poor countries has put scarce natural resources to a severe strain. An increase in human population exerts enormous pressures on our environment, which finds it difficult to cope with. The western countries say that they have taken measures to minimize its environmental problems, mainly those of air and water pollution, by the application of advanced pollution control measures, where as the third world countries have not taken any such measures. Again, they say that they provide a cleaner atmosphere to their people.

The debate on the scale of accountability of developed and developing countries for the global environmental degradation continue to date. The worst victims of this debate are people and the environment. Unless a serious effort is made at global level, there is no hope for an early resolution of the conflict of perspective on the use of renewable resources.

6

TRANSITION TO SUSTAINABILITY

Retrospects and Prospects

Sustainable development is a new paradigm for the world. It is a term that unfolds basically two concepts: the concept of needs and concept of limits. It is based on the premise that the needs of the present and future generations must be met with the full use of human ingenuity but within the limits of a stable biosphere. Translating these two concepts into practice shall achieve two critical objectives. These critical objectives are satisfying the basic needs and conserving and enhancing the resource base of the poor (WCED, 1987), with emphasis on both inter-generational and intra-generational equity. From the point of forests, sustainable development is required to be undertaken in such a fashion that it does not jeopardise ecological functions of forests. Again, we should not loose sight of the critical objectives of sustainable development. In other word, sustainable development of forests emphasises on deriving benefits from forests for meeting the basic needs of people as well as expanding the resource base in an intra-generational and inter-generational framework.

Sustaining both forests and development simultaneously is a daunting task. However, steps have already been initiated at every levels to address this task. The journey from old paradigm of unsustainability to new paradigm of sustainable development, though a protracted one, has already begun. National and international initiatives, measuring to the intensity required, are already afoot. The Earth Summit constituted a watershed in the field of natural resource management. Considerable progress has already been made since then through a series of national initiates as well as bilateral and multilateral treaties.

This chapter highlights major initiatives—international and regional, governmental and non-governmental to promote sustainable forest development. A short account of natural resource use with a historical perspective has been appended in the beginning of this chapter. The focus of this chapter is on developments over the past ten years, many of these efforts were initiated at the behest of UNCED. A detailed discussion about the Earth Summit (1992) has been presented with a specific focus on forest development. The steps taken in international arena in the post Rio period has also been enumerated to a reasonable length as to provide a distinct perspective on changes in forest policy, legislation, management and practices.

Conservation: A Historical Perspective

Conservation of natural ecosystem has a long and chequered history. Modern conservation attitudes and practices have evolved largely in the context of western society. In other words, conservation policies were modelled on the basis of major political, economic and intellectual revolutions that western society experienced. But they are different from the oriental approach. In the East conservation was well rooted in culture and civilisation. But it took a back seat because the solution to immediate problems in the East emerged from mindless exploitation of resources. In the beginning it appeared to the politicians and environmentalists that conservation means negation of economic growth. The East remained silent while the policies of conservation were formulated at different world fora. Such a posture still continues in many parts of the globe till date. These trends continue today to shape the practice of conservation in many western countries.

Western viewpoints about conservation are conditioned by basic western philosophy rooted in the Judeo-Christian view of man and nature. It combines two ideas like (1) The right of exploitation, and (2) The responsibility of stewardship.

A fundamental Judeo-Christian belief is that nature was created to serve the human race. Hence, the exploitation of nature is a legitimate and natural pursuit. This view does not endow the environment and its inhabitants with protective spirits that prohibit exploitation. The question of exploitation of natural resources ingrained in the Judeo-Christian belief can also be understood in the context of wider global perspective. Until the 1700's, the rights and rewards of exploitation of the natural world remained largely in the hands of an elite aristocracy. The democratic revolution of the late 1700's, including the American Revolution of 1775-1783 and the French revolution of 1789-1799, triggered a restructuring of a societal framework throughout western societies. With this change came the increased access of individuals to productive resources and increased ability to use them for improving economic and social status. This apart, the legitimate right of exploiting nature was also extended to individuals at large in society.

At nearly the same time that is in mid 1700s – Industrial and Scientific Revolution begun in Europe. On the industrial side, machines and sources of energy were harnessed to enable resources to be processed on new scales and increased efficiency. With the introduction of steam engine a new chapter was added to the exploitation of nature. Railroads and steamships provided opportunity to open up new regions to exploitation. On the scientific side, discoveries led to a revolutionary change in the basic concept of nature and its use by mankind. All of a sudden a world in which all was created and overseen by God was replaced by the world that functioned according to the operation of basic laws of physics and chemistry. The Industrial and Scientific Revolution gave individuals an enormously expended ability to exploit resources and create material wealth for the people of western countries. The eighties were the culmination of a period of worldwide spread of western culture through colonisation and establishment of world trade. The western concept and system of exploitation thus spread widely, so it affected people, even in areas where the basic philosophical view of human and nature was quite different.

By the middle decades of 19th century biology was undergoing a revolutionary change in its view of the natural world *i.e.* the replacement as static and creationists view of life by an evolving mechanistic view. This change is best exemplified by the emergence of the theory of evolution by natural selection, presented jointly by Charles Darwin and Alfred Wallace. The concept of natural selection replaced the creationist view of the original living species with a mechanistic process of interaction within nature. The evolutionary view also opened the eyes of many to the fact that change in the environment, including changes caused by humans, could bring about the extinction of many kinds of organisms, as the fossil record demonstrated.

World War I and II, suddenly diverted attention from conservation issues. It initiated an era of unparalleled economic expansion and explosive growth of technology and human population. Technology provided a better living through chemistry in the form of synthetic fibres, plastics, inorganic pesticides, mineral fuels and many other products that sooner or later caused the introduction of toxic and biological active materials into the environment. To this explosion of technology was added the human population in the postwar period. The end result was large-scale degradation of natural productive systems and resources. Again over the years, the human activity enormously increased, leaving the ecosystem functions of the biosphere in topsy-turvy. This concern is best reflected in the amount of literature that has addressed itself to the problem of environment during that period. A list of such literature which created an impact on the world opinion is presented in Table 6.1. Apart from concern voiced by a world genre at different times, Indian cultures and philosophy also left an indelible mark on world opinion. The ecological overtone of Indian culture and philosophy is self evident in many religious and social practices.

Table 6.1: List of Literature Reflecting the Concern for Environment and its Conservation

Year	*Writer's Name*	*Name of Work*
1948	Fairfield Osborn	Our Plundered Planet
1948	Willium Voyd	Road to Survival
1958	The Princeton Conference Report	Man's Role in Changing the Face of the Earth
1962	Radiel Carson	Silent Spring
1965	Jean Dorst	Aqant que nature meure
1968	Paul Ehrlich	The Population Bomb
!972	Denis and Donella Meadow	The Limits to Growth
1974	Robert Heisbroner	An Enquiry into the Human Prospect

The Indian theory of nature and ecology recognises that *every element, object and living being in the universe is created by the same Supreme Being; and the man has no special domination over nature.* The Hindu religion has enshrined respect for nature in three basic elements: (1) faith in God, (2) non-dualistic view of Purush and Prakriti, and (3) a set of rules for duties and worship. Vedas, Upanishads, Puranas and other scriptures give a detailed description of trees, plants and wildlife alongwith their importance in the community. Trees have been considered as an essential part of dwelling in Indian homes. Significance of plants and trees to human life is further exemplified in Varah Puran which advocates regular plantation as a means to achieve haven. In Machya Puran and Padma Purana also there is a description of great plantation ceremony – Vriksha Mahotsava. In Matsya Puran planting of a tree has been equated with progeny of ten sons.

Indians accept nature as divinity. Various tees and plants are used in religious ceremonies and worship. Some trees and plants are considered so scared that it is assumed that particular Gods and Goddesses have made their abode in them. In Narsingha Purana tree has been personified as God (Brahma) itself. Atharvaveda considers Pepal tree as abode of various Gods. Names of various trees and their associations with God and Goddesses are given in Table 6.2.

Table 6.2: Trees and Associated Gods/Goddesses

Sl. No.	*Name of Trees*	*Associated God /Goddesses*
1	Ashoka	Budha, Indra, Vishnu
2	Peepal	Vishnu, Laxmi, Vana Durga
3	Tulsi	Rama, Narayana, Vishnu, Krishna, Jagannatha, Laxmi
4	Kadamba	Krishna
5	Ber	Shiva, Durga, Surya, Laxmi
6	Vata	Bramha, Vishnu, Shiva, Kal, Kubera, Krishna.

The various trees and plants are not only worshipped but cutting green trees has been prohibited and punishments prescribed for the offender. To Indians, relationship with the nature and animals is not a subject of domination and subjugation but rather a relationship of mutual respect and kindness. The Indian culture, in ancient and mediaeval times, provided a system of moral guidelines towards environmental conservation. Environmental ethics as propounded by ancient scriptures and the seers continued to exist in society and was practised by not only common man but even by rulers and kings. These principles remained deeply embedded in the social milieu of the Indian society.

From time immoral, our sages and saints have been moving to mountains, meadows, and streams and experiencing elevation of mind. They felt the exhilaration of the clean and crisp air and found 'tongues' and books in running 'brooks'. They understood that man and nature were not two separate entities but an enmeshed part of the same organic entity, the same divine spirit. They believed that the basic elements of nature constitute the Cosmic Being—the mountains His bones, the earth, His flesh, the sea His blood, the air His breath and fire His energy. They propagated: "the Earth is our mother and we are its children". One of the earliest Vedic hymns, composed over 4000 years ago, gave the message of what we termed as sustainable development

"Whatever I dig of you, O Earth,
May you of that have quick replenishment,
O Purifying One, may my thrust never,
Reach right unto your vital points, your heart I"

The carrying and recouping capacity of the Earth were reverentially recognised and given a strong spiritual underpinning. That is why India, for centuries together has remained a treasure house of natural and cultural wealth.

Sustainable Forest Development

The concept of sustainable development gained prominence in the year 1980 when International Union for the Conservation of Nature (IUCN) published the World Conservation Strategy (WCS). The world Conservation Strategy had the objective of achieving development through the conservation of natural resources. The strategy laid emphasis on the fact that development could be sustained only if human activities operate within the reality of resource limitations and carrying capacities of ecosystems. In other words, the Conservation Strategy primarily emphasised on biophysical sustainability of ecosystems. Apart from the merits, it had many pitfalls. It failed to recognise the fact that development process has political and social overtones which in many cases, act as impediments to the conservation. After conservation, the concept of eco-development was introduced in natural resource management. Eco-development focussed on the satisfaction of basic human needs while maintaining ecological health (Sachs, 1979, p. 21). Gradually, the doctrine of eco-development, besides fulfilling the basic human need as the core component, encompassed the aspects like decentralisation, community participation, use of indigenous knowledge, and the adoption of appropriate technology. But the demerit in eco-development concept was that it limited itself to development at local scale only. However, the basic approach of eco-development like enhancing the resource base and intra-generational and inter-generational equity was instrumental in shaping present thinking on sustainable development.

The concept of sustainable development took concrete shape in the report of World Commission on Environment and Development in the year 1987. This report, popularly known as the Brundtland Report, defined sustainable development as "development that meets the needs of the present without compromising the ability of future generations to meet their own needs" (WCED, 1987). The June 1992 United Nations Conference on Environment and Development (UNDP) at Rio focussed on sustainable forest development and recognised that problems like poverty, food security, over-consumption of forest products and external indebtedness of some developing countries were linked with forest decline. In addition to it, the Summit found that such problems reduced their capacity to manage their forest resources sustainably.

The issues that dominate the politics and policies of this twenty-first century are: stabilisation of human habitat, population control, development, poverty eradication, gender equity, food security and social infrastructure. The most fundamental and urgent among them is the need to stabilise the human habitat where man lives. Forest, being an important component of human habitat, assumes stupendous significance. It constitutes an important component of human habitat. Improved forest management arrangements and practices are required not only to sustain forest indefinitely and but also to contribute to more equity in the distribution of benefits from their use. Efforts to conserve forest resources were initiated in the beginning of last century. Such efforts continued, but they received a definite direction and support only after Rio Summit.

International/Regional Agreement or Convention on Protection of Forest

International community has been thinking about protection of environment seriously since 1972 (Kiss, 1983; UNEP, 1991). Many studies have shown that number of agreements on protection of forests and environment increased manifold in the last thirty years. The period before 1972 was a formative phase marked with intense debate but few agreements. The year 1972 marked a watershed in international agreement/convention on forest protection and convention. Further, in the last decade, world witnessed a series of institutions/arrangements/conferences/conventions, related to forest and environmental conservation. Some of the important agreements/conventions/world institutions/programme, which deal with forest and environmental conservation in the last century, are discussed below:

Convention Relating to the Preservation of Flora and Fauna in their Natural State, 1933

This convention was adopted in London and came into force in the year 1936. Its objectives are to preserve the natural flora and fauna of certain parts of the world, particularly Africa, by establishing national parks and natural reserves and regulating hunting and species collection. It also proposed control of all human settlements in those areas. To date, only nine countries have become parties to the convention. These countries are Belgium, Egypt, India, Italy, Portugal, South Africa, Sudan, UK and Tanzania.

International Convention for the Protection of Birds, 1950

This convention was adopted in Paris in 1950. It came into force in the year 1963. The avowed objective of the convention was to protect birds in their wild state. The convention focussed on the principle that birds should be protected because they are important from the point of science, protection of nature and economy of each nation. The delegates emphasised on establishing reserves, which would act as breeding ground for birds. There were only ten countries, which remained signatory parties to the convention. The member countries were Belgium, Iceland, Italy, Luxembourg, Netherlands, Spain, Sweden, Switzerland, Turkey and Yugoslavia.

United Nations, 1945

United Nations (UN), created after Second World War, played a major role in protection of natural resources. The Food and Agricultural Organisation (FAO), established in the year 1945 as an umbrella organisation under UN played a dominant role in conservation of natural resources. Forestry has been a part of FAO's mandate from the inception of its establishment, and is specially mentioned in the global goals of the organisation in terms of its contribution to economic and social progress and also in relation to the conservation, improvement and sustainable utilisation of natural resources. Forestry also contributes strongly to the mission of FAO to " .... help build a food-secure world for present and future generation", and to assist member nations to "........ reduce food insecurity and rural poverty; ensure an enabling policy and regulatory framework for food and agriculture; fisheries and forestry; secure sustainable increase in the supply and availability of food; conserve and enhance the natural resource base; and generate knowledge on food and agriculture, fisheries and forestry". FAO urges all the member countries to (1) promote national and international action in the field of conservation of natural resources, and (2) adopt improved methods of forest protection and production. Other agencies of UNO that actively participated and took considerable interest in forest conservation were United Nations Environment Programme (UNEP), United Nations Development Programme (UNDP), United Nations Conference on Trade and

Development (UNCTD), the United Nations Industrial Development Organisation (UNIDO).

International Union for the Conservation of Nature (IUCN) in 1956

After the formation of United Nations as a world body, a series of international environmental agreements and framework of international environmental organisations began to emerge. This eventually evolved into the International Union for the Protection of Nature (IUPN), in 1949. It became International Union for the Conservation of Nature (IUCN) in 1956.This organisation played an important role in developing the modern concept of sustainability.

World Wildlife Fund (WWF) was set up in 1961 as a fund raising organisation to support IUCN. But, with the passage of time, this organisation emerged as a powerful player in the field of conservation on its own. Initially IUCN focussed on nature protection, but afterwards, it embarked on major environmental programme. By the end of the 1960s, IUCN had begun to show a greater concern for economic development and holistic approach to conservation. IUCN, along with UNEP established after Stockholm conference, prepared the World Conservation Strategy. UNEP and WWF not only contributed to development of basic themes of conservation and development but also provided financial support to translate such concerns into action.

The Stockholm Conference, 1972

The Stockholm Conference is the landmark in the field of global environmentalism. It marks the coming of age of the environmental movement. It assumed significance because of the legitimacy that afforded to environmental issues in international relations (Thomas, 1992). The conference led to the Stockholm Declaration with 29 principles and provided a permanent basis for international environmental co-ordination and diplomacy. The importance of this conference is indicated from the fact that representatives of about 113 countries and 19 inter-governmental agencies attended the conference. The scale of this international gathering itself symbolised the significance of environmental issues. The conference ended with a decision to set up the United Nations Environmental Programme (UNEP). It also initiated the process of forming the Convention on International Trade in Endangered Species (CITES). The conference also helped to strengthen environmental groups and expand their roles.

Meeting of non-governmental organisations and the interaction with governmental representatives provided a forum for international networking of these groups. This helped the groups to broaden their interests and move away from narrow concerns such as species protection. This encouraged the groups to take up wider issues such as funding policies pertaining to environment and development. All this led to an emergence of the concept of sustainability. Apart from this, the conference initiated changes in many fields. Some of the changes are as under:

- It promoted the development of national environmental policies.
- It helped the setting of separate environmental agencies and ministries in many countries.
- It promoted a formal dialogue between developed and developing countries over their environmental concerns.
- It initiated a process of thinking environmental and developmental problems interconnectedly.
- It led to a realisation among the nations that a synthesis between conservation and development is the answer to environmental as well as economic crisis.

World Conservation Strategy (WCS), 1980

The World Conservation Strategy (WCS) was lunched simultaneously in 40 countries in the year 1980. It reflected compromises, both among conservationists, and between conservationists and 'practitioners of development'. The strategy focussed on three main groups of potential users – governmental policy makers, conservationists and those directly concerned with living resources and developmental practiceners including aid agencies, industry and trade unions.

Conservation was redefined as 'the management of human use of the biosphere so that it may yield the greatest sustainable benefit to present generations while maintaining its potential to meet the needs and aspirations of future generations' (IUCN *et al.*, 1980). Three main objectives of conservation are:

- To maintain essential ecological processes and life supporting system.
- To preserve genetic diversity.
- To ensure the sustainable utilisation of species and ecosystem.

Therefore, conservation focussed 'preservation, maintenance, sustainable utilisation, restoration, and enhancement of the natural environment'. The conservation strategy emphasised on practical benefits that would stem from the preservation of genetic diversity and sustainable utilisation of ecological resources. It also laid stress on the fact that human benefits would follow from appropriate forms of environmental management. Essentially, the strategy succeeded to a great extent to reconcile conservation and development goals by incorporating conservation principles into development rather than opposing development.

World Commission on Environment and Development (WCED)

The Conservation Strategy lunched the theme of 'conservation' the intrinsic principle behind the concept of sustainability. But, the concept got a major boost with the publication of the report of the World Commission on Environment and Development (the Brundtland Report) in 1987 (WCED, 1987). The commission was established by the United Nation's General Assembly in 1983. The said commission had the mandate (1) to examine critical environmental issues, (2) to formulate proposals for dealing with them, (3) to propose new forms of international co-operation, and (4) to raise levels of understanding and commitment to action on the part of individuals, corporations and governments.

Brundtland's Report coined the word 'sustainable development'. It focussed on how development should be achieved. It also emphasised on the fact that environment degradation is inimical to development and economic growth. What is noteworthy is the fact that the report placed distinct emphasis on sustainable development. Besides, the report provided an interpretational and functional framework to sustainable development. The commission defined sustainable development as the development that meets the needs and aspiration of the present without compromising the ability to meet those of the future. It also advocated the continuation of economic growth as a means of solving the environmental problems. It accepted economic growth as key to solving poverty and underdevelopment. Sustainable development requires meeting the basic needs of all and extending to all the opportunity to fulfill their aspirations for a better life (WCED, 1987; 8). The report highlighted distributional issues like inter-generational, intra-generational and wide chasm between 'have nots' and 'haves' in tackling environmental problems. It emphasised on the fact that economic growth should use the available stock of capital on sustainable basis and should not deplete the stock by using unsustainably. It sensitised the world community about the concept of sustainable development.

The Second World Conservation Strategy, 1991

The concept of sustainability became more popular with the publication of the second Conservation Strategy (Caring for the Earth) in 1991. It was prepared by IUCN, UNEP and WWF. The strategy has two aims. One is to promote a new ethic for sustainable living, and to translate its general principles into practice. The other is to integrate conservation and development. It is said that the first strategy emphasised on the fact that conservation was not anti-development and the second strategy sought to extend and embolden the concept by popularising the theme that conservation is development friendly. Therefore, the second strategy outlined few principles for building sustainable society (See Table 6.3). It provided a broader view of environment in its developmental context. It laid emphasis on developmental and distributional aspects. It also sought to promote ethics in economic development. Emergence of ethics led to the acceptance of a fact that purely technical solutions to environmental problems are not likely to succeed.

Regional Arrangements on the Subject of Forest

Many regional arrangements were also made on the subject of forest protection and conservation. Among the regional arrangements, the following merit special attention.

Convention on Nature Protection and Wildlife Preservation, 1940

A regional agreement on nature protection and wildlife preservation in the Western Hemisphere was adopted in 1940 and entered into force in 1942. El Salvador, Guatemala, Haiti, the United States and Venezuela were the initial parties and they were later joined by Argentina, Brazil, Chile, Panama, Peru, Trinidad, Tobago and Uruguay. The objective of the arrangement was to preserve all species and genera of the native American fauna and flora from extinction and to preserve extraordinary beauty, striking geological formation, or aesthetic, historic or scientific value. Article 2 obliges parties to establish National Park, Nature Reserve Monument and strict wilderness.

Table 6.3: Second World Conservation Strategy: Principles of a Sustainable Society

Principle	*Action*
Respect and care for community of life.	• Develop the world ethic for a sustainable living. • Promote world ethic for sustainable living at national level. • Implement the world ethic through action in all sector of society. • Establish a world organisation to monitor implementation of the world ethic and to prevent and combat serious breaches in its observation.
Improving the quality of human life.	• In lower income countries, increase economic growth to advance human development. • Provide the service that will promote a long and healthy life. • Provide universal primary education and reduce illiteracy. • Develop more meaningful indicators of life. • Enhance security against natural disasters and social strife
Conserving the earth's vitality and diversity	• Adopt a precautionary approach to pollution. • Cut emissions for greenhouse and other gases. • Adopt integrated approach to land and water management, using the drainage basin as the unit of management. • Maintain as much as possible of each country's natural and modified ecosystems. • Take pressures off natural and modified ecosystems by protecting the best farmland and managing it in ecologically sound ways. • Halt net deforestation, protect large areas of old-growth forest, and maintain a permanent state of modified forest. • Complete and maintain a comprehensive system of protected areas.

(*Contd.*)

(*Contd.*)

Principle	*Action*
Conserving the earth's vitality and diversity	• Improve conservation of wild plants and animals. • Improve knowledge and understanding of species and ecosystems. • Use a combination of in-situ and ex-situ conservation to maintain species and genetic resources. • Harvest wild resources sustainably. • Support management of wild renewable resources by local communities and increase incentives to conserve biological diversity.
Keeping with the Earth's carrying capacity.	• Increase awareness about the need to stabilise resource consumption and population. • Integrate resource consumption and population issues in national development policies and planning. • Develop, test and adopt resource efficient methods and technologies. • Tax energy and other resources in high consumption countries. • Encourage 'green consumer' movements. • Improve maternal and child health care. • Double family planning services.
Changing personal attitudes and practices.	• Ensure that national strategies for sustainability include action to motivate, educate and equip individuals to lead sustainable lives. • Review the status of environmental education and make it an integral part of formal education at all levels. • Determine the training needs for a sustainable society and plan to meet them.
Enabling communities to care for their own environments.	• Provide secure access to resources and equitable shares in managing them.

(*Contd.*)

(*Contd.*)

Principle	*Action*
	• Improve exchange of information, skills and technologies. • Enhance participation in conservation and development. • Develop more effective local governments. • Care for the local environment in every community. • Provide financial and technical support to community environmental action.
Providing a national framework for integrating development and conservation.	• Adopt an integrated approach to environmental policy, with sustainability as the overall goal. • Develop strategies for sustainability and implement them directly through regional and local planning. • Subject proposed development projects, programmes and policies to environmental impact assessment and to economic appraisal. • Establish a commitment to the principles of a sustainable society in constitutional or other fundamental statements of national policy. • Establish a comprehensive system of environmental law and provide for its implementation and enforcement. • Review the adequacy of legal and administrative controls and of implementation and enforcement mechanisms. • Ensure that national policies, development plans, budgets and decisions on investments take full account of their effects on the environment. • Use economic policies to achieve sustainability. • Provide economic incentives for conservation and sustainable use.

(*Contd.*)

(Contd.)

Principle	*Action*
	• Strengthen the knowledge base, and make information on environmental matters more accessible.
Creating a global alliance	• Strengthen existing international agreements to conserve life support systems and biological diversity.
	• Conclude new international agreements to help achieve global sustainability.
	• Develop a comprehensive and integrated conservation regime for Antarctica and South Ocean.
	• Prepare and adopt an universal declaration and covenant in sustainability.
	• Write off official debt of low-income countries and retire enough of their commercial debt to restore economic progress.
	• Increase capacity of lower income countries to help themselves.
	• Increase development assistance and devote it to helping countries develop sustainable societies and economies.
	• Recognise the value of global and national non- governmental action and strengthen it.
	• Strengthen the United Nations system as an effective force for global sustainability.

Source: Compiled from IUCN/UNEP/WWF (1991) *Caring for the earth. A strategy for sustainable living*. Gland, Switzerland.

The Conservation of the Nature of South Pacific, 1976

The Conservation of the Nature of South Pacific, a regional agreement was established in 1976. It took concrete shape in 1990. It has six signatory countries: Australia, the Cook island, Fiji, France, Papua Guinea and the Western Samoa. The objective is to take action to promote conservation, utilisation, and development of natural resources in the South Pacific region. Articles 2-5 of the agreement focuses on conservation of forest. Article 2 enjoins parties to create Protected Area to safeguard representative sample of natural ecosystem. Article 3 prohibits National Park from being altered with out complete investigation. Article 4 enjoins upon the signatory countries to make the natural reserve inviolate as far as practicable.

The Treaty for Amazonian Co-operation, 1978

The regional treaty, though adopted in 1978, came into force in the year 1980. The signatory countries are Bolivia, Brazil, Columbia, Equator, Guyana, Peru, Surinam, Venezuela. The treaty has the following objectives:

- To promote the harmonious development of Amazonian region, to preserve the environment, to foster the conservation and rational use of natural resources and to permit equitable distribution of the benefits of such development among themselves.
- To emphasise international co-operation and recognition of the exclusive sovereign right of each country to use the natural resources within the territory of each party.
- To acknowledge the complete freedom of the Amazonian rivers for commercial navigation.

The Convention on the Conservation of European Wildlife and Natural Habitats, 1979

The convention, though adopted in 1978, came into force in the year 1982. The member countries are Austria, Belgium, Burkina Faso, Cyprus, Denmark, Finland, France, Greece, Hungary, Ireland, Italy, Liechtenstein, Luxembourg, the Netherlands, Norway, Portugal, Senegal, Spain, Sweden, Switzerland, Turkey, UK, and the European Community as parties. The objectives of the convention are to preserve wild fauna and flora and their natural habitat. The convention underlined the need for setting nature reserves to achieve the avowed objectives.

The Benelux Convention on Nature Conservation and Landscape Protection, 1982

The convention came into force in the year 1983.The Benelux countries like Belgium, Netherlands, Luxembourg are parties to the convention.

The objectives of the convention are to preserve nature, natural areas, and the landscape. The convention focuses on protection of trans-boundary natural areas and landscapes.

The ASEAN Agreement on the Conservation of Nature and Natural Resources, 1985

The convention was adopted in 1985 by the Association of South-East Asian nations like Brunei, Darussalam, Indonesia, Malaysia, Philippines, Singapore and Thailand. The objectives of the agreement are to undertake unilateral and bilateral initiatives to promote conservation and management of natural resources of the South-East Asian region. This is the most comprehensive agreement ever made in the field of nature conservation. It provides greater details of how its objectives are to be accomplished. The convention asked the parties:

- To preserve genetic diversity by ensuring conservation and preservation of all species within their jurisdiction;
- To maintain harvested species through sound management and suitable uses;
- To promote soil conservation, improvement and rehabilitation,
- To promote ecological process, by reducing, controlling or preventing environmental degradation and pollution;
- To set-up protected areas to conserve biological diversity, specially of endangered species to ensure that conservation and management of natural resources become an integral part of the development planning at both national and regional levels; and
- To harmonise the use of shared resources without prejudices to the environment avoiding harmful international environmental effects.

The agreement is still to come into effect. But all the countries of South-East Asia signed it.

International Tropical Timber Agreement (ITTA), 1983

This agreement was signed in November 1983. It is a unique trade agreement. It established the International Timber Trade Organisation (ITTO) to take up the task of promoting the trade in tropical timber as well as the work of encouraging sustainable use and conservation of tropical forests and their genetic resources and maintaining ecological balance. It entered into force on 1 April 1985. ITTO is a independent organisation controlled by a council made up of member countries. Renegotiations of the ITTA (International Tropical Timber Agreement) take place under the auspices of UNCTAD in Geneva.

All of the agreements/conventions that took place under the aegis of ITTO focussed on nature conservation. However, principal purpose of entering into such instruments was not to conserve and but to operationalise management of forest resources with a focus on tropical timber trade. The only international agreement to date that specifically provides for a broad framework governing a certain types of forests, even though principally for the purpose of co-operation and consultation between contracting parties is the International Tropical Timber Agreement adopted in 1983. This came into force in the year 1985. To date, 48 countries have joined as parties. The agreement provides for establishment of the International Tropical Timber Organisation in order to administer the provisions of the treaty. This organisation functions through International Tropical Timber Council. The council arranges for consultations within the United Nations and other non-governmental organisations. Apart from this, under the aegis of the council, there is one committee on economic information and market intelligence, another on reforestation and forest management and another on forest industry. The agreement aimed at (1) increasing international co-operation by facilitating co-ordination between countries producing and consuming tropical timbers, (2) promoting research and development to improve forest management and use, (3) encouraging national policies compatible to sustainable use and conservation of tropical forests and their genetic resources, and (4) maintaining ecological balance in the regions concerned.

Conservation for the Protection of Natural Resources and Environment of the Pacific Region, 1986

The Conservation for the Protection of Natural Resources and Environment of the Pacific Region was adopted in 1986. It came into force in 1990. Its objective was to protect and manage the natural resources and environment of the South Pacific Region. Article 14 of the agreement asks the signatory countries to take all appropriate measures to protect and preserve rare ecosystem and endangered flora and fauna as well as their habitat. There were 10 parties to this convention. The countries are Australia, the Cook Island, the Federated States of Micronesia, Fiji, France, the Marshall island, Newsland, Papua New Guinea, the Solomon Island and the Western Samoa.

The Tropical Forestry Action Plan (TFAP), 1985

In 1985, the Food and Agricultural Organisation of the United Nations (FAO) published a document that attributed tropical deforestation to the poverty of the people living in or around them, and proposed more food production, higher incomes and greater employment through increased harvesting and processing as remedies. Later in 1985, a task force was formed by the United Nations Development Programme (UNDP) to look into these issues. The World Bank and the World Resource Institute (WRI) published a document called 'Tropical Forests: A Call for Action', which advocated policy changes inside and outside the forestry sector to address the multiple causes of deforestation, and increasing donor investment in tropical forest projects. The subsequent merger of these two initiatives led to the constitution of the Tropical Forestry Action Plan (TFAP).

The action plan was launched in 1985, by the World Bank, UNDP, FAO and the World Resources Institute (WRI). The initiative was an emergency response to the crisis of tropical forest resources. It calls for massive development assistance to the forestry sector. A permanent TFAP secretariat was recently established at FAO headquarter in Rome. Under TFAP secretariat projects are developed as a result of national planning exercise, which includes the review of problems facing the forest sector in the country concerned. The level of development from the member of the countries has increased to $1 billion, up from $500 million per year before the adoption of the plan. However, TFAP has not been able to deliver satisfactory result in most of the countries. It's critique believes that its failure is due to "Top-Down", approach which provides inadequate participation for the people who live in and depend on the tropical forest and for non-governmental organisations.

TFAP is a combination of previous development agenda (modernisation, and meeting basic needs) and issues that had gained prominence more recently such as the conservation of biological diversity, the need for policy and institutional reforms, and the realisation that the causes of deforestation originate mainly outside the forestry sector itself. The TFAP was intended to work at two levels: internationally it was to promote consultation and co-ordination between the donor agencies; and the nationally it was to mobilise support for a country–level development planning process and stimulate investment to implement the resulting plans. It is now being implemented in more than 80 developing countries, with varied inputs.

Priority Areas in TFAP

- *Forestry as Land Use*: Activities aim at the interface of forestry and agriculture and at more rational land use through community forestry, integrated watershed management and desertification control and land assessment and multipurpose trees on farms to help combat declining soil fertility and shortages of poles, fuelwood and other forest products.
- *Forest-based Industrial Development*: Activities aim at promoting appropriate forest-based industries: small scale 'cottage' enterprises and other forest-based incomes generating activities in rural areas, as well as industrial plantations and the expansion of forest product exports.
- *Fuelwood and Energy*: Activities aim at restoring a balance between fuelwood supply and demand, by increasing production of and reducing demand for woodfuels; as well as programmes to develop wood-based systems to generate energy.
- *Conservation of Tropical Forest Ecosystem*: Activities aimed at conserving, managing and using forest genetic resources, such as management of protected areas and of forests for sustainable production.
- *Institution Building*: Activities aimed at removing the institutional constraints to conserving and managing tropical forests, including support for training, research, extension; greater institutional support to NGOs and the business community; the strengthening of public forestry agencies; and the revision of laws and policies to integrate forestry into national planning.

The Earth Summit, 1992

Much of the deterioration in the earth's environment is caused by patterns of production and consumption, especially of the industrial countries. In developing nations, which altogether contain almost 80 per cent of the earth's population of 6 billion, poverty, population growth, and environmental damage are closely linked. Every country feels that protection of local as well as global environment must form an integral part of the development process everywhere.

It is in this context, the United Nations General Assembly decided to hold the Rio Conference, and established its mandate and the basis for its Resolution GA 44/228 of 22nd December 1989. Therefore, United Nations decided to host a Conference on Environment and Development (UNCED) in Rio de Janeiro, Brazil, in June 1992. The occasion also marked the 20th anniversary of the United Nations Conference on Human Environment, which was held in Stockholm in June, 1972.

The General Assembly made it clear that the linkages between development and environment must be tackled through fresh international consensus on global issues and in particular, the revitalisation of development in the developing countries on an environmentally sound basis.

The nations of world met at Rio de Jeneiro for Earth Summit in the year 1992. This was the most important International Conference on environment after Stockholm Conference on Environment and Development in 1972. The Earth Summit made far-reaching promises to save the world's environment. It represented an unique opportunity to put the human society on a path to a more secure, equitable, and sustainable future. The unprecedented involvement of government and non-government organisations in the deliberations was the hallmark of the conference.

Five documents were agreed at Rio: The Rio declaration consisting of a political statement of 27 principles guiding environmental and development activities; a statement of principles on forestry, two conventions negotiated in parallel with the UNCED process (one on Biological Diversity and the other on Climate Change) and a comprehensive and far-ranging programme of action known as Agenda 21.

The Framework Convention on Climate Change has been signed by 153 National Governments and European Government. This is a legally binding agreement on a framework for dealing with the threat of global warming. The Montreal Protocol on substances that deplete the ozone layer in the year 1987 and the first meeting on Inter-governmental Panel on climate change in the year 1988 played as the precursor for the framework convention on climate. In both these occasions, the realities of the problems were widely accepted and different participating countries emphasised on the dire need of adopting precautionary approach in the maters of trade and industrial development. The framework convention aimed at stabilising emission at their 1990 level by the year 2000. There was no agreement with regard to distribution of costs involved in reducing the emissions by the South.

The second convention centered on bio-diversity conservation. The convention encompassed two aspects: (1) conservation of bio-diversity, (2) the modalities of how the North, with its enormous interest in biotechnology, can ensure access to the diversity of species in the South, over which individual countries assert sovereign rights.

The convention accepted the following facts:

- States have their own sovereign rights over their own 'biological resources'.
- States have their own responsibilities for maintaining 'biological diversity'.
- States have the right to use the biological diversity on a sustainable way.

Sustainable management of biological diversity necessitates enormous financial resources. The South which is home to enormous diversity lacks necessary finance. In this backdrop the North agreed on the need to finance such biodiversity conservation projects in the South. It also agreed in principle to an equitable exchange of genetic resources in return to access to, and transfer of, technology to South. However, the convention failed to evolve any comprehensive action plan to stem erosion of biodiversity.

The Forest Principle

A set of general principles for the management, conservation and sustainable development of all types of forests was proposed. These principles were expressed in a 'non-legally binding authoritative statement'. However, sustainable development was declared as the goal to which the principles were directed and sound management and conservation are said to be of concern to the governments of the countries to which they belong and are of value to local communities and to the environment as a whole.

The issue of tropical deforestation attracted the attention of the conference. The North raised the issue vehemently. This created an impression among the states of South that North is interested in conservation of tropical forests because it wants to use it as a 'sink' for emissions of carbon dioxide and to evade responsibility for reducing emission of greenhouse gases. A lot of discussion took place but no agreement was reached about controlling deforestation. As a result, there occurred a non-binding statement, called 'Principles of Forest Management'. It dwelt more on importance and relevance of forests for the well being of human society in general and for biodiversity and climate, in particular (See Box 6.1).

BOX 6.1: FORESTRY PRINCIPLES ADOPTED IN EARTH SUMMIT: 1992

Some of the most important forest principles are:

- Forest resources and forest lands should be sustainably managed to meet the social, economic, ecological, cultural and spiritual needs of present and future generations.
- Forest policies should be integrated with economic and trade policies.
- The right of states to exploit their own resources is recognised, along with their responsibility to ensure that activities within their jurisdiction do not cause damage to the environment of other states.

Agenda 21 or Rio Declaration

Agenda 21 is an Earth Charter setting out basic principles and programmatic action required to move towards sustainability. It established a negotiated framework for co-operative action between government agencies, and programme of the United Nation's system, Non-governmental Organisations and the private sectors. It laid an emphasis on people, communities and organisation in all matters of natural resources management. This approach is called as 'bottom –up approach'. It stresses that most effective planning evolves gradually thorough participatory process that allows different social groups to debate the gains and losses in reconciling development and environment (David Reid, p. 188).

The programme of action on environment and development is divided into four main sections. They are as follows:

- Social and economic development encompassing issues of inequities between rich and poor; wasteful consumption; the population explosion; integration of development and environment.
- The conservation and management of resources for development.
- Strengthening the role of major groups involved in achieving sustainable development.
- Means of implementation.

Chapter 38 of Agenda 21 calls for the establishment of a Commission on Sustainable Development (CSD) that will facilitate the active involvement of organs, programme and organisation of the United Nation's system, international financial institutions and other relevant inter-governmental organisations, and encourage the participation of non-governmental organisations, including industry, the business and scientific communities. The most relevant functions of the commission are as under:

- To monitor progress in the implementation of Agenda 21;
- To consider the information submitted by governments, including their national reports;
- To review progress in the implementation of commitments contained in the Agenda 21, such as those related to provision of financial resources and transfer of technology and to receive and analyse relevant inputs from competent non-governmental organisation, including the private and scientific sector.

The agenda focuses on the role of national governments in promoting sustainable development. It urges on every government to prepare a national strategy for sustainable development, which should integrate development and environment policies at all levels and at all sectors of economy. It also advised all governments to build a national consensus on every issue pertaining to sustainable development of resources. Besides, it called upon South to devise ways and means of 'capacity building', so that the environmental problems are appropriately dealt with.

Capacity building is a major theme in the section—Means of Implementation. It involves developing the abilities and resourcing of institutions to manage the various changes and activities required of them. The ways suggested for capacity building are as follows:

- Developing human resources.
- Strengthening the capacity of existing institutions in research and development.
- Developing management techniques for programme implementation.
- Undertaking and co-ordinating reviews of sectoral needs.
- Addressing the larger issues of technology transfer and delineation of terms for such transfer.
- Negotiation over intellectual property rights.

Earth Summit Plus-1997

A five-year review of Earth Summit took place in 1997. The Summit was called Earth Summit Plus Five (ESPF). The objective of this summit was to assess the impacts of the Earth Summit held in 1992. Heads of Governments from 42 countries participated and representatives from other countries attended the conference.

The Summit passed a resolution which required countries to take steps for the implementation of Agenda 21 as well as some of the other declarations like (1) Copenhagen Declaration on Social Development, (2) the International Conference on Population and Development, (3) the Beijing Platform Actions regarding Women Participation, (4) the UN Conference on Human Settlements' (Habitat II) recommendation on sustainable human settlements, and (5) the report of the Ad Hoc Intergovernmental Panel on Forests (IPF). The Summit did not bring desired results. The progress was proposed to be reviewed again at another Summit in 2002.

Eight Years after Rio—An Appraisal

The performance in the post-Rio phase does not match with the commitment shown in the wake of Rio Conference in the year 1992. The Rio Summit roused a lot of expectations from participatory countries. Over the years, the number of poor people has increased, the profligate life styles of the rich have barely altered, and the pressures on the depleting natural resources have increased manifold. Notwithstanding the enormous problems, the Rio Summit generated a good deal of awareness about values of environmental conservation and significance of ecosystems in the biosphere. It motivated world institutions to initiate systematic inventories of world bio-diversity resources and inspired many countries to evolve national bio-diversity strategies.

The period after Rio is distinctly marked with less action compounded with lack of funding to world environmental projects. The Framework Convention on Climate Change, the instrument to deal with problem of global warming, has seen little action in controlling greenhouse gas emissions of the developed North. The bio-diversity convention, established to protect the world's threatened bio-diversity, has not yet been signed by the U.S., the world's largest user of bio-diversity resources and knowledge. The grandiose Agenda 21, the Global Action Plan for Environment has gone largely unfunded. The total global funding for environment has, in fact, declined in the post-Rio phase. The commitment made by the developed countries at Rio with regard to the Overseas Development Assistance (ODA) target of 0.7 per cent of GNP, is yet to be fulfilled. It was agreed that new and additional financial resources should be available, but, in the contrary, there is a continuing decline in ODA. All these indicate that there is yet any action on the part of the rich countries to match the commitment made in the Summit.

There are many reasons for failures in the performance front. The most important one is the fact that the agenda adopted in Rio Summit was a Northern agenda. The participation of Southern countries was weak and unassertive. There has been little progress on the Bio-diversity Convention. It is argued that the extraordinary clause in the treaty which stipulates that any country or company taking genetic resources from another country will have to share on the use of that resources with the donor countries dampened the spirit of developed countries.

In the treaty to curb global warming, time bound commitment to the industrialised countries to contain greenhouse gas emissions was discussed. There was emphasis on evolving a time table for applying the cut on emissions. There is an all out effort to push a deadline for reduction. There is also a move to bring India and China into the folds of commitments as it is apprehended that firms in the North, which emit greenhouse gas, will be tempted to move into such countries.

The Forest Principle–though a non-binding to countries also received no acceptability. However, it put forward a framework for the management of world's forests. This still remains in the inter-governmental agendas. In the year 1995, an Inter-governmental Panel on Forest was set up under the Commission on Sustainable Development (CSD). After eight years of the formation of the commission, again the same principles, which constituted the forest framework, were discussed. What is more disturbing is the fact that the debate whether the said principles are required or not continued in the Summit. However, a greater realisation has come about the fact that keeping forest intact is a cheaper option to reduce future greenhouse gas emissions than cutting down the number of cars in US and Europe.

The globalisation of economy has led to emergence of a strong private sector, particularly the multinational companies who have more control than government over financial resources, technology and information. The key to success in sustainable development process lies with the private sector. Therefore, it is imperative to bring the multinational companies under the fold of sustainable management of resources. Having understood the need of the hour, business world have started adopting attitudinal changes towards sustainable use of natural resources. The World Business Council for Sustainable Development, a network of 120 international communities from 35 countries encouraged business enterprises to set their own priorities in accordance with the principles of sustainable development. What is more heartening to know that the business enterprises have started taking a holistic view of the development? The business circle focuses on the following features:

- Trade and environment.
- Sustainable production and consumption.
- Climate change and energy issues.
- Ecólogical efficiency.

In the changed situation, the government role is weakening day-by-day. The traditional reliance on government action through regulatory and economic policy in areas such as environment is declining. There is a need to manage the resources of the societies collectively in a globalised world.

Apart from the failures, there are many achievements. One is the emergence of awareness among people about environment problems. In spite of economic pre-occupations and compulsions, there are more people today to say that economic growth should be sacrificed, if necessary to ensure the protection of the environment. Besides, more and more people are realising the need to organise themselves and act collectively to influence social change, which will finally bring sustainable development.

In the post-Rio Phase, a wide range of experiences and practices consistent with the principles of sustainable development has emerged. Many fora for discussion and co-ordination have been established in the government systems. At the global level, the UN Commission on Sustainable Development has provided important openings for all the stakeholders to influence the global policy dialogue on sustainability. Associations and networks of stakeholders have established themselves to reach out more widely to share information and resources and adopt common programmes. Many business councils and associations have developed voluntary sustainability code. Of late, civil society organisations or non-governmental organisations play a variety of role to inform, catalyse and promote the local, national and global public interest.

Chapter 28 of Agenda 21 requires each country to undertake a consultative process with a wide cross-section of people and achieve a consensus on 'local agenda 21' for their community. To date, about 1800 local governments in 64 countries are currently implementing 'local agenda 21'. The local agenda encompasses the following features:

- A mechanism to facilitate and institutionalise public participation in the preparation, implementation and monitoring of local action plan based on principles of sustainable development.
- A comprehensive review of developmental issues, including baseline data on economic, social and environmental issues against which changes can be measured.
- An action plan which sets specific targets for achievement and carries activities that different actors in the community should implement.
- A monitoring and reporting framework, including local performance indicators, which are used by all the stakeholders to assess the progress.

Chapter 8 of Agenda 21 recommends that each nation should adopt a national strategy for sustainable development based on, *inter alia*, the implementation of decisions taken at the UNCED Conference. The strategy should build upon and harmonise various sectoral economies, social and environmental policies and plans that are operating in the country. Against this backdrop of commitment, many countries have responded to this by preparing a strategy, 'A National Agenda 21' or an equivalent action plan. More than 100 countries have now prepared National Sustainable Development Strategy or National Environmental Action Plan. The rationale behind evolving national sustainable development strategy is as follows:

- The importance of setting priorities, economic as well as ecological basis, because of the fact that financial and human resources are limited and government can only respond realistically to a few targets.
- The need of developing national ownership to create the necessary political climate for effective action and policy change.
- The significance of participation by public and relevant sections of the society.

The most daunting task in the post-Rio Phase is the setting of an effective institutional mechanism to ensure the implementation and monitoring of the programmes of sustainable development. Chapter 8 and 38 of Agenda proposes the establishment of National Council for Sustainable Development (NCSD) to oversee the implementation and monitoring work. To date, about 80 countries have more or less some sort of national institution either at government or non-government or both levels.

The Summit at Rio fostered a process of internalising environmental concerns into the mandates of many international institutions. It established the fact that there is an intimate relation between social development, economic upliftment and environmental conservation.

The Summit has succeeded in bringing a lot of change in thinking of international funding institutions. The World Bank has started mainstreaming the environmental dimensions into all its operations. Apart from this, all UN programmes have incorporated the elements of environmental conservation.

Both Agenda 21 and Uruguay Round agreements which paved the way for establishment of World Trade Organisation (WTO) call upon countries to realise that trade liberalisation and sustainable development are mutually supportive. However, after UNCED the economic and trade sectors are more aware of the importance of the environmental agenda. There has been little progress in integrating environment with development till now.

Nevertheless, what is more important is the fact that there has been a commonality in thinking about the role of environmental management in development all over world. This apart, there is also awareness about the fact that eradication of poverty is the key to sustainable development. A commitment to eradicate poverty was in the social summit. But there is no progress in poverty reduction. Today more people live in abject poverty than in the wake of Rio Summit in the year 1992. Therefore, there are unfulfilled commitments of the Rio Summit today. More importantly, they are (1) eradication of poverty, (2) the new and additional financial resources for funding sustainable development programme, and (3) transfer of technology to developing countries in concessional terms.

UN Convention to Combat Desertification, 1992

The decision to adopt the Convention to Combat Desertification (CCD) was taken at Rio in 1992, with the persistent demand of countries from Africa, where two-thirds of the land area is either desert or dry land. The main elements of the convention are as under:

- Establishment of a global legal framework.
- Creation of a system for exchanging information on ways to combat desertification.
- Principles that include a 'bottom-up' approach to ensure participation of local population in combating desertification.
- Mobilisation of finances through bilateral and multilateral aid as well as the Global Environment Facility (GEF).

Convention on Biological Diversity (CBD), 1993

Concern for conservation of bio-diversity at global level figured for the first time in the discussions at the UN Conference on the Human Environment held in Stockholm in 1972. Though UNEP identified conservation as a priority area in 1973, it was only towards late 1980 that systematic and concerted efforts to look at bio-diversity conservation profile at international level started with constitution of an Ad Hoc Working Group of Experts on Biological Diversity by UNEP in 1987. Eventually, an Expert Group was constituted by UNEP, which started its work in 1989 culminating in the Convention on Biological Diversity (CBD) at the UN Conference on Environment and Development (UNCED) held at Rio de Janeiro in June, 1992. This Convention entered into force on

29th December, 1993. At present 175 countries are parties to the Convention.

This international treaty is a historic treaty because it reflects the commitment of global community for conservation and sustainable use of benefits arising out of utilisation of genetic resources with the countries of origin. The three principal objectives of the Convention captured in Article 1 reflect this. According to this, the main objectives of the Convention are:

- The conservation of biological diversity.
- The sustainable use of the components of bio-diversity.
- The fair and equitable sharing of benefits arising out of the utilisation of genetic resources.
- The preservation of knowledge and practices of indigenous communities.

The objective of equitable sharing of benefits has to be further seen in the reaffirmation of sovereign rights of States over their own bio-diversity which entitles a country to equity and fairness in sharing of benefits arising out of the utilisation of their genetic resources. The Convention recognises and reaffirms certain basic principles and values (See Box 6.2). The implications of the Convention and obligations of the contracting parties are presented in Box 6.2.

The Convention recognises and reaffirm:

- The intrinsic value of biological diversity;
- The sovereign rights of States over their biological resources;
- The fundamental requirement of in-situ conservation of ecosystems and natural habitats;
- The supporting role of ex-situ measures;
- The vital role of local communities and women in the conservation and sustainable use of biological diversity;
- The desirability of sharing equitably the benefits arising from the use of traditional knowledge, skills, innovations and practices;
- The importance of and the need to promote regional and global co-operation for conservation; and
- The requirements of substantial investments to conserve biological diversity.

BOX 6.2: IMPLICATIONS OF THE PROVISIONS OF THE CBD AND THE MAIN OBLIGATIONS OF THE CONTRACTING PARTIES

- Parties are required to take measures for in-situ conservation of biological diversity, promote rehabilitation and restoration of degraded ecosystems, and ensure protection of threatened species (Article 8).
- Parties are obliged to respect, preserve and maintain knowledge, innovations and practices of indigenous and local communities and encourage the equitable sharing of benefits arising from the use of such knowledge, innovations and practices (Article 8).
- Parties are also to adopt measures for ex-situ conservation of components of biological diversity, for complementing the in-situ efforts (Article 9).
- Parties are to facilitate access to genetic resources on mutually agreed upon terms with prior informed consent of the country providing these resources (Article 15).
- The recipient country is to share in a fair and equitable way the results of research and development and the benefits arising from the commercial and other utilisation of genetic resources with the party providing such resources.
- The Convention calls for transfer of relevant technologies, including biotechnologies on fair and most favourable terms from the developed to the developing nations, which provide genetic resources used for the development of these technologies (Article 16).
- It also calls on the private sector to facilitate access to and transfer of such technologies developed by them (Article 16.4).
- The contracting parties and other intellectual property rights are supportive of and do not run counter to the objectives of the Convention (Article 16.5) Recombinant technology (or genetic engineering) are increasingly gaining ground and are being seen as potentially useful for various sectors by experts. Recognising that introduction of these biotechnologies requires utmost care and caution based on precautionary principle, outlined in Agenda 21,

particularly because recall of an introduced organism in nature would not be possible.

- The Convention commits the parties to adhere the Convention protocol for safe transfer, handing and use of any living modified organism resulting from biotechnology (Article 19.3).
- Parties are also to take measures for facilitating access on a fair and equitable basis and on mutually agreed upon terms to the results and benefits arising from biotechnologies based upon genetic resources provided/ transferred (Article 19.2).
- The developed country parties are to commit to contribute to a fund to enable developing country to meet the agreed full incremental costs' for implementing the provisions of the Convention (Article 20.2).
- The financial mechanism is to operate within a democratic and transparent system of governance and function under the authority of the Conference of the parties (Article 21).

What is noteworthy about the Convention is the fact that the facilitation of access by developing countries is linked with equitable sharing of benefits. Technology flows are also founded on the principle of equity with the developing countries providing resources and traditional technologies, and developed countries sharing and transferring technologies including biotechnologies and providing financial resources to help developing countries meet their commitments and realise benefits. It is amply clear that the Convention is the first global comprehensive agreement to address all aspects of biological diversity – genetic resources, species and ecosystems—which would have revolutionary and far reaching implications. Being based on considerations of equity and shared responsibility, the Convention envisages reciprocity of arrangements between developed and developing countries, thereby promoting a renewed partnership between them.

The main implementation measures for the Convention are to be through national strategies, plan or programmes. Although qualified with phrases like 'as far as possible' and 'as appropriate' throughout its text, the Convention commits the Contracting Parties to take substantive action in many areas including:

- Development of national plans, strategies or programmes for conservation and sustainable use of bio-diversity; and integrating these into relevant sectoral or cross sectoral plans, programmes and policies;
- Inventorisation and monitoring of components of bio-diversity and of processes adversely impacting it; developing and strengthening of in-situ mechanisms for bio-diversity conservation both within and outside protected areas;
- Development of ex-situ measures for bio-diversity conservation as a complement to in-situ approaches;
- Restoration of degraded ecosystems and recovery of endangered species;
- Adopting measures to avoid and minimise adverse impacts on bio-diversity;
- Protecting and encouraging customary use of biological resources that are compatible with conservation or sustainable use requirements;
- Adopting economically and socially sound measures that act as incentives for conservation and sustainable use of components of bio-diversity;
- Promoting and encouraging research contributing towards achieving the objectives of the Convention;
- Developing educational and public awareness programmes with respect to conservation and sustainable use of bio-diversity;
- Facilitating access to genetic resources on mutually agreed terms and prior informed consent; and taking measures for fair and equitable sharing of benefits arising from utilisation of the resources thus transferred;
- Facilitating access to and transfer of technology, including biotechnology to developing countries under fair and most favourable terms;
- Facilitating exchange of information relevant to bio-diversity;
- Promoting scientific and technical co-operation with other Parties;
- Consideration of a protocol for safe transfer handing and use of living modified organisms resulting from biotechnology; and
- Providing new and additional financial resources by the developed country Parties to enable the developing country Parties to meet the agreed full incremental costs for implementing the provisions of this Convention.

The International Conference on Population and Development (ICPD), 1995

The International Conference on Population and Development was held in Cairo in 1995. Representatives from 183 nations participated and agreed to an action plan to stabilise the human population by the year 2020. They also agreed to provide greater equality to women along with improved reproductive health care. But the Conference failed to draw a meaningful framework for operationalising the decisions taken.

The Fourth World Conference on Women, 1995

The World Conference (Fourth) on Women was held in Beijing in September 1995. This adopted a bill of Rights for women. It was ratified by about 160 nations by 1997. The Conference emphasised, *inter alia*, on aspects of empowering women to take part in development process.

The Berlin Climate Summit, 1995

The Berlin Climate Summit was held in March 1995. The objective of the Summit was to strengthen the Framework Convention on Climate Change signed at Earth Summit. The decision is called as Berlin Mandate. It acknowledged the fact that the existing commitments to curb GHG emissions in developed countries were inadequate to meet the Convention's goal. It sought a protocol to strengthen the commitments. The protocol endorsed the ban on the production of ozone-depleting chemicals.

The World Food Summit, 1996

The World Food Summit was held in Rome in November 1996. This highlighted eight commitments pertaining to conditions for economic and social progress conducive to (1) food security, (2) poverty eradication and access to adequate food, (3) sustainable agriculture, complementarity to food security, (4) preparedness for food famines, (5) human resource development, (6) rural development, (7) global co-operation in implementation, and (8) ensuring follow-up action.

The G-8 Countries' Action Programme on Forests, 1997

The heads of states of the G-8 countries (Canada, France, Germany, Italy, Japan, the Russian Federation, the United Kingdom and the United States) first proposed the creation of an action programme on forests at their

Summit in Denver, United Sates in June 1997. It was subsequently approved at the next Summit, held in Birmingham, United Kingdom in May 1998. The action programme commits the G-8 countries to take action in five important areas:

- *Monitoring and Assessment of Forests*: Monitoring and assessment of G-8 forests using agreed national criteria and indicators; support of Forest Resource Assessment (FRA)-2000; working with partner countries to build national forests assessment capacity; improving access to remote sensing data and geographic information system technology.
- *National Forest Programme*: Encouraging partner countries to develop effective national programmes; focusing technical and financial assistance on counties that give priority to sustainable forest management; improving in-country donor co-ordination.
- *Protected Areas*: Working to achieve consensus on the purposes and categories of Protected Forests Areas; identification of key forest types not sufficiently represented in Protected Area system; strengthening the effectiveness of Protected Area management.
- *Private Sector*: Encouraging the private sector to develop voluntary codes of conduct that support sustainable forest management; promoting private investment in sustainable forest management, including innovative financing mechanism.
- *Illegal Logging*: Sharing information and assessment on the nature and extent of international trade in illegally harvested timber; implementation of effective measures to combat bribery and corruption in international business transactions.

The Kyoto Protocol, 1997

The Kyoto Protocol, 1997 was a landmark convention in the history of world. It was signed at the Third Conference of the Parties to the UN Framework Convention on Climate Change (FCCC) in December 1997. It has important forestry dimensions. The convention said that quantification of forests' potential contribution to reduction of greenhouse gas emissions through reduced deforestation and reforestation will require comprehensive accounting of the associated carbon sources. The organisation also said that comprehensive analysis of other environmental and socio-economic criteria that influence forest management choices and the feasibility of fossil fuel substitution by bio-energy are also needed.

The Kyoto Protocol has made the role of the forests prominent in mitigating global climatic change. The deliberation at the Fourth Conference of the Parties in Buenos Aires, Argentina in November 1998 laid emphasis on forests. It establishes legally binding commitments for reduced emissions of greenhouse gases from industrialised countries and permits the use of limited activities in the land use and forest sector to meet these commitments. The protocol provides to industrialised countries incentives to invest, in their own as well as in other countries, in forestry activities, which increase carbon sequestration and/or reduce carbon emissions. The FCCC recognised that countries had 'common but differentiated responsibilities'. The Convention decided that industrialised countries, with larger historical and current 'greenhouse gases (GHGs)' emissions, would be the first to reduce GHG emissions and allow developing countries to promote industrialisation. Under the resulting Kyoto Protocol, industrialised countries agreed to reduce their emission in the 2008-2012 period by 5.2 per cent compared to 1990 levels. Though many details of the Kyoto Protocol remain to be clarified, the treaty if ratified should offer possibilities for many rich countries to arrange investment in forestry. To date, 84 countries have already signed it but it is not yet in force.

Inter-governmental Panel on Forests (IPF), 1997

The post UNCED international dialogue on forests led by the Inter-governmental Panel on Forests (IPF) from 1995 to 1997 resulted in over 100 negotiated proposals for action. Work continues under the Inter-governmental Forum on Forests (IFF). IPF will present its final report to the United Nations Commission on Sustainable Development on its three major areas of work.

- The implementation of IPF's proposal for action.
- Issues on which international consensus has yet to be achieved;
- The identification of possible elements and initiatives towards developing consensus on international agreements and mechanisms for the management, conservation and sustainable development of forests.

Some of the key Environmental Treaties and Conventions discussed in the aforesaid paragraphs are presented on a tabular fashion (See Table 6.4)

Table 6.4: Major Environmental Treaties and Conventions: 1933-97

Treaty or Conventions/ Subjects	*Date of Formulation*	*Place*	*Number of Signatories and Ratifiers*
Convention related to the Preservation of Flora and Fauna in their natural state.	1933	London	9
The Convention on Nature Protection and Wild life Preservation in the Western Hemisphere.	1940		13
International Convention for Birds	1950	Paris	10
Antarctic Treaty	1959	Washington	39
Nuclear test ban in the atmosphere, outer space and under water	1963	Moscow	120
Wetlands of International importance	1971	Ramsar, Iran	84
Prohibition of Biological and Toxins Weapons	1972	London, Moscow, Washington D.C.	122
Protection of World Cultural and Natural Heritage	1972	Paris	120
Prevention of Marine Pollution by Dumping	1972	London, Mexico City, Moscow, Washington	73
International Trade in Endangered Species	1973	Washington D.C.	111
The Convention on the Conservation of Nature in the South Pacific	1976		6
Prevention of Pollution from ship	1978	London	65
The Treaty for Amazonian Co-operation	1978		8
Transboundary Air Pollution (Europe)	1979		29

(*Contd.*)

(*Contd.*)

Treaty or Conventions/ Subjects	*Date of Formulation*	*Place*	*Number of Signatories and Ratifiers*
Conservation of Migratory Species	1979		47
Convention on the Conservation of European Wild life and Natural Habitat.	1979		24
Conservation of Antarctic Marine Life	1980		27
U.N. Law of the Sea	1982		126
The Benelux Convention on Nature Conservation and Landscape Protection	1982		3
International Tropical Timber Agreement.	1983		
Vienna Convention. Protecting the Ozone Layer	1985	Vienna	103
The ASEAN Agreement on Conservation of Nature and Natural Resources.	1985	–	7
Convention for the Protection of Natural Resources and Environment of the South Pacific Region, 1986.	1986		10
Montreal Protocol on Ozone layer	1987	Montreal	96
Control of Transboundary Hazardous Wastes	1987	Basel	58
Convention on Biological Diversity	1993	Nairobi	175
Convention on Climate Change	1993	New Work	143
Oslo Protocol on Sulphur Emission	1994	Oslo	–
UN Framework Convention on Climate Change	1994/97	Kyoto	84

FAO Strategic Plan for Forestry, 1999

Food and Agricultural Organisation (FAO) began a process of consultation with member countries, institutions and individuals in February 1996. This process has come to an end recently with the formulation of strategic plan for forestry. The objective of this plan is to orient the programme and policies of FAO in forestry related matters. This strategic plan aims at linking forestry programmes to the mandate, corporate strategies and objectives of the overall FAO Strategic Framework, which was approved by the member countries at the thirteenth session of the Conference of FAO in November 1999 (FAO, 1999). In other words, it aims to build on the ability of FAO to address the full spectrum of environmental, economic and social challenges of sustainable forest management and to provide linkages and cross-fertilisation with other relevant disciplines. Besides, it provides overall direction on which the more detailed departmental implementation plans-the Biennial Programme of Work and Budget—will be based. Highlights of 'FAO Strategic Plan for Forestry' are presented in Box 6.3.

BOX 6.3: HIGHLIGHTS OF 'FAO STRATEGIC PLAN FOR FORESTRY'

FAO Forestry Mission

- To enhance human well-being through support to member countries in the sustainable management of the world's trees and forests.

Forestry Goals

- The contribution of trees and forests to sustainable land use, food security and economic and social development and cultural values at national, regional and global levels.
- The conservation, sustainable management and improved utilisation of trees and forest systems and their genetic resources.
- The increase in worldwide access to reliable and timely forestry information.

Strategies

- Continue to execute mandated role efficiently.

- Set clear priorities for work
- Build mutually beneficial partnerships with other organisations.

Medium-term Objectives

- Strengthen the information and database on forest and tree resources.
- Strengthen natural forest policies.
- Strengthen the technical foundation for sustainable forest resource conservation and development and forest development and utilisation.
- Improve and maintain the health and condition of the forests.
- 'Strengthen countries' institutional, legal and financial frameworks for forestry sector.
- Improve regional and international discussion and collaboration on forest policy and technical issues.
- Strengthen partnerships with other groups working in forestry.

Current Priority Activities

- Global forestry statistics and information. Development of a forestry information system: Global Forest Resources Assessment (FRA 2000); forestry sector outlook studies.
- Technological and methodologies for the conservation and sustainable use of trees, wooded lands and forests. Technical support to sustainable forest and wild life management, including developing and harmonising criteria and indicators of sustainable forest management; support to activities in afforestation, especially in countries with low forest cover; encouraging the adoption codes of environmentally sound harvesting and utilisation practices, and increasing conversion efficiency; promoting non-wood forest products, including their management, utilisation and marketing.
- Policy and institution strengthening. Support to national forest programmes, especially capacity building; Community Forestry Programme.
- Support to international processes influencing forests. Support to the post-United Nations Conference on Environment and Development (UNCED), international dialogue on forests, including the UNCED Conventions,

the Ad hoc Open-ended Inter-governmental Forum on Forests (IFF), the Inter-Agency Task Force on Forests (ITFF) and the International Year of Mountains, 2002.

FAO's Commitments for Future

- Maintaining and increasing its effectiveness in the forestry sector over the next 15 years using the Strategic Plan as a guide.
- Continued leadership and partnership promoting the sustainable management of world's trees and forests.
- Striving to be innovative, abreast of new developments, able to anticipate trends and able to work in a truly cross-sectoral fashion.
- Continued synergy of field programme and normative activities.

Vision for the Future: The Scenario to Aim for

- Increase in the area of sustainably managed forests
- Slowing of rate of deforestation in the tropics.
- Decrease in forest degradation world-wide.
- Increase in global areas of trees and forests through afforestation and reforestation, especially of degraded land.
- Enhanced knowledge of the location, extent, composition, health and value of goods and services represented by forest ecosystem and trees in the landscapes.
- Further use of informed and constructive debate among a wide range of interest groups to develop consensus on forest management, particularly in defining sustainable forest management and striking a balance between environmental and developmental objectives.
- Policy changes that will help to remove restrictions on forestry development, promote participatory approaches towards their management and encourage the equitable distribution of benefits.
- Enhancement of the role of trees and forests in contributing to food security (including the wood energy required for cooking food) and environmental protection.
- Increased flow of investment into the sector, particularly in developing countries and countries with economies in transition.

Source: FAO Strategic Plan for Forestry: 2000.

UN Millennium Summit 2000

UN Millennium Summit 2000 was an important milestone in the field of development and environment. World leaders including 100 heads of state and 47 heads of state government, three crown princes, five vice presidents and three deputy ministers attended the UN Millennium Summit 2000. The Summit adopted a 'visionary declaration' on the future of the body. The Summit declaration said, "We solemnly reaffirm, on this historic occasion, that the UN is the indispensable common house of the entire human family, through which we will seek to realise our universal aspirations for peace, co-operation and development". The declaration spelled out values and principles as well as goals in the key priority areas of peace, development, environment, human rights, protecting the vulnerable, special needs of Africa, and strengthening the UN. The declaration said in its opening section, "For while globalisation offers great opportunities, at present its benefits are very unevenly shared, while its costs are unevenly distributed". The opening section of the declaration identified six core values as essential to international relation. These core values are as under:

- Freedom,
- Equality,
- Solidarity,
- Tolerance,
- Respect for nature and shared responsibility.

Initiatives in the New Millennium

FRA 2000: Summary Findings

FRA 2000 is the most comprehensive and technologically advanced assessment in FAO's 50 years history. The Global Forest Resource Assessment 2000 (FRA 2000) provides a perspective on the world's forests through an appraisal of their state in the year 2000, and changes since 1980s. The assessment is the key source of factual information on forests for use by national institutions and international for a such as the Convention on Biological Diversity, the United Nations Framework Convention on Climate Change and the Convention to Combat Desertification in seeking solutions to environmental concerns. The thematic content of the assessment is broader than ever, covering forest area status and change, biological diversity, timber volume and forest biomass, non-wood forest products, trees outside the forest, forest fires and other tropical issues. For the first time, comparable trend information on tropical deforestation from two successive assessment periods has been obtained through the use of statistical sampling and satellite remote sensing. Therefore, FRA 2000 is a milestone in the journey towards sustainable forest management.

The Global Forest Resources Assessment 2000 (FRA 2000) collected and synthesised a vast amount of information on the status and trends in forest cover worldwide, on forest management, and on additional forest-related variables. It also provides information on the status of forest inventories. Such valuable information are required for policy-making and forest management decisions that underpin countries efforts to work towards sustainable forest management. Some major conclusions of FRA 2000 are as follows:

- The total forest area for the year 2000 was 3.9 billion ha, of which 95 per cent was natural forest and 5 per cent was forest plantation.
- About 47 per cent of forests worldwide were tropical, 9 per cent sub-tropical, 11 per cent temperate and 33 per cent boreal.
- The world's natural forests continued to be converted to other land uses at a very high rate. During the 1990s, the total loss of natural forests (*i.e.* deforestation plus the conversion of natural forests to forest plantations) was 16.1 million ha per year, of which 15.2 million ha occurred in the tropics.
- The area of forest plantations increased by an average of 3 million ha per year during the 1990s. Half of this increase was the result of afforestation on land previously under non-forest land use, whereas the other half resulted from conversion of natural forest.
- The net annual deforestation rate globally for the 1990s was an estimated 9.4 million ha per year (or 0.2 per cent of total forest). This was the combined effect of a gross deforestation rate of 14.6 million ha per year and a gross expansion rate of 5.2 million ha per year.
- The independent FRA 2000 remote sensing survey of forest cover change studied the entire tropical region through a 10 per cent sample of the forest for the periods 1980 to 1990 and 1990 to 2000. The survey provided information on changes in tropical

forests at the pan-tropical and regional levels, including on the patterns of forest and related land use change, over the past 20 year.

- For the first time, a uniform definition of forest was used in FAO's global forest assessment. The application of a uniform definition resulted in forest cover figures for some countries that were significantly higher than those of previous assessments. This does not indicate a real increase of forests. FRA 2000 recalculated the 1990 forest cover figures using the same definitions and methodologies used for calculating the 2000 figures, in order to make the comparison between 1990 and 2000 possible. This sets a new baseline for forest cover in 1990.
- The above-ground woody biomass in forests amounts 420 billion tonnes (dry), of which 27 per cent is in Brazil alone. The standing volume of forests is highest in Central America and Central Europe.
- The concept of sustainable forest management continued to gain momentum around the world. Most countries were involved in international initiatives related to sustainable forest management and areas under forest management plans were increasing. As of 2000, 149 countries were involved in international initiatives to develop and implement criteria and indicators for sustainable forest management. However, data on key indicators were missing for many of these countries. National. figures were not available from many developing countries, including many of the larger countries in Africa and some key forest countries in Asia. Nevertheless, results obtained so far indicated that at least 6 per cent of the total forest area in developing countries was covered by a formal, nationally approved forest management plan with duration of at least 5 years. Some 89 per cent of the forests in industrialised countries were managed according to formal or informal management plans.
- FAO used the best available and most relevant information on forest resources for FRA 2000. Although the number of reports on forest resources increased in the 1990s, many countries still lacked the basic data needed to assess accurately the state and changes in their forests. Some countries, however, have notably improved their inventories over the past decade. Most countries updated their forest cover estimates during the 1990s, often

through remote sensing mapping approaches, but in many cases the methodology was not directly compatible with previous surveys, making change estimates difficult. Future global assessments should strive to improve both the accuracy and depth of the information provided, and decision-makers must be fully involved in defining further information needs to support policies and programmes in sustainable forest management.

United Nations Forum on Forests (UNFF)

The countries of the world were much divided on forest issues at UNCED. In order to advance beyond the agreements contained in the "Forest Principles" in Chapter 1 and Chapter 11 (Combating deforestation) of Agenda 21, Inter-governmental discussion and debate continued, first under the Inter-governmental Panel on Forests (IPF) and then under the Inter-governmental Forum on Forests (IFF). IFF recently completed its work and has put fourth a proposal for an international arrangement on forests, including the establishment of the United Nations Forum on Forests (UNFF).

Strengthening of Linkages and Regional Initiatives

The terms for three international conventions were agreed on at UNCED: the Convention on Biological Diversity, the Framework Convention on Climate Change and the Convention to Combat Desertification. The past few years have brought further progress in their implementation as well as strengthened links with one another, with IPF and IFF, and with longer-standing conventions, including the Convention on International Trade in Endangered Species of Wild Fauna and Flora (CITES) and the Ramsar Convention

While international discussions and agreements on forests have intensified since UNCED, regional co-operation in forest issues also increased. Regional initiatives have been witnessed among countries like Congo Basin/Central Africa, Southern Africa, Central America, the Amazon Basin, Asia and Europe. Increased co-operation is also occurring at the ecoregional levels. Initiatives for co-operation among countries with a low forest cover and for mountain forests are most notable. Cutting across geographic regions, such initiative serves to increase inter-country collaboration based on ecological imperatives.

In agreeing to the Forest Principles of UNCED's Agenda 21, countries committed themselves to working towards the sustainable management of all types of forests to ensure the continued availability of the goods and environmental and social services that they provide. The need to define what sustainable forest management actually means in practice and to provide tools to measure progress gave rise to the development of criteria and indicators for sustainable forest management. Model and demonstration of forest programmes have been established in many countries to illustrate what sustainable forest management looks like in practice as well as the processes that may be employed to work towards it. This apart, recognition of the fact that sustainable forest management cannot be achieved in the absence of an enabling institutional framework has led to increased international support for national forest programmes.

Non-governmental Initiatives

Integral to the concept of sustainability is the issue of social development and equity, which necessitate widespread participation in decision-making so that stakeholder can represent their own interests. NGOs (including those representing the interests of various civil society sectors) have become major recognised voices in international discussions on this topic and are key catalysts for action at the local level.

The Inter-governmental Forum on Forest (IFF) and UNFF Processes

IFF achieved notable progress in building consensus on international forest policy issues through the intensive deliberations carried out during its term, from July 1997 until April 2000. As a result, the wide gap that existed between North and South at the UNCED Conference in 1992 and at the Rio+5 Special Session of the UN General Assembly in 1997 has narrowed considerably. Although a number of issues related to forests remains controversial, complex and politically sensitive, countries agree that the main priority for the next few years is the implementation of the proposals for action adopted between 1995 and 2000 by IFF and its predecessor (See the topics of the proposals for action in Table 6.5). Contributing to this enhanced international dialogue has been the active participation of non-governmental and indigenous peoples' organisations, which have taken a leading role in a number of regional and global initiatives and international meetings of experts (FAO, 2001).

Table 6.5: Topics of the IPF and IFF Proposals for Action

Programme element		*Description*
IPF	*IFF*	
I.A.		Progress through national forest and land use programmes
I.B.	II.D.1	Underlying causes of deforestation and forest degradation
I.C.	II.D.2	Traditional forest-related knowledge
I.D.		Fragile ecosystems affected by desertification and drought
I.E.		Impact of airborne pollution on forests
I.F.		Needs and requirements of countries with low forest cover
II.A	II.A	Financial resources
II.B	II.C	Transfer of environmentally sound technology to promote sustainable forest
III.A		Assessment of the multiple benefits of all types of forests
	II.D.8	Assessment, monitoring and rehabilitation of forest cover in environmentally critical areas
	II.D.3	Forest conservation and protected areas
III.B	II.D.4	Forest research
III.C	II.D.5	Valuation of forest goods and services
	II.D.6	Economic instruments, tax policies and land tenure
	II.D.7	and demand for wood and non-wood forest products and services
III.D		Criteria and indicators for sustainable forest management
IV	II.B	Trade and environment
V		International organisations and multilateral institutions and instruments, including appropriate legal mechanisms
	II.E	Forest-related work by international and regional organisations and under existing instruments
	III	International arrangements and mechanisms to promote the management, conservation and sustainable development of all types of forests
	I.A	Promotion and facilitation of the implement of the IPF proposals for action
	I.B	Monitoring of progress in implementing the IPF proposals for action

Source: FAO, 2001.

IFF recognised that increased financial resources, the transfer of environmentally sound technology, and capacity building to support national forest programmes were essential elements in the implementation of the IPF and IFF proposals for action. The continued coordination of the forest-related activities of international organisations and instruments was also recognised as important. The Informal Interagency Task Force on Forests (ITFF), set up in 1995 as a coordination mechanism for support to IPF by international organisations, was acknowledged as one of the main institutional legacies of the IPF/IFF process.

One of the most controversial issues facing IFF was how to establish an international arrangement and mechanism on forests, including the question of a legally binding instrument on all types of forests. After long and intense deliberations, IFF reached an agreement on the establishment of a new inter-governmental body. More specifically, IFF's recommendations were for the Economic and Social Council (ECOSOC) and the UN General Assembly to:

(a) "Establish a new inter-governmental body which may be called the United Nations Forum on Forests (UNFF);
(b) Invite the executive heads of relevant organisations of the United Nations system and heads of other relevant international and regional organisations, institutions and instruments to form a collaborative partnership on forests to support the work of UNFF and to enhance co-operation and co-ordination among participants.
(c) Within five years, consider with a view to recommending the parameters of a mandate for developing a legal framework on all types of forests.
(d) Take steps to devise approaches towards appropriate financial and technology transfer support to enable the implementation of sustainable forest management.

At its eighth session in April-May 2000, the Commission on Sustainable Development (CSD) endorsed IFF's conclusions and proposals for action. CSD invited ECOSOC and the UN General Assembly to take action on the proposed terms of reference for an international arrangement on forests, as recommended by IFF. In its resumed session in October 2000, ECOSOC created an international arrangement on forests, including UNFF, which was established as a subsidiary body of ECOSOC. At the organisational meeting of UNFF, held in February 2001, it was decided, among other things, to base the UNFF Secretariat in New York. UNFF's first substantive session was held in June 2001.

Conference of Parties-5 (COP-5) to CBD: 2001

The fifth meeting of the Conference of the Parties (COP-5) to the Convention on Biological Diversity (CBD), which was held in Nairobi, Kenya in May 2000, highlighted the need to expand the focus of the Convention's programme of work in forest biological diversity from research to action-oriented activities. COP-5 called on Parties, governments and organisations to take practical actions to do this within the scope of the existing work programme. The aim is to propose an action-based, integrated and holistic approach to the conservation and sustainable use of forest biological diversity.

Johannesburg Summit-2002

An international commitment to work towards sustainable development was made almost a decade ago at the United Nations Conference on Environment and Development (UNCED) which took place in Rio de Janeiro, Brazil in June 1992. After this, a lot of international, regional and national initiatives have been taken in the field of sustainable forest management. Some of the initiatives are still continuing to date. Again, certain special initiatives are emerging in the international, regional and national level also. One among such international initiatives is World Summit on Sustainable Development—which was held in Johannesburg of South Africa from 26th August to 4th September of 2002. This is otherwise known as the Rio +10 Conference. Beside head of governments of many countries or their representative, over 8,000 civil society participants attended the Summit, reinforced by parallel events which included major groups, such as, NGOs, women, indigenous people, youth, farmers, trade unions, business leaders, the scientific and technological community and local authorities as well as Chief Justices from various countries. This Summit took stock of the progress made over the past ten years towards meeting the commitments made at UNCED. The review focussed on the implementation of Agenda 21, the Plan of Action produced by UNCED and identified measures for its further implementation. The Summit, *inter alia*, redeemed the resolve to (1) achieve by 2010 a significant reduction in the current rate of loss of biological diversity, and (2) accelerate implementation of the IPF/IFF proposals for action by countries and by the Collaborative Partnership on Forests, and intensify efforts on reporting to the United Nations Forum on Forests, to contribute to an assessment of progress in 2005. Key outcomes of the Summit are presented below:

- The understanding of sustainable development was broadened and strengthened as a result of the Summit, particularly the important linkages between poverty, the environment and the use of natural resources.
- Governments agreed to and reaffirmed a wide range of concrete commitments and targets for action to achieve more effective implementation of sustainable development objectives.
- Energy and sanitation issues were critical elements of the negotiations and outcomes emerged to a greater degree than in previous international meetings on sustainable development.
- Support for the establishment of a world solidarity fund for the eradication of poverty was a positive step forward.
- The views of civil society were given prominence at the Summit in recognition of the key role of civil society in implementing the outcomes and in promoting partnership initiatives.
- The concept of partnerships between governments, business and civil society was given a large boost by the Summit and the Plan of Implementation. Over 220 partnerships (with $235 million in resources) were identified in advance of the Summit and around 60 partnerships were announced during the Summit by a variety of countries.

Forest Management: Current Trends and Prospects

Over the years, significant changes in the field of forest management have taken place worldwide. National priorities and international commitments with relation to forest management have changed in response to the call given by United Nations Conference on Environment and Development (UNCED) in 1992. A broader approach to forest management has been evolved in most of the countries, balancing social, economic, and environmental objectives. The concerns of a wider range of interest groups are being taken into consideration and local communities are increasingly becoming directly involved in forest planning and management.

Signs of improvement are conspicuous in areas like management objectives, policy and legislative environment, availability and consumption of forest products, certification and emergence of civil society. Presently, changes on a global scale have been observed in the following areas:

- Forest management objectives.
- Policy, Legislative and Institutional framework.
- Community based forest management.
- Standards and benchmarks for Sustainable Forest Management (SFM).
- Forest resources: consumption and availability trends.
- Forest product certification.
- Emergence of civil society.

Forest Management Objectives

Objectives of forest management are undergoing a sea change. In the past, more emphasis was laid on production of wood. It is because wood had a primary economic value to society. With the passage of time, non-wood forest products gained importance. Again with the growing realisation about the imperatives of life-supporting services of the forest ecosystem, protection and conservation values of forest are increasingly appreciated. The concept of sustainable development further strengthens the changing ethos of forest management and helps to develop a trade-off not only between different multipurpose objectives but also intra and inter-generational requirements. Re-balancing of forest management objectives has led to changes in management practices and reallocation of forest areas between different uses.

Forest management objectives and practices have changed drastically in many countries. There is an increased emphasis on environmental values of forests. As a result, there has been a significant expansion of protected areas in some countries over the past few years. What is more important is the fact that greater emphasis on management of forest for multiple purposes and increased attention to environmental factors have led to reduced intensities in timber harvesting and establishment of low-impact logging practices. Owing to greater emphasis on the use of natural forests for environmental protection, there is an increased focus on conservation of biological diversity and eco-tourism. This apart, more reliance is also being laid on plantation for increasing wood supply.

There is a change in the field of operationalisation, silviculture, forest ownership, private sector and local community participation in forest management. Operational guidelines and codes of practice for forest management have been adopted in Europe and North America. New silvicultural systems have been developed for temperate and boreal forests in North America and for tropical forests. Codes of forests, most notably in the Asia and the pacific region have been put on practice (FAO, 1999). Visible changes in forest ownership are emerging. Grater participation of private sector in forest management has been witnessed in many countries. Local communities are being increasingly given responsibilities for forest planning and management. Changes leading to increased community participation in forest management are as follows:

- A proliferation of new mechanisms for the devolution of forest management to local communities or user groups.
- Increased recognition of the claims of indigenous people for use of the forest resource.
- Restoration of lands including forest lands of underprivileged communities.

Emphasis on social and environmental services of forests has increased manifold. More focus is being laid on mountains, dry lands and Small Island and low forest cover countries, as they symbolise fragile ecosystems in different parts of the globe. Environmental and social functions of such forests are being increasingly recognised in forest management practices world wide. Role of forests in conservation of water has been highly recognised, because there has been a great crisis of fresh water world wide. This role, along with the ecological role, shall gain unprecedented prominence in the near future. The role of forest in mitigating global climate change has received unprecedented prominence with the adoption of the Kyoto Protocol of the framework Convention on Climate Change in 1997.

Policy, Legislative and Institutional Framework

A lot of changes are taking place in forest policy, legislation and institutional front. The trend in forest policy reform consists of the following elements:

— Emphasis on ecological services of the forests.
— Restoration of multi-tier structure and multipurpose functions of forests.

— Increased focus on Non-Wood Forest Products (NWFP) including medicinal plant resources.
— Privatising state forests resources and forest based public companies.
— Increasing participation of private sector in sustainable forest management.
— Community participation in sustainable forest management practices and decentralisation of certain functions of government forest administration.
— Elimination of some 'perverse subsidies' including the under-pricing of forest concessions.
— Application of information technology into forest management practices.

There has been significant changes in legislative environment too. The process of revision of forest laws has set in all over the world in recent years. Some of the changes reflect commitments to: (1) promotion of people's participation in forest management, (2) enhancement of environmental functions of forests, (3) reinforcing the process of forest management planning, (4) increasing consideration and incorporation of environmental and social issues in management plans, and (5) supporting public participation in the planning and management process (see Box 6.4).

BOX 6.4: PUBLIC PARTICIPATION GIVEN LEGAL RECOGNITION

In June 1998 member states of the United Nations Economic Commissions for Europe (UN-ECE) signed a Public participation convention to regulate relations between the public and governments in environmental matters. The Convention has three pillars:

- *Access to information*: A general right for everyone to access environmental information held by public authorities.
- *Public participation*: Public participation in environmental decision-making through public participation mechanisms in range of activities.
- *Access to justice*: Judicial or administrative procedures to provide remedies that are fair and equitable.

Source: UN/ECE, 1998.

Institutional changes are distinctly visible in the forestry sector. Privatisation of certain forest sector activities and devolution of forest management responsibilities to the local communities have taken place in many countries in response to the changes made in policy and legislative environment. New institutions have been built up at local, national and global level to plan and monitor forest management practices.

There are many international initiatives aimed at fostering sustainable forest management. Some of the significant initiatives are (1) establishment and management of model and demonstration forests, (2) ITTO's 'Year 2000 objective', and (3) G-8 countries' action programme of forests, which was approved in, May 1998. Implementation of three international conventions arising from UNCED (the Framework Convention on Climate Change, the Convention on Biological Diversity and the Convention to Combat Desertification) and the International Tropical Timber Agreement provide the necessary support to the process of sustainable forest development on a global scale.

With the change in policies about natural resource management, the framework for institutional and administrative arrangements for forest management in states is undergoing a transformation. Such changes include modification in the role of forest organisation and manager, evolution of new social micro and macro level institutions, decentralisation and privatisation of sustainable forestry. Many developed countries have moved substantially towards privatisation and decentralisation. Changes are taking place in ownership regime of forests. Forestry sector is now increasingly recognised as a multi-stakeholder environment whose multiplicity of stakeholders like village community, forest organisation, non-government organisation (NGO), private sector, political parties, are demanding a greater role not only in decision-making about forests but also in the implementation. The existence of multiple and conflicting interests undoubtedly adds to the richness of the forestry debate. Therefore, the role of forest institutions as facilitators among a range of stakeholders has become increasingly important in pursuing the goals of management.

Community based Forest Management

The involvement of communities in forest management is now a significant feature of national forest policy and practice and of internationally supported forestry programmes throughout the world. For forestry organisations, greater reliance on resources at local community levels is a potential solution to a growing resource problem. Large-scale community based initiatives began in South Asia in the 1980s. By such programmes the community gained access to many areas of management. This form of community involvement in management, *i.e.* user-centered co-operation, defines local interests as those of user interests (FAO, 2001). Attention has now shifted to recent initiatives in community forest management in Africa, especially in the Gambia and the United Republic of Tanzania. Policy and legal changes and implementation on the ground are gaining momentum in this region. This is different from the Asian model of user centered approach. The emerging model in Africa is to support the custodian interests of the community. The basic premise on which this is based is that forest adjacent communities have custodian interests in ensuring that the forests do not become degraded. The intention is to make the local communities stakeholders of the forests, not simply users of its products. As with other forest managers, the community-based stakeholders must address a range of forest management goals, including forest protection, production and poverty alleviation, or economic benefits (FAO, 2001). Presently, community based management systems are very much in a stage of evolution. The transformation of present stage of limited participatory mode of forest management to a multiple stakeholder and community based approach is an uphill task. But, efforts are on to accomplish it.

Standards and Benchmarks for SFM

Many international initiatives have been taken with an aim to foster sustainable forest management. One important initiative is development of standards and benchmarks for SFM. Since the Earth Summit, there have been concerted inter-governmental efforts to develop criteria and indicators. More than 110 countries are participating in eight inter-governmental process to discuss the scientific and policy aspects of SFM and develop and implement national level criteria and indicators (C&I).

Criterion describes a state or situation, which should be met to comply with sustainable forest management. Indicator is a quantitative, qualitative or descriptive attribute that, when periodically measured or monitored, indicates the direction of change. Criteria and indicators for sustainable forest management are still in the process of their evolution. Presently, it is at a slower pace. It has began with economic criterion and slightly moved towards incorporating the ecological and social dimension of sustainability. Generally speaking, it is the social issues including participatory management, which are most difficult to grapple with.

All international initiatives in this area are being co-ordinated by the Centres for International Forestry Research (CIFOR), the International Tropical Timber Organisation (ITTO) and the African Timber Organisation (ATO). These processes have resulted in the development of the following eight sets of criteria and indicators for sustainable forest management. The eight inter-governmental processes for the development of SFM C&I are:

- International Tropical Timber Organisation (ITTO) covering most forested countries in the tropics—27 countries.
- The Helsinki Process—39 European countries.
- The Montreal process—12 Non-European counties with boreal and temperate forests.
- The Tarapoto proposal—8 countries in the Amazonian co-operation treaty.
- Lepaterìqui—7 Central American Nations.
- Sub-Sahel Dry Zone Africa—28 sub-Saharan countries.
- North Africa and Near East—20 countries stretching from Morocco to Afghanistan.
- Central—13 countries of the African Timber Organisation.

Many nations are using international sets of criteria and indicators to develop a more detailed set of C&I that is specific to their forests and situation. Some governments are translating these criteria and indicators into national and sub-national forest legislation. The question of definition of criteria and indicators and minimum acceptable standards of logging were extensively debated by the Inter-governmental Panel on Forests which recommended *inter alias* the need for a broad spectrum of qualitative and descriptive indicators covering social, cultural, economic, ecological, institutional, legal and policy elements.

Some indication of the increasingly complex range of factors that needs to be taken into account by forest policy decision-makers can be gauged from the criteria that were proposed for the Amazon region countries under the Tarapoto Process. The proposed criteria cover:

Environmental Criteria

- Biodiversity (genetic, species, ecological and landscape).
- Productivity of the ecosystem.

- Soil conservation.
- Water conservation including water quality and quantity.
- Forest ecosystem health and vitality (ecosystem functioning and processes).
- Contribution to carbon sequestration and other global ecological services.

Socio-economic Criteria

- Institutions and infrastructure to facilitate SFM.
- Long-term supply of social benefits.
- Long-term output of multiple economic benefits.
- Recognition of full spectrum of forest functions and uses.
- Recognition of and respect for indigenous rights and knowledge of historical and archaeological sites.

International Tropical Timber Organisation (ITTO) processes have formulated guidelines for the sustainable forest management of natural tropical forests in the year 1992. Such guidelines have specified criteria and indicators for sustainable forest management. More importantly, seven criteria have been identified as essential elements of sustainable forest management. Those seven criteria are as follows:

- Criterion 1: Enabling conditions for sustainable forest management.
- Criterion 2: Forest resource security.
- Criterion 3: Forest ecosystem health and condition.
- Criterion 4: Flow of forest produce.
- Criterion 5: Biological diversity.
- Criterion 6: Soil and water conservation.
- Criterion 7: Economic, soil and cultural aspects.

Different indicators have been identified and formulated under each criterion so that a change in any one of them would give information necessary to assess the progress towards sustainable forest management. However, these indicators are more of preliminary and indicative in nature rather than exhaustive. Again, looking at the changing needs of forest management practices, a different set of criteria and indicators, which is able to measure the effects of sustainable forest management, can be formulated.

Forest Resources: Consumption and Availability Trends

Trends in consumption and resource availability have influenced the course of forest management. Presently nearly about one-half (1,563 million hectares) of the area of natural forests worldwide is considered to be available for wood supply under current legal and market conditions (FAO, 1998). The area of natural forests that is currently available for wood production is diminishing because of deforestation and reallocation of some more areas for conservation purposes. Timber harvesting is gradually shifting from forests undisturbed by humans to semi-natural forest, plantations and TOF (Trees Outside Forests) areas. Factors driving this shift include deforestation and pre-eminence of conservation over timber production. This shift has already taken place in Europe, where an estimated 85 per cent of forests are considered semi-natural. The areas of semi-natural forests, plantation and trees outside forests are expected to increase in developing countries. The impact of sustainable forest management on future wood supply is also gradually becoming visible. Member countries of the International Tropical Timber Organisation (ITTO) which account for more than 80 per cent of world's tropical forests and more than 95 per cent of the global tropical timber trade, have made commitment to have their exports of tropical timber and tropical timber products come from sustainably managed sources by the year 2000 (State of World's Forests, 1999). To achieve the goal of sustainability, more than 150 countries are participating in regional and eco-regional process to establish criteria and indicators for sustainable forest management. It is expected that implementation of sustainable forest management may not only affect the wood supply on a short run but also increase management cost of wood harvesting on an average of 5 to 25 per cent. However, with the adoption of sustainable management practices in its totality, the long-term supply of wood shall improve as well as the management cost decreasing. The State of World's Forests report 1999 predicted that in the tropics much of this increase is expected to be realised through improved harvesting method leading to their maintenance of site productivity and prevention of damage to immature stems. In the temperate forests the long-term increase is expected to be less pronounced because of high level of productivity already reached (See also Tables 6.6 and 6.7) .

In the forest product sector, there have been a lot of changes. The most significant is the effort to meet the needs for wood and non-wood forest products while at the same time fulfilling demands for environmental and social services from forests. Increased importance is being attached to non-wood forest products (NWFPs), whose main importance currently lies in their contribution to household and local economies, particularly among the poor in developing countries. Regional and international forums have addressed the needs to conserve non-wood resources while ensuring local people's equitable access to and use of the resources. The medicinal plants have emerged as the most valuable NWFPs from forests. Their value provides additional incentives for sustainable management of forest resources and for conservation of specific habitat.

Table 6.6: Production and Consumption of Wood Products in 1996

Forest Products	*Production/ Consumption (million cubic meter)*	*Distribution in percentage*	
		Developed Countries	*Developing Countries*
Fuelwood and charcoal	1860	10	90
Industrial round-wood	1498	70	30

Fuelwood and charcoal still continue to be one of the important sources of household energy in developing countries. Developed countries continue to dominate heavily in production and consumption of industrial wood products. FAO (1999) has projected in its report 'State of World's Forests' that demand for industrial round-wood will increase by 1.7 per cent annually between now and the year 2010, driven both by population increases and economic growth (See also Table 6.7).

Plantations are becoming increasingly important sources of industrial wood in the future. This will reduce the intensity of timber harvesting in the natural forests, thereby promoting conservation of forest ecosystem. Today there are 60 million hectares of forest plantations in the world. The area of forest plantations established for industrial wood supply can help compensate for an anticipated reduction in production from natural forests. Over the years, gains in productivity of forest plantations have been made through improved management, tree breeding and tree improvement. Recent advances in biotechnology are increasingly being applied to the

Table 6.7: Current trends in Timber Harvesting

Country	*Current Trends in Timber Harvesting*
United States	Banned or severely restricted timber harvesting in primary forests.
India	Banned timber harvesting in hills and severely restricted timber harvesting in primary forests.
Philippines	Banned logging in 'old growth and virgin forests' and placed such forests under National Integrated Protected Area System.
New Zealand, Srilanka, Thailand	Banned or severely restricted timber harvesting in primary forests.
China	Imposed ban on timber harvesting in natural forests on July 1998.
Surinam	Natural forest area extending about 1.5 million hectares (one-tenth of the countries total land area) were set-aside as wilderness/ Nature Reserve in 1998.
Brazil	Government of Brazil announced its intention to put 25 million hectares of rain forests under Protected Area status.

Source: State of World's Forests — 1999 and other government records.

forestry sector, resulting in improved yield. Extent of plantation in different parts of the world is presented in table 6.8.

Table 6.8: Extent of Plantation in Different Parts of the World

Name of Continent/Countries	*Extent of Plantation in million hectares*
European countries	29.00
United States	Over 13.00
Japan	10.00
New Zealand	1.50
Australia	1.00

Source: State of World's Forests, 1999.

However, not all plantations have been established for wood production. Many have been planted for protection function, such as soil and water conservation, watershed conservation and wind protection. Almost 75 per cent of forest plantations are located in Asia and Pacific region, while about 10 per cent in Africa (DFID, 1996). They, being a source of raw material for wood based industry, provide relief to the natural forests. Otherwise, the demand for industrial wood might have impacted on the forest adversely. Plantations, therefore, play an important role in the process of sustainable forest management.

Forest Product Certification

Certification is one such area, which is growing rapidly in the field of sustainable forest development. Some international process like ITTO Guidelines, Helsinki Process, Montreal Process, Tarapoto Proposal, FAO Region Process are assisting countries to develop national frameworks to determine progress on sustainable forest management. Some countries like Bolivia, Mexico, Brazil, Indonesia, the Nordic countries, U.K., Germany, the Netherlands, Belgium, Switzerland have set up national certification programme for imported and domestically produced woods. Since only 20 per cent of the forest products enter the international trade, there is equally an urgent need for establishing standards for certification for domestically traded products. All countries producing forest products are making serious efforts to develop criteria and indicators specific to their situation and need.

Many forest product consumers in Europe, U.S.A. and Japan, who account for more than 60 per cent of world consumption of manufactured forest products, have started increasingly insisting that the products they purchase should be derived from forests certified as being managed sustainably. Therefore, it is relevant to emphasise on the fact that the process of certification has already begun in many countries (See Box 6.5 and 6.6).

BOX 6.5 : CERTIFICATION PROCESSES

Following are some of recent developments in the area of forest certification process:

- The area certified by accredited certifiers of the Forest Stewardship Council (FSC) has reached 22.0 million hectare from the 10.3 million hectare reported for 1998 in the State of the World's 1999. Most of this is in Europe and the United States. Sweden and Poland, alone account for 61 per cent of the total, and the United States for another 11 per cent.
- Outside the FSC process there has been an even more rapid increase: 21 million ha of Finland's forests (95 per cent of the country's forest area) have been certified under the Finnish Forest Certification System; a further 6.9 million hectare in Norway and Sweden have been certified under national certification schemes;

and some 44.0 million hectare of forest land in Canada has been certified according to the ISO 14001 standard of the International Organisation for Standardisation.

- This last certification procedure indicates that the companies involved conform to the ISO 14001 Environment and it can be seen as a step towards. Although it does not provide for forest management certification, it can be seen as a step towards gaining certification. Many of the Canadian companies adhering to this standard are now working towards the additional requirements needed to achieve Canadian Standards Association (CAS) certification. This is an ISO-based system that includes forest management performance requirements. Some 5 million hectare are already reported to have been certified according to the CSA standard.
- A new European certification process, the Pan European Forest Certification Framework (PEFC), has been established to provide a framework for voluntary forest certification and a mechanism for mutual recognition among different European national systems. National PEFC governing bodies have been established in 15 European countries.
- The Indonesian Ecolabelling Institute (LEI) has developed criteria and indicators for the auditing of forest management on logging concessions, as well as the ecolabelling of products from these concessions. The LEI system is based on the International Tropical Timber Organisation (ITTO) guidelines for sustainable forest management. A memorandum of agreement has been signed with FSC, and this may lead to joint certification by the two processes.
- Malaysia has formed a National Timber Certification which is establishing a national set of criteria and indicators, also based on the ITTO framework. It has entered into discussions and trials with other organisations to widen the acceptance of its system.
- The area covered by the American Forest and Paper Association's Sustainable Forestry Initiative, by which its member companies commit themselves to move towards sustainable forestry, has continued to expand. Although this is not a certification process, the principles and guidelines that companies commit themselves to are now being used as a basis for certification by independent bodies. Some 12 million hectares of forest have been verified by third party auditors and 20 million hectares are currently reported to be undergoing assessment.

Source: State of the World's Forests, 2001 (FAO, 2002).

BOX 6.6: MUTUAL RECOGNITION OF CERTIFICATION

The following points indicate mutual recognition of various certification schemes is increasing

- A decision has been taken by B&Q, a leading home improvement chain in the United Kingdom and a member of FSC and of the United Kingdom WWF 1995+Group, to accept Finnish timber certified under the Finnish Forest Certification System. This national certification process has been developed in competition with the FSC system in Finland.
- A wide range of interest groups in the United Kingdom, including the Forestry Commission, timber growers associations the timber traders, retailers and a number of NGOs, have reached an agreement on the recognition of the United Kingdom Woodland Assurance Scheme (UKWAS), a certification standard for forests in the United Kingdom.
- Pan European Forest Certification Framework (PEFC) is actively encouraging mutual recognition between different European national systems and also has provision for recognising non-European certification schemes.
- The International Forest Industry Roundtable, an informal network of forest industry associations from 16 forestry nations, is developing an international framework for mutual recognition between different performance standards and certification systems; and the Confederation of European Paper Industries (CEPI) is supporting mutual recognition efforts through the development of a comparative matrix of different certification systems as an educational tool for its members and for pulp and paper.
- The American Forest and Paper Association's Sustainable Forestry Initiative and the American Forest Foundation's Tree Farm System, which is the system of certification of forests in the United States and has 66,000 non-industrial private forest landowner members, have signed a mutual recognition agreement under which they recognise each other's standards for sustainable forest management. About 10 million ha are certified under the Tree Farm System.

Source: State of World's Forests, 2002 (FAO, 2002).

Certification is perhaps the most powerful 'soft' policy instrument to be designed and implemented outside government sector. It is already making positive impact on private sector forestry. It is a procedure by which written assurance is given that a product comes from a forest, which is managed in conformity with, specified environmental and social standards. Certification links market demands for sustainably produced forest products with producers who can meet these demands.

The International Organisation for Standardisation (ISO), through its ISO 14,000 series, offers a framework for certification of forest management system among other environmental management systems. The ISO approach offers potentiality for assessing the environmental sensitivity of forest management.

Certification has begun to show result. Many multinational companies whose operations are now certified have started adopting sound forestry practices. Certification is having the effect of recognising and rewarding the performance of these companies by enabling them to maintain and improve their market share and marketability of their products.

Emergence of Civil Society

One of the impressive developments of the last two decades has been the emergence of civil society in national and global affairs. Increased public involvement in forestry and environmental issues is evident in all regions of the globe. Civil society organisations are increasingly spearheading action in support of conservation and sustainable management of forests. As democratisation and decentralisation trends continue worldwide and new technologies improve communication, the 'environment' for successful civil society action improves (FAO, 2002). Though the civil society has emerged from the stage of being the governed, it has not still reached the stage of active interest and involvement in governance. There is need to improve governance mechanisms to permit citizens to have more structured participation in the policy making and management of forests. Institutional changes are taking place worldwide to improve governance mechanisms. This is definitely going to be an important beginning to what will increasingly be recognised as a foundation of 21st century civilisation.

India's Forays into the Field of Sustainability

India has made great dent in the sustainability front. It has great traditions that strengthen the process of establishing an environment conducive to operationalisation of sustainable development. It has taken long strides in the field of sustainable development in the post-Independence era.

India has a great tradition of environmental conservation. It teaches people to respect nature and to take cognisance of the fact that all forms of life — human, animal and plant — are closely interlinked and that disturbance in one gives rise to an imbalance in other's. There were many environmental laws enacted during the last centuries (See Box 6.7). Even in modern times conscious efforts have been made to maintain environmental security along with developmental advances. The Indian Constitution has very robust provisions for matters relating to environmental conservation.

BOX 6.7: LAWS ENACTED DURING LAST CENTURIES

- The Madras Elephant Preservation Act of 1873 and 1879.
- The Nilgiris Game and Fish Preservation Act of 1879.
- The Wild Birds and Game Protection Act of 1887.
- The Wild Birds and Game Protection Act of 1912.
- The Bengal Rhinoceros Preservation Act of 1927.
- The Indian Forest Act, 1927.
- The Punjab Wild Birds and Wild Animals Protection Act of 1933.
- Wildlife (Protection) Act, 1972.
- The Environment (Protection) Act, 1986.
- The Wildlife (Protection) Act, 1972 amended in 1983, 1986 and 1991.
- The Water (Prevention and Control of Pollution) Act, 1974, amended in 1988.
- The Water (Prevention and Control of Pollution) Cess Act, 1977, amended in 1991.
- The Forest (Conservation) Act, 1980, amended in 1988.
- The Air (Prevention and Control of Pollution) Act, 1981, amended in 1988.
- The Motor Vehicle Act, 1938, amended in 1988.
- The Public Liability Insurance Act, 1991.
- A Notification on Coastal Regulation Zone, 1991.

In recognition of the felt need for environmental protection and sustainable management, various regulatory and promotional measures have been taken in India over the past twenty years. A list of institutions and legal instruments relating to forest conservation is given in Box 6.8 and 6.9.

BOX 6.8: LIST OF INSTITUTION RELATING TO FOREST CONSERVATION

- Department of Environment in 1980 and the integrated Ministry of Environment and Forest in 1985, Department of Science and Technology, Department of Agriculture and Cooperation, Department of Biotechnology, Department of Ocean Development, Department of Space. Department of Non-Conventional Energy Sources, Energy Management Center, Council of Scientific and Industrial Research etc. at the Center, Departments of Environment at the State and Union Territory level.
- Central Pollution Control Board and State Pollution Control Boards.
- Central Forest Board.
- Indian Council of Forestry Research and Education with specialised institutions for research in arid zone forestry, moist and deciduous forests, wood technology, genetics and tree breeding and deciduous forests.
- Forest Survey of India (FSI) and the Wildlife Institute of India (WII) in addition to the existing organisations like Botanical Survey of India (BSI) and Zoological Survey of India (ZSI).
- National Land Use and Wasteland Development Council.
- National Wastelands Development Board.
- Indian Board of Wildlife
- National Museum of Natural History, Center for Environmental Education, Institute for Himalayan Environment and Development and Centres of Excellence in specialised areas are among the various institutions set up.

BOX 6.9: LIST OF IMPORTANT MEASURES RELATING TO FOREST CONSERVATION

Conservation and Sustainable Management of Forests and Wildlife

- Adoption of a new Forest Policy (1988) with the principal aim of ensuring ecological balance through conservation of biological diversity, soil and water management, increase of tree cover meeting the requirements of the rural and tribal population, increase in the productivity, efficient utilisation of forest produce, substitutions of wood and people's involvement for achieving these objectives.
- Under the Forest (Conservation) Act, 1980 stringent provisions for preventing diversion of forest land for any other purpose.
- Setting up of the National Wastelands Board to guide and oversee the wastelands development programme by adopting a mission approach for enlisting people's participation, harnessing the inputs of science and technology and achieving interdisciplinary coordination in programme planing and implementation.
- Formulation of a National Wildlife Action Plan.
- An exercise for preparation of National Forest Action Programme.
- Establishment of National Parks and Sanctuaries covering about 4 per cent of the country's area.
- Eco-Development plans for sanctuaries and National parks.
- Identification of biogeographical zones in the country for establishing a network of protected areas including seven Biosphere Reserves set up so far.
- Management Plans for identified wetlands, mangrove areas and coral reefs.
- Formulation of a National River Action Plan.
- Initiation of Joint Forest Management (JFM) programmes in all States/Union territors.

Land and Soil

- Surveys by the All India Soil and Land-Use Survey Organisation.

- Treatment of catchment in selected river valley projects and integrated watershed management projects in catchment of flood prone rivers.
- Assistance to States to control shifting cultivation.
- Assistance for reclamation and development of ravine areas.
- Drought prone areas programme.
- Desert development programme.

Environmental Impact Assessment

- Establishment of procedures for environmental impact assessment and clearance with regard to selected types of projects requiring approval of the Government of India.
- Prior clearance of projects requiring diversion of forests for non-forest purposes under the Forest (Conservation) Act, 1980.
- Formulation of Environmental guidelines for projects in various sectors.

Other Activities

- Eco-Task Forces of ex-servicemen for ecological restoration through afforestation and soil conservation.
- National Environmental Awareness Campaigns for creating environmental awareness through non-governmental Organisations.
- Surveys and research studies.
- Training programmes, workshops and seminars for building up professional competence and for creation of awareness.

Out of the aforesaid actions taken by India, three measures have made definite contribution in creating enabling conditions necessary for building the edifice of sustainable forest management. They are: (1) The constitutional provisions, (2) National Forest Policy–1988, and (3) The National Conservation Strategy and Policy Statement on Environment and Development (1992).

Constitutional Provisions

The Indian Constitution incorporates comprehensive guidelines for the citizen as well as governments with regard to protection of the country's environment. Much of the incorporations date back to 1976 when the 42nd Amendment to the Constitution came into force. These provisions are enshrined in the Directive Principles of State Policy (Part IV) and Fundamental Duties (Part IV A). Part XI of the Constitution deals with the distribution of legislative powers between the Union and States. The three lists in the Seventh Schedule to the Constitution provide details of various subjects of environmental legislation under Article 246 of the Constitution.

Directive Principles of State Policy

The directive principle, constitute, *inter alia*, the major guidelines for the protection of environment. These principles are applied while making laws on the subject. Articles 48A and 49 in Part IV of the Constitution wherein directive principles of State policy are enshrined, provide as follows:

- Article 48A: Protection and improvement of environment and safeguarding of forests and wildlife

  > ***"The State shall endeavour to protect and improve the environment and to safeguard the forests and wildlife of the country."***

- Article 49: Protection of monument and places and objects of national importance.

  > ***"It shall be the obligation of State to protect every monument of place or object of artistic and historic interest and declare it under law by parliament to be of national importance, and protect it from spoliation, disfigurement, destruction, removal, disposal or export, as the case may be."***

Fundamental Duties

Fundamental duties of the citizens of India are enshrined in Part IVA of the Constitution, which provides Article 51A(g). The article asks citizen: "*to protect and improve the natural environment including, lakes, rivers and wild life, and to have compassion for living creature.*"

The National Forest Policy, 1988

The national forest policy declared by the Government of India in

December 1988 is a unique expression of intent on the part of central government to preserve and conserve the precious forest wealth of the country. It recognises poverty to be the main reason of forest loss. Poverty compels people to claim forest land for cultivation as well as to take to axe for domestic fuel which together snowball into a wholesale destruction of forests and biodiversity. The policy document encompasses three parts; (1) the nine basic objectives, (2) essentials of forest management, and (3) the strategies to deal with the problems in different areas of forestry. Of the nine basic objectives governing the National Forest Policy, few important objectives are as follows:

- Maintenance of environmental stability through preservation and where necessary, restoration of the ecological balance that has been adversely disturbed by serious depletion of the forests of the country
- Conserving the natural heritage of the country by preserving the remaining natural forests with vast variety of flora and fauna, which represent the remarkable biological diversity and genetic resource of the country.
- Increasing substantially the forest/tree cover in the country through massive afforestation and social forestry programmes, specially on all denuded, degraded and unproductive lands.
- Creating a massive people's movement with the involvement of women, for achieving these objectives and to minimise pressure on existing forests.

Essentials of Forest Management

The policy objectives are sought to be achieved through recasting of the forest management principles. The major principles concerning conservation of forests and biological diversity, as highlighted in the Policy, are:

- Existing forest lands should be fully protected and their productivity improved. Forest and vegetal cover should be increased rapidly on hill slopes, in catchment areas of rivers, lakes and reservoirs and ocean shores and on semi-arid and desert tracts.
- For the conservation of total biological diversity, the network of national parks, sanctuaries, biosphere reserves and other

protected areas should be strengthened and extended adequately.

- Minor forest produce provides sustenance to tribal population and to other communities residing in and around the forests. Such produce should be protected, improved and their production enhanced with due regard to generation of employment and income.

Strategy

The policy resolves to maintain at least one-third land area of the country under forest or tree cover with a minimum of two-third of the hilly tracts being maintained under such cover in order to ensure stability of the fragile ecosystem. The Policy advocates total preservation of forest cover in the ecologically sensitive areas and to manage such forests only under scientifically prepared and duly approved working plans conforming to the National Forest Policy. It also cautions against production forestry programmes entailing clear felling of adequately stocked natural forests or introduction of exotics unless such introduction is backed by research.

Matters having an indirect but important bearing on biological diversity have also been addressed to in the Policy. As regards rights and concessions available to the people from forests, the Policy states that the extent of their enjoyment should be related to the carrying capacity of forests and that the holders of such rights and concessions should be involved in the protection and development of forests. The Policy stresses the need to recognise domestic requirements of the forest dwellers for fuelwood, fodder, MFP and timber. While stressing on the need to maintain forest cover as a national asset, the Policy advises against indiscriminate diversion of forest land for non-forestry purposes. It also, for the first time, recognises the symbiotic relationship between tribals and forests and emphasises the need to maintain and strengthen tribal culture and economy.

The Policy also emphasises the need to have forest management plans, which adequately safeguard and take special care of wild fauna. In order to maintain genetic continuity between artificially separated sub-sections of migrant wildlife, the Policy stresses on the need to provide for "corridors" linking the protected areas.

Wood substitution, liberal import of wood and restriction on the use of natural forest as raw material for forest based industries are some other areas having a bearing on the biological diversity in natural forests of the country, which have been specially dealt with in the policy.

To sum up, the National Forest Policy is clearly oriented towards preserving the natural heritage of the country. The foresight of the Policy makers can be appreciated from the fact that most of the objectives, principles and strategies of forest management envisioned in the National Forest Policy in 1988, were duly recognised as vital issues of forest management in the Earth Summit held in Rio de Janeiro, Brazil during June, 1999.

BOX 6.10: CRITICAL ELEMENTS OF NCSPSED

The National Conservation Strategy and the Policy Statement on Environment and Development has the following sections:

1. *Environmental problems.* Nature and dimension.
2. *Action taken, in the field of environment.*
3. *Constraints and agenda for action*: Under this section, it is mentioned that "conservation is the key element of the policy for sustainable development. Development requires the use and modification of natural resources, conservation ensures the sustainability of development for the present and future. The conservation strategy aims to serve as a management guide for integrating environment concerns with developmental imperatives."
4. *Priorities and strategies for action*: The priorities and strategies for action are (I) Population control, (II) Conservation of natural resources, like land, water, air, bio-diversity, other bio-mass.
5. *Development policies from environmental perspectives.* The developmental policies from environmental perspectives are: (1) Agriculture and Irrigation, (2) Animal Husbandry, (3) Forestry, (4) Energy generation and use, (5) Industrial Development, (6) Mining and query, (7) Tourism, (8) Transportation, and (9) Human settlement.
6. *International cooperation*
7. *Supply Policies and systems*
8. *Conclusion*

The National Conservation Strategy and Policy Statement on Environment and Development, 1992

Apart from the New Forest Policy (1988), the National Conservation Strategy and Policy Statement on Environment and Development, (1992) is a land mark policy enunciation on the part of India. This latest policy statement embodies the core issues of forest policy, among other aspects pertaining to all sectors having relevance to environment.

In June 1992, the Ministry of Environment and Forest, Government of India, released a policy statement outlining India's National Conservation and Development approach. "Sustainable development" is the key phrase in the agenda for action. The basic aim of the agenda is "to ensure sustainable and equitable use of resources for meeting the basic needs of the present and future generation without causing damage to the environment."

Government of India has already adopted legislative and administrative action in several key areas. Environment is a state subject and forest is in concurrent list. The National Conservation Strategy and the Policy Statement on Environment and Development is in response to the need for laying down the guidelines that will help to weave environmental consideration into the fabric of our national life and development process. It is an expression of our commitment for reorienting policies and action in unison with the environmental perspective (NCSPSED, 1992). Therefore, in order to understand the contours of policy statement pertaining to sustainable development, it is necessary to discuss it threadbare.

However, looking at the limitations of space, the national conservation strategy is discussed very succinctly. The strategy has been designed to ensure survival and well being of the country based on sustainable socio-economic, industrial and other development processes. It classifies environmental problems in the country into two broad categories *viz.*, very process of development and those arising from conditions of poverty and under development, which are inter-related. It enumerates the galloping population, spiraling malnutrition, fast eroding grasslands and pastures, degrading forest cover, biological impoverishment, degradation of wetlands and coastal areas, indiscriminate exploitation of marine ecosystems, global atmospheric changes resulting in altered climatic conditions and atmospheric pollution as the major environmental problems confronting the physical, biological and cultural components of India's environmental system (See Box 6.10).

PART III

SUSTAINABLE FOREST MANAGEMENT: PRINCIPLES AND PRACTICES

PART III

SUSTAINABLE FOREST MANAGEMENT PRINCIPLES AND PRACTICES

7

SUSTAINABLE FOREST MANAGEMENT

Concept, Principles and Objectives

Forests constitute the planet's largest and most important terrestrial ecosystem. They have profound influence on the structure and functions of human habitat locally and globally. They constitute the largest reservoir of plants and animals on the land. They sustain much of world's diversity of life embodying stupendous genetic wealth developed over evolutionary time. They provide innumerable goods and services to human society. They provide the means for their livelihoods as well as succor to millions of people who live close to forests. They affect the quality of atmosphere and temperature regime, which in turn regulate global and local climate. They provide spiritual, aesthetic and symbolic value for millions of people.

Conservation and sustainable development of forests have now emerged as priority area in national and as well as international agenda. But, policy makers face the challenge of reconciling the role of forests in meeting national socio-economic and environmental objectives as well as global environmental interests of the community of nations. Ecological considerations are now viewed not as subordinate but as an integral part of economic policy and planning (Ullesten, 1991). This apart, sustainable forest management is emerging as critical consideration in the international trade of forest products too. Therefore, now it is imperative on every county to adopt and operatianlise sustainable forest development.

Sustainable forest management is the operational part of sustainable forest development. Sustainable development (SD) of forest resources is possible, if they are managed on the basis of sustainability principles. It necessitates an elaborate management system and practices which aim at maximising the achievement of objectives of SD for the benefits of society at large and consolidating them on a sustainable basis. The ensuing chapter deals with the different facet of sustainable forest management. It dwells upon genesis, principles and objectives of sustainable forest management. It delineates contours of current trends in sustainable forest management.

Sustainability in Context

Forests: The Constant Natural Capital

Economic analysis of sustainable development focuses on the concept of 'constant capital'. The idea is the capital stock that ensures the capability of future generations must not be worse off than the current generations. Hence, the capital stock should be held at least constant and preferably growing through time. Growth of capital is especially important if population growth, which lowers capital per capita, is expected to be faster than technological change, which raises productivity of capital.

The concept of constant capital underscores the conventional principles of business profitability. That means the profit or net income should not involve the depreciation of the capital base if the business is to be sustainable. Many authors have discovered a relationship between sustainability, which has been defined as non-declining utility, and the underlying capital stock. There are two schools of thought with respect to constant capital stock. The first school is based on neo-classical economic analysis. It argues that all forms of capital are substitutable. It says that there are three forms of capital stock. The first one is human made capital; second is human capital *i.e.* stock of knowledge and skills, and the third is 'natural capital', which includes renewable and non-renewable. The case of natural capital assumes significance in this context. It is said that a country relying heavily on a non-renewable natural resource such as oil, coal, and soil should reinvest rents from exploitation, which leads to degradation of those resources. This helps the country to maintain the real consumption at a constant rate and resultantly the obligation of inter-generational equity is fulfilled. But in case of forests, there is a peculiarity. The biodiversity is non-renewable and forest as such is renewable to the point of carrying capacity, but beyond it, it is more of non-renewable in nature. Again once the biodiversity is eroded, then renewable base of forest is also degraded. The second school of thought propounded by London School of Economics argues that there is limited substitutability for at least some forms of natural capital. In case, where there is no substitute, natural capital is called as 'critical capital'. Both the schools of thoughts on natural resources hinge on degree of sustainability. Both the approaches emphasise on a host of uncertainties that are germane to the life supporting functions and services of natural capital. The biodiversity is a case in point. If it is lost, it cannot be recovered. So also, the natural forests, if lost, it can not be recovered.

Forest ecosystem, on which the society depends, is an amalgamation of ecological and socio-economic systems. It is an ecological system because it encompasses the components and attributes of an ecosystem. It is part of a socio-economic system because the benefits from forests in the form of goods and services enter into the consumptive basket of the society and dynamics of supply and distribution of goods and services follow the rule of economics to a great extent. Therefore, the forest ecosystem always has a primary goal which aims at maximising the social value of forests without eroding the socially relevant properties of ecosystem.

Socially Relevant Properties of Forest

Forests, apart from their ecological characteristics, have many social values. These values have several measurable components. These components could be their capacity to produce goods and services to satisfy the needs of the society, their distribution among the community and ability to sustain the benefits not only for the present but also for the future. In other words, these components could be described by different ecosystem properties. These properties are:

1. Productivity

Productivity emphasises maximisation of present benefits, both in terms of goods and services. Efficient use of resources is the main focus under productivity. This apart, efficiency must also emphasise on physical, social, economic and ecological front. It is imperative to evolve a trade-off among these sub-components.

2. Equity

It encompasses four main aspects. They are basic needs, equitable distribution, equal accessibility and rational use of resources. The aspect of basic need focuses on the fact that resources have to be used to satisfy basic needs like, fuelwood, minor forest produces, timber before they are used for other purposes. Equitable distribution lays stress on the fact that resources should be distributed among human beneficiaries on an equitable basis. Equal accessibility puts on emphasis on the rights of each members of the present as well as prospective community to access to the resources system. The aspect of rational use of forest resource aims at ensuring that neither the welfare of the people is affected nor it leads to depletion and degradation of the resource base.

The most important aspect is inter-generational and intra-generational equity. Even, in the conceptual level, it is difficult to circumvent the conflicts between the interests of present and future generations. While needs are assessed differently from one society to another and from one country to another in the same generation, how future generation will estimate their needs is well beyond the imagination of the present generation. The issue of intra-generational and inter-generational equity, therefore, remains in the fore front of all discussions relating to sustainable forest management.

3. Sustainability

Sustainability is a principle or value which guides and directs our thinking/decisions today. It is based on the principle that the needs of the present generation should be met without compromising the ability of the future generations to meet their own needs. It encompasses all aspects of productivity and equity in an 'inter-temporal' context. There are three sub-components of sustainability. They are stability, resilience and non-declining natural stock.

Stability symbolises the elements of 'constancy' of capital as well as productivity of the biological production system. In other words, it is the ability of the system to maintain equilibrium in response to normal fluctuations in the environment. Coefficient of variation is the measure of stability. Stability indicates the state of dynamics in an ecosystem. Likewise resilience is the capacity of the biological system to maintain its structures and patterns of behaviour in the face of 'external disturbances' which, with passage of time, emerge as stress and shocks. Thus resilience is the ability of a forest ecosystem to withstand such prospective disturbing forces. Forces of resilience act against forces that try to disturb the system. In such cases, the ecosystems develop their own defense system. Such defense mechanism differs from one ecosystem to another. Non-declining natural capital stocks are those natural resources whose decline affects the productive capacity of the system. Soil, vegetation, water and biodiversity are the natural capital stock, required for ensuring productivity and sustainability of the forests.

4. Resilience

Resilience is a measure of degree or intensity to which a given system can respond to and absorb 'stresses' and 'shocks'. Generally stress appears in a forest ecosystem because of human interventions. These interventions may be in the form of management practices or anthropogenic pressures. The symptoms of stress appear in the form of soil erosion, deforestation and erosion of biodiversity. Such stresses may be frequent, or continuous or discontinuous. But they all built up to impart a cumulative negative effect on the forest ecosystem. Likewise, measure events like, drought, epidemic, flood constitute 'shocks', *i.e.* a force relatively large and unpredictable. On account of such stress or shocks, the productivity of the system declines. That means the forest ecosystem is neither capable to control the external agents nor able to evolve systemic changes to overcome the effects. The system that is unable to respond to such stress or shocks is dubbed as unsustainable. Resilience, therefore, is a necessary condition of sustainability.

Productive capability of the critical natural forest resources lies in 'diversity' of its capital. Biodiversity in the living system acts as 'insurance' against such external agents. In economics it is known as portfolio effect. The uncertainty in sustained production of goods and services from a forest ecosystem is reduced, if we have a varied diversity, like that of varied and large portfolio. As a result, the return to the composite package of renewable natural assets will have reduced variability in comparison with individual components. Retention of greatest possible diversity in a biological resource system will maximise the portfolio effect, thereby assessing the least quantum of risk in biological production system.

These four distinct properties are not mutually exclusive. Each property facilitates the other one. For an example, equity facilitates production and *vice versa*. Likewise, sustainability facilitates productivity and equity. However, forest management aims at maximising 'social benefits'. Therefore, equity and sustainability become the maximising criteria. It means element like equitable distribution, equal accessibility and rational use of benefits/resources maximise the productivity and stability and control natural capital stock. This apart, distribution of benefits of forest production among the poor requires a control and regulation because the capability among the poor people to maximise the 'social welfare' as marginal utility for consumption is very high.

Stretching the same logic to the intra-generational and inter-generational context, there is a need to regulate the direction, accessibility as well as the use of the biological productive system. Therefore, in a context of forest ecosystem which aims at achieving higher social value, the best approach is to strike a trade-off between all the properties. Striking a balance, however, is not an easy task. It requires an enabling and compatible political, social and economic environment.

Sustainable Forest Development

What Does it Mean?

Forest provides social, economic, cultural and environmental benefits to society. In order to maintain this broad spectrum of benefits from forests, it is imperative to adopt a forestry paradigm which is different from the old one. Sustainable development is the developmental paradigm, which, if followed, has the potentiality to deliver the broad spectrum of benefits in the form of goods as well as services.

The World Commission on Environment and Development in 1987 defined "sustainable development" in the following way:

> "Development that meets the needs of the present without compromising the ability of future generations to meet their own needs."

Sustainable development has also been defined by Food and Agricultural organisation as "... the management and conservation of natural resource base and the orientation of technological and institutional change in such manner as to ensure the attainment and continued satisfaction of human needs for the present and future generations. Such sustainable development (in the agriculture, forestry and fisheries sectors) is environmentally non-degrading, technologically "appropriate, economically viable and socially acceptable" (FAO, 1997).

Sustainable development is a new paradigm for the world. It is a term that unfolds basically two concepts: the concept of needs and concept of limits. The needs of the present and future generations must be met with the full use of human ingenuity but within the limits of a stable biosphere. Translating these two concepts into practice shall achieve two critical objectives. These critical objectives are satisfying the basic needs and conserving and enhancing the resource base of the poor (WCED, 1987), with emphasis on both inter-generational and intra-generational equity. So for the sustainable development of forests is concerned, this requires that if we want to benefit from the material goods and services of the forests, it has to be done in a way that does not jeopardise their ecological functions. In other word, sustainable development of forests emphasises on deriving benefits from forests for meeting the basic needs of people as well as protecting and expanding the resource base in an intra-generational and inter-generational framework.

The concept of sustainable development recognises that utilisation of resources is necessary, but that utilisation should be within the carrying capacity of the system. It emphasises that use of forests is important for achieving social goals, such as poverty alleviation. But such uses must take care of the fact that the ability of the future to meet their own needs is not impaired. In other words, the paradigm of development should be based on a trade-off between present and future.

The concept of sustainable forest development takes sustenance from the definitions of SD. It is more concerned with integrated forest management *i.e.* maintaining the ecological integrity of the forest environment, meeting basic needs of the present generation and keeping future options open. This does not imply that ali forests everywhere should be managed for all benefits simultaneously. Keeping in mind the above objectives, forest development can be accomplished by adopting different management practices in different regions.

Sustainable development of forest land and its multiple economic and environmental values involve maintaining indefinitely, without unacceptable impairment, the productive and renewal capacities as well as the species and ecological diversity of forest ecosystems (Maini, 1989). The acceptable threshold of 'unacceptable impairment' is determined by the choices and decisions made by individuals, institutions and nations as well as by the international community. Generally it is based on our present understanding of both ecological and socio-economic principles and imperatives. What is acceptable under a specific socio-economic and ecological condition may be totally unacceptable under another set of condition. Consequently, in order to achieve the avowed objectives, choices and trade-offs are made.

Sustainable forest management is the operational part of sustainable forest development. The process of evolving management approaches to sustainable forest development requires the harmonisation of human activities with the biological and physical aspects of forest ecosystems. Human activities and forest ecosystem as well as the interactions between the two are dynamic and change over time and space. Consequently, monitoring the two systems and their interaction is crucial when practicing sustainable forest development, and it involves a number of ecological, socio-economic, technological and political considerations (Maini, 1991).

While forests are resilient ecosystems, there are limits to their ability to withstand environmental change, and they degrade when these limits are exceeded. Understanding these limits also allows us to enhance various forest outputs through silviculture. This apart, forests are also exposed to environmental stresses associated with other human activities such as industrial manufacturing and the use of fossil fuels. The impacts of some of these stresses are restricted and local, others are global. Therefore, sustainable forest management means recognising these limits of forests to withstand environmental changes, individually and collectively, and in managing human activities to produce the maximum level of benefits obtainable within these limits. A number of parameter may be used to assess the status of forests with regard to individual species and ecosystems (Jordan, 1989; Rapport *et al.*, 1985; Woodwell, 1970).

The Genesis of the Sustainability Concept

The concept of sustainability was first placed on the international agenda by the Brundtland Report in 1987 (WCED, 1987), which defined sustainable development as 'meeting the requirements of present generations without compromising the ability of future generations to meet their own needs'. The concept has received widespread acceptance as an ethically laudable goal with respect to the use of natural resources. Over the years, myriad of definitions have been added to explain the meaning and connotation of sustainable forest management.

In the context of forestry, the concept of sustainability first received international attention in the statement of Forest Principles and Chapter 11 of Agenda 21, which were formulated at the 1992 UN Conference on Environment and Development (UNCED). The Forest Principles, a 'non-legally binding authoritative statement of principles', aimed to 'contribute to the management, conservation and sustainable development of forests' and noted the need for setting relevant standards for forest use.

The importance of considering the needs of future generations while managing a forest resource has in fact been recognised in the ancient past. A definition of sustainability was provided by the German forester Hartig as early as 1804 (Schmutzenhofer, 1992):

> '...to utilise [forest stands] to the greatest possible extent, but still in a way that future generations will have at least as much benefit as the living generation'

These words are clearly echoed in more recent definitions, such as that given by Duerr and Duerr (1975):

> "To fulfill our obligations to our descendants and to stabilise our communities, each generation should sustain its resources at a high level and hand them along undiminished".

This definition implies that there are social and economic aspects to an overall concept of sustainability, within forestry. The concept of sustainability was for many years equated with the principle of sustained yield. But only in the last few decades the concept broadened to include environmental and socio-economic aspects.

Defining Sustainable Forest Management (SFM)

Sustainable forest management is the forestry component of sustainable development. It is about operationalisation of the concept of sustainable development in the realm of forestry. In other words, it is managing forest development in such a way that it is economically viable, environmentally benign and socially beneficial and at the same time, it balances present and future needs. More precisely speaking, sustainable forest management is the process of managing forests to achieve one or more clearly specified objectives of management with regard to the production of a continuous flow of desired forest products and services, without undue reduction of its inherent values and future productivity and without undue undesirable effects on the physical and social environment (ITTO, 1998).

Defining and re-defining sustainable forest management has evolved into a process. With the change in time and societal needs, more and more aspects relating to socio-economic and ecological imperatives are added to precepts of sustainable development day-by-day. This apart, the concept of sustainability and sustainable development is also evolving in the context of prevailing social and economic condition of the society.

All such developmental concepts based on sustainability are integrated into forest management framework. Therefore, the concept of sustainable forest development put in a management framework is called as sustainable forest management.

A number of authors have recently attempted to define sustainable forest management in general terms or certain facets of it. Some of the examples are as follows:

(i) Gale and Cordray (1991) raised the question 'What should forests sustain?' and indicated that the answer varied depending on:

- the maintenance of a dominant product or product mix;
- the sustenance of production capacity;
- the conservation of total forest ecosystems rather than specific components of such ecosystems;
- the maintenance of human systems that are forestry-dependent.

(ii) According to Poore (1993) the sustainable management of forests comprises three components:

- the condition of the forest must not deteriorate irreversibly;
- management of the forest should be environmentally and socially acceptable and economically viable;
- the process of management itself requires that a well defined policy must be in place with the resources and ability available to implement it.

(iii) The definition developed by Poore for the ITTO is as follows (ITTO, 1992):

'Sustainable forest management is the process of managing permanent forest land to achieve one or more clearly specified objectives of management with regard to the production of a continuous flow of desired forest products and services without undue reduction of its inherent values and future productivity and without undue undesirable effects on the physical and social environment'.

(iv) Sustainability may also be viewed in terms of forest functions, which may include products, services and values. At the management unit level, management of a certain forest may be considered to be sustainable when it guarantees the continuity of all recognised principal functions of a particular forest without undue effects on other functions (DBB, 1994).

(v) Heuveldop (1994) defined sustainable forest management as follows:
Sustainable forest management comprises all those direct and indirect measures of protection, tending and utilisation, which ensure the permanent conservation of forests. Sustainable management maintains the natural plasticity and diversity of life forms, which enable forests to evolve and provide human benefits from their ecological, economic, social and cultural functions in perpetuity.

(vi) Upton and Bass (1995) defined sustainable forest management by the three dimensions of sustainability; these dimensions are (1) environmental sustainability, (2) social sustainability, and (3) economic sustainability. These three dimensions are explained below:

Environmental Sustainability

This entails an ecosystem being able to support healthy organisms, whilst maintaining its productivity, adaptability and capability for renewal; it requires that forest management respects and builds on natural processes.

Social Sustainability

This reflects the relationship between development and social norms: an activity is socially sustainable if it conforms with social norms, or does not stretch them beyond a community's tolerance for change.

Economic Sustainability

This requires that benefits to the group(s) in question exceed the costs incurred, and that some form of equivalent capital is handed down from one generation to the next.

(vii) United Nations Commission on Sustainable Development

(UNCSD) has defined Sustainable Forest Management as: management to meet the social, economical, ecological, cultural and spiritual needs of present and future generations. In other words, Sustainable Forest Management (SFM) aims at ensuring that the values derived from the forest meet present-day needs while at the same time ensuring their continued availability and contribution to long-term development needs. The values can be forest products like wood, fruits, etc. and services like soil and water conservation and life supporting services. Forest management involves planning the production of wood for commercial purposes as well as meeting local needs for fuelwood, poles, food, fodder and other purposes. It includes the protection or setting a side of areas to be managed as plant or wildlife reserves, or for recreational or environmental purposes." (FAO, 1993 a). "Sustainable management is considered under the headings of wood conservation, wildlife management, the conservation of biological diversity, forest protection and climate change; policy, institutional and legal aspects, socio-economic aspects and research needs." (FAO, 1994)

The term 'Sustainable Forest Management (SFM)' has been in vogue since Rio Earth Summit in 1992. It is a widely used phrase in political, scientific, environmental, economic and social context. Many perspectives on SFM exist today. Some of the views about broad connotations of SFM are as follows:

- A production of continuous flow of desired forest products without loss of inherent productivity.
- It is all about maintaining and enhancing the ecosystem functions, without entailing production or extraction.
- It is nothing but wise management.

Transition to Sustainable Forest Management (SFM)

Classical Forest Management

Forest management has been defined differently by many authors embodying basic ingredients in different proportion and varying emphasis. Some of the definitions are presented below.

Forest management has been defined as the practical application of the scientific, technical and economic principles of forests. (Anon, 1953.) Over the years forest management assumed an important role in overall forestry. It has been recognised as the branch of forestry whose function is the organisation of a forest property for management and maintenance, by ordering in time and places the various operations necessary for the conservation, protection and improvement of the forest on the one hand, and the controlled harvesting of the forest on the other. In other words, it emphasised on protection, controlled harvesting, especially of wood and their utilisation. It did not lay stress on economic, social and cultural aspects of forestry. However, things changed rapidly in the last two centuries. Forest management assumed wider connotations. All the aspects of sociology, economics, human development, political science, public administration, ecology and management have entered into the domain of forest management. Consequently, the definition of forest management has undergone a drastic change. The FAO definition in the year 1991 is a testimony to this. FAO (1991) defined forest management as dealing with "... the overall administrative, economic, legal, social, technical and scientific aspects involved with the handling of conservation and use of forests. It implies various degrees of deliberate human interventions, ranging from action aimed at safeguarding and maintaining the forest ecosystem and its functions, to favouring socially or economically valuable species or groups of species for the improved production of goods and environmental services".

Defining Scientific Management

Scientific management is the hallmark of forest management in all countries in the world. By definition scientific management is "that kind of management which conducts business or affairs by standards established by facts or truths gained through systematic observation, experiment, or reasoning" (Babcock, 1927). If we go by the history of scientific management, Taylor (1967) in his book 'The Principle of Scientific Management' said that, "The principal object of management should be to secure maximum prosperity of the employer, coupled with the maximum prosperity for the employee". Further Taylor proposed four principles of scientific management, as outlined in Table 7.1. First, the manager should develop a science of every job based on the rules of motion, standardised work tools, and proper working conditions. Second, the manager should select workers with the best possible skills for the specific job. Third, the manager should train these workers to do the job scientifically and to motivate them with piecework incentives. Fourth, the manager should support the workers with good planning and other management practices.

Table 7.1: Taylor's Principle of Scientific Management

Sl. No.	*Taylor's Principle*
1	Develop a science for each job with standardised work implements and efficient methods for all to follow.
2	Scientifically select workers with skills and abilities that match each job, and train them in the most efficient ways to accomplish tasks.
3	Ensure co-operation through incentives and provide the work environment that reinforces optimal work results in a scientific manner.
4	Divide responsibility for managing and for working, while supporting individuals in work groups for what they do best. Some people are more capable of managing, where others are better at performing tasks laid out for them.

Source: Holt, David. *Management Principles and Practices*, 22nd Ed. (Englewood Cliffs, N J.: Prentice Halls, 1990.

Scientific management made a number of contributions to forestry in many countries. The European foresters who initiated scientific management of forestry focussed on: (1) developing a science of every forestry job based on the rules of motion, standardised work tools, and proper working conditions, (2) selecting forest staffs with the best possible skills for the specific job, (3) training these staffs to do the job scientifically and motivating them with appropriate incentives, and (4) supporting the staffs with good planning and other management practices.

However, there are many limitations found in scientific management. First of all, the systematised methods of scientific management have been found to have their applications mainly in structured and stable work environments and have less application in dynamic and complex organisations like forest departments. Secondly, they placed too much emphasis on the so-called rational and economic nature of man, overstating man's desire for money and understanding the desire for social and self-actualisation needs. Finally, they tried to apply universal, management principles to every work situation, without recognising the uniqueness of some work environments.

Defining Sustained Yield

Sustained yield has been an age-old concept of forest management world over. It pertains to production of timber and other measurable forest produce on a sustainable basis. This principle has been accepted as the basis for evolving timber management practices in the past. However, sustained yield has been defined and explained variously by different agencies or authors. Few of such definitions/explanations are as follows:

- *Sustained yield*: (a) The material that a forest can yield annually or periodically in perpetuity. (b) As applied to policy, method or plan of management, it implies continuous production with the aim of achieving at the earliest practical time at the highest practical level an approximate balance between net worth and harvest by annual or some what longer periods" (Anon, 1957).
- "The regular, continuous supply of the desired produce to the full capacity of the forest".
- "The yield of timber or other forest produce from a forest which is managed in such a may as to permit the removal of approximately equal volume or quantity of timber or other forest produce annually or periodically in perpetuity".

The concept of sustained yield has been evolved from the basic consideration that the later generations may derive from the forest at least as much of the benefits as the present generation. The principle of sustained yield envisages that a forest should be so exploited that the annual or periodic felling does not exceed the annual or periodic growth, as the case may be (Ram Prakash, 1979).

The Concept of Normalcy

Normalcy has been an old concept of forestry. It symbolises sustained yield of timber from forests. However, the concept has been subjected to a plethora of interpretations all over the world. Normalcy or normality, in general forestry parlance, implies a regular distribution of same variable associated with the production of timber. In forestry practice, normality aims at sustained production of wood from a forest management unit (FMU). In other words, it implies an equal annual production of wood from the unit of the forest. However, the doctrine of normalcy can be extended, as has been done by many foresters, to such concepts like normality of production unit *i.e.* growing stock or normality of wood production as a whole, normality of production by species or size classes, normality of annual revenue, normality of annual production of wood and non-wood products and services. However, interpretation and definition of normality has undergone a progressive change over the time on account of changing perspective on forests and their ecological overtones.

Foresters belief that if a forest is irregular and abnormal in its stand composition, it can be steered towards normalcy with the help of management practices. In the past, there have been many efforts to reach normalcy by resorting to different management regimes. Despite the preoccupation with normality in forestry, it is a curious thing that it has seldom been achieved, although considerable financial sacrifices have been made in efforts to improve the age class distribution or to balance the annual production in one sense or other (Johnston, D.R., *et al.*, 1978). Therefore, no part of the globe has ever witnessed normalcy in any point of time in the history.

The causative factor that led to the evolution of this concept of normality or normalcy is attributable to the history of forest management in Europe in the seventeenth and eighteenth centuries. During this period, there occurred widespread destruction of forests on account of increasing population and local industries, such as glass making and iron smelting. Such industries depended upon continuing local supplies because in that age it was impossible to transport wood for a long distance over the land. In the face of over cutting and destruction, the first concern of forest managers was to conserve and rationalise supplies so that forests could be regenerated and made continuously productive (Johnston, D.R., *et al.*, 1978). In many tropical countries, the concept of sustained yield in the beginning of this century was based on long conversion periods or rotations fixed on the basis of maximum mean annual increment (MAI) of various timber species. Since 1950, the economic forces have constantly been compelling the foresters in India to reduce the conversion/rotation periods and not to base decision purely on MAI. (Pant, M. M., 1977).

Increased emphasis on aspects like 'Utilisation of forest produce' in the forest management plans bears testimony to the fact that the influence of market on the forest management was on a steady rise. In old management plans, it has been found that there is a gradual decrease in conversion period or rotation of the crop in each revision of the plan. This resulted into increase in areas of forests for felling and numbers of trees leading to higher production. The need to such as act might have been arisen on account of pressure for increasing the revenue or improving the falling yield in comparison to the last plan. Besides, the trend for timber production, during those olden days, was a response to market demand. Over and above, the concept of sustained yield evolved with an objective to maximise timber production from forests.

Normality is a concept, which has gone through a process of radical alternation. Initially, it evolved as a response to the needs of the market, rather than the ecological compulsion of forests. The factors like cost of production, transportation of wood to industry and market conditions played major role in shaping the concept. With the change in government policies in many countries, depletion of forest resources, and increasing valuation of forests, the concept has evolved into a holistic perspective. The concept then transcended the traditional boundary of definition to encompass the principles of non-wood and other ecological services of forests. Such benefits include wood, nón-wood forest products and life supporting services. Considered in the present context, normality can be deemed to have evolved into the present concept of 'sustainable benefits – economic, social, political, and ecological – from the forests'. Therefore, practice of doctrine of 'sustained yield' is becoming increasingly synonymous with sustainable benefits of forests.

The Transition to SFM

The transition from sustained yield management for wood to sustainable forest management in a broader sense is now the main challenge. It is, as some says, an impossibility (Jacob, 1988). There is no gainsaying of the fact that SFM for wood is an uphill task. In this context the task of combining and synchronising not only sustainable yield of wood with the unimpaired production and protection of the many other non-wood forest products, but also services and values of forests on a holistic basis is the most daunting and challenging job today.

United Nations Commission on Sustainable Development (UNCSD) has defined Sustainable Forest Management as: management to meet the social, economical, ecological, cultural and spiritual needs of present and future generations. In other words, Sustainable Forest Management (SFM) aims at ensuring that the values derived from the forest meet present-day needs while at the same time ensuring their continued availability and contribution to long-term development needs. The values can be forest products like wood, fruits, etc. and services like soil and water conservation and life supporting services. Forest management involves planning the production of wood for commercial purposes as well as meeting local needs for fuelwood, poles, food, fodder and other purposes. It includes the protection or setting aside of areas to be managed as plant or wildlife reserves, or for recreational or environmental purposes" (FAO, 1993 a).

In sustainable forest management, timber production should not be the sole aim and that the sustained provision of a wide range of environmental, social, cultural and economic needs must be included. In the past system of working, the gap between sustained yield for wood and multipurpose sustainability in forest management was glaring. The science and practice of forestry is largely simultaneous conservation and use of forests for the welfare and development of human societies. The difficulties arise mainly from attempts to combine conservation with potentially destructive uses. Using forest for wood productions only is potentially the most destructive uses of forests.

However, wood is the most important product of the forests. The sustainable management of forests for wood production is based on the simple principle that harvesting the wood should be done at an average annual rate that is no greater than at which the forest in question can grow it and without harming the forest's capacity to supply other goods and services. Elucidating this principle is easy, but the problem lies in its application. The increment being physically inseparable from the trees, with which it is produced, must be harvested by felling a part of the forest equal in amount. Here lies the complexity of sustainable management.

Determination of annual wood increment and identification of appropriate part of the crop to be felled as equivalent of increment on the first two elements of sustained wood production. The two elements have been taken care of in the past. The practice continues today also. The third element is concerned with regeneration or silvicultural part. This has gone beyond the control of the present system of management. The fourth is the harvesting or using the forest. In practice, it is not easy to devise measure, apply or monitor any one of these, and the difficulties are compounded because all elements have to work together and simultaneously. The difficulties increase with the ecological and structural complexity of the forests to be managed and their economic and social environment (Janzen, 1975).

Sustainable forest management encompasses an array of objectives and activities whose significance changes with the change in socio-economic and political environment. These activities are as follows:

- The production of wood on a sustained basis.
- Conservation and harvesting of Non-Wood Forest Products (NWFP and other genetic resources on sustainable basis).
- Meeting local needs for fuelwood, poles, food, fodder and other purposes.
- The protection or setting aside of areas to be managed as Protected Areas (PAs) or plant or wildlife reserves or for recreational or environmental purposes.
- Regeneration of wastelands and degraded forests.

Over the year, it was felt that SFM, apart from the aforesaid activities, should include two other aspects like maintaining ecosystem integrity and well being of the local people. It is a well recognised fact that in order to make forest resources sustainable, it is indispensable that the aforesaid objectives are fulfilled and suitable activities are carried out not only to maintain or improve the ecological integrity but also to contribute to people's well being both now and in future. Ecosystem integrity has been defined as the ability to support and maintain a balanced, integrated, adaptive biological community having a species composition, diversity and functional organisation, comparable to that of natural habitat in the region (Schneider, 1992). Likewise, well being encompasses the economic, social and cultural aspects of people's lives as influenced by forest management. Therefore, apart from carrying on activities or determining objectives for forest management, it is necessary to ensure that two conditions are satisfied. These conditions are: (1) ecosystem integrity is maintained now and in the future, (2) well being of people is maintained or enhanced now and in future.

Objectives of Sustainable Management

Sustainable forest management necessitates integration of environmental, social and economic dimensions of forests into policies and practices for utilising and managing forests, so that economic and social needs are met while leaving forests capable of fulfilling their environmental functions enduring (WCFCD, 1999). There is no gainsaying of the fact that many of the root causes of forest decline originate outside the technical realm of forestry. The effect of population growth on the forest resources and consequent pressure on forest land for agriculture and timber production indicate that the causes of forest decline lie in the policy and practice undertaken for development of society. Therefore, it is necessary to understand that solutions to most of the forest problem lie in areas beyond the scope of forest management and traditional forest sector operations. Nevertheless, it is also necessary that approaches to forest management adjust to the needs of ecological improvement in the forest ecosystem. Therefore, we need to be certain that within the forestry sector itself, all the possibilities for sustainable forest management are explored and reflected in management practices. Forests being renewable should be capable of providing their services in perpetuity. But, forest land are finite, and whether the forests renew themselves or not depend upon how we affect their resilience. The sustainable forest management practice should address these areas.

Traditional forest management was supposed to be based on managing forests for a combination of forest values, but timber and other tangible products and profits derived from these have dominated. Sustainable forest management reflects a shift towards forest practices that have a stronger ecological and social focus compared to the past. It requires integrating concerns for economic and ecological viability of forests, while ensuring that their use and management contribute to the social objectives of societies. In order to secure this range of economic, ecological, social and political values, sustainable forest management must reflect the following objectives.

- To indefinitely satisfy needs for timber, and non-timber forest products.
- To ensure conservation of soil and water.
- To sustain the resilience and renewal capacity of forests.
- To support the food security and livelihood needs of marginalised communities that are dependent on forests.
- To conserve biological diversity.
- To strive and realise a more equitable sharing of benefits from the uses to which forests are put.
- To organise management, cultivation, harvesting and utilisation of Non-Wood Forest Products (NWFP) as mainstream practices of forest management to sustain livelihoods.
- To reduce industrial pollution which is inimical both to soil and atmosphere, affecting the forests and biodiversity.
- To manage effluents that have serious degrading effects on forest ecosystem.
- To secure traditional rights of the millions of people living in villages near forest areas as a means to promote conservation.

- To achieve all the above objectives which are compatible with the incremental productive capacity of forests and the requirements of ecological security.

Essentials of Sustainable Forest Management

Sustainable forest management is still an evolving concept. Situation in any country cannot be equated to another one. The social, cultural, economic, political and cultural factors, which provide the bedrock on which forests are managed, differ from country to country. Therefore, it is very difficult to delineate universal essentials, which will govern sustainable forest management. However, assuming a combination of circumstances, an attempt has been made at Helsinki in 1993 to hammer out a set of essentials on the basis of definitions and general criteria of sustainable forest management. The following are few important essentials of SFM:

- It is an integral part of sustainable development process.
- Forest resources should be maintained and enhanced for the health and vitality of forest ecosystems as well for global carbon balance.
- Forest should be tended for the biological diversity of forest ecosystems and to advance the socio-economic functions and conditions of forests.
- Wood and non-wood productive functions of forests should be encouraged.
- Integrated ecosystem approach.
- Sustainable use and non-destructive harvesting practices.
- Synchronisation of wood and non-wood products.
- In-situ and ex-situ conservation and propagation.
- Backward and forward linkages between stages in sustainable use.
- Managing the forest resources on a sustainable basis with the help of well-defined criteria and indicators (C&I).
- It requires long-term commitment and adequate arrangements for its execution and for co-operation on all types of forests at global, national, regional and local level.

The sustainable forest development recognises three critical parameters: productive capacity, renewal capacity and species and ecological diversity.

Productivity Capacity

Productive capacity is a function of the number of species and individual trees growing on specific location, soil fertility status, species and climate. In addition to soils, forest biomes constitute an important reservoir of the total nutrients of a given forest land. Removal of forest biomes through harvesting may represent a net loss of nutrients from a site during the rotation period.

Renewal Capacity

Renewal of a forest ecosystem, following a harvest or other forms of disturbances, is dependent on the nature and intensity of disturbances and the mode of reproduction of species located on the site. Under many tropical conditions, forest revegetation by seed or vegetative means is rapid and is completed with in a few months with high species diversity (Lamb, 1990). Depending on management objectives, it is important to maintain the ecological process of forests renewed by appropriate natural and artificial regeneration.

The sensitivity of forest ecosystems to stress is determined by the type of forest ecosystem, *i.e.* resilient or fragile, and by the form of stress, *i.e.* type, duration and intensity. Forests, which work under stress beyond their tolerance limits, if subjected to recovery, witness three levels of pattern. The recovery patterns are as follows:

- *Self renewal*: At moderate level of degradation, following the withdrawal of the stress factor, forest ecosystems are able to renew themselves, returning to relatively quickly without human intervention to more or less original state.
- *Rehabilitation*: At an intermediate level of degradation, the forest ecosystem may require long periods to recover naturally, but this period often may be shortened through positive human intervention.
- *Restoration*: At certain level, forest degradation becomes virtually irreversible, at least with in a human time frame, and is characterised by a combination of total or near total loss of forest cover (*i.e.* deforestation) and species diversity as well as soil degradation and consequent reduction in the overall productive capacity of the site. In such an extreme situation, the recovery process may take centuries as a result of natural processes, or decades with positive

human intervention. While it would be impossible to recreate the 'original natural' state of the forest, it may be possible to create forest plantation consisting of multiple strata and diverse species, and providing an ecological semblance of natural forest.

Species and Ecological Diversity

Forests constitute the rich repository of planet Earth's genetic heritage. Tropical forests contain more than 50 per cent of all plant and animal species in about 6 per cent of the world's surface area (Poore and Sayer, 1991). The species diversity apparently decreases towards the higher latitudes, as compared to the tropical forests, composed of hundreds of trees species. Species diversity and ecological diversity are closely related and their preservation is an integral component of efforts to maintain future options (Maini, 1991).

Principles of Sustainable Forest Management

There are certain principles, which govern sustainable forest management. These principles are complex, varied and multidisciplinary in nature. They pertain to disciplines like ecology, sociology, public administration, economics and management. They are not well defined but have wide implication in natural resource management. Being interdisciplinary in nature, it is very difficult to define any facets of such principle within their broad framework. However, an attempt has been made to lay bare certain broad principles that govern sustainable forest management.

1. Holistic Landscape Management

The earth's natural resource base is finite. It has a definite carrying capacity. Use of natural resource beyond the threshold limit leads to impairment of the resource base. Therefore, there is a 'limit to growth' with respect to use of natural resources. Forest is an inalienable component of the earth's natural resource.

With escalating human demand on a shrinking natural resource base, it is vital to ensure that planning for meeting human demand takes all aspects of the landscape together in totality. In other words, to deal with the range of essential needs, to integrate economic, environment, and social aspects of development, and to anticipate and deal with the feedback from one sector to another, we require a form of planning which takes all aspects of the landscape together in totality. Managing forests for sustainability must emerge from such considerations and fit in within a broader approach to planning for and managing the overall landscape. A process of planning must lead to identification of how the requirement of forests for conservation and of community for basic needs without entailing the future generation's potentiality to get at least same quantum of social welfare can be met. This method of planning must be conducted in conjunction with the context of other natural resources in the ecosystem. In other words, the planning should encompass all aspects of natural resource management in such a way that the execution of plan leads to increase in natural capital, including forest. Therefore, there is a need to embark on a pattern of holistic planning of the landscape, in which forest is a vital component.

BOX 7.1: REQUIREMENTS OF LANDSCAPE PLANNING

Three elements of planning are essential for environmentally sound and socially acceptable forest management:

- That areas of forest to provide for all these uses should be set in wider, national or bio-regional, land-use context which provides adequately for all of them in suitable locations;
- That forests should be available to meet the various needs of society; and
- That each areas of forest is carefully managed for the purpose for which it is suited and intended.

The exact details will very greatly from country according to the area and nature of its forests, its population density, its state of development and many other conditions. This pattern should retain or even enhance the 'potential' of forests and give them the flexibility to respond to changing conditions whether social, economic or ecological. The best use of a forest cannot be considered in isolation. For example, forest plantations play an important part in producing timber and may thereby reduce pressures on natural forests; if established on degraded lands they may also increase biological diversity. In general, planning for agricultural expansion, for new settlements and for roads should take into account the possible effects of these developments on adjacent forests.

Source: World Bank, 1998.

2. Ecosystem Management

Ecosystem management is all about managing the forest resources on purely ecological criteria. It involves ecological site classification that identifies ecologically significant variations in climate, soil vegetation and ecosystem functions, across the landscape. Site-specific management objectives and practices are then developed for the ecologically distinct portion of the landscape. The objective and practices of such management patterns are consistent not only with the necessities of ecology and the individual landscape units but also with imperatives of the forest management.

Ecosystem management is also concerned with pattern and rate of harvest of forest products in the forest, effect of such operations on watershed and downstream rivers and rivulets, wildlife habitat and all such physical and functional component of the ecosystem. No single set of prescription will be appropriate to all contexts. Retention of large dead tree and decomposing log as habitat for small mammals, amphibians and other organisms and removal of less wood per hectare during the time of harvest in order to maintain site productivity, carbon storage and organic resource status in the forest soil, are some of the examples of strategy for ecosystem management.

The important ecological aspects behind such management are limiting factors, homeostasis, dynamism, resilience and carrying capacity of the ecosystem. In the context of ecosystem management, it is important to understand the relevance of such aspects.

To begin with, in an ecosystem, various environmental factors like light, temperature, humidity, wind speed, availability of food, nutrients etc., keep changing. These changes affect the well being and survival of the organism in an ecosystem as they can thrive only if all factors essential for life are available. These environmental factors then become a limiting factor for the plant's growth and survival. There are two laws, which explain the organism's response to these environmental changes.

- *The Law of Minimum*: This law states that the growth and well being of an organism is ultimately regulated by that environmental factors which are in its lowest supply relative to what is required. The most deficient resource is, therefore, called the limiting factor.
- *The Law of Tolerance*: This law states that for each physical factors in the environment, a minimum and maximum limit

exists. This limit is called tolerance limit, beyond which the organism does not thrive or survive. In other words, either too little or too much of any required factor like food, energy, heat, vitamins, minerals, water or oxygen threatens the survival of organisms and even the entire species.

Ecosystem is a dynamic system. All the components of the ecosystems are operationally inseparable. They interact with each other on a continuous basis to form a functional unit. This initiates a vital process of production, consumption and decomposition in a functional unit. There is inherent functional and structural harmony among all the components in the ecosystem. Apart from harmony, each ecosystem has the capacity for self-maintenance and self-regulation. In other words, the ecosystem has an in-built system of internal control. Nevertheless, with the increase in human intervention in the resource use system, there is an attempt to disrupt the natural control system and to substitute artificial mechanisms with natural mechanisms. But, every biological system, to a great extent, resists change and remains in a state of equilibrium or homeostasis. Homeostasis means inherent capacity of a system to revert to its normal state after a period of perturbation. The homeostatic mechanisms are established in the ecosystems after a protracted period of evolutionary process.

A homeostatic mechanism exists at different levels of biological organisation. Besides, there is an equilibrium between living things and the environment. This homeostatic mechanism has the propensity to resist any change to a great extent. These mechanisms at structural and functional levels symbolise 'balance of nature'. However, beyond a limit, the homeostasis mechanisms or the equilibrium system collapses. Violent interventions of man into the 'nature's system of production, consumption and decomposition not only weaken the homeostatic mechanisms but also accelerate the resource use beyond the upper limit that environment imposes on the production system itself.

The capacity of the living community to recover from any kind of disturbance is known as resilience. In nature, the physical environment poses continuous challenges to the life forms with disturbance of various kinds. Apart from the natural disturbance, the human factor also inflicts major disruptions in the communities. The recovery of the communities to its original state after a span of time reflects the community's resilience, *i.e.* inherent tendency and capacity of the community to attain a dynamic equilibrium. In ecological parlance, homeostasis is in-built in community resilience.

The concept of carrying capacity has strong relevance to ecosystem management. It aims at explaining the upper limit of resource utilisation in an ecosystem. It denotes the maximum limit of use of resource imposed by the environment. In other words, carrying capacity is the threshold limit of any human activity beyond which physical capacity is diminished and ecological capacity is degraded. The knowledge about carrying capacity is necessary for scientific planning and management of natural resource use. This concept has been widely accepted in principle but difficulties in measuring the thresholds have restricted its operationalisation. A blend of factors relating physical and ecological capacity, along with existing social realities, helps to determine the optimum carrying capacity for any resource.

In human environment, carrying capacity is primarily influenced by the following factors:

- Level of science and technology
- Institutional innovations
- Increasing hopes and aspirations of the people for better standard of life.

In any ecosystem, the carrying capacity depends on the available resources and the ability of the system to cope with the residual waste. The conceptual model of carrying capacity comprises:

- *Supportive Capacity*: This symbolises the ability of the ecosystem to allow withdrawal of resources like raw materials, water, infrastructure, without causing permanent damage to the environment.
- *Assimilative Capacity*: This symbolises the ability to absorb without ill effects, a certain amount of wastes.

Carrying capacity of a region is described as the number of persons that can be supported by a unit area of land while assimilating the wastes. The human population has shown manifold increase, which necessitated an ever-increasing demand on resources. The propensities of the societies to over-consume the critical resources lead to depletions of the productive resources *i.e.* the base itself. This phenomenon is synonymous with ecological equivalent of deficit financing. Likewise, the assimilative capacity can absorb wastes, to some extent but cannot regenerate the land productivity or recover the ecosystem functioning, or replenish the water regimes or restore the lost biodiversity. However, the carrying capacity is subject to change. The expansion of ecological boundaries of carrying capacity is possible in consequence to natural evolutionary forces transforming both physical resources and composition of life forms. But the pace of evolutionary process is so slow and the forces acting on the ecosystem is so negative that it is unthinkable to expect a positive change in the carrying capacity of the system. Nevertheless, a progressive change in the carrying capacity can occur as a consequence to advancement in human society. This is possible if we introduce new eco-friendly technology, bring institutional innovations, and enunciate appropriate government policy.

3. Participatory Management

Sustainable forest management transcends beyond the domain of technical forestry. Therefore, the task of managing the forest sustainbly involves myriad issues like betterment of human condition, social equity, poverty reduction, gender roles, and governance structure. Such issues lie at the heart of the forest crisis and conflicts. Addressing these human issues requires the participation of a broad spectrum of people who live near and interact with the forest, in the process of forest planning and management.

In order to embark on participatory management, there is a need to put in place a proper governance mechanism to open up the decision-making process and involve not only community affected by forest use but also civil society which expresses concern for their management. Improved participation in decision-making in the field of forest use and management will not itself deliver the goods, but it is definitely the cornerstone for sustainable development. In other words, it is a prerequisite for more effective community participation in sustainable forest management practices.

4. Maximisation of Agro-forestry Potential

One of the main reasons for forest degradation is mounting pressure on forest products like timber, fuelwood and fodder. In the time to come, scarcity of such products will be a big challenge all over the globe. The population, especially in the developing countries is increasing at an alarming rate. On account of rising demand of food and urbanisation, diversion of non-forest land to forest growing is also not a practical proposition. Therefore, the only solution to the problem lies in harnessing the agro-forestry potentials of the country.

With the degradation and disappearance of common property resources, farmers have sought to shift the production of timber and tree products into their own land by protecting, planting, and managing trees of selected species alongside their normal agricultural activities. Many farmers depend on their own tree resources for their own fuel and timber requirement. Recently, the process of adding trees to farming systems has been accelerated by the growing commoditisation of fuelwood and other tree products and consequent emergence of growing trees as a cash crop. Such a practice of on-farm tree cultivation has picked up in many parts of Asia and Africa. The practice of agro-forestry is well entrenched in the culture and social milieu of such region.

The types of systems used are consequently diverse and complex. The main agro-forestry systems that are being adopted in such regions can be categorised as:

- Agro-silvicultural (crops and trees)
- Silvipastoral (trees and pasture/animals)
- Agro-silvipastoral (crops, trees and pasture/animals)

Agro-forestry holds considerable potential as a major land management alternative for conserving the soil and maintaining soil fertility and productivity of land use system. There is now a wealth of scientific information to indicate that agro-forestry farming system incorporating trees and medicinal herbs/plants makes a significant contribution to maintaining and improving the fertility and overall productivity of the soil. Resultantly, it helps to increase the productivity of agriculture, generate rural incomes and benefits and maintain forests on a sustainable basis.

5. Verifying Sustainable Forest Management

Sustainable management practices necessitate periodical verification. Therefore, it is imperative to develop methods, process and frameworks for measuring and verifying sustainability. Such methods, process and frameworks have been useful in catalyzing effort and commitment towards sustainable forest management. They aim at operationalising the process of verifying SFM by establishing principles, criteria, and indicators and developing mechanism for its certification.

Criterion describes a state or situation, which should be met to comply with sustainable forest management. Indicator is a quantitative, qualitative or descriptive attribute that, when periodically measured or monitored, indicates the direction of change. Criteria and indicators for sustainable forest management are still in the process of their evolution. Presently, it is at a slower pace. It has began with economic criterion and slightly moved towards incorporating the ecological and social dimension of sustainability. Generally speaking, it is the social issues including participatory management, which are most difficult to grapple with. The measurement process throws many challenges. As the forest types changes, there will be a change in ecological criterion and indicators. Further, criterion and indicators encompass both quantitative and qualitative aspects. Such aspects have to be context specific including social dimensions like equality, gender roles, women empowerment, etc.

ITTO guidelines for the sustainable forest management of natural tropical forests (1992) have specified criteria and indicators (C&I). Seven criteria have been identified as essential elements of sustainable forest management. These seven criteria are as follows:

- Criterion 1:Enabling conditions for sustainable forest management.
- Criterion 2: Forest resource security.
- Criterion 3: Forest ecosystem health and condition.
- Criterion 4: Flow of forest produce.
- Criterion 5: Biological diversity.
- Criterion 6: Soil and water conservation.
- Criterion 7: Economic, soil and cultural aspects.

Different indicators have been identified and formulated under each criterion so that a change in any one of them would give information that is necessary to assess the progress towards sustainable forest management. However, these indicators are more of preliminary and indicative in nature rather than exhaustive. Again, looking at the changing needs of forest management practices in specific area, a different set of criteria and indicators (C&I), which are able to measure the effects of sustainable forest management, can be formulated.

Criterion 1: Enabling Conditions for Sustainable Forest Management

This criterion covers the general institutional requirements for sustainable forest management to succeed. It addresses policy, legislation, economic conditions, incentives, research, education, training and mechanism for consultation and participation. Many of the indicators are descriptive. Taken together, the information gathered indicates the extent of country's political commitment to sustainable forest management.

Criterion 2: Forest Resource Security

This criterion relates to the extent to which a country has a secure and stable forest estate, which could include plantations, to meet the production, protection, biodiversity conservation and other social, cultural, economic and environmental needs of present and future generations. This is necessary for long-term sustainable forest management.

Criterion 3: Forest Ecosystem Health and Condition

The criterion relates to the condition of a country's forests and the healthy biological functioning of forest ecosystems. Forest condition and health can be affected by a variety of human actions and natural occurrences, from air pollution, fire, flooding and storms to insects and disease.

Criterion 4: Flow of Forest Produce

The criterion is concerned with forest management for the production of wood and non-wood forest products. Such production can be sustained in the long-tem if it is economically and financially viable, environmentally sound and socially acceptable.

Forests earmarked for production are able to fulfil a number of other important forest functions, such as environmental protection and conservation of biological diversity. These multiple roles of forest should be safeguarded by the application of sound management practices that maintain the potential of the forest resources to generate the full range of benefits for the society.

Criterion 5 Biological Diversity

This criterion relates to the conservation and maintenance of biological diversity, including ecosystem, species and genetic diversity. At the species level, special attention should be given to the protection of endangered, rare and threatened species. The establishment and management of geographic system of protected areas of representative forest ecosystems can contribute to maintaining biodiversity. Biological diversity can also be conserved in forests managed for other purposes, such as for production, through the application of appropriate management practices.

Criterion 6: Soil and Water

This criterion deals with the protection of soil and water in the forest. The importance of this is two folds. First, it has a bearing on maintaining the productivity and quality of forest and related aquatic ecosystems. Secondly, it also plays a crucial role outside the forest in maintaining downstream water quality and flow and in reducing flooding and sedimentation. The environmental and social effects of mismanagement (landslides, flooding, water pollution) can be enormous. National level data for indicators will normally be derived from the aggregation of data collected at the forest management unit level. Extent of protection: (1) extent and percentage of total forest area managed primarily for the protection of soil and water, (2) extent and percentage of area to be harvested for which off-site catchment values have been defined, documented and protected before harvesting.

Criterion 7: Economic, Social and Cultural Aspects

This criterion deals with the economic, social and cultural aspects of the forest, besides those mentioned under criteria 4, 5 and 6. As a renewable resource, the forest has the potential, if sustainably managed, to make an important contribution to the sustainable development of the country.

Broadening the Scope of Sustainable Management

The general scope of the sustainable forest management has broadened. Stable economic growth is possible when the development paradigm is based on principles of environmental, social and cultural sustainability. People are increasingly aware of this fact. Public support for sustainable development is gaining momentum in every nook and corner of the world. There is an irrepressible desire among communities to pass on the legacy of welfare and well being from one generation to another.

Sustainable forest management is not confined to implementing different elements and specific programme. It is now required to address the complex question of balancing a myriad of objectives or interests. It necessitates balancing of following interests/objectives:

- Private and public interests.
- Socio-economic and environmental needs.
- Present and future generation's needs.
- Timber and non-timber forest products needs.
- Human and animal rights.
- Interests of poor people and rich people.

Current Trends in Sustainable Forest Management

Significant changes in forest management practices have taken place worldwide. National priorities and international commitments with relation to forest management have changed in response to the call given in United Nations Conference on Environment and Development (UNCED) in 1992. A broader approach to forest management has been evolved in most of the countries, balancing social, economic, and environmental objectives. The concerns of a wider range of interest groups are being taken into consideration, and local communities are increasingly becoming directly involved in forest planning and management practices. Some of the important changes in the field of sustainable forest management are enumerated below.

- There is an increased emphasis on environmental values in forest management. This has resulted into significant expansion of protected areas system in many countries over the past few years.
- There is greater emphasis on management of natural forests for multiple purposes.
- There are changes in the field of forest policy, legislation and institutional environment and framework.
- There is an increased attention to environmental protection, conservation of biological diversity and eco-tourism. This apart, distinct focus has been laid on forest plantation and exploration of other sources of wood supply in some countries. This has led to reduced intensity of timber harvesting in natural forest and changes in management practices. Even in some countries logging has been banned.
- There is an increased visible effort to improve the stewardship

of forest designated for wood production. This encompasses silvicultural improvement, adoption of environmentally sound timber harvesting practices, formulation of operational guidelines and codes of practice for forest management in countries of Europe, North America and few countries of Asia. New silvicultural systems have been developed for temperate and boreal forests in North America and for tropical forests. Codes of practices and guidelines for forest harvesting have recently been drafted for tropical forest, most notably in Asia and the pacific region.

- There are many countries that have adopted operational guidelines and code of practices for forest management.
- There is a changing pattern of forest ownership in many parts of the globe. Firstly, greater participation of the private sector in forest management has taken place. Secondly, changes are taking place leading to increased local community participation in forest management.

Current trends in the field of SFM are presented below:

1. Forest Management Objectives and Practices

Forest management objectives and practices have changed drastically in many countries. There is an increased emphasis on environmental values of forests. As a result, there has been a significant expansion of protected forests in some countries over the past few years. What is more important is the fact that greater emphasis on management of forest for multiple purposes and increased attention to environmental factors have led to reduced intensities in timber harvesting and establishment of low-impact forest management practices. Owing to increased emphasis on the use of natural forests for environmental protection, there is increased focus on conservation of biological diversity and eco-tourism. This apart, more reliance is being laid on plantation for wood supply.

2. Forest Management Code

Operational guidelines and codes of practice for forest management have been adopted in Europe and North America. New silvicultural systems have been developed for temperate and boreal forests in North America and for tropical forests. Codes of forests, most notably in the Asia and the pacific region have been put on practice (FAO, 1999). Visible changes in forest ownership are emerging. Grater participation of private sector in forest management has been witnessed in many countries. Local communities are being increasingly given responsibilities for forest planning and management practices. Changes leading to increased local forest management in various countries include:

- A proliferation of new mechanisms for the devolution of forest management to local communities or user groups.
- Increased recognition of the claims of indigenous people for use of the forest resource.
- Restoration of lands including forest lands of underprivileged communities.

3. Emphasis on Social and Environmental Services

Emphasis on social and environmental services of forests has increased manifold. More focus is being laid on mountains, dry lands and small Island and low forest cover countries, as they symbolise fragile ecosystems in different parts of the globe. Environmental and social functions of such forests are being increasingly recognised in forest management practices worldwide. Role of forests in conservation of water has been highly recognised, since there has been a great crisis of fresh water worldwide. This apart, uses of forest as a social security system has also emerged prominently. The role of forest in mitigating global climate change has also received unprecedented prominence with the adoption of the Kyoto Protocol of the framework Convention on Climate Change in 1997. These roles, along with the ecological role, shall gain unprecedented prominence in the near future.

4. Changes in Forest Product Sector

In the forest product sector, there have been a lot of changes. The most significant is the effort to meet the needs for wood and non-wood forest products along with fulfilling demands for environmental and social services from forests. Increased importance is being attached to non-wood forest products (NWFPs), whose main importance currently lies in their contribution to household and local economies, particularly among the poor in developing countries. Regional and international communities have addressed the needs to conserve non-wood forest resources while ensuring local people's equitable access to and use of the resources, to improve market information and to develop appropriate and fair pricing mechanisms for NWFPs. The medicinal plants have emerged as the most valuable NWFPs from forests.

Fuelwood and charcoal still continue to be one of the important sources of household energy in developing countries. Developed countries continue to dominate heavily in production and consumption of industrial wood products. FAO (1999) has projected that demand for industrial round wood will increase by 1.7 per cent annually between now and the year 2010, driven both by population increases and economic growth.

5. Changes in Policy, Legislation and Institution

A lot of changes have taken place in forest policy, legislation and institutional environment and framework. The trends in forest policy reform consist of the following:

- Increased community participants in forest management.
- Privatising state forests resources.
- Increasing participation of private sector participation in sustainable forest management.
- Privatising public forest based companies.
- Decentralisation of certain functions of government administration.
- Elimination of some 'perverse subsidies' including the underpricing of forest concessions.

There have been significant changes in legislative environment, too. The process of revision of forest laws has set in all over the world in recent years. The legal changes reflect commitments to; (1) promotion of local forest management, (2) enhancement of environment functions of forests, (3) reinforcing the process of forest management planning, (4) increasing consideration and incorporation of environmental and social issues in management plans, (5) supporting public participation in the planning and management process.

Institutional changes have come in forestry sector. Privatisation of certain forest sector activities and decentralisation and devolution of forest management responsibilities to the local communities have taken place in many countries in response to the changes in policy and legislative environment.

6. International Initiative

Many international initiatives have been taken with an aim to foster sustainable forest management. One important initiative is development of criteria and indicators. More than 150 countries are participating in international process to develop and implement national level criteria and indicators for sustainable forest management. These initiatives are being co-ordinated by the Center for International Forestry Research (CIFOR), the International Tropical Timber Organization (ITTO) and the African Timber Organization (ATO). Other significant initiatives are (1) establishment and management of model and demonstration forests, (2) ITTO's 'Year 2000 objective' and G8 Countries' Action Programme on Forests, which was approved in May 1998.

Implementation of three international convention arising from UNCED (the Framework Convention on Climate Change, the Convention on Biological Diversity and the Convention to Combat Desertification) and the international Tropical Timber Agreement provide the necessary support to the process of sustainable forest development on a global scale.

8

ELEMENTS OF SUSTAINABLE FOREST MANAGEMENT PRACTICES

Sustainable forest management has been defined as the process of managing forest to achieve one or more clearly specified objectives of management with regard to the production of a continuous flow of desired forest products and services without undue reduction of its inherent values and future productivity and without undesirable effects on the physical and social environment. It entails the balancing of the economic, environmental and social functions and values of forests for the benefit of present as well as future generations. In other words, it implies provision of a range of goods and services not only for the present generation but also for the future. While all the benefits from forests, by their nature, are generally multipurpose, the range may differ from one place to another. The range of benefits that emanates from forests depends upon the forest policy, management strategy and objectives. With the passage of time, more and more emphasis is given to widen the range of benefits from forests. Many initiatives are taken towards achieving the objective of sustainable forest management. But the goal is met only after having synchronised many processes that are initiated in that direction.

Every country adopts its own forest policy. Within that policy, broad framework of management objectives and strategies are enumerated. Most of the managed forests have primary management objectives like production (of wood or non-wood products), protection (mainly of soil and water conservation) or conservation of biological, cultural heritage, etc. Realisation of one primary objective affects the prospect of other objectives. Likewise, achievement of one objective in the present generation may affect its prospect for the future generation. Therefore, balancing of multiple objectives in intra-generation or inter-generation framework is an important exercise for practicing sustainable forest management. However, the very exercise of balancing is a complex, protracted and challenging task. Again in the face of the earth's rapidly expanding population and increasing demands for products and services, the task becomes more intractable day-by-day.

Therefore, it is the need of the hour to evolve certain basic trade-off between not only economic imperative and environmental necessity but also needs of present and future generations. We cannot afford to neglect it further. Forest polices helps to do this job, but because of conflicting objectives in the policies, the task becomes difficult. There is already inordinate delay in finding a viable solution to this vexed problem. Many initiatives, nationally and internationally, have been taken towards achieving the objective of sustainable forest management. But the goal is met only after having synergyised many such processes that have been initiated in that direction.

Considered things in this perspective, a framework of critical elements of forest management practices has been hammered out. This chapter primarily aims at presenting an overview of critical elements of sustainable forest management practices. There may be certain elements, which will be highly appropriate to a situation in county, and certain elements may not be relevant. Again the degree of relevance of any element to a country should be determined in the context of that country or locality's need.

Sustainable forest management practices have many critical elements. All such elements are embedded in a framework, which encompasses political, social, cultural, economic and environmental aspects of sustainable development. These elements are either complementary to each other or in some cases non-complementary to each other. In case where certain elements are not complementary to each other, some amount of balancing has to be done to develop a compatible framework. Few of the critical elements of sustainable forest management practices are; (1) Legal and policy framework, (2) Sustained and optimal production of forest goods and services, (3) Protecting the forest ecosystem, (4) Well-being of people, and (5) Verifying effects of sustainable forest management practices. With the change in societal needs, incorporation of new elements or recasting of the aforesaid elements with differential focus on a wide range of aspects may be necessary. Few of the important and critical elements and sub-elements are enumerated below:

1. *Legal and Policy Framework.*

    - Compliance with all existing legislation and regulation.

- Formulation of policy/guidelines compatible to sustainable forest management.
- Amending the legislation, rules and regulation on the basis of evolving social, economic and environmental needs of the society.
- Property and Use Rights.
- Forest organisations' commitment to policy.

2. *Sustained and Optimal Production of Forest Goods and Services*

- Management and action planning.
- Sustained yield of forest products.
- Plantation management.
- Protection of the forest from illegal activities.
- Optimizing benefits from forests
- Monitoring the effects of management.

3. *Protecting the Forest Ecosystem*

- Environmental Impact Assessment.
- Conservation of Bio-diversity
- Maintenance of ecological sustainability.
- Soil and water conservation.
- Minimising the harvesting impact.
- Minimizing the use of chemicals.

4. *Well-being of People*

- Consultation and participatory process.
- Social analysis.
- Social impact assessment.
- Recognition of rights and culture.
- Relation with labour/workers and forest staff.
- Contribution to development.

5. *Verifying the Effects of Sustainable Forest Management Practices*

Sustainable management practices necessitate periodical verification. Therefore, there is an imperative need to develop methods and frameworks for measuring and verifying sustainability. Such processes have been useful in catalysing effort and commitment towards sustainable forest management. They aim at establishing principles, criteria, and indicators for sustainable forest management and mechanism for its certification.

Implementing the aforesaid elements initiates a process, which, if synchronised with other process, shall go a long way in achieving the mission of sustainable forest development. Few critical elements discussed in detail with reference to the objective of SFM are enumerated below.

Legal and Policy Framework

Use of forest is influenced by a wider political, social and economic climate prevailing in the country, more particularly by national policy and institutional and legal framework. Again, on account of rising importance of forest resources, globally, regionally and locally, it is now increasingly influenced by international and regional conventions also. Decisions on how forestland should be allocated and forest resource should be used determine the success of sustainable forest management. However, there are many issues and aspects, which influence forest organisation's responsibility towards sustainable forest management practices. Some of the important issues and aspects are enumerated below:

Compliance with all existing Legislation and Regulation

Compliance with all existing laws and regulation is the key to the success of sustainable forest management. The government enacts laws for smooth implementation of policies. Such laws are forest legislation, forest management codes, environmental protection laws, conservation and wildlife laws, labour laws, tax laws and other legislation regulating use of land and forests. All forest organisation, therefore, should work within the legal and regulatory framework and respect the laws and regulations of the country.

Compliance with international laws is also a necessary requisite for success of forest management. Normally international conventions are ahead of national laws. So when a national government signs an international convention, it incorporates the provision into national legislation. However, there is always a time lag between signing of international convention and adoption of appropriate laws or regulations. The forest organisation, therefore, should have the in-built capacity and commitment to adopt the said principles and regulation. The main international conventions are: (1) Convention on International Trade in

Endangered Species (CITES), (2) International Tropical Timber Agreement (ITTA), (3) UN Convention on Biological Diversity (UNCBD), and (4) International Labour Organisation (ILO) Conventions 87 and 98.

Apart from complying national and international laws, there is also a need to enforce the forest practice code and implement the decisions taken after management planning and environment and social impact assessment exercise.

Formulation of Policies and Guidelines Compatible to SFM

Sustainable forest management is an evolving process. Principles and practices keep on changing on the basis of changing needs of society and forest. Besides, sustainable forest management encompasses myriad sectors, which have a bearing on forestry and natural resource management. Therefore, in order to succeed in sustainable forest practices, there is an imperative need not only to keep on recasting the existing laws and regulations but also to evolve pragmatic policy for providing a guided direction to thinking and activities.

Amending the Legislation, Rules and Regulations/Guidelines

The needs of forests and people keep on changing with the passage of time. Therefore, amending forest legislation, rules, regulations and guidelines should be a continuous process. It makes the existing laws and rules/regulations always relevant and appropriate to the need of the time. This requires amendment of existing acts and rules on the basis of changing.

Property and Use Rights

Sustainable forest management is a long-term exercise. It requires not only a protracted time frame but also consistent flow of investment and continuous protection of forest resources through out the span of management. The issue of rights and culture are at the core of the well-being of the people living near the vicinity of forests. Therefore, there is a great necessity of respecting the traditional and indigenous use and access rights of people living in/near forests. Therefore, recognition of rights (including distinct property rights and culture) are critical for ensuring people's interest in forest management. Towards this end, long-term tenure or distinct use rights for the forest user is essential for the successes. When the ownership of the forest lies with the government, then it becomes more important on the part of the government to ensure that both the legal and traditional rights of local communities are recognised and respected. Normally such rights are not reflected in national laws perfectly. Therefore, such traditional rights and privileges are required to be reflected adequately in forestry regulation and practice codes. Use rights for indigenous people depending on forests are generally explicated by rights settlement documents or agreements.

Apart from the aforesaid commitment the Government or forest organisation must prove the intention with appropriate actions. Local communities and indigenous people with legal or customary tenure or use rights should be able to maintain these rights with respect to any forest management operations on their land. Management activities must not threaten or diminish the resource rights, use rights or tenure rights of local and indigenous communities. Similarly, the use of such rights should be within the threshold of carrying capacity of the forests. Otherwise, the very productive base of forests will be diminished.

Forest Organisation's Commitment to Policy

Sustainable forest management is a long drawn affair. It requires inputs from all fronts. It requires continuous investment in forestry and allied fields. Commitment is needed to ensure that adequate investment is made to help develop the management capability of staff, maintain the ecological productivity and integrity of the forests, support sustainable development of local communities. Again commitments are also required for ensuring reinvestment of financial benefits from production into the maintenance of the system.

Apart from the investment and reinvestment into the forestry, there is also a need to show commitment to sustainable forest management at all level of the organisation. Every person of the organisation involved in the process must understand forestry practices in its totality and commit himself or herself toward the goal of the organisation. Further, commitment particularly assumes more importance at higher level. It is because of the fact that strategic decisions are taken at higher levels. However, it is also necessary on the part of lower level functionary to understand and support sustainable forest management, because their activities directly and significantly affect the way the forest management programme is carried out.

Commitment of the organisation can be demonstrated in the form of policy, resolution, and management plan. Such documents outlines the broad principles of forest practices and operation. Apart from this, commitment can be demonstrated in the course of collaboration and communication with stakeholders.

Sustained and Optimal Productions of Forest Goods and Services

Sustainable forest management goes beyond sustained production of tangible forest products like timber and on-timber forest products from the forests. It involves achievement of multiple management objectives, which may be short-term or long-term in nature. Overall planning of forest operation, harvesting the sustainable yields, protection of forest from illegal activities, monitoring the effects of management on forests, and optimisation of the range of benefits derived from the forest are all necessary components of sustainable forest management process. These components are as follows:

Management and Action Planning

Sustainable forest management involves the achievement of multiple management objectives. These objectives should be clearly spelt out and defined in a management plan. Likewise, means of achieving such objectives should also be indicated clearly in the management plan. Every forest management unit should have a management plan. A forest management unit (FMU) is an area of forest under a single or common system of management.

Management planning is the foundation of a well-managed forest. It lays out the details of works, their rationale, and location. Management plan is the document, which provides guidelines for day-to-day working. It is available to every body who is involved in decision making process. It is an indispensable tool for planning sustainable forest management operation. It states objectives clearly so that every one involved in managing the forest shall work towards the same end. A management plan contains: (1) the objectives of management, (2) a description of the resources available, and (3) the proposed methods of achieving the objectives.

Based on the size of forest operations, management plan can be categorised into three types. They are as follows:

- *Strategic Plan*: It is the forest management plan prepared for an entire forest management unit (FMU), over a long-term, such as an entire rotation, or a period of twenty-five years.
- *Tactical Plan*: The forest management plan that sets out the activities planned, normally over a five-year period, in more detail. It may coincide with business plans.
- *Operation Plan*: The forest operation plan or annual plan of operation contains the details of the precise activities to be carried out over the next year. This will include month-to-month activities and should provide the direct control over operations. It is essential to carry out operations in consonance with forest management plan. It is generally taken up along with annual budgeting.

The tactical and operational plans are not only compatible with the strategic plan but also derived from it. They provide more detailed information and procedure. In many counties the strategic and tactical plans are amalgamated to form a "management plan" or "working plan', which covers a period of 10 to 20 years. A written management plan is revised periodically to ensure that it does not become static, irrelevant and unworkable. It also provides an opportunity to assess and revise objectives and methods of SFM. Revision of management plan should be a continuous process taking into account the changing situations within and out side the ambit of forestry. Induction of new technology and practices like information technology and bio-technology into the management process should be done periodically. Again with the increasing awareness of the public and need for community participation in management planning, the management plan should be made public. By making the management plan or a short summary of the management plan public, transparency and accountability of forest operations will be improved. This will go a long way not only in promoting better communication with myriad stakeholders but also in restoring confidence of local community in forest organisation.

Sustained Yield of Forest Products

A prerequisite of sustainable forest management is that removal of forest product must not exceed the limits of regeneration or replenishment. In production forests where the major product is timber, this requires calculating sustained yield and implementing SFM for timber. This requires information showing growing stock levels and regeneration rates and such information can be used as a basis for calculating sustainable harvestable levels. In case of forest where harvest of non-timber forest products is an important management objective, inventory data and calculations will be required to determine the sustainable harvest limit of NWFP. However, methods for calculating sustainable NTFP yields are not yet fully developed in any part of the world. This poses a great deal of problem for operationalizing SFM.

Apart from the direct benefits like timber and non-wood forest products, forests provide a range of social and economic benefits and ecological services including life support services. Such benefits and services are indirect. Some of the benefits are alleviation of poverty, livelihood security, increased food security and enhanced well being for the rural poor living in and around forests. A livelihood comprises the capabilities, assets and activities required for a means of living. A livelihood is sustainable when it can cope with and recover from stresses and shocks, and maintain or enhance its capabilities and assets both now and in future, while not undermining the natural base (Carney, 1998) (See also Box 8.1). The ability to move out of poverty is critically dependent on access to assets. Food insecurity arises when people lack access to sufficient amounts for food and are therefore not consuming the food required for normal growth and development. This may be because of lack of access to food – because of unavailability, insufficient purchasing power, inappropriate distribution or inadequate utilisation at the household level.

A total contribution of forests and trees to livelihoods is difficult to quantify. A significant proportion of forests produces is consumed by those who collect them, with the amount collected varying according to season and available options. Increased income alone is insufficient as a criterion of poverty, increased income is clearly relevant to the economic sustainability of the household. Earnings from forest products are often important as a complement to other income. Very large number of households generate some of their income from selling forest products, often on a part-time basis when farm production is not enough to provide food self-sufficiency all the year round. Income from forest products is often used to obtain inputs for other activities that contribute to livelihoods: to purchase seeds, hire labour for cultivation or generate working capital for trading activities (*e.g.* Leach and Fairhead, 1994, cited in Byron and Arnold, 1999). The rural poor often produce, process and sell forest products in the absence of other farming households.

BOX 8.1: FORMS OF CAPITAL REQUIRED FOR SUSTAINABLE LIVELIHOODS

- *Natural capital*: Privately owned assets such as land, forests, water and pasture.
- *Physical capital*: Privately owned assets that can be used to increase labour and land productivity (such as farm animals, tools and machinery) and publicly owned economic infrastructure (*e.g.* roads, electricity supply) and social infrastructure (*e.g.* schools, hospitals)
- *Financial capital*: Cash (income and savings) and readily convertible liquid capital.
- *Human capital*: Health, nutritional levels, educational standard and skills.
- *Social capital*: The set of social relationship on which people can draw to expand livelihoods options. These include kinship, friendships, patron-client relations, reciprocal arrangements, memberships of formal groups and membership of organisations that provides loans, grants and other forms of insurance.

Source: Carney, 1998.

Improved Food Security: Food security is the key element of livelihood. Forests are the source of a variety of foods that supplement and complement what is obtained from agriculture. Probably the majority of rural households in developing countries, and a large proportion of urban households, depend on plant and animal products of forests to meet some part of their nutritional, cooking and/or health needs (Byron and Arnold, 1999). Therefore, forests play an important role in improving food security to the rural poor.

Reduced Vulnerability: Poor people often live precariously, with no cushion against adversity. Non-wood forest resource have an important role as a reserve or safety net, providing both subsistence and income in times of crop failure, shortfalls during particular seasons in the year. Energy –rich forest foods such as roots, tubers, rhizomes and nuts are especially important in emergencies such as floods, famine droughts.

Increased Well-being: Forestry initiatives that supports access to non-wood forest resources, participatory decision-making and equity assist in increasing the well-being, especially that of the poor. Forests provide non-material goods that contribute to livelihoods by enhancing social and human capital. Sense of well-being is affected by numerous factors including sense of involvement and control, access to resources and political enfranchisement.

Notwithstanding sustainable development, the integration of non-wood forest products with timber production holds stupendous prospect to rural employment and wood industry. This option, apart from being socially sustainable, appears to be economically feasible and environmentally sustainable. Sustainable management for non-wood products means balancing optimal productivity and controlling ecological change so that environmental equilibrium is maintained (Wickens, G.E., 1994). The range of management requirements for forest species providing non-wood products may complicate their management process, and their integration with timber production system may decrease the revenue outturn from timber sale but could make the practice more environmentally efficient. But, sustainably managed forests for non-wood forest products provide a range of environmental services as well as goods. One of the best known of these services is soil and water conservation and other ecological services. Moreover, income generation, livelihood security, increased food security and enhanced well-being are some of the important social benefits that might nullify the increased cost of management of such forests.

Management requirement for determining sustainable yield of forest products is as follows:

- Sustainable levels for timber and NTFP yield should be determined separately. However, such determination process is a complex one. It is because of the fact that such sustainable levels are likely to change with the improvement in forest growth and technology to harvest.
- Authentic forest inventory data should be collected in order to determine the level of sustainable harvest. Proper recording and documentation should be undertaken to assist monitoring and evaluating the trend. Firstly, the information needs for undertaking calculation of sustainable yield should be assessed. Essential data required are: (1) forest inventory data which provides information about the quantity of harvestable resources currently available, (2) information about growth and yield pattern in order to determine how fast the resource will be renewed after harvesting, (3) information about seed production and method of natural regeneration from studies and background knowledge and secondary sources, (4) information about NTFPs

and their pattern of exploitation and rate of replenishment. Growth and yield prediction requires analysis of results obtained from permanent sample plots. Big forest organisation maintains a research organisation to conduct research and development in forestry. But forestry inventories are carried out by all organisations whether small or big.

- There must be a reliable method and sound rationale for the calculation of the rate of harvest. Normally the 'Annual Allowable Cut' or 'Annual Cut' method is adopted to determine sustainable limit of timber yield. The annual cut is the volume of timber, which may be cut in one year in a given area. Calculation of annual cut is based on the volume of timber in the area, which can be harvested, while leaving enough stems to provide the next crop. It depends on the currently exhisting growing stock and the growth rate. The harvest level should be set conservatively where growth and yield data are unreliable. By doing this, we follow the precautionary principle in practicing forest management.
- There should be acceptable and reliable method of control of such harvest operation. It is needed to ensure that the production rate is kept below the level decided. This necessitates maintenance of records regarding level of wood and non-wood products for each compartment of the forests. Records should be reconciled against predicted yield in order to ensure that annual cut is not exceeded. Besides, records in forestry practices play an important role in continuity of management practices.
- Periodic revision of sustained yield is also a necessity in sustainable forest management practices. It is required for the reasons such as: (1) changes in forest ecosystem after undertaking harvest operation, (2) changes in socio-economic landscape which exerts influence on the use of forest resources, and (3) improvement in knowledge and technology which is expected to provide better understanding of growth and yield pattern.
- The silvicultural system and regime should be distinctly discussed and its application should be sufficiently justified. Therefore, a comprehensive discussion on applicability and justification of silvicultural system should be undertaken in the management plan. The act of justifying the choice of silvicultural system helps to ensure that all levels of management understand

what they are doing and why they are doing.

- Proper execution and supervision plays an important role in sustainable forest management practices. It is necessary to ensure that all silvicultural and harvesting operations are carried out according to the plan and operational guidelines. This is possible through proper supervision.

Plantation Management

Plantation provides an array of benefits to society. It not only provides goods but also a range of ecological services. But they lack all the benefits of natural forests. Planting trees may also entail negative impacts on few families. It also entails social and economic costs. Therefore, in order to minimise social and economic cost, it is necessary to undertake plantation management.

Plantation management aims at maximising the benefits and minimising the negative externalities. It encompasses planning, implementation and control of plantation. Plantations are normally assiduously planned and designed to complement the management of adjoining natural forests. Besides, it is also ensured that such plantations are integrated with other land uses in order to conserve native flora and fauna, to maintain ecological sustainability and to maximise social benefits, while providing a productive resource base.

Plantation management covers all aspects pertaining to plantation, its harvesting, and managing local biodiversity and use. Generally it encompasses the following aspects of forestry:

- plantation planning;
- species selection;
- soil and site management;
- planting and maintenance;
- crop management;
- pest and disease management.

Monitoring the Efforts of Management

Monitoring is a part of forest management and is fundamental to the continual improvement aimed for. It is the process of collecting and analysing information about how effectively management prescriptions are being implemented, and what effects those prescriptions are having on forest management. It is an essential part of the management process. It helps the manager to ensure that action proposed is taken as per the plan. It also helps ensure that the avowed objectives are met. The results of monitoring provide a feedback into the planning process which is further improved to provide better service to forest and the society. Therefore, monitoring should be a regular activity of any organisation involved in sustainable forest management. Moreover, environmental, financial and social aspects require constant monitoring.

The intensity of monitoring which should be carried out by an organisation depends upon its size, the criticality and complexity of operations and performance standards, as well as the resources available. Monitoring is carried out in a forest organisation at two levels. One is at operational level and the other at strategic level.

Operational monitoring helps forester or forest manager to identify whether practices are being properly implemented, or where the effects of certain operations are not as expected. It helps to identify successes and failures in forest management practices, to provide a basis for modifications to future management and to identify areas where corrective steps are required. The activities which are covered under operational monitoring are harvesting, forest road construction, silvicultural operation, etc. Besides, post-harvest assessments are also a particular type of operational monitoring. It is because of the fact that harvesting and extraction operations have the greatest potential for environmental damage of any forest operations. Post-harvest assessment may cover the following activities:

- Implementation of harvesting plan and guidelines.
- Environmental effects of harvesting operations.
- Regeneration of species harvested.
- Effect of harvest on the growth of forest stand.

Post-harvest assessments are generally taken on a sampling basis. Different harvesting sites are selected randomly on the basis of a statistical model. This is usually done about a year after the year of harvest operation. This provides damaged saplings time to die, so that a clear picture of regeneration emerges. Such exercise needs a clear method and procedure. The results of the assessment are analysed and inferences are drawn. Based on such inferences, necessary steps are taken to improve upon the coming harvesting operation and silvicultural programmes.

Strategic monitoring is a long-term process. It needs repeated and continuous observations or measurement of the environmental or social effects of forest management. It provides data about the long-term effects of the forestry operation, so that those potential problems can be identified in proper time and resolved forthwith. Strategic monitoring of yields, growth rates and regeneration is especially important to ensure that harvest levels are sustainable. Strategic monitoring aims at providing information about the results of management, which can be fed back into the planning process of the management system. Before undertaking any such monitoring exercise, decision about parameter of monitoring is essential. Generally certain key elements as the indicator are focussed in monitoring exercise. The subjects covered under strategic monitoring are site productivity, soil and water conservation, wildlife population, ecological restoration, regeneration of forests, social development. Key areas of strategic monitoring in forest practices include growth and yield monitoring, environmental monitoring, social monitoring and forest cover monitoring.

Record and data produced in the process of monitoring helps in improving the control system. Therefore, records should be produced and maintained properly to facilitate monitoring and evaluation of activities further. Apart from this, monitoring procedures should be developed to facilitate speedy working. As far as possible, a comprehensive monitoring programme should be drawn for the forest organisation. The following activities can be taken under that programme.

- Timber and NTFPs yields.
- Growth rates of forest stand.
- Regeneration status of the forests.
- Impact of forest management on flora and fauna in the forest.
- Environmental, social and economic impacts of forest practice.
- Cost, productivity and efficiency.
- Effect of management practices on soil and water conservation status of the forest.
- Impact of protection measures on illegal activities in forests.

Monitoring of Social Impacts

Along with the monitoring of the production and environmental effects of management, the social effects of forest management practices carried out by the organisation need to be constantly monitored and improved. This helps the management to assess the progress in the field of social issues. A systemic monitoring system also takes care of the changing social values in the society. Basic monitoring of social impacts by the forest organisation itself enables it to know the real position of its enforcement and implementation. This helps the forest organisation to identify problems and opportunities for development.

Participatory approach to monitoring helps to obtain perception of local community about impacts of management. It helps the organisation to review and recast its policies and programmes. In other words, it provides the forest organisation an opportunity to learn from its failings and shortcomings, so that necessary improvement can be made in the on going management practices. Apart from this, monitoring of social issues provides a firm platform for regular face-to-face contact with divergent stakeholders. This itself promotes understanding, mutual respect, trust, communication and consultation and collaboration.

Social Issues and Approaches to Monitoring

If the issues are fairly clear and scale of monitoring required is small, then the forest organisation can undertake internal monitoring exercise with little or no external help. Some useful social issues to consider are given in Box 8.2.

BOX 8.2: SOCIAL ISSUES

- Recognition of and respect for rights and culture.
- Consent by local people for forestry operations.
- Impact of forestry activities on poverty and unemployment.
- Impact of participatory forest management on gender, empowerment and democratisation in the rural sector.
- Respect and recognition of belief system, cultural practices, customs and religious sites by forest organisation.
- Adherence of environmental laws, rules and regulation by people.
- Work procedure, public grievances redressal mechanism and complaint disposal system.

Participatory monitoring is a modern method. It involves developing a process for gathering, analysing and using information. Before undertaking the exercise, the issues to be monitored should be defined and a consensus of stakeholders should be brought out. Besides, in the context of objectives of the organisation indictors of good forest management are decided after consulting with people and other stakeholders. Monitoring of such indicators should be done and results obtained should be fed into the forest planning process. The method of participatory monitoring is still in a process of evolutionary improvement. A prescriptive framework for conducting participatory monitoring is given in Box 8.3.

BOX 8.3: SUGGESTIVE FRAMEWORK FOR PARTICIPATORY MONITORING

- Deciding the objective of monitoring.
- Identifying the target group *i.e.* the specific community.
- Identifying the theme/objectives/outputs/activities which have social impacts.
- Identifying the indicators of progress and failure.
- Selection of Specific, Measurable, Action-oriented, Realistic and Time-framed (SMART) indicators. For example number of man-days (Employment), yield of NTFPs.
- Selection of monitoring method depending on the nature of work, availability of time and skill.
- Formulation of monitoring programme containing details about collection, compilation, analysis and dissemination of information, area and community where the exercise is to be conducted, time table and costs to be incurred.
- Finalisation of monitoring methods and train stakeholders in their use.
- Implementation of the monitoring programme.
- Documentation of the whole exercise and its analysis.
- Application of inferences and results into the management process for improvement in the project performance. Separate programme can be developed to alter the inimical activities of villagers.

Protection of Forest from Illegal Activities

Sustainable forest management is a long drawn affair. It necessitates constant protection and vigil. There are many forces of destruction acting on the forest resource system. All such forces are incompatible to the goals of sustainable forest management. Many of such forces are anthropogenic in nature. Therefore, forest needs to be protected from such destructive and illegal activities. What is more important is the fact that in the past forest management failed due to constraints emanated from protection of forest resources. Therefore, success of sustainable forest management lies with effective tackling of protection problems.

The forest resources must be protected from all such illegal activities like encroachment, illegal felling, land clearance, grazing, illegal hunting irregular and illegal collection of NTFPs etc. All such activities are totally inconsistent with the broad objectives of sustainable forest management. Take for example the menace of forest encroachment. This problem poses a serious threat to long-term ecological sustainability of forest resources. Like this, uncontrolled and repeated fire incidences destroy the young seedlings in the forest floor and capacity of forest to regenerate. Besides, it degrades the forest crop and opens up the canopy, changing the microclimate. Over the years, instances incendiary behaviours of people living near the forests have increased manifold. Such behaviour has proved highly incompatible with the goals of sustainability. Likewise, forest plantation requires utmost protection from destructive activities. Therefore, there is every need to protect forest from such activities, along with the protection of traditional user rights or customary rights. Of late there has been a realisation that the best means of resolving conflicts and solving problems lie with involvement of people in forest management. Such involvement of people aims at:

- To arrive at a consensus or compromise over a difference or problem which has the potentiality to tell upon the forest sustainability.
- To encourage the local communities to assert control over management of community use rights.
- To improve upon the forest regulatory regime.
- To sensitise people about the destructive effects of illegal activities.

Optimising Benefits from the Forest

Forest management aims at optimising and maximising production of wood and non-wood benefits respectively. However optimising the mix of products ands services from forest remains central to sustainable forest management. Optimising benefits in the long run involves making trade off between benefits, which can be reaped today, and those, which should be left, for future. Besides, it requires a balance between forest goods such as timber, and NTFPs and vital ecological services of forest like watershed protection, biodiversity services. These services do not have a market and therefore the services do not attract sufficient attention from forest organisation.

In order to meet the goals of sustainable forest management, the forest organisation must be economically viable. Economic viability means the capacity of the organisation to arrange financial resources and to promote reinvestment required for the maintenance of the system and the additional costs due to protection of the forest ecosystem and equitable distribution of social costs and benefits of forest management.

Forest management with short-term goals is never economically viable nor environmentally benign, nor socially desirable. Traditional thinking on forest management does not give any weight to non-financial services provided by forest, such as watershed conservation, biodiversity, etc. However in the long run, such non-financial resources are considered to be essential prerequisites of sustainable forest management. Therefore, forest organisation must ensure that multiple benefits of forests are safeguarded, and more importantly the trade-off between present need and future need and commodity value and non-commodity value of forest are maintained.

In the context of prevailing socio-economic condition of developing countries, there is a need to promote multiple use forestry. Multiple use benefits of forests are soil and water resources, food, wood-fuel, fodder, social benefits like employment, income generation, and poverty eradication. However, while pursuing this goal one should not loose sight of optimal use of the forest's multiple product. Over-reliance on a single or a few timber species can lead inefficient and unsustainable harvesting, leading to genetic degradation of the forest crop. Therefore, a wider range of species should be preferable in order to prevent over-reliance and over-harvesting of particular species. Besides, the aspects of marketing and merits of local processing of forest products are also important to sustainable production of both timber and non-timber products. Local processing is intended to increase opportunities for local people to benefit from forest management, through increased employment and income generation from processing activity. Such processing unit, if established in rural sector, can act as a nucleus for the development of supporting economic activities, promoting further development.

Protecting the Forest Ecosystem

Forest plays a major role in ameliorating the macro and micro-environment. Therefore, sustainable forest management should focus on maximisation of environmental benefits and minimisation of adverse effects of forest practices on environment. These objectives can be met only when the forest is fully protected.

Protecting the forest mainly includes maintaining its ecological functions, conserving biodiversity, conserving soil and water resources and minimising ill effects of forestry practices. The main thrust areas for protecting the environment are: (1) environmental impact assessment, and (2) conservation of biodiversity, and ecological sustainability.

Environmental Impact Assessment

An environmental and social impact assessment (ESIA) is a combination of environmental and social impact assessment. An environmental impact assessment (EIA) is an exercise to: (1) identify actual and potential impacts on the environment as a result of forest operations, (2) plan to minimise or avoid negative environmental impacts and maximise positive environmental impacts. Similarly a social impact assessment aims at: (1) identifying actual and potential impacts on people as a result of operations, and (2) to plan minimise actual or avoid negative impacts and maximise positive impacts on stakeholders and others. Therefore, a social impact assessment involves collecting information about stakeholders and their interests, and then considering their actual, or possible, impacts of forest operations on these interests in order to propose mitigation measures. Because environmental and social impacts often overlap, a social impact assessment is often undertaken along with environmental impact assessment (EIA). Environmental and social impact assessment (ESIA) examines forest management in terms of the effect it has on both the environment and people. It is indispensable to the forest organisation as a means of identifying its positive and negative impacts, both currents and potential. It acts as a guide to the forest organisation in setting its objectives and targets and provides a basis of planning process. The assessment is also used as a base line study to monitor actual impacts of forest operation against potential impacts predicted by ESIA.

An environment and social impact should be carried out before any field operations are carried. Where operations are being carried out, an ESIA should be undertaken for all existing and future operations. Such practices are in vogue in few countries. But such practices are yet to begin in many counties. Apart from this, another study called as ecological impact assessment (EIS) is generally conducted along with environmental impact assessment (EIA). Ecological impact assessment is commonly concerned with impacts on the natural environment, fauna and flora and ecological processes. It aims at determining sensitivity of fauna, flora, habitats and ecosystem to physical or chemical impacts (Spellerberg Ian F, 1992).

There are two types of assessments with respect of environmental and societal impacts. They are:

- One is in-depth environmental and social impact assessment of the physical, biological and social implications of a proposed operation or management regime. Normally before undertaking a plantation project, an in-depth ESIA is carried out either by an internal assessment group comprising forest managers working in the organisation or by an external agencies or team comprising of natural and social scientists who have acquired the professionalism to assess the probable impacts of a proposed operation.
- Second is on-site assessment carried out by the internal managers of the organisation. This is a rapid assessment exercise of possible impacts to ensure that planned actions aim to minimise negative impacts. This helps to develop an aptitude among forest managers for considering environmental and social impacts always before they occur. Consequently, it helps to minimise the chances of any negative effects.

A social impact assessment requires extensive consultation with stakeholders. It can therefore, be a good means of developing consultation and participation amongst stakeholders. Social impact assessment includes the following processes:

- Identification of stakeholders and their interests;
- Identification and evaluation of potentially significant social impacts;
- Consideration of options for avoiding or mitigating negative impacts and optimising positive impacts;
- Prioritisation of activities required to address impacts;
- Incorporation of activities into the management planning process.

Results of the ESIA should be clearly documented and integrated into forest management planning. The information obtained is helpful in setting management objectives and targets.

BOX 8.4: PHASES OF ESIA

- Consultative phase, to discuss with stakeholders the possible impacts of the operations and therefore the scope of the ESIA;
- Identification of potentially significant environmental impacts;
- Evaluation of impacts;
- Consideration of alternatives to proposed management actions;
- Consideration of options for minimising impacts;
- Consultation about options and alternatives;
- Development and description of mitigation measures to be implemented.

Conservation of Biodiversity

Tropical forests are particularly rich in plant and animal spacies. So their value for biodiversity conservation is high. Deforestation leads to loss of biodiversity. This has assumed stupendous proportion all over the world. Therefore, there is an urgent need to address the task of biodiversity conservation. Biodiversity requires to be tackled at three levels *i.e.*, (1) ecosystem level; (2) species level; and (3) genetic level.

BOX 8.5: ISSUES ARISING FROM THE ESIA WHICH NEED TO BE ADDRESSED DURING PLANNING PROCESS

- Description of expected impacts;
- Description of measures to mitigate negative impacts;
- Commitment to and who and when they will be implemented;
- Definition of responsibilities for implementing measures.

Forest management must address to conserve biodiversity at all levels *i.e.* ecosystem, species, and genetic level. Conservation efforts must be integrated into the forest management system. The forest manager or forester must visualise the impending effects of silvicultural regime on the biodiversity. Silvicultural system with an objective of timber production promotes few timber species at the cost of diverse mosaic of tree species. Very often this makes few rare species unviable. Therefore, while evolving suitable silvicultural regime, there is a need to retain viable population of all species. Apart from this, management guidelines for harvesting should be formulated and implemented to ensure conservation of biodiversity. The objective can be accomplished by undertaking: (1) protection of representative forest areas, (2) protection of rare and endangered species, and (3) protection of features of special biological interest, such as seed trees and keystone species.

The establishment of protected area is an essential component of a national conservation strategy. Every country has a network of protected areas. Apart from this, conservation zones are normally set up inside forest management unit (FMU). Not withstanding this, representative areas of commercial forest types should also be identified and protected. The proportion of such conservation zones or representative areas depends on local situation, dependence of people on forests. However, ITTO guidelines for the conservation of Biological Diversity recommends that a system of small (approximately 100 hectares each) undisturbed and protected forest reserve is recommended, to act as conservation zone. Natural forests, including primary forests should not be replaced by tree plantation or other land use method.

There is a need to protect rare and endangered species and their habitats, including their nesting and feeding sites. Few of the basic steps required are as follows:

- Consult with local people to determine which species are rare and endangered in the region;
- Conduct surveys, preferably linked to forest resource inventories, to establish whether rare species are present in the forest management unit;
- Develop and implement a plan to protect any rare species which have been identified;
- Monitor the performance of the species and adjust the plan if necessary.

Maintenance of Ecological Sustainability

Ecological sustainability necessitates perpetuation of essential resources and support processes of the ecosystem. Important life supporting processes are:

- Regeneration, succession and nutrient cycling;
- Soil and water conservation.

Harvesting operation has its accompanying hazards in the form of disturbance. Such disturbance has the potential to impact on ecological sustainability. Forest road construction and transportation of forest products are two distinct factors in the disturbance regime. Maintenance of ecological sustainability requires that such negative impacts on the ecological condition of the forests be minimised.

Regeneration, ecological succession and nutrient cycling are important processes that sustain the forests. Forest management activities affect these ecological processes to a greater or lesser extent. Therefore, forest management should focus on ways to maintain ecological processes in spite of such activities. The following points should be considered for:

- Sufficient seed trees of different species should be left in the forest during harvesting in natural forest.
- Criteria for marking suitable seed trees of all species should be developed.
- There should be no preferential selection of timber trees while marking. This may lead to genetic degradation.
- Natural regeneration status should be measured periodically for each compartment and measures for remedial action should be considered.
- In forest areas where natural regeneration is deficient, appropriate measures for supplementing natural regeneration should be taken. Guidelines should be evolved to spell out the critical limits at which natural regeneration should be supplemented.
- The scale and pattern of harvesting assume relevance in the context of sustainable forest management. They should be appropriate to the natural dynamics of forest type and ecological entity. Where ecological requirements are not distinctly determined, it is prudent to take steps to keep canopy opening at minimum.
- Keystone species should be marked and protected during felling operation. Where commercial timber species are suspected to be keystone species, all care should be taken to maintain enough trees in an area to support population of dependent animal.
- Some habitat trees may also need to be retained during

harvesting. Habitat trees provide nesting space for birds and living space for insects and other animals. These trees may be of poor quality, defective, diseased and old. These trees play a key role in maintaining the ecological processes.

Soil and Water Conservation

Conservation of water resources plays an important role in forest ecosysten management. It promotes productivity and quality of forest ecosystem. Besides, it ensures downstream water quality and quantity. Therefore, soil and water resources should be conserved at any cost. All care should be taken to protect soil and water resources during all forest operations. In order to make conservation measures more practical, it is necessary to define slope limits and soil types for particular operations and to suggest site-specific management prescriptions as a remedial measures.

Minimising the Harvesting Impact

Timber harvesting and extraction operations leave a trail of destruction in the forest. Therefore, they are of such activities, which have the maximum potential for damage to soil and water conservation, regeneration processes, and biodiversity conservation. Considered from this backdrop, it is essential to evolve management guidelines for sustainable management of harvesting operation and to operationalise. The basic approach behind managing harvesting operation and post- harvesting operations is to keep the impacts of such operation on forest structure and functioning at minimum. Therefore guidelines should fundamentally address at: (1) harvesting planning, (2) tree marking and felling, (3) extraction, and (4) post-harvest restorative operation.

Another area of importance lies in minimising the waste of harvested timber, such as broken logs, large off-cuts, broken trees, abandoned wood pieces and other forest products. All such wastes should be disposed properly. While undertaking harvesting, it should be ensured that harvesting and logging operations are not wasteful. Efficient harvesting is an important component of sustainable forest management practices. It minimises waste and reduces costs and increases revenue.

Minimising the Use of Chemicals

Chemical like fertilizer, insecticides, herbicides, fungicides and hormones are generally used in different forest operations. Such chemicals have many potentially damaging effects in the environment. Apart from the surface effects, these chemicals enter into the nutrient cycle of the forest ecosystem and damage it ecologically and genetically. Therefore, there is a need to control and minimise use of chemicals in forest management practices.

Use of chemical in forest management should be allowed to the extent, which is bare minimum. It is also necessary to adjust the timing of application of use of chemicals in such a way that it should have maximum effect on the target and the minimum effect on the ecosystem. Besides, use of fertilizers should be matched to meet the deficiency and growing needs of the plant.

Towards minimising the use of chemicals, the following steps should be taken:

- Integrated pest management should be encouraged. This means using preventive measures along with curative measures to control pests. The strategy aims at preventing pest outbreaks by good forest practice and forest hygiene measures. If preventive steps fail, then biological, silvicultural and chemical control may be considered to control outbreaks.
- Minimum use of chemical has been in vogue in forest management. But, over the years, in order to boost timber production chemicals are used. Such chemical impairs the natural biological control processes of the forest ecosystem. Therefore, use of chemicals should be bare minimum in natural forest. However, it may be necessary to use chemical in the forest nursery. Here also the number and the quantity of chemical being used can often be reduced by a combination of good nursery planning and preventive measures in nursery management.
- Chemical should not be used in environmentally sensitive areas such as: (1) wetlands, (2) streamside buffer zones, (3) conservation zones, (4) sites of special ecological and biodiversity significance, and (5) habitats of rare or endangered species.
- Dangerous chemical like chemicals contained in the World Health Organisation type 1A and 1B lists, chlorinated hydrocarbons, persistent and toxic pesticides such as DDT and pesticides banned under international conventions should not be used.

- Biological control measures agents may be used but it should be closely monitored.

The Well-being of People

Forestry contributes towards economic development of the community. With the degradation of forests, impoverishment of people sets in. Forest management has failed in the past because of the fact that people have not been involved in the working of the forests. Community living near the forests was not given opportunity to participate in shaping and implementing forestry projects. The conflict between forest dwellers and forest organisation takes its roots in planning and controlling the use of forest resources. This alienated the people from the forest organisation. Therefore, in order to operationalise sustainable forest management practices, it is essential to involve people in forest management mechanism and address the contentious issues like equity, user rights, usufruct sharing, sustainable use of forest products and democratisation of forest management. Therefore, forest organisation owes a responsibility to the society to address and resolve such contentious social issues at the social plane.

Why Social Issues are Important?

Social issues have assumed immense significance over time. They are important because of the following reasons:

- People's rights to forests: people have a range of rights, which directly concern their life, forest and its use. Such rights are: (1) territorial rights, (2) rights of access such as grazing, collection of firewood, timber and NTFPs, (3) rights to protection of cultural heritages, and (4) intellectual property rights. These range of rights and privileges conflict with life supporting services of forest. Therefore, this situation creates problems for forest managers for management.
- *Good socially acceptable management practices*: When social issues are not resolved, conflicts, dissention, social tension, unfulfilled demands create problem for the forest managers. These problems can be manifested in the form of legal challenges, compensation claims, unrealistic demands for infrastructure development, confrontation of stakeholders with management,

encroachment, damage to forest plantation, and negative publicity of good forestry programme. By addressing to social issues that mar the prospect of forest management, the forest managers increase the potential social benefits that come support from others.

- *Legal reasons*: Apart from the rights bestowed on people by different national laws, there is a number of legally binding international agreements to which many countries are parties. These agreements are: (1) UN Covenants on Economic Social and Cultural Rights 1966, (2) UN Covenant on Civil and Political Rights, 1966, UN Declaration on the Human Right to Development, 1986, International Labour Organisation 169 concerning Indigenous and Tribal Peoples in Independent Countries, 1989, and UN Convention on Biological Diversity-1992.
- *Contribution of forest resources to sustainable development*: Sustainable forest management contains social, economic and environmental dimensions. All such dimensions are inter-linked to each other structurally and functionally. Forest management, which only addresses silvicultural issue side stepping other dimensions, cannot solve the problem of forest and people. Therefore, addressing social issues as well as implementing silvicultural programs can play an important role in development. However, all social issues cannot be solved by the local forest managers. Larger issues need to be addressed at national level.

How to Address Social Issues

Many social issues defy easy solutions. Towards finding a solution, the following aspects assume significance:

- social analysis;
- consultation and participation processes;
- social impact assessment;
- recognition of rights and culture;
- contribution to development;
- Relation with staff working for sustainable forests management.

Social Analysis

Social analysis is the methodology, which provides guidelines for studying and identifying the social, economic and political factors that may affect or be affected by project activities as well as the people who are expected to benefit, particularly local population. On the basis of this information, there is a need to identify potential problems that may emerge during implementation of the project or plan and suggest ways in which they can be addressed.

The application of social analysis implies that development projects have social objectives. Underlying this is a belief that sustainable development means increasing the potential of rural people to influence and control their future on a long-term basis, a goal that can be achieved by strengthening capacity, supporting equity and fostering empowerment (Gow, 1988). For social analysis to make a significant contribution to design and implementation at both programme and projects levels within this broader context of sustainable development, a framework that is simple to capture the complexities and constraints that characterise development interventions is called for. The emphasis should be on concerns involving the environment and natural resource base, the political dimension of forest protection and resource use, institutional implications, national, regional and local. Social analysis is generally grouped under three major components:

1. Social feasibility
2. Institutions and organisations
3. Social and distributional impact.

Social feasibility analysis focuses on the extent to which planned interventions respond to local needs, conditions, and potentials and capabilities. A project or plan is socially feasible if it is sufficiently adapted to local conditions and people can see the advantages of making changes and modifying their practices to attain new benefits.

Consultation and Participatory Process

The word "stakeholders" has become used in recent years to describe all the people who are (directly or indirectly) affected by, or interested in, forest management. Different stakeholders have different objectives and interests. They influence forest management practices. Some stakeholders put constraints on the process of sustainable forest management and others facilitates the processes by playing catalytic role.

Consultation and participation are now recognised as core aspects of sustainable forest management practice. Therefore, without initiating the process of consultation and participation, no headway can be made in forest management front. However, while undertaking the process of consultation and participation it is also necessary to ensure that unrealistic expectations are not raised among the forest community. Again in the case of conflicts, communication and coordination, is the key to resolution.

Consultation is a two-way flow of information between forester/forest manager and few stakeholders. It involves participation of people or stakeholders in forest planning, implementation and control. It provides appropriate mechanism required to resolve grievances and creates compatible atmosphere for resolving the issue of compensation in cases of damage or loss of property rights, loss of human or domestic animal or resources or livelihoods on account of any forest operation or incident.

Social Impact Assessment

Social Impact Assessment (SIA) is an assessment of social impact of forestry operations on the society. It involves collecting information about stakeholders and their interests, and then considering the actual or possible impact of forest operation on these interests in order to propose mitigation measures.

The exercise necessitates intensive and extensive consultation with stakeholders. It includes the following processes.

- Identification of stakeholders and their interests;
- Identification and evaluation of potentially significant social impacts;
- Consideration of options for avoiding or minimising negative impacts and optimising positive impacts;
- Prioritisation of activities and their integration into the management planning process.

After identifying the possible negative impacts, there is a need to take appropriate steps to avoid them. Therefore, planning and assessment of alternative activities should be considered as the part of the social impact assessment. Where alternatives are not found mitigating measures to reduce or minimise impacts must be implemented. After this, social issues relating to forest management should be clearly brought out and documented in the management plan.

Recognition of Rights and Culture

The issue of recognition of rights and culture is central to promotion of welfare of people living near forest. Therefore, forest organisation must recognise such rights/concession and culture of the community. Towards this end, there is a need on the part of forest organisation to have policy, which lays emphasis on rights and culture of such communities.

After having a policy, it is also necessary to create such an environment where the local communities and indigenous people with legal or customary use rights should be able to maintain their rights with respect to forest management practices. Forest practices must not threaten or diminish or affect the resource use rights, or use rights or tenure rights of local and indigenous people.

Sites of specific cultural, ecological, economic or spiritual significance to indigenous people must be protected from damage by forest operations. Towards this end, there is a need to develop a system to identify, record and protect such sites, in co-operation with local and indigenous people. These sites if any, should be protected as conservation area.

If traditional knowledge of any indigenous community is used for development and biodiversity conservation, then adequate compensation should be given to such community. This assumes relevance in the context of increasing possibilities of forest organisation considering commercial harvest of traditionally utilised non-timber forest products and medicinal plants with potentials for use in pharmaceutical, biotechnology and agro-industries.

Relation with Labour/Worker and Forest Staff

Sustainable forest management depends upon efficient management of human resources who are engaged in execution of forest operation. Forest workers, and staffs are all stakeholders in forest management. Workers capability and willingness to work efficiently and honestly helps not only to improve the forest condition but also to minimise the negative impacts of forestry activities on the ecosystem. In order to achieve the goal of labour and staff welfare, the forest organisation must muster all necessary financial resources and observe all laws, regulation, procedures pertaining to labour and staff welfare.

Training and skill up-gradation plays an important role in improving the efficiency of the staff engaged in forest management. It is essential at all levels of the organisation to ensure that the capacity to carry out the tasks of sustainable forest management is available with the staff and labour. More importantly, increasing skill level and training provides a motivating force and helps to improve the level of confidence, efficiency and professionalism.

Contribution to Development

The broader goal of rural development cannot be achieved by the forest organisation alone. It requires synergy of many other organisations under the fold of government. It is because the factors of development are normally beyond the control of forest organisation.

However, the forest organisation can facilitate the role of state in rural development. This is possible if the forest organisation incorporates social issues in forest management and takes steps to work towards human centric forest activities. Towards this end, the forest organisation should strive for equitable distribution of cost and benefit of forest management, between state and the local communities.

Forest organisation should encourage the development and diversification of local forest enterprises. This will entail local processing and marketing of wood and non-timber forest products. It helps the local community in two ways. First is development in such fashion shall prevent over dependence by the local economy on forest. Second is the prospect of gainful employment generation out of such local processing and marketing activities.

Verifying Effects of SFM Practices

Sustainable management practices necessitate periodical verification. Therefore, there is an imperative need to develop methods and frameworks for measuring and verifying sustainability. Such processes have been useful in catalyzing effort and commitment towards sustainable forest management. They aim at establishing principles, criteria, and indicators for sustainable forest management and mechanism for its certification.

Criterion describes a state or situation, which should be met to comply with sustainable forest management. Indicator is a quantitative, qualitative or descriptive attribute that, when periodically measured or monitored, indicates the direction of change. Criteria and indicators for sustainable forest management are still in the process of their evolution. Presently, it is at a slower pace. It has began with economic criterion and slightly moved towards incorporating the ecological and social dimension of sustainability. Generally speaking, it is the social issues including participatory management, which are most difficult to grapple with. The measurement process throws many challenges. As the forest type changes, there will be a change in ecological criterion and indicators. Further, criterion and indicators that encompass both quantitative and qualitative aspects have to be context specific including social dimensions like equality, gender equality, women empowerment, etc.

ITTO guidelines for the sustainable forest management of natural tropical forests (1992) have specified criteria and indicators for sustainable forest management. Seven criterias have been identified as essential elements of sustainable forest management. Seven criterias are as follows:

- Criterion 1: Enabling conditions for sustainable forest management.
- Criterion 2: Forest resource security.
- Criterion 3: Forest ecosystem health and condition.
- Criterion 4: Flow of forest produce.
- Criterion 5: Biological diversity.
- Criterion 6: Soil and water conservation.
- Criterion 7: Economic, soil and cultural aspects.

Different indicators have been identified and formulated under each criterion so that a change in any one of them would give information that is necessary to assess the progress towards sustainable forest management. However, these indicators are more of preliminary and indicative in nature rather than exhaustive. Again, looking at the changing needs of forest management practices, a different set of criteria and indicators, which are able to measure the effects of sustainable forest management, can be formulated.

Criterion 1: Enabling Conditions for Sustainable Forest Management

This criterion covers the general institutional requirements for sustainable forest management to succeed. It addresses policy, legislation, economic conditions, incentives, research, education training and mechanism for consultation and participation. Many of the indicators are descriptive. Taken together, the information gathered indicates the extent of country's political commitment to sustainable forest management.

Criterion 2: Forest Resource Security

This criterion relates to the extent to which a country has a secure and stable forest estate, which could include plantations, to meet the production, protection, biodiversity conservation and other social, cultural, economic and environmental needs of present and future generations. This is necessary for long-term sustainable forest management. The indicators are as follows:

- Description of resource base *i.e.* Extent and percentage of total land area under primary forests and secondary forests, plantation.
- Extent (Area) and percentage of total land area under each forest types.
- Length and percentage of external boundaries of forest area demarcated or clearly defined.
- Area of forest converted for non-forest use and rate of such diversion.
- Forest protection procedures *i.e.* existence of procedures to control encroachment, fire, grazing and illicit exploitation of forests.

Criterion 3: Forest Ecosystem Health and Condition

The criterion relates to the condition of a country's forests and the healthy biological functioning of forest ecosystems. Forest condition and health can be affected by a variety of human actions and natural occurrences, from air pollution, fire, flooding and storms to insects and disease. The indicators are as follows:

- Area of forest damaged by human activities and degree of damage. The various human activities like encroachment, agriculture, roads, mining, dams fire, grazing, illicit felling, should be enumerated and the extent of damage should be determined.

- Area of forest damaged by natural causes. The various natural causes like wild fire, drought, flood, cyclone, pest and diseases.
- Conservation and protection procedures relating to eliminating the human activities or to minimising the effect of damage due to natural causes.

Criterion 4: Flow of Forest Produce

The criterion is concerned with forest management for the production of wood and non-wood forest products. Such production can be sustained in the long-term if it is economically and financially viable, environmentally sound and socially acceptable.

Forests earmarked for production are able to fulfil a number of other important functions, such as environmental protection and conservation of biological diversity. These multiple roles of forest should be safeguarded by the application of sound management practices that maintain the potential of the forest resources to yields the full range of benefits to society. The indicators are as follows:

- Resource assessment (1) extent and percentage of forests for which inventory survey procedures have been used to define the quantity of the main forest products and resource rights, (2) estimate the level of sustainable harvest for each wood and non-wood forest products for each forest type, (3) quantity of wood and important non-wood forest products harvested for each forest type.
- Planning procedures with respect to (1) forest management plan and forest harvesting (operational) plans, (2) extent and percentage of forest production area covered by management plan, (3) existence of long-term strategy, and plans for production, and (4) availability of historical records on the extent, nature and management of forests.
- Management guidelines for each of the main wood and non-wood forest products to be harvested, the assessment of natural regeneration, and measures to supplement natural regeneration where necessary, the mechanism to review the management guidelines.

- Monitoring and evaluation with respect to implementation of procedures for management, to assessment of damage to the residual stand and post-harvest survey to assess the effectiveness of regeneration.

Criterion 5: Biological Diversity

This criterion relates to the conservation and maintenance of biological diversity, including ecosystem, species and genetic diversity. At the species level, special attention should be given to the protection of endangered, rare and threatened species. The establishment and management of geographic system of protected areas of representative forest ecosystems can contribute to maintaining biodiversity. Biological diversity can also be conserved in forests managed for other purposes, such as for production, through the application of appropriate management practices. The indicators are as follows:

- *Ecosystem Diversity*: (1) Number and extent of forest type covered, (2) percentage of forest area under category of protected area, and (3) percentage of total number of protected areas connected by biological corridors.
- *Species Diversity*: (a) Existence and implementation of procedures to identify endangered, rare and threatened species of forest flora and fauna, and (b) Number of endangered, rare and threatened forest dependant species.
- *Genetic Diversity*: Existence and implementation of a strategy for *in-situ* and *ex-situ* conservation of the genetic variation within commercial, endangered, rare and threatened species of forest flora and fauna.
- *Management Guidelines*: (1) Existence and implementation of management guidelines to keep undisturbed a part of each production forests, (2) Protect endangered, rare and threatened species of forest flora and fauna, and (3) Protect features of special biological interest, such as seed trees, nesting sites, niches and keystone species.
- *Monitoring and Evaluation*: Existence and implementation of procedures for assessing changes of biological diversity of the production forests, compared with areas in the same forests type kept free from human intervention.

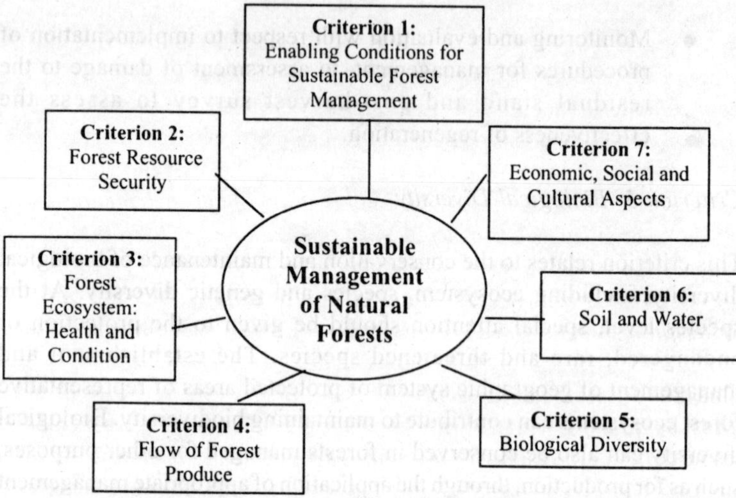

Fig. 8.1: Schematic Tabulation of Criteria

Criterion 6: Soil and Water

This criterion deals with the protection of soil and water in the forest. The importance of this is two folds. First, it has a bearing on maintaining the productivity and quality of forest and related aquatic ecosystems. Secondly, it also plays a crucial role outside the forest in maintaining downstream water quality and flow and in reducing flooding and sedimentation. The environmental and social effects of mismanagement (landslides, flooding, water pollution) can be enormous and restoration very costly. National level data for indicators will normally be derived from the aggregation of data collected at the forest management unit level. The indicators are as follow:

- *Extent of protection*: (1) Extent and percentage of total forest area managed primarily for the protection of soil and water, (2) Extent and percentage of area to be harvested for which off-site catchment values have been defined, documented and protected before harvesting.
- *Conservation and protection procedures*: (1) Existence and implementation of procedures to identify and demarcate sensitive areas for the protection of soil and water, (2) availability

and implementation of guidelines for forest road lay-out, including drainage requirements and conservation of buffer strips along streams and rivers.

- *Monitoring and evaluation*: Existence and implementation of procedures for assessing and changes in the water quality of streams emerging from production of rests as compared with streams emerging from the same forest type kept free from human intervention.

Criterion 7: Economic, Social and Cultural Aspects

This criterion deals with the economic, social and cultural aspects of the forest besides those mentioned under criteria 4, 5 and 6. As a renewable resources, the forest has the potential, if sustainably managed, to make an important contribution to the sustainable development of the country. The indicators are as follows:

- *Socio-economic aspects*: (1) Value and percentage contribution of the forestry sector to the Gross Domestic Product, (2) Quantity (Volume) and value of wood and non-wood forest products for subsistence use, including fuel, (3) Efficiency of wood utilisation in terms of the percentage of felled volume processed, (4) Existence and implementation of mechanisms for the effective distribution of incentives and the fair and equitable sharing of costs and benefits among the stackholders involved, (5) Employment in the forestry sector with respect to number employed, percentage of total workforce, average wage rate, etc., (6) Number and extent of forest sites available primarily for research, education, direct use and benefit of local communities and recreation, (7) Number of people dependent on the forest for subsistence uses and traditional and customary lifestyles, (8) Area of forest upon which people are dependant for subsistence uses and traditional and customary lifestyles, (9) Number of visitors to forest for recreational purposes.
- *Cultural aspects*: (1) Number of important archaeological and cultural sites identified and mapped, (2) Number of important archaeological and cultural sites protected.
- *Community Participation*: (1) Extent to which user rights over the forest are documented and recognised, (2) extent to which forest planning and management practices and processes

consider and recognize legal customary rights with resect to indigenous people and local communities, forest villagers and forest dependent communities, (3) Extent of participation by indigenous people and local communities, forest villagers and forest dependent communities in forest-based economic activities, (4) Number of Memorandum of Understanding (MOU) or agreements involving local communities in management responsibilities.

9

SUSTAINABLE FOREST MANAGEMENT

Policies and Conditions

Sustainable development requires integrating economic viability and human development with the necessity to protect the environment and sustain indefinitely the natural resource base. Considered in this backdrop, sustainable forest management requires integration of environmental, social, economic dimension of forests into the policies and practices for utilising and managing forests, so that economic and social needs are met while leaving forests capable of fulfilling their environmental functions enduring.

Forest management, of late, has become far more complex by the emphasis on aspects of ecological, social and economic sustainability. In order to address this, it is necessary to initiate, among other things, major reforms in policy and legislative environment. What is more important is the fact that supportive environment and conditions are also required to make the policy and legal framework to work in the desired direction. This chapter focuses on critical policy elements along with the conditions, which hold key to success of sustainable forest management. Policy issues for the new era have also been discussed at length.

While discussing major policy and legal aspects of forest management, it is necessary to clarify the shift from the traditional sustained yield concept to that of sustainable forest management for multiple benefits. This shift consists of a change from production techniques designed to ensure a sustained commodity flow over time to a broadened focus that encompasses socio-economic benefits, the participation of rural people, environmental benefits and ecological stability in holistic continuity of multiple flows while maintaining the potential to respond to evolving needs. A concern for sustainability was already present in sustained yield concept but this concern now embraces systematically the economic, social and ecological roles of forests in development. To translate these concerns into action, a robust policy is indispensable.

The need of a sound forest policy for every country has been emphasised in many international conventions. The most important and recent one is the non-legally binding authoritative statement on forests, that "national policies and strategies should provide a framework for increased efforts, including the development and strengthening of institutions and programmes for the management, conservation and sustainable development of forests and forest lands". The dynamic nature of development in a world of pressing and competing needs requires that policies, legislation, regulations, conditions and institutional arrangements are kept under a continuous process of monitoring and adaptation that act as an effective incentive framework for sustainable forest management.

Need of a Sound Policy Framework

A sound policy framework is a *sine qua non* for sustainable forest management. It deals with forest resources and their management when treating socio-economic factors related to increasing the performance of the sector; the role of the forest and tree resource in land use and rural development; and nature conservation and environmental protection. Generally existing forest policies have been formulated to address simpler situations than those prevailing today. Forest policies in the past focussed principally on wood production and, at best, on the concept of sustained yield. But today, the things have changed drastically. The objectives of forest management have changed. Forests are now required to produce a whole range of goods and services. Therefore, forest must be managed in much interdependent and complex context, which requires a collaborative process among all-major actors and beneficiaries. For this to happen, it is essential that forest policies recognise the diversity of interests related to forest conservation and utilisation. It is also necessary to accept major interest groups in forest management decisions through consultations in which they can express their expectations and ensure their role. The prevailing political system in each country will have to determine how divergent interests are to be harmonised and how the costs and benefits are to be shared among the main actors and beneficiaries.

As every country, over the years, has shown a modicum of political will to stabilise existing forests and increase forest resources, the moot point remains how to go about. The important questions that come across before we embark on the journey to sustainability are; how much forest should be maintained to meet the desired economic, social, conservation and environmental objectives ? How these resources should be classified and managed to reflect both the productive and the protective functions of forests like protected areas, forests for timber production, forests for recreation purposes, forest for non-wood forest product and areas for social forestry. Answers to these questions go beyond the realm of traditional forestry. Solutions are found in the domain of ecological, ethical, economic, socio-political considerations. Everybody wants that all remaining natural forest should remain intact, but preserving them all intact would be unrealistic given the increasing needs of many developing countries for social and economic development. Therefore, the best possible course for many countries would be to manage forest for multiple uses, balancing conservation and development objectives.

Eventually each country must develop its own forest conservation and development policy and create conditions conducive for effective implementation of such policy. When such policy is based on principles of sustainable forest management, then it is called as sustainable forest management policy. Such policies are the public expression of forestry organisation or country's commitment to the goals of sustainable forest management. They express the intentions that forest management will be carried out in ways, which are environmentally responsible, socially beneficial and economically viable. The policy statement forms the basis of relationships between the government organisation, local communities and other stakeholders.

The forest policy describes a broad set of economic, social and environmental objectives. It outlines how the organisation intends to achieve the objectives and what benefits will be for the people and society and other stakeholders. Towards this end, every government or organisation needs: (1) a national land use policy aiming at the sustainable use of all natural resources, (2) a national forest policy forming an integral part of the comprehensive national land use policy, assuring a balanced use of forests. Therefore the forest policy should be formulated by a process which seeks consensus of all the actors/stakeholders involved in forest management and use. Considerations in a forest policy include the needs of determining the objective of forest management, needs of deciding the proportion of land under forests, needs of protection and conservation of biological diversity; needs of strengthening forest management systems for single or multiple use, needs of creating property rights and correcting market and policy failures; needs of developing forestry institutions and human resources, needs of adopting environmentally friendly technologies; needs of involving private sector in forest management; needs of implementing conservation measures; needs of expanding environmental education; needs and aspirations of present and future generations and the needs of determining a place for forestry in national economic planning. Besides, countries should take the values of conserving forest for future into account while formulating policies and programmes for sustainable forest management. The features of the forest policy or the land use policy or environmental policy should be developed on the basis of the societal and environmental needs of that country.

Critical Elements of SFM Policies: A Multilevel Framework

International Tropical Timber Organisation (ITTO) guidelines for sustainable forest management of natural tropical forests have defined 'sustainable forest management' as the process of managing forest to achieve one or more clearly specified objectives of management with regard to the production of a continuous flow of desired forest products and services without undue reduction of its inherent values and future productivity and without undue undesirable effects on the physical and social environment.' In order to put the said process in the work, we need suitable policies, programmes and activities. To begin with a holistic approach to understand relevant policies, programmes and activities that enable effective coordination of desired influences to effect sustainable forest management is necessary. Towards this end, a multilevel classification of elements of forest policies is imperative. It helps to undertake a systematic analysis of issues involved. Apart from this, it helps to explore preventive and mitigational options while addressing anthropogenic influences on the system and phenomenon governing sustainable forest management. A broad classification of critical components or elements of SFM Policies is presented below.

1. *Ecosystem Components*

   - Recognition of forests as a major renewable natural resource of value for present and future generation.
   - Application of principles of ecosystem management, more specifically the 'Malawi Principle'.

- Application of ecosystem principles, specially Precautionary Principles (PP).
- Assessment of implication of transitory and permanent equilibria, threshold effects on the sources and sink capacities of forests.
- Implications for the economic systems on forest ecosystem management.
- Assessment of bio-geophysical externalities.

2. *Macro-economic System Components*

- Application of demand and supply management with respect to forest products.
- Integration of domestic and international policies in respect of trade, debt and export obligation.
- Internalisation of various provisions of international environmental and multilateral trades agreements.
- Application of the Polluter Pays (PP) principle.
- Providing guidance to regional and local institutions regarding varied policies for SFM.
- Institutionalising green taxes or equivalent fiscal policies for environmental protection.
- Forming institutions for enhanced equity and productivity of forest resources.
- Reduction of poverty and fulfillment of basic minimum needs.
- Support of R&D and technical innovation.
- Internalisation of costs of economic and environmental externalities.
- Identification and assessment of possible negative impacts of agricultural/industrial programme or privatisation policy on forest resource conservation.
- Identification of areas of market development that work against sustainable forest management and policies and modify forest use rights.
- Sustaining forest management becoming an important element in the overall development objectives of optimising land uses while ensuring environmental stability.
- Integration of social, environmental and economic objectives of development with the forest policy.

3. *Sectoral Components*

- Devising policies and operational programmes conducive to sustainability and sustainable development.
- Recognition of inter-sectoral linkages and internalisation of externalities.
- Assessment of income distributional implications of policies and programmes.
- Provision of pricing systems and pricing policies which ensure internalisation of incremental costs and other externalities.
- Control of features affecting global commons.
- Enhancing innovative management practices and utilising people's participation.
- Monitoring of inputs and interactions particularly in areas bordering on forests, in order to induce and develop consistency and complementarities with forest management activities and to minimise the negative impacts of pricing and to initiate incentive measures in other sectors to promote forest management and sustainable use.

4. *Territorial Components*

- Integration of national, international, regional, and local policies and systems to move in harmony.
- Inter-regional and inter-sectoral consistency of policies and programmes.
- Actions to control environmental deterioration
- Utilisation of indigenous resources.

5. *Socio-economic Components*

- Human centered development approach
- Ensuring gender equality.
- According priority to the needs of women and children.
- Recognition of poverty eradication in association with environmental development.
- Investing in people and human capital formation.
- Strengthening social capital in communities.
- Focussing on the behaviour of the various social groups that share an interest in the use of forest resources and encouraging actions that support sustainability.

- Recognising different groups of users who depend on the various outputs from the forests and encouraging flexible approaches that promote sustainable development across a variety of tenure, use, and a management regimes in different ecological, socio-economic and political context.
- Attaining economic growth without ignoring the requirements of social justice or improved income distribution policies.
- Protecting the cultural integrity of their forest heritage and encouraging the design and implementation of management approaches that enable local communities to involve themselves as preferential partners and beneficiaries.
- Ensuring upliftment of the 'weaker' sections of the society.

6. *Institutional Components*

- Promoting a proactive 'facilitator' role for government.
- Supporting democratisation of institutions, and rule of law.
- Strengthening market institutions, private sector, and public or government sector to effect catalytic support and provide a complementary role rather than substitutory role.
- Encouraging people's institutions and genuine non-government organisations (NGOs) at different levels of the governance of social, political and economic areas.
- Promoting governance and administrative systems for improved integrative effects, which recognise cross-departmental linkages and reduce transaction costs.
- Promoting performance and accountability at various levels of the government bureaucracy to ensure management of objectives.

7. *Technology Components*

- Promoting elements of information technology including application of Geographical Information System (GIS), Geographical Positioning System (GPS), Management Information System (MIS), Internet and strategic communication technology in forestry.
- Promoting elements of biotechnology in the field of improved plant production, disease protection system, tree improvement, etc.
- Adopting new technologies in plantation, logging, forest utilisation, etc.

Formulating Forest Policy

Forest policy is the key to effective management of forest resources. The objectives of forest management need to be clearly defined and effective means of achieving them require to be identified in the policy. This apart, policy making should be a continuing process in order to keep pace with changing conditions (Gane, 1983). If the policy is too flexible, ephemeral or transient, then it may fail to convey the impression of long-term commitment that forest management requires. Therefore, forest policies should be coherent, comprehensive and consistent. General prescriptions for forest pollicies are presented in Box 9.1.

BOX 9.1: PRESCRIPTIONS FOR FOREST POLICIES

- Forest policies need to be strengthened and implemented more rigorously.
- Forest policies should give more emphasis to the needs and wishes of people.
- There must be close co-ordination between forest policies and other policies.
- Forest policies must be treated as coherent whole.
- National policies should recognise the growing importance of forestry's international dimension.
- Those responsible for forest policy should do what they can do to protect forests against avoidable damage and destruction.
- Forest administration and individual forest officer should become more outward looking, and become more concerned with people.

Source: Compiled from Hummel (1984).

Formulation of forest policy is a complex process. There is a need to integrate many policies to make it pragmatic and down to earth. No forest policy stands in isolation. Various other agricultural, economic and social policies are likely to be in operation at the same time. It has been proved difficult to harmonise the various internal elements of other natural resource policies. Adequate integration of such elements requires efforts at the intra-sectoral and inter-sectoral levels. If serious conflicts arise between forest and other sector's policies, then problem arises in the relationship between forest resource use and other policies. Such policies may have a far greater impact on the extent and condition of the forest than forestry policies. Therefore, all efforts should be made to harmonise different elements of other sector's policy and integrate them into the forest policy. If it is not possible then other sector's policy should be suitably amended.

Forest policy and practices in developing countries focus on concessions and subsidies. They, in turn, exacerbate market limitations. They do not promote sustainable use of forest resources. This apart, many policies and measures, applied to forest as well as other sector activities, have unintended consequences that are detrimental to forests (See Box 9.2). Therefore, forest sector policies should arise from considerations that go well beyond forestry, anticipating the inevitable increase in demands for a wide range of goods and services.

The forest policy should be supported by appropriate legislation, which should, in turn, be in harmony with laws concerning related sectors. Therefore, laws, regulation, and management codes at appropriate national and local levels should be enacted or revised to support the established forest policy. Apart from this, there should be firm mechanism for regular revision of policy in the light of new circumstances and/or availability of new information.

Bringing policy changes is a complex process. Policy changes to rectify market and price distortions require strong public support and political will. This apart, many policies relating to use of forests fall out side the forest sector. Policy reforms could require the sacrifice of some benefits in the short run. Some time policy reform becomes more intractable because of consideration like externality. Externality costs associated with forest use may have regional and global consequences, but sovereign governments can be expected only to address the domestic externalities in their pricing and taxation policies. Global externalities need to be dealt at global level.

Beyond the critical policy elements, there is also a need to adapt the policy framework regularly in response to real changes; so that it continues to provide an effective incentive for the long-term management of forests for sustainable development. This requires a process of regular consultations among interested parties or stakeholders for the early identification of issues and possible constraints arising from current policies as well as of the need for reforms or adaptations both in policy formulation and implementation.

The process of policy evolution is a unique mix of continuity and change, success and failure, progress and introspection as well as a process of learning and maturing for the entire nation. The salient features of any forest policy can be summed up under the following parameters:

- *Symbolising political will and vision*: Forest policy is a testimony to resolute political will. Each forest policy embodies vision, which aims at betterment of human society. It symbolises political will and vision.
- *Flexible and open ended*: The policy provides a course to achieve the intended goal. It indicates a broad direction and strategy to guide planners, managers and people to direct their efforts in the right direction at the right pace.
- *A holistic approach*: It adopts a holistic approach to natural resource management rather than accepting forests as separate entity. Therefore, the landscape and ecosystem approach is taken for planning and management of forests.
- *Mix of continuity and change*: The process of policy evolution is a strange mix of continuity and change. Certain elements continue to dominate whereas some changes are brought in the policy to reflect societal change. Therefore, the process of continuity and change is an intrinsic part of any policy evolution.

Elements of Wildlife Management Policy

Wildlife management needs a distinct focus. But in the past, the sector suffered from a variety of problems like governmental neglect, insufficient financial resources and incentives, lack of training and conservation education and poor or non-existent regulatory structures. Many countries don't have an official wildlife policy and most existing forest policies scarcely state the value of wildlife conservation. There is no more important tool available to the wildlife managers than a clearly articulated and well-reasoned national policy for the management of the wildlife resource. Without policy support and 'political will' management efforts for wildlife conservation are destined to fail.

The specific elements of Wildlife Policy will vary from country to country. However, as a minimum, a policy should describe the status and role of wildlife in the country and articulate the variety of reasons for regulating wildlife. These should include food values, economic motivations, aesthetic and moral concerns and cultural and historical reasons such as the protection of the national animals, human health and the conservation of genetic resources. The policy should describe the major factors affecting wildlife populations and the institutional and structural means for conserving them. It should spell out government intentions with regard to wildlife management and describe the anticipated benefits. Much attentions should be directed towards providing local communities with a greater measure of control over natural resources in recognition of the fact that, without their involvement, wildlife conservation afforts are destined to fail, apart from some strict nature reserves. Besides, the policy should also focus on many other aspects of sustainable management. It should take into account the impacts of non-wildlife laws as well as fiscal law and local government law on wildlife management and use. Sometime, the impacts of other legislation may have a greater impact than the resource-specific law itself (Moore, 1985).

A wildlife policy can be an exclusive national wildlife policy or part of national forest policy or national conservation strategy. With the growing recognition of the importance of the management of wildlife resources for a variety of reasons, greater emphasis must be placed on the development of more effective and appropriate regulatory mechanisms. We should emphasise on providing an adequate and sustainable stream of benefits to local communities and preserving the viability of threatened wildlife populations. An explicit expression of government policy on management of wildlife is necessary to begin with the process of sustainable forest management. Along with this, the legal and regulatory structure for wildlife management should also be evaluated to determine whether or not it provides the needed incentives, especially to local communities for proper management.

Enabling Conditions for Sustainable Forest Management

Every country has a range of options for forest use. In one end of the range, complete exploitation of forest lies to meet the immediate needs and wants as well as short-term economic goals. In the other end lies the option to keep all forests under protection for future generation. Between these two extremes lies conservation, which implies using the forest to produce goods and services while protecting the environment and resource base on which sustainability of the production system depends.

Conservation conflicts with economic growth in the short-term. But, in the long run these two options are complementary in nature. Moderation and balance in the use of resources is the hallmark of both conservation and sustainable development. In the transition to sustainable development of forest, trade-off between short-term economic gains and long-term development must be made. By balancing conservation and development goals, sustainable development protects the interests of current and future generations in the use of forest resources and links consumption to needs of the society. Merging conservation and economic development goals is definitely a difficult proposition, but it is indispensable for the sustainable development and welfare of humans. The task requires host of policy initiatives for determining a course towards sustainable forest development. This apart, it also requires that enabling condition and supportive environment are created for the policy to work. Therefore, unlike that of sustained yield which mainly depends on technical and ecological elements, sustainable forest management *inter alia*, depends on many such aspects most of which lie beyond the control of a forest organisation.

BOX 9.2: EXAMPLES OF POLICIES, WHICH CONTRIBUTE TO FOREST DECLINE

- Timber concession terms with under-price of wood encourage waste or condone poor forestry practices.
- Subsidies that encourage destructive forestry or forest land conversion to other uses.
- Policies that require forest land clearing as a condition for obtaining legal titles to land ownership.
- Road construction into forest areas.
- In some cases, log export bans that may reduce domestic prices of wood, and therefore reduce incentives to plant trees and also lead to conversion of natural forest lands to other uses.
- Subsidies to industrial wood processing that lead to economic inefficiency.
- Plantation subsidies that may induce natural forest conversion.
- Price controls and taxes that discourage investment in forest planting or conservation.
- Policies to boost mining without simultaneously enforcing strict environmental safeguards.

Source: Our forests: Our future (1999).

Some of such aspects when translated into action provide a supportive environment or act as enabling conditions for facilitating sustainable forest management practices. The appropriate policy may be in place but it does not work because the enabling conditions for implementation of the said policy do not exist. Some of the important enabling conditions on which the execution and success of policy depend are illustrated below:

Laws and Regulations

Laws and regulations constitute one of the important conditions necessary for the success of sustainable forest management. They are the result of policy formulation processes as well-being the basis for their implementation. Changes in national policy, putting more emphasis on sustainable forest management must lead to a systematic review and to modification of legislation. Presently forest law generally tends to refer to sustainable forest management only in the context of wood production. Therefore, the law and regulation should address the conservation and management of forest ecosystems as a whole.

Legislation of particular importance to sustainable forest development includes: (1) legislation referring to the general and specific aspects of environmental protection, including national environmental protection codes and legislation related to environmental pollution control, soil and water conservation, (2) legislation principally concerned with renewable natural resources, including sector-specific legislation related to land use practices like agriculture, animal husbandry, fisheries, and land rehabilitation, (3) legislation dealing with social and economic measures for the development of rural areas, including land tenure legislation, land use planning legislation, regional and national development and investment laws as well as tax legislation, and (4) legislation on nature of protection, including laws protecting flora, fauna and undisturbed landscapes and to a considerable extent, hunting, wildlife, forest and biodiversity conservation.

Traditional legislations on conservation and development of forests do not significantly reflect the principles of sustainability. Indeed, many laws and regulations are inconsistent and often contradictory to long-term forest management. Therefore, periodic and systemic review of laws, regulation and objectives of SFM and their modification in response to evolving needs is necessary. Such an adjustment or modification reinforce existing provisions and improve enforceability.

Population Control

Population growth has been the single most important factor responsible for forest degradation in developing countries. The population has reached a level, which leads to use of forest ecosystem beyond its carrying capacity. Unless it is controlled, no matter whatsoever measures we take to operationalise sustainable forest management, it is not possible to achieve it. Therefore, population control measures constitute an enabling condition for implementing sustainable forest management policies.

Gender Equity

Gender equity is a fundamental issue of governance. It is necessary to make appropriate governance arrangements in any society to ensure that constitutional provisions, legal frameworks, equitable policies, sensitive programmes and responsive administration are put in operation. This constitutes an enabling condition for the forest policy to work successfully.

Gender roles define how women and men perform different tasks for the households, earn income in different ways, have different levels of control over their respective incomes, allocate time differently, have different legal and traditional rights, and possess different types of knowledge. While women normally have multiple, often disproportionate responsibility, they have little ownership or control over productive resources. This imbalances in the ownership and control over resources *vis-a-vis* gendered responsibilities place women in a subordinate and dismembered position relative to men as they persistently depend on men and run a greater risk of being excluded from their homes and livelihoods. As a consequence, women and men develop different perceptions about priorities and goals of life. Therefore, different developmental interventions aimed to improve womenfolk affect them differently.

Women have negligible ownership of private resources and poor rural people have a higher dependence on common natural resources for meeting their survival needs. In this context, the participatory forest management mechanisms would go a long way in empowering women and ensuring their specific needs. The constitutional commitment of a society to gender equality should be reflected in the arrangements for participation, decisions-making and management of forests. These arrangements should be supported by a range of policy measures. This range of policy measures could be:

- Silvicultural and management options responsible to meet

diverse livelihood needs, instead of maximising timber production, need to be developed in order to be more sensitive to interests of women.

- Strategies for increasing self-confidence and empowerment of women and marginalised groups need to be developed to increase the voice of voiceless.
- Organisational change and improved gender balance within forest departments need to be observed to make their functioning more conducive to gender sensitive participatory forest management.
- Education in support of gender equity goals.

Demand and Supply Management

Rapid population growth and accelerated economic growth will lay pressure on the decreasing forest resources. To meet this challenge every country should improve their management of forest resources, recognising the needs of present and future generation. Demand-supply management implies managing the supply of goods and services in such manner that it increases to a level of required demand.

There are two types of demands for forest resources and products. First is the demand for environmental protection, which includes biodiversity conservation, habitat protection, carbon sequestration, climate regulation and watershed protection. The second is the demand for forest land (conversion of forest areas to support other economic activities like agriculture, mining or infrastructure development) and forest products. The second demand constitutes the basic human needs of people living near forests. Sometime, the demand for revenue from the sale of forest produce falls in the second category. These are two categories of demands that compete for each other in the short-term. But, in the long run, both categories of demand stand complementary to each other. In other words, managing both the demands on a long-term basis symbolises conservation and sustainable development of forests.

Therefore, countries should emphasise on sustainable management of natural forest and expansion of forests through afforestation and farm forestry. This apart, they should also focus on management of demands by (1) linking consumption to needs, (2) practicing conservation in the use of forest products, (3) improving the use of fuelwood, (4) promoting efficiency in wood processing industries, (5) promoting efficient pricing of forest products, and (6) promoting timber substitutes.

Supply management is also important for sustainable forest management. Forests will continue to be an important source of economic and environmental goods and services. Tree planting in degraded forests should be encouraged to augment forest resources. Restoration of degraded forests and improvements in the management of tropical forests could ensure a steady supply of tropical timber and reduce pressure on existing forests. Enhancement of productivity in potential forests as well as plantations will be other important areas for increasing supply of forest goods.

Education

Education plays an important role in promoting sustainable forest development. It provides the underpinnings for the direction, which a society decides to take. It prepares citizens for occupying the political space which governance arrangements provides. It inculcates the values and ethics in a society. Education is fundamental to reducing both individual and national poverty and has a close relationship to the pressing issue of human population growth. It is a means to achieving the development goals of health, higher labour productivity, more equitable economic progress and the broader objective of social integration through participation in political and cultural affairs. It is central to orienting a society towards sustainable development. Education is also the means through which individual citizens will appreciate the multiple functions for which forests are important and public policies which governments formulate to ensure continuation of these functions. It is public awareness through education that would lead to appropriate consumption patterns and levels for individuals and societies. Therefore education is central to any efforts to sustainable forest development.

There are immediate and exciting possibilities in the field of education. The growth of distance education, the spread of Internet Technology, and encouragement of 'lifetime learning' has broken down the classroom barriers and allowed many adults to re-discover their potential. When these developments are linked to the need to increase awareness of environmental issues, the opportunities to engage societies in sustaining forests and development are apparent. The education sector, therefore, is a potentially vital avenue through which the objective of sustaining forests specifically and sustainable development more generally can be advanced. It needs to be factored into any policies/programme that is intended to promote sustainable forest management.

Information and Communication

Information and communication play an important role in sustainable forest management. Both the aspects help to spread knowledge, reinforce the social base of sustainability through understanding and dialogue and gradually strengthen technical skills and capabilities.

Information involves documenting positive ideas and developments and diffusing the information in appropriate formats to generate support for suitable solutions. Of late, there has been a wider realisation among the forest managers/officers that some of the misconceptions regarding forest management stem from a lack of public relation capacity. Adequate information activities are essential to build up common understanding and interaction among all stakeholders concerned with sustainable forest management and to ensure support from policy makers and the public.

The information base of the forest organisation worldwide is narrow. There is inadequacy of forest data. This apart, there is incompatibility in definitions and measurements employed by those agencies involved in forest data gathering and analysis. A sound information base is a boon to any forest organisation. It is very useful to policy makers. It helps forest officers and managers to take proper decision in the right context.

Apart from this, there is enormous scope for enhancing the use of information technology in the management of information. The potential of Geographical Information System (GIS) and Global Positioning System (GPS) has started to unfold in the forestry sector. Training in data processing, archiving and retrieving will also be necessary to make possible use of increased and improved satellite data. This is an important element in the process of sustainable forest management. Ecotechnologies based on a blend of traditional wisdom and technologies, and frontier technologies like biotechnology, information, space and renewable energy technologies, will be needed to stimulate the process of sustainable forest management. Hence, the tools of the information age should be fully harnessed for empowering rural families with the needed information and skills.

Communication involves consultation and dialogue with the various stakeholders in forest management. Such a process must specially enable forest dwellers and others forest dependent rural communities to express their needs, expectations and experiences from the early stage of forest management preparation. This will facilitate two-way communication to stimulate participation and support in implementing the forestry plans. This apart, communication generates convergence among groups when different interests require negotiations and mediation.

Management Arrangements and Practices

A robust forest policy with a weak management arrangements and practices will miserably fail. It is because we need a strong management framework to carry out the sustainable forest management practices. Improved forest management arrangements and practices are needed to sustain forest indefinitely and to contribute to more equity in the distribution of benefits from their use.

Liberation of the Civil Society

Liberation of full potential of the civil society is another condition for success of any policies. Forestry sector needs short-term as well as long-term measures. Removal of perverse subsidies, increased transparency in decision-making, improvement in community participation in forest management practices are some of the short-term measures. Likewise, there are some measures, which are possible in the long run. For example, creation of market mechanisms, which can allow wide range of values, placed on forests should be reflected in the economic sphere. Again choices are made in contemporary societies through the operation of political and economic forces. The weak and dismembered segments of society are destined to become more so, unless the politics and policies of countries provide space for them at the decision-making level. Private interests shall outplay public interests unless the government and the civil society are vigilant about the discharge of responsibilities to hold forests in trust. Here lies a great challenge to government organisation as well as civil society in the new era. Therefore, it is widely believed that the full potentiality of the civil society should be liberated through compatible policies and measures that would facilitate the process of sustainable forest management.

Further, opening of decision-making and management process to civil society participation will not by itself reverse the decline of forests, because many of the causes of decline originate outside forestry sector. However, participatory management is a necessary measure of achieving greater social equity, which is so essential to sustaining human societies and to achieving sustainable development. New forms of governance and institutions to permit wider and more equitable participation are required at all levels. Therefore liberation of the civil society has to be inbuilt in the social policy and agenda of the country.

Objectives of Forest Management

The objectives of forest management should undergo a radical change. The objectives should shift from sustaining timber yields to sustaining forests as well as a range of products and services, and more importantly from securing private or group interests to assuring the public interests. The public interest goes beyond the material interests of a single group or private interests of a community and it exceeds the sum of all group interests. The public interests involve securing all the environmental functions of forests, which are essential for humankind as a whole. The society at large shares the benefits that emanate from the environmental function of the forests, collectively and indivisibly. Such benefits go beyond individuals to communities, beyond communities to entire societies, beyond humankind to well-being of all other species, and beyond present to future generations. Thus the objective of forest management should reflect the ecological, economic and social significance of forests.

Over the years, forest management objectives and practices have changed drastically in many countries. There is an increased emphasis on environmental values of forests. What is more important is the fact that greater focus on management of forest for a range of goods and services including environmental have led to reduced intensities in timber harvesting and establishment of low-impact forest management practices.

Operational guidelines and codes of practice for forest management facilitate implementation of sustainable management practices. New silvicultural systems are also required to be developed for temperate, boreal and tropical forests. Greater participation of private sector in forest management is also indispensable to promote sustainable forest management on a holistic basis. It is also necessary to devolve responsibilities for forest planning and management to local communities. Now the concern for the local people has increased. There is a need to provide increased recognition to the claims of indigenous people for use of the forest resource. All these objectives of management should be clearly spelt out in forest policy and strategy papers.

Correcting the Property Regime

Present market mechanisms are unable to reflect the ecological and social values of forests. Such values symbolize public values. The existing divergence between private values and public values discourages investment and encourages economic decisions away from conservation and sustainable development. In addition to it, it distorts the pattern of consumption and production of forest goods and services. As a solution to this problem, we should establish secure and enforceable property rights, which are fundamentally required for minimising the divergence between private values and public values.

Governance Framework

The causes of forest decline have their roots in economic and political arrangements and values. They constitute policies, patterns of use and management, and distributions of benefits from forest. Prevailing governance arrangements generally exclude from consideration decision-making and other groups who are directly on affected by forest policies, uses and management practices.

New governance arrangement will be an important enabling condition for successful implementation of any policies to address the forest crisis. Therefore, government needs to create new governance framework that would be conducive for operationalising the said policies. The new and better forms of governance arrangements are required to reflect the range of needs and interests, to resolve inevitable conflicts, to contribute to equity and democracy, to allow the public interests to emerge and to be made the principal purpose for which forests are managed. In such a framework, there is a need to establish institutional mechanisms to encourage, catalyse and support a larger public role in dispensation of forests.

Organising civil society is one such area by which the governance mechanism can be strengthened. Over the years, there has been an active engagement of civil society in local, national and global affairs. Citizens are taking initiatives through non-governmental and civil society organisations to address some difficult aspects of forest policies and practices. This is particularly evident in environmental matters. Such efforts contribute more effectively towards finding a balance between competing demands and objectives, and conservation and sustainable management of forests. Therefore, more mechanisms are required for civil society participation in policy making and execution to enable the pubic interests in forests to be fully expressed.

Integrating Economic Needs with Environmental Imperatives

Management of forests shall be improved by integrating economic needs with environmental imperatives and social objectives. Many of the forces, which underlie forest decline, originate in non-forest sector like energy, agriculture, irrigation, and human settlement. So it is not simply the decisions that are made about forests alone would sustain them or not. It is now imperative that forestry sector itself urgently adopts suitable approaches and practices in the evolving context where the objective is to sustain both forests and development. Development of people and eradication of poverty provide the necessary synergy for sustainable forest development. Towards this end, it is necessary to adopt the principles of landscape planning and management, and focus on ecosystem-based management practices, participatory decision-making, poverty eradication and human development (See Box 9.3). Therefore, in order to find a panacea for the present forest crisis we must transcend the threshold of classical forestry and get forest management practices and issues assessed in their environmental, economic, political, social and cultural context.

Presently a linear and sectoral approach to policy making and planning is adopted. This has already proved to be inadequate and inappropriate in a complex landscape on which the natural, economic and human worlds juxtapose to each other. Therefore, a landscape planning and ecosystem management approach with people's participation will stand a better chance to the conservation efforts. It provides a stable base for a variety of entrepreneurial activities. It holds key to successful human, social, political and economic development. This approach to planning and management will enable societies to restore stability and assure a future that operates within the biophysical limits of a finite and fragile Earth.

This requirement implies that policy analysis and planning for use of forestlands require radical changes. Development planning on a sectoral basis is not equal to the task of satisfying basic human needs. Planning for forests requires projections for satisfying a variety of needs like food, water, energy and services for living and infrastructure development. It also now requires consideration for where the largest public interests lie.

BOX 9.3: REQUIREMENTS OF LANDSCAPE PLANNING

"Three elements of planning are essential for environmentally sound and socially acceptable forest management:

- That areas of forest to provide for all these used should be set in wider national or bioregional land-use context which provides adequately for all of them in suitable locations;
- That forests should be available to meet the various needs of society; and
- That each area of forest is carefully managed for the purpose for which it is suited and intended.

The exact details will vary greatly from country according to the area and nature of its forests, its population density, its state of development and many other conditions. This pattern should retain or even enhance the 'potential' of forests and give them the flexibility to respond to changing conditions whether social, economic or ecological. The best use of a forest cannot be considered in isolation. For example, forest plantations play an important part in producing timber and may thereby reduce pressure on natural forests; if established on degraded lands they may also increase biological diversity. In general, planning for agricultural expansion, for new settlements and for roads should take into account the possible affects of these developments on adjacent forests."

Source: World Bank, 1998.

Another area, which needs attention, is correct identification of public interests in areas of forest management. This helps to safeguard the functions of forests. If this is done, then it will be a leap towards integration of the environmental, economic and social benefits, which are derived from forests.

Establishing an Ethical System

Establishing a sound ethical system is also a necessary condition for successful implementation of sustainable forest management. Ethical factors like excessive concentration of wealth and power, both within countries and internationally; patterns of corruption, of consumption of natural resources, of inequity, and of cultural discrimination can be detrimental to the sustainability of forest. Ultimately, economic and other pursuits cannot be separated from such ethical concerns. Corrupt and illegal practices that are rampant in forest organisation jeopardise the financial capacities of government and societies to sustain both forests and development. Again excessive consumption of natural resources, including forest products and rising consumptive behaviour of people, especially in developed countries weakens the remaining strands of ethical system, which promotes sustainability. Therefore there is a need to establish a sound ethical system in consonance with requirements of sustainable forest development, democracy, equity, gender equality; transparency, conservation sustainable utilisation and overall sustainability.

Political Will and Leadership

Political will and leadership constitute an important condition for successful implementation of sustainable forest management in any country. The need for attention to different forest issues is so urgent that new and potentially more effective mechanisms, either in government or non-government sector, are necessary to accelerate the required reforms. Commitment by government to signal the requisite political will and leadership is prerequisite for urgent and effective action to deal with the forest issues.

Institutional and Organisational Aspects

The implementation of policies and laws and their impact on forests depend on the attitudes and capacities of people at national and local levels. This is why any progress in policy and regulations requires critical examination of institutional arrangements. Institutional arrangements therefore constitute important instruments for implementing national forest policies through forestry laws and regulations. Assertion of that instrument provides a supportive environment for sustainable forest management.

In developing countries, forest management has been the sole responsibility of government forestry institutions. These institutions have suffered deep financial problems. Such problems can be addressed to by allocating proportionate resources to match the responsibility of the institutions, injecting new dynamism by adopting new policies in the evolving context, increasing the management skill, transferring management responsibilities from government to communities, adopting innovative approach and methods, specially while dealing with the socio-economic aspects of forest management under high demographic pressures. Again, institutional capacities to manage public forests need to be increased by creating requisite infrastructure, downsising bureaucracy, promoting a system of rewards for professional capacities improving career prospects for the officers, and weeding out corruption from the public institutions.

Emerging Policy Issues for the New Era

The major issues that shaped the policies of twenty-first century have been discussed in major international conferences during the last decade. Primarily these issues are: stabilisation of human habitat, population control, poverty eradication, ensuring sustainable development, gender equity, food security, community participation and social infrastructure. In all such issues, the forests play a central role.

In specific environment and forest related conventions, a whole range of issues to which the fate of forests is linked has been deliberated. These issues are population control, poverty eradication, development, social infrastructure, governance, empowerment, consumption and public *versus* private interests. Without addressing these issues, sustaining forests is not possible.

Improved forest policies and management practices are required to sustain forests indefinitely and to contribute to more equity in the distribution of benefits from their use. There is no gainsaying of the fact that causes of forest decline go beyond the forestry sector. Therefore, to sustain forests requires removing the causes of forest decline which generally derives sustenance from current policies and prevailing economic and political arrangements.

There is a prospect of short-term and long-term improvement in forest polices and practices. Apart from this, a robust political and economic arrangement, which creates enabling conditions for policies to work effectively is necessary. The short-term measures can be (1) increased transparency in decision-making in forest management, and (2) improvement in community and civil participation.

Civil society's participation in forest management is very important. It is a general trend that private interests outclass public interests unless the government and civil society is vigilant about the discharge of responsibilities to hold forests in trust. It is believed that the full potential of the civil society is liberated through policies and measures that would remove obstacles in their way. Experiences in the field have emboldened the fact that opening of the decision-making and management process to participation will remove the causes of forest decline, that generally originate outside the ambit of forestry operation. This apart, participatory process is a necessary measure of achieving greater social equity, which is essential to sustaining human society and to achieving sustainable development. The priority to find new form of governance and institutional framework promoting wider and more equitable participation, therefore, has to be high on political and social agenda in the twenty-first century. Periodical changes are also required to focus on the primary objectives of forest development *i.e.* sustaining multifarious benefits for the present as well as future.

Empowerment of the downtrodden and oppressed class is also a necessary condition for effective use of policies. It is multidimensional social process that helps people gain control over their own lives. It is a process that fosters power and responsibility in people, for use in their own lives, their communities, and in their society, by acting on issues that they define as important.

Sustainable management of forests is possible by integrating economic needs with environmental imperatives and social objective. Many of the forces, which underlie forest decline, originate in non-forest sectors, associated with the need for agriculture, energy, transportation and human settlements. Therefore, it is not simply the decisions that are made about forest that would sustain forests or not, but we must reach the domain of economics and natural resource management on a holistic basis.

In order to translate the principles of sustainable forest development into perceptible action, two things are necessary. Firstly, it is required to specify policy objectives and actions, appropriate to scale and significance of the prevailing forest crisis. Secondly, it is necessary to summon the required commitment on the part of government and international community to pursue them with urgency. The World Commission on Forest and Sustainable Development (WCFSD, 1999) has proposed the following policy objectives and actions in the form of ten resolutions (See also Box 9.4).

1. That radical and urgent attention be given to arrest the decline in forests, since forests, their products and services, are threatened.
2. That conserving and sustainably managing the world's forests go hand in hand with the priority of reducing poverty and

sustaining livelihoods of millions of poor people and numerous communities who depend heavily on forests.

3. That the public interests in a stable and secure environment becomes paramount in decisions about use and management of forest lands.
4. That we get to the roots of the crisis by bringing prices and policies in line to better reflect the range of values and uses of forests.
5. That the threshold for responsible forest stewardship be raised to reflect the new responsibilities of forest management to integrate economic, environmental and social considerations and to make the public interest paramount.
6. Those new measures be created to keep track of the value of the capital stock of forests and to create a basis for compensation to countries for ecological services of forests.
7. That participatory planning for the use of landscapes, not just forests, be instituted to assure conservation objectives.
8. That the information base about forests be enhanced and made more directly useful and applicable to policy makers, and in education programmes for the public.
9. That research and training be adapted and accelerated to support the new responsibilities of forest management.
10. That additional avenues for political and policy leadership be explored to accelerate progress towards solutions.

BOX 9.4: RESOLUTIONS AND ACTION POINTS

Resolution 1

That radical and urgent attention be given to arrest the decline in forests, since forests, their products and services, are threatened.

- A target to avoid further destruction or degradation of remaining primary forests, in order to secure their environmental services for all societies and species from what is left, now and for the future.
- Allocation and management through participatory land-use planning of forest land for different purposes: conservation, corporate production, and community forestry.
- Intensify wood production through expansion of plantation

forestry on degraded and vacant lands and improve productivity in secondary forests.

- Reduce pressure on forest land for agriculture through improved productivity in farming by supporting efforts towards a New Green revolution.
- Extensive support to community agro-forestry to reduce the pressures on primary forests for supplying small-scale subsistence products.

Resolution 2

That conserving and sustainably managing the world's forests go hand in hand with the priority of reducing poverty and sustaining livelihoods of millions of poor people and numerous communities who depend heavily on forests.

- Intensified agro-forestry efforts through application of technologies already developed and tested.
- Rapid afforestation and reforestation programmes, targeted to reducing poverty of about on billion of the world's poorest people, through community forestry.
- Removal of obstacles to community forestry ensuring secure titles, tenure and access to forest lands and resources.
- Supports for community forestry through credit facilities, technology, technical assistance, marketing.
- Subsidies to support community forestry made available through a percentage of revenue from timber sales and timber concessions and licenses.
- Creation and expansion of markets for non-timber forest products.
- Support of entrepreneurship for small and medium forest - based enterprises.
- Removal of policy bias towards large-scale timber production by introducing intensities in favour of community forestry, incorporating subsidies that favour communities rather than corporations.
- Support for village-level institutions required for sound management.
- Involvement of communities in the decision-making about allocation of forest lands.
- Creation of a Forum for indigenous people under the UN Commission on Sustainable Development.

Resolution 3

That the public interests in a stable and secure environment become paramount in decisions about use and management of forest lands.

- Creation and support of mechanisms that encourage and catalyse a larger role for non-governmental organisations and civil society that would permit scrutiny of the ways in which benefits from the use of forests are distributed.
- Creation of structured processes for civil society participation in policy making and management.
- Creation and use of participatory processes by governments for policy making for forests.
- Creation of arrangements for gender equity in decision-making, management, entitlements, access to credit, technical assistance and marketing supports.
- Creation of mechanisms for conflict resolution.
- Governance of mechanisms for conflict resolution.
- Governance and other reforms that would limit opportunities for corruption and imposition of heavy penalties for corrupt practices.
- Creation of a Forest Ombudsman mechanism as a civil society body for resolving conflicts among different groups and passing judgement on the implementation of sustainable development policies in the forest area.

Resolution 4

That we get to the roots of the crisis by bringing prices and policies in line to better reflect the range of values and uses of forests.

- A comprehensive review of subsidies and other incentives, which originate within and outside the forestry sector.
- Reform or removal of subsidies that have perverse effects on forest lands and forest resources.
- Public sale or timber concession, licenses and leases through open auctions.
- Stumpage prices that properly reflect the diverse range of forest values.
- A review of policies in agriculture, transportation, settlements,

energy, and water, to alter those which have negative consequences for forests.

- A review of land and resource tenure arrangements to make them more conducive to conservation.
- Support for work to value forest functions and to create market mechanisms for them.

Resolution 5

That the threshold for responsible forest stewardship be raised to reflect the new responsibilities of forest management to integrate economic, environmental and social considerations and to make the public interest paramount.

- Involvement of communities in all stages and implementation of forestry projects.
- Stipulating criteria for management and indicators of performance for all forest operators – public or private, corporate or community, domestic or foreign, large, or small.
- Prescribing codes of conduct for timber companies, which are consistent with the objectives of conservation, sustainability, equity and transparency.
- Imposing penalties for non-compliance with established standards.
- Adherence to social and ethical accounting practices by timber corporations
- Investment in research to increase efficiency in the timber corporations.
- Investment in research to increase efficiency in the timber industry and to establish ancillary economic activities that make use of all 'waste' products from forestry operations.
- Adoption of third-party certification schemes for both domestically traded and exported products.
- Product labelling in accordance with certification standards and accompanied by consumer education programmes.
- Establishment of mechanisms for including local communities in monitoring performance through Forestwatch.
- Harmonising the various sets of criteria and indicators of sustainable forest management and co-ordinating forest certification systems through Forest Management Council.
- Special efforts to reforest deforested land and land abandoned by agriculture through establishment of plantation and woodlots.
- Recognition and reward to communities, corporations and countries for good practice in conservation and sustainable management of forests through a Forest Award Mechanism.

Resolution 6

Those new measures be created to keep track of the value of the capital stock of forests and to create a basis for compensation to countries for ecological services of forests.

- Development of the concept of Forest Capital.
- Development and use of a Forest Capital Index.
- Creation of financial mechanisms on the basis of such an Index to compensate countries for ecological services from forest.

Resolution 7

That participatory planning for the use of landscapes, not just forests, be instituted to assure conservation objectives.

- Opening up a new realm of analysis and research on landscapes and how to keep them stable and functional in support of the human endeavour.
- Implementing integrated planning and management approaches at the landscape level.
- Improvement in the reliability of time-series data for a variety of goods and services (food, fuel, fibre, water for domestic and industrial use, energy sources and services, living space and infrastructure).
- Creation of mechanisms that would enable public administration systems to overcome the limitation of sectoral organisation and approaches
- Creating and maintaining forest resource inventories.
- Engaging in participatory land-use planning.

Resolution 8

That the information base about forests be enhanced and made more directly useful and applicable to policy makers, and in education programme s for the public.

- Efforts by UN and other international agencies involved in observation, measurement, monitoring and mapping of forests to achieve more compatibility in their definitions and terminology, more comparability in their coverage and data.

- Better organisation and dissemination of information concerning forests to enable reliable monitoring of the state of forests.
- Emphasis on public awareness of the role of the forests within formal and non-formal education.
- Campaigns for public education about forests, their role in meeting basic human needs, the pressures on forests, the part which consumption plays in those pressures.
- Incentives for reducing, reusing, recycling forest-related products.
- Incorporating indigenous and local knowledge in forest management.
- Disseminating forest-related information to local communities and forest users.

Resolution 9

That research and training be adapted and accelerated to support the new responsibilities of forest management.

- Establishment by existing institutions and programmes of an international network within which research for sustainable forest management can be enhanced and training can be accelerated.
- Support by corporations of such a network as a means of enabling them to satisfy sustainable forest management requirements, standards and certification systems.

Resolution 10

That additional avenues for political and policy leadership be explored to accelerate progress towards solutions.

- Constitution by those countries which dominate forest cover, production, trade and consumption of forest products of a Forest Security Council, to provide leadership in working out the economic, policy and planning reforms required, and to seek solutions in a multilateral context which could be eventually extended to all countries.
- Undertaking a focussed programme of actions by the Forest Security Council within which the contributions of governments, corporations, NGOs, communities, universities research institutions, scientists and foresters are unified.

- Exploration of ways and means to curb the excesses of multinational timber corporations.
- Assessment of the extent to which liberalised trade negates efforts towards conservation and sustainable forest management.
- Providing feedback from these pilot efforts to on-going inter-governmental and international processes in order to have more widespread application of approaches, policies and measures.

10

SUSTAINABLE FOREST MANAGEMENT

Dynamics and Strategy

Success in sustainable forest management depends on policies, legislation and strategies. We have already discussed about policies and legislation in our previous chapters. Strategies are very critical to success of SFM. They translate the policies into actions on the ground. They set the objectives for carrying out activities, which ultimately lead to attainment of the goal. This chapter dwells on strategy. It deals at length with dynamics of technical aspects of sustainable forest management and few important strategies required to address the silvicultural and management issues. However, in the outset an account of actions required to tackle the social and economic aspects of SFM has been enumerated. The economic, social and environmental dimensions of strategies have been discussed. Along with it, the management needs for implementing different strategies have been enumerated.

For years the military used the word 'strategies' to mean grand plans made in the light of what is believed an adversary might or might not do. While the term 'strategies' still usually has a competitive implication, executives usually use it to reflect broad areas of an enterprise operation. There are three common definitions used in management parlance to define 'strategies': (1) general programmes of action and deployment of resources to attain comprehensive objectives, (2) the programme of objectives of an organisation and their changes, resources used to attain these objectives, and policies governing the acquisition, use and disposition of these resources, and (3) the determination of the long-term objectives of an enterprise and the adoption of course of action and allocation of resource necessary to achieve these goals. In general terms, for instance a conservation strategy consists of the overarching direction for conservation, sustainable use, and equity in use/benefit-sharing.

Likewise, a SFM strategy consists of a broad direction for forest conservation, development, sustainable use, equity based benefit sharing, etc. The purpose of evolving strategies is to determine and communicate a picture of the kind of working, that an organisation visualises. Strategies do not attempt to outline exactly how the enterprise or organisation should accomplish its objectives, since this is the task of countless major and minor supporting programmes. But they furnish a framework for guiding thinking and action.

Different Strategies for Different Countries

Forest management, as we have discussed earlier, is a programme of interventions aimed at optimising production of certain benefits. Such benefits primarily consist of wood, non-wood forest products, biodiversity, livelihood security, recreation and life-supporting capacities. All such benefits are indispensable for the survival and well-being of man. But different society derives different benefits or different combination of benefits at different scale. The developed countries use primary forests basically as a source of industrial goods, biodiversity, recreation and life supporting services. They rarely look at forests as source of energy and livelihood security. In such countries forests face the problem from pervading pollution and urban expansion. But in developing country, the scenario is different. Here, forests have multiple uses. Majority of people depends on forests for their basic needs like household timber, fuelwood, bamboo, and most importantly livelihood security. The economic dependence of poor people on forests is primarily due to pervasive poverty. Such a pattern of dependence on forests has led to depletion of forest resources. Therefore, depletion and degradation of forests in developing countries can be primarily attributed to root causes like poverty and population explosion. Apart from this, there can be many proximate reasons for forest loss. In case of developing and tropical countries, intervention strategy should, therefore, always be focussed on reducing the degree of dependence on forests in one hand, and expanding the forest cover and increase the productivity of forests, in the other. Again the strategy for reducing dependence should take umbrage in social, economic, cultural and political development of the people living near forests. In other words, the overall strategy should be so formulated that it to sustains forests as well as development.

Identifying the measures for sustaining development *vis-à-vis* forests is a complex job. It needs understanding of the special conditions prevailing in a country or a sub-state level. Again, the developmental measures can be of two types. Firstly, it is rural development measure focussed on infrastructure development in the area and income generation of the poor communities. It encompasses programmes like poverty elimination, education, promoting local participation in natural resource management, rural empowerment, removing gender inequality, strengthening local institutions, expanding cottage industry. Secondly, it is more of creating conducive conditions necessary for implementing SFM. Some of the actions points related to the second category is listed in Table 10.1.

Table 10.1: Actions Needed at the Local, National and Global Levels

Type of Action Needed	*Local Level*	*National Level*	*Global Level*
Promote commitment and participation	• Involve local people from the earliest identification and design stages in programmes. • Identify local capacities and strengthen those that are weak. • Initiate environmental education programme	• Establishing strong political commitment to programmes for sustainable development and use of forest resources. • Ensure participation of other sectors in meeting forest conservation objectives.	• Adopt common agenda for sustainable development of forest resources. • Provide grants and concessional funds. • Support global initiatives such as TFAP, ITTO, and GEF.
Establish legal and policy frameworks related to tenure rights, management responsibilities, etc.	• Develop local common property and open access management strategies. • Establish links between local management groups and higher level authority. • Enforce local conservation related mechanisms and rules. • Use self-policing approach to control.	• Develop and adopt a multi-sectoral approach, recognising that most key issues surrounding forest use and misuse involve other sectors. • Develop appropriate inter-sectional policy linkages. • Establish appropriate links between national, regional, and local authority and management. • Establish environmentally sound national land use laws and accompanying cadastral system to clarify rights.	• Develop a global perspective on forest policy. • Provide financial, technical, and managerial support for forest areas designated as world heritage sites. • Develop international legal measures for cost sharing and benefit distribution related to global benefits derived from forest (e.g. genetic materials, carbon storage)
Consider explicitly equity and gender issues.	• Involve local people involved in local forest management.	• Establish laws that promote equity on gender and other bases.	• Contribute to the direct and indirect costs of maintaining preservation forests.

Type of Action Needed	*Local Level*	*National Level*	*Global Level*
	• Address the needs of indigenous peoples. • Consider resolutions to local situations.		• Support projects that benefit the poor and tribal groups
Develop appropriate institutional mechanisms that take into account true account and true scarcity values associated with forest outputs (goods and environmental services)	• Promote strong local NGO planning and action. • Link local governmental and NGO action programmes. • Develop local tree management and conservation incentives. • Establish buffer zones. • Strengthen common property resource management.	• Develop concession and forest fee systems for national lands that promote sustainable use of forest resources. • Develop national incentive mechanisms to encourage tree planting and management. • Establish effective mechanisms to encourage tree planting and management. • Establish effective mechanisms for implementing national and use policies and programs.	• Reduce trade barriers. • Establish guidelines and 'best practice' code for sustainable management of natural forests. • Support research and training. • Expand knowledge on forest ecosystems, the interaction of people with forests, and social environmental impacts of deforestation. • Promote better valuation of forests.

Source: Narendra Sharma, *et. al.* (1992).

The intervention strategies for economic development and creating conducive environment shall not be sufficient to bring fourth improvement in the forests. There is a need to undertake strategies focussed on silvicultural and management needs of forests. In other words, forests are required to be managed in such a manner that it sustains the forests as well as the development.

Most of the tropical countries are poor and so they are dependent on forests for many basic needs like energy, timber, non-wood forest products (NWFP) etc. Looking at the scale and range of requirement in tropical countries, there is a problem of mismanagement and deficiency of forest resources. Therefore, the solution to most of the forest problems in such developing counties lies with not only improving the management of forests but also expanding the forest resource base. Sustainable forest management programme, being multidisciplinary in nature, fits into the scheme of things required. Again under the broad programme of SFM, there are different strategies/programmes to achieve different management objectives. Such strategies focus on silvicultural and management aspects of forestry. Along with the rural development strategies, such silvicultural and management initiatives aim at managing the forests on holistic basis.

In this chapter we shall be discussing more on strategies or programmes focussed on technical and management aspects of forestry. While delineating the strategies every aspects of silvicultural management along with environmental, social and economic dimension of sustainability are dealt with. The strategies suggested in the ensuing paragraphs are applicable to tropical forests.

Silvicultural and management strategies aim at managing the structural and functional aspects of forest sustainably. There may be many such strategies. Each such strategy again aims at achieving a common management objective. However, there are many such aspects in silvicultural management, which are seemingly distinct but mutually correlated in the broad framework of sustainable forest management.

While discussing different critical elements of the strategy, different sustainability dimensions will also be dealt with. The issues of sustainability assume importance because the society today faces twin challenges of environmental degradation and rural impoverishment. In much of the developing world, conservation for the sake of conservation has become an anachronism. There is an increasing awareness and acceptance of the fact that if the natural resource base is to be sustained, it must be done so in a productive manner which benefits the local population. That means conservation is only possible through sustainable utilisation of resources.

Some of the important strategies or programmes focussed on silvicultural and management aspects of forestry under the broad framework of Sustainable Forest Management (SFM) are discussed below.

1. SFM for Wood Production
2. SFM for Non-Wood Forest Products (NWFP)
3. SFM for Biodiversity Management
4. SFM for Ecosystem Management.

SFM for Wood Production

Timber production remained in the center stage of forestry during the last centuries. It shaped the science and practice of forestry. This trend continued until the end of last century. Along with timber production, management of forest for multiple purposes evolved slowly in the last leg of the twentieth century. Again, within the spectrum of multiple use, many options of forest management emerged. One among is sustainable management of forest for wood production. In other words, SFM for wood production is a strategy, which aims at producing timber and other wood products without sacrificing multiple benefits of forests. While delineating a strategy, the discussion shall be confined around how the management objectives shall be achieved.

Sustained yield management remained the traditional principle of forestry. Basically, it was always understood that forests were valuable from the point of wood only. Of late, the values of forests have widened considerably. The concept of sustainability, with respect to over all potentiality of the forests as well as broad range of benefits, has been added to forest management. The journey to sustainability, not only of wood but also a broad range of goods and services, has just begun in the fag end of the last century.

The journey from sustained (wood) yield management to sustainable forest management in a broader sense including wood, non-wood products and services) is replete with challenges. Some says that it is impossibility. (Jacob, M. 1988). There is no gainsaying of the fact that sustainable wood management without sacrificing other benefits from the forests is definitely a daunting task. The performance of tropical forests in developing countries corroborates this premise. Given this, the task of harmonising sustainable wood management with the system of unimpaired supply of a broad range of non-wood products, and services and values to constitute an integrated management system looks gigantic. As things stand today, there is an imperative need to address this problem.

Basic Principles of Wood Management

Sustainable forest management for wood production is based on principle that: ' Harvesting of wood at an average annual rate that is no greater than that at which the forest can grow it and without harming the forests' capacity to supply other goods and services.' (Leslie, A.J., 1996.) This concept laid emphasis on two facets. The first is 'sustained yield of wood'. This principle concurs, to a great extent, the concept of 'timber sustainability' practiced in the olden days. The second facet is that managing the forest should be in such a manner that it does not affect the capacity of the forest to supply other goods and services to the society. When both facets are applied into practice, then it must be in unison with each other. But, in this framework the structural and functional integrity of the forest takes precedence over timber production. This is how sustained timber or wood production is different from the old concept of sustained yield.

Addition of the second facet in wood management is a recent one. This is in response to the concern of the people and world communities for maintaining forests not only for wood but also for other goods and services. It appears that the approach is to imbibe the principles of 'over all sustainability', more specifically ecological sustainability, into the concept of sustained timber yield. Therefore, the concern is now with sustaining the forests and all of its values rather than just its wood-producing capacity (Leslie, A.J., 1996).

Presently, the concept of SFM for timber or wood has the following fundamental elements:

- Ascertaining the wood increment.
- Identifying the appropriate part of the forest to be felled as being equivalent to increment.
- Replacing that part of the forest to be felled in conjunction with the harvesting operation.
- Adopting such methods of harvesting so that no serious and permanent damage results to other goods and services or to the forest's capacity to continue supplying them in the future.

As said earlier, there is a lot of polemics on the practicability of such principles. However sound the principles of wood management be, there are problems in implementation. Leslie A.J., (1994) opined that timber harvesting, even under effective sustained yield management for wood, puts most of the other aspects of sustainable management at risk, simply because, it disrupts the forest structure, the forest and social environment and the ecosystem for more than one occasion. Apart from the aforesaid ecological problems, there emerges a problem related to management practices too. Such problems pertain to determining increment, identifying it correctly, and replacing that part with new crop and undertaking low impact harvesting practices.

There is a great degree of difficulty in harmonising the previously mentioned four elements while evolving the management prescriptions for any forests. Problem emerges at every step. First, it is difficult to determine the increment of wood exactly. In a selection forest the problem is further compounded because there is diversity in growth patterns, species composition, and age distribution. Secondly, it is difficult to separate the increment from the trees with which it grows. Thirdly, it is again difficult to replace that part of increment with new regeneration. Fourthly, it is difficult to replace the increment by felling trees without harming the overall ecological sustainability of the forests. Therefore, sustainable management of forests for timber or wood necessitates a thorough understanding of principles and practices.

Sustainability Dimension in Wood Management

SFM for wood production has distinct sustainability dimensions. It encompasses elements of environmental, economic and social sustainability. But the degree of such elements may differ.

Environmental Dimension

Environmental sustainability in SFM for wood production revolves around the four fundamental elements of wood production. All the elements are intertwined with each other in such a manner that only an emphasis on all the elements on a synchronised pattern can lead to sustainability. Exclusion of any one of those four elements shall lead to development of unsustainability in the forest system. While planning and executing the sustainable forest management, each element needs to be worked out, measured and evaluated (See Table 10.2).

Table 10.2: Elements of Wood Management and Methods/Technique of Measurement

Sl. No.	*Elements of Management*	*Methods/Technique of Measurement*
1.	Determination of annual wood increment	Inventory making and yield regulation
2.	Identification of appropriate part of the crop to be felled as equivalent to annual increment	Marking of trees
3.	Replacing the appropriate part of the crop equivalent to increment	Regeneration
4.	Felling and removing of the crop found equivalent to increment	Harvesting of the crop

All the four elements along with their dynamics are explained below:

The Wood Increment

Wood increment in an unit of forests is the function of site quality and past management system and its effects on the forests. If the management practices followed are sound, then the increment will be conspicuous. In selection system, if the felling cycle is fairly large, then the big sized timber will be the result. If the felling cycle is short, then small sized timber will be the output.

Measuring the increment in tropical forest is a daunting task. This is done by adopting sample plot, growth ring and yield regulation analysis. The standard practice of determining age on the basis of diametric growth is not absolute. The basis of incremental measurement still largely depends on repeated measurement of differential growth pattern of individual species, distribution of size classes and the protracted time horizon *i.e.* the long rotation of the crop. Apart from this, the methods of measurement are not accurate but approximations. Therefore, measuring the correct increment of wood is definitely a challenge, which is yet to be solved.

The Distribution of Size Classes

Selection forests have a distribution of size classes or age classes of the trees producing the type of wood required over a unit of a forest. This element indicates the limit to which allowable cut of wood requires to be harvested in order to keep the sustained yield in a balanced state. The intensity of harvest depends, among other things, on the condition and productivity of the forests. A higher cut is possible where the stem distribution in a forest is skewed towards larger size classes but, in a forest where stem distribution is skewed in the opposite direction, the allowable cut should be set lower than the increment.

The Method of Regeneration

Regeneration is central to forest sustainability. The method of regeneration used to replace a part of the crop is very important. It is because two major factors affect regeneration: firstly, it is availability of light on the floor of the forests at optimum level and secondly, it is anthropogenic pressure on the forests beyond the threshold limit. The first requirement is fulfilled by silvicultural management system, which comprises regeneration felling and low-impact harvesting practices. Nevertheless, the problem comes while fulfilling the second requirement. It is because of the fact that the forests are under tremendous anthropogenic pressure and use of the forest is being carried beyond the carrying capacity of the system.

Looking at the present system of development and demographic trend in developing countries one can safely conclude that in future the pressure on the forests is going to mount at a faster pace. Consequently, increasing anthropogenic pressure on forests shall mar the prospects of natural regeneration in the forest floor. Therefore, augmenting natural regeneration requires to address the problem of how to decrease the pressures on forests.

Over the years, it has been found that harvesting operations damage the regeneration found in the floor of the forests or create conditions not compatible to promoting regeneration. Apart from this, logging operations impair the system of sustainable flow of other forest goods and services. Therefore, it is also necessary to adopt a low impact harvesting system or reduced impact logging (RIL) in order to promote regeneration and ensure supply of other forest products and services at a scale that is consistent with the carrying capacity of the ecosystem as well as management objectives.

Low impact harvesting or reduced impact logging (RIL) is the use of environmentally sound timber harvesting practices. It is a method, which aims at minimising the adverse impact of tree felling operation on the forest and its supply of other non-wood products and services. It can reduce environmental damage associated with felling and skidding practices, extraordinarily large gaps or the excessive use of forest land or infrastructure. It can also reduce stand damage significantly (Bach, 1999). In this method, the cost of logging may be higher. It may also happen that the market may not be in a position to absorb the high economic rent because of increased cost of harvesting. Consequently, the logging operation may push the cost of sustainable management practices far beyond the threshold of economic efficiency. However, the cost of low-impact logging is the unavoidable price the society has to pay for pursuing sustainable forest management. Therefore, the moot point is whether sustainable forest management is worth emulating because of its cost involved. Possibly, the answer is always 'yes'.

Low impact harvesting method or reduced impact logging (RIL) includes (1) low felling intensity *i.e.* felling of few trees per hectare, (2) minimum damage to the standing crop, advance crop and established regeneration, (3) protection of trees having ecological or religious or cultural significance or groves of trees having cultural import, (4) conservation of strip of forests along river and rivulets from the point of soil and water conservation, (5) confinement of felling in production areas, (6) delineation of protection areas within production forest unit, (7) maintaining timber extraction path according to ecological requirement, rather than the economic norms, (8) optimising the disturbance owing to timber felling in space and time (this can be possible by prolonging the felling cycle, reducing the felling intensity and limiting the period of felling and other operation within minimum time frame, specially completing all operations before the onset of rainfall in tropical forests), (9) adoption of a silvicultural system which promotes diffused felling over the entire area of the production unit, and (10) adoption of silvicultural principles in place of economic criterion, improvement of productive potential of forests in terms of growing stock and not merchantable part of the forests.

Ensuring the Supply of Other Products and Services

Along with low impact logging, it is also imperative to ensure the supply of other products and services from the said unit of forests. Therefore, apart from the practices, which lead to sustainable production of wood, it is also necessary to ensure that the flow of products and services, which the forest is capable to supply, is not disturbed. The primary objective of such management is to produce timber on a sustained way but without impairing the structural and functional integrity of the forests.

The Economic Dimension of Wood Management

The wood management has a distinct economic dimension. Over the years, this dimension emerged as an important aspect in sustainable forest management. In most of the cases, in spite of the fact that the elements of environmental sustainability are incorporated in such a management framework, they still do not fulfil the norm of economic standard or economic viability. In a market economy, any thing, which is not economically viable, takes a backseat. Consequently the prevailing market structures, pattern and opportunities force the system of management to opt for higher output at lower cost. This leads to high impact logging which runs counter to the principles of environmental sustainability. It has also been found in many cases that the management system tends to adjust to the economic regime rather than to the standard of ecological sustainability. In the process of adjustment and readjustment with the prevailing economic regulation, the scale of sustainable management tilts towards unsustainability. Resultantly, it leads to development of many unsustainable practices. However, allocation of higher financial resources to forestry operations can minimise the unsustainable practices to some extent. But, such higher allocation for sustainable forestry is not the long-term solution, though it is in practice in many countries. It is therefore, necessary to look for economic sustainability in wood production also.

Price of Sustainable Wood

If sustainability is the goal in forest management, then the society must be ready to pay for the price of sustainable wood. Sustainable wood is a product of a complex forest management process. Ecological, social, management and economic principles govern the process. Before delving into the aspects of social costs of sustainable wood, it is pertinent to discuss three factors, which stand out conspicuously as determinants of success in sustainable management. Such factors are as follows:

- Interaction between the elements of yield regulation and element of regeneration.
- Distribution of all age classes in the same degree *i.e.* normal distribution of stems.
- Cushion against the forces, which try to tilt the balance towards 'unsustainable development'.

Managing the forests for sustainable wood production without affecting the potentiality of forest to provide other non-wood forest products and services is definitely a difficult proposition. Nevertheless, this is not impossible. In order to meet the multipurpose sustainability of forests, it may be necessary on the part of the society to pay the price for it. The price may be in terms of higher cost of management of forests. However, if we want timber management to absorb the cost, then it will have adverse fall-out on forest ecosystem. Likewise, if we want timber yield to reflect the cost in the market place, then it will increase the market price of wood. If this happens then it is a welcome development. But there is always a genuine doubt about the capacity of the market to absorb the higher cost of management and logging. It is so because the wood market is imperfect and unorganised. However, a study of price increase in timber over the last thirty years in India indicates that the market is quite capable of absorbing the additional cost of sustainable management to a great extent. But the market is not in a position to absorb full cost of sustainable management. Societies in developed countries are in a better position to absorb the additional costs of sustainable management. The prospect of such a trend looks bleak at least in developing countries toady. However, a change is imminent in future.

Social Dimension of Wood Management

Sustainable wood management has a social dimension too. A forest managed on the sustainable basis may entail less wood production in comparison to traditional 'timber yield management practices'. But it will have strong intra-generational as well as inter-generational sustainability. On a long-term basis, the production of wood will be sustained. That means, wood management practices shall emanate a sustained flow of social benefits, spread over a period of many generations, in the form of employment, non-timber forest products, fuelwood and timber to villagers living in and around forests. In other words, sustainable management of wood is a potential tool to provide social security to the needy people on a fairly long-term basis. Apart from this, it shall have certain social costs also. If we keep the objective of management as 'sustainable wood production', then it will have to compromise certain benefits like non-wood forest products (NWFP), biodiversity, and ecological services. Loosing all such benefits, though at different intensity, shall involve social costs to the society.

Management Needs of Wood Production

The management needs for wood production require emphasis on two areas; first it is primary forest and the second it is secondary forest. We shall be dealing here with primary forests only. The case of secondary forests or plantation shall be dealt with separately. Wood production can be one of the management objectives in primary forests. But in such forests, other management objectives like soil and water conservation, biodiversity conservation and NWFP production should also go along with the primary objectives of wood production. But in such situation, it becomes difficult to prioritise different objectives and develop the silvicultural regime accordingly. If we aim to maximise the wood production, then it may conflict with other management objectives. Likewise, if we optimise production of NWFP and other ecological services, then it may reduce wood production. Therefore, there is a need to evolve a balance between different management objectives. If the primary objective of management in a unit of forests is wood production, then other objectives shall remain subordinate to the primary.

Considered in this context, the strategy for wood production is evolved in the following ways:

Wood Production in Primary Forests

Wood production in primary forest is still a practice in most of the countries. In the past the management objective used to be maximisation of wood production. However, with the widening importance of forests, there is now a trend to shift wood production gradually from the primary forests to secondary forests. This will reduce the pressure on such primary forests and resultantly, such forests shall provide ecological and other planetary services required for survival of the mankind. However, till the alternative strategy for boosting wood production is not evolved, it is necessary to develop sustainable forest practices for timber production in such primary forests.

Sustainable forest management strategy for timber production in primary forests necessitates a series of intervention into the forest ecosystem. Now the question arises whether to sustain yield or to sustain the capacity of the forests to produce timber and other forest products. In the past, the emphasis was on production of timber out-put on a sustained basis. Now the emphasis is on maintaining the potentiality of the forest system and in the course of this, the yield may vary from time-to-time. The merit of the later system lies in the fact that the forest maintains its potentiality to produce forest products and services for the present as well as for the future generation also. Where as the previous one runs the risks of loosing a part of the potentiality of the forest system in the course of obtaining timber yield on a sustained basis.

The strategy should contains the following components:

1. There should be minimum interference into the forest ecosystem.
2. Timber management should not be practiced at the cost of soil and water conservation and biodiversity.
3. There should be minimum or no differentiation between valuable

and non-valuable species. All species have their own significance in the ecosystem. Preferential treatment promotes gradual domination of preferred species in the composition and eliminates the species not preferred from the ecosystem. Therefore, all measures regarding preferential treatment of timber trees should be stopped forthright.

4. In the past, subsidiary silvicultural systems like improvement felling were adopted to improve the timber content of the growing stock. But such measures do not result into any substantial improvement in the growing stock. Rather, in the process of such 'so called improvement' forest loses valuable biodiversity. Again deformation in the crop is generally because of the genetically make-up of the tree species. Therefore, any attempt to correct and improve the timber quality and content of the trees by adopting management practices does not bear fruit to the point it is expected.
5. Hygienic operation should be minimised. It deprives the forest ecosystem of its biodiversity. Lack of diversity leads to erosion of resilience which is required to counter any natural adverse development
6. In the past, a lot of emphasis was laid on monoculture or a semblance of monoculture. Monoculture was adopted to maximise the wood production potentiality of the forests. As a result, forest ecosystem, being deprived of diversity, suffered from lack of dynamism and resilience.
7. Evaluation of the forest should be done on a holistic basis and not on timber resources. Ecological characters like biodiversity, status of soil erosion, stand sustainability, normal age distribution, normal distribution of age classes, species composition should define the evaluation pattern of such forests.
8. Non-destructive method of logging should be adopted.
9. There should be distinct system of control and monitoring of marking, felling, and transportation of wood.
10. While manipulating growing stock to increase the timber output, the objective should be fuller site occupying, less mortality, greater control of individual tree growth and better selection of species, optimum promotion of timber species.
11. Adopting correctly determined rotation of maximum volume production.
12. Retaining a fair amount of diversity in tree composition is an

insurance against pest and disease. It helps to improve the stability and resilience of the ecosystem.

13. There should be a trade-of between timber production potentiality of the crop and the stability of the forest system. The timber production should not transcend the threshold limit of resilience of the ecosystem. For an example, in mixed forests, if any attempt is made to raise mono-crop, then in the initial stage the forest system shall tend to revert back to the stage from where it was changed. In order to continue in the changed stage, it requires continuous intervention for about a decade. Secondly, the site productivity shall decline. Therefore, in the long run, changing the existing crop composition goes against the principles of sustainability. As a result, indicators of unsustainability shall emerge.
14. Use of silvicultural systems like shelterwood and selection – which maintain forest cover at all times is desirable. It leads to slightly lower in timber yield but shows optimum sustainability.

Wood Production through Plantations

Plantation holds immense possibilities for timber production in many parts of the globe. Large-scale plantation forests are mostly a 20th century phenomenon, though there are antecedents in both temperate and tropical countries. Majority of the world's plantation forestry has been established in the past half-century.It provides new source of wood and it relieves pressure on primary forests. It represents the most intensive form of commercial forest management, and many expect them to become an increasingly important source of industrial wood and fibre in the coming century (WCFSD, 1999). The role of plantation forests in sustainable forest management was emphasised in Inter-governmental Forum on Forests held in Santiago, Chile in April 1999 (IFF, 1999). Simple plantation forestry—the relatively intensive management of simplified forest systems for a range of wood products—can return commercial wood yield many times greater than natural forest system (WCFSD, 1999).

It is said that yields over time in forest plantation management are well documented. Well-managed plantation forests are likely to continue as a major component of the productive forest resources in many countries, as long as they produce competitive returns on investment. It is generally argued that plantations are relatively deficient in attributes like diversity, wildlife, and release of carbon, soil and moisture conservation. It is a fact that some important functions, especially ecological ones, cannot be provided by plantations. There is, therefore, a need for a more discriminating appreciation of what values can and cannot be secured by plantations.

Secondary forest is emerging as a major source of wood worldwide. The management needs for wood production through plantation or secondary forests focus on the following areas:

1. No plantation should be created by/through conversion of any remaining primary forestland.
2. Plantation should be planned and managed precisely to reduce pressures on remaining natural forests.
3. There is a need for more discriminating appreciation of what values can and cannot be secured by plantations. Without this, a lot of adverse public debate begins.
4. There should be greater involvement of local people in the planning and management, and in the sharing of benefits and products. The envisaged plantation models should incorporate diverse species composition and a wider range of products so that it could meet local needs. Decisions about their location, establishment and management should be made in a framework of participatory land use planning.
5. Plantation should be promoted as an acceptable form of land use for production forests. Such plantations should be raised by using degraded lands.
6. Plantation forestry should be promoted in developing countries as a major vehicle of economic development. Many pockets in tropical belts are suitable to fast tree growth.

SFM for Non-Wood Forest Products (NWFP)

Non-wood forest products are an integral part of the survival and development strategy for the continuing well-being of man, and his environment. Tenth World Forestry Congress (1991) concluded, 'while still not fully appreciated, there is an increasing awareness of the richness and diversity of forest resources other than wood". The harvesting and processing of forest products other than timber are underrated as sources of employment and income, and are generally undertaken without damage to the environment. Given the present state of scientific development, one can envisage the strategy of Non-Wood Forest Product as a potential tool for sustainable development and rational utilisation of the resources.

Active management is required for forest conservation, development and the sustainable utilisation NWFPs. The preservation of forest resources through strict protection and non-intervention will neither meet the felt need of the people nor sustain those resources. Therefore, there is an imperative need for a strategy, which will sustain the forests as well as sustain the supply of NWFPs to the people.

Characteristics of Non-Wood Forest Product (NWFP)

The important non-wood forest products are: edible parts of the plant, fodder, and grasses, bamboo, canes, medicinal products, spices, essential oils, insecticides, resins, gums, commercial leaves, natural dyes and tannins, starches, oil and fats, fibres and flosses and animal products like lac, silk, honey etc. According to Wickens (1994) non-wood forest products refer to all the biologically material (other than wood) that may be extracted from natural ecosystems and managed plantations and that can be utilised within the households, be marketed or have social, cultural, or religious significance. Such products include plants used for food, beverages, forage, fuel, medicine, fibre and bio-chemicals; and animals, birds and fish used for food, fur and other feathers; as well as their products such as honey, lac, silk. Ecosystem use for recreation, nature reserve and catchment management is regarded as forest service." (Wickens, G.E., 1994). Some of the important characteristics of non-wood forest products (NWFP) are presented in Box. (10.1).

Recommendations at the Rio Earth Summit

The Rio Earth Summit discussed the subject at length and advised countries for sustainable development of non-wood forest products. Agenda 21 recommends countries for :

1. Promoting, popularising non-wood forest products,
2. Conducting research on properties of non-wood forest products and their use to improve their utilisation,
3. Scientific investigation on their development and improved sustainable utilisation of harvesting and process residue,
4. Maximising the use of waste to improve the value of non-wood forest products,
5. Promoting and supporting the downstream processing to increase retained value and their benefits,

6. Promoting appropriate small scale forest based enterprises for supporting rural development and local entrepreneurship,
7. Regeneration/cultivation of wild species for improved rural income and employment, ensuring economic and social benefits without harmful ecological impacts, and
8. Promoting/improving market for, and trade in forest products through relevant institutions, policies and facilities.

BOX 10.1: IMPORTANT CHARACTERISTICS OF NON-WOOD FOREST PRODUCTS (NWFP)

- A larger quantity of NWFP is directly used, consumed, or bartered away by the people in and around forest areas.
- There are substantial quantities and number of NWFPs available in the forest but investigations are required to know their uses or development and utilisation.
- A large number of NWFP are not collected and are wasted because people do not find their uses remunerative. Like wise, few NWFPs are over exploited and consequently, there has been a lot of erosion of their resource base.
- Most of the NWFPs are perishable. Due to poor storage and preservation quality, deterioration is a common phenomenon.
- In the past, NWFPs were collected for trading in such small quantities that they made an insignificant contribution to economy. Now their products have acquired major importance.
- The growing commercialisation of NWFPs appears to be a worldwide phenomenon. The quantity collected, traded, price obtained has registered increase in market demand.
- There is unsustainable practice in harvesting of NWFPs. Generally, plants are uprooted or heavily debranched and burnt to harvest the produce. This causes the decrease in resource base.
- Majority of the supply of NWFPs depends solely on wild resources from the forests. Regeneration of species, which produce NWFPs, is a great problem. Forest requires ample protection from unsustainable use.

The Framework of the Strategy

Sustainable management for non-wood products means balancing optimal productivity and controlling ecological change so that environmental equilibrium is maintained (Wickens, G.E., 1994). Considered things in this perspective, it is necessary to hammer out a separate strategy to produce NWFPs optimally as well as sustainably without changing the structural and functional integrity of the forests. In the previous strategy, the primary objective was wood management and the secondary was supply of other goods and services. In contrast to this, the present strategy of NWFP should have the primary objective of optimal production of NWFPs. The wood production shall remain subordinate to the main.

Integrating these two objectives in this fashion is a difficult problem, but not an impossible one. Such integration of non-wood forest products with timber production holds stupendous prospect to rural livelihood security as well as urban wood industry. This option appears to be not only socially desirable but also economically feasible and environmentally sustainable.

The framework of the strategy consists of the following components:

- Augmentation and development of NWFP resources.
- Non-destructive harvesting practices
- Sustainable utilisation with people's participation.

Technology for Augmentation of NWFP Resources

A range of technology falling in the ambit of silviculture, ecology and biotechnology can be applied to augment and develop the NWFP resources in the forests. But, since there are myriad of NWFP resources, one type of technique for maximising the production of a single species antagonises the augmentation process of other NWFP. Certain technique acts on species at individual level, other acts on population level and other acts at community or ecosystem level. Therefore, one type of technique may lead to maximising production process of one type of product, and consequently it may lead to diminution of the supply of another product in the forest system. Therefore, before embarking on a management strategy for NWFP, it is imperative to decide upon the objectives of the management and the target products and to analyse the prospective fallout of such an operation on the overall function and potentiality of the forest ecosystem. After deliberating on these issues and strategies comprehensively, the technology for optimum production of targeted NWFP should be adopted and put into action. Some of the general and simple techniques suitable to most of the NWFP resources are as follows.

Fire: Fire is a traditional management tool. It augments vegetation growth after the initial burn. The impact of fire on fauna survival is also important. Flightless insects, eggs and immature animals are generally destroyed. Overly frequent fires may result in long-lasting or permanent faunal change (Bigalike and Willian, 1984).

Coppice Growth: Coppicing is a unique character of most of the plants in the tropical countries. Coppicing of a number of tree species and shrubs on a rotation can also be used to maintain sustainable yields of many fruits, seeds, leaves, barks, etc. It can be used to prolong the life span of the individual species.

Improvement of NWFP Resources: Natural variation found in multipurpose trees, shrubs and herbs offers diverse management opportunities for conserving, developing and utilising plant resources. Recognition of taxonomic varieties with significant differences in the phonology of flowering, fruiting and leaf flush shall lead to the possibility of deliberately extending the period of fruit and vegetable availability, increasing productivity and selecting the desired pattern and yield season. Fruit availability can be increased substantially by methods of vegetative propagation like budding and stem cutting. Biotechnology also plays an important role in augmentation process. Apart from this, different varieties may require different management objectives and practices.

Management Process: Presently, the management process is heavily tilted towards timber production. The parameters iike felling regime, rotation system, selection of trees, subsidiary silvicultural regime, etc, lead towards building up of a management process which augments wood production at the cost of NWFPs. Therefore, in order to initiate an appropriate management process, which leads to optimum augmentation of NWFP resources, the elements responsible for promoting wood content in the trees or timber trees should be properly identified and developed.

Management Needs to Conserve and Develop NWFP Resources

There is a wide variation in management requirements associated with augmentation of non-wood forest products. The present system of management does not reflect the varied environmental requirements of habitats of the species concerned. It also poorly reflects the varying diverse concerns and interests from individual, communities, traders, local institutions and government on the matter of environmental conservation. There can be no single answer to the management problems related to non-wood forest products. Therefore, there is a great necessity to develop site specific and requirement specific management practices.

In the present context, the following elements/components have been found to constitute the management needs:

1. Identification of Forest Produce which needs Immediate Attention

- There is a need to strengthen research to find out alternate natural resources for heavily exploited products and improved methods of extraction, processing and marketing.
- There is a need for more practical and effective methodology for making assessment of the availability of important NWFPs.
- There is a need to identify all-important products, which are required by the local communities, trade and industry.
- There is a need to increase research and management efforts to develop efficient utilisation of waste products and under-utilised products for value addition.
- Considering the widening importance of certain non-wood forest products in socio-economic development and their increasing demand in trade and industry, it is necessary to increase their production by way of planting in places of their occurrence and in some other suitable places.

2. Research and Management Requirements

- There is a need to focus on few limited important species and elite wild fruit trees in order to raise productivity through selection of superior planting material and vegetative propagation.
- There is a need to compile the available information and classify all the non-wood forest products according to their use and prepare a comprehensive database with relation to cultivation of these species in forestland and outside.
- There is a great need to carry out research programme to sustain productivity of bamboo forests, reduce the cutting cycle and improve their harvesting and processing technique. It is also necessary to take urgent steps to promote natural regeneration of bamboo in the forests. It is also necessary to integrate productivity of bamboo with timber and other minor forest produce.
- There is a need to carry out research on multiple use management of naturally regenerating and mixed species.

- There is a need to identify the endangered species of medicinal plants, multiply in laboratory through tissue culture appropriate for them in their natural habitat.
- There is a need to determine research priorities in consultation with end-users, including private sector, companies, small-scale growers.
- There is a need to grow non-wood forest products as mixed crop with timber species to sustain interests of rural communities in forest resources and to derive sustainable optimum return from the land resources.

3. *Marketing and Socio-economic Aspects*

- There is a need to develop proper post-harvest technology and to undertake market survey to ensure proper returns to the tribals engaged in collection and processing of minor forest produces.
- There is a need to ensure people's participation through joint forest management for economic development of the tribals.
- There is a need for scientific and technological inputs for improving the processing of the minor forest produces.
- There is a need for skillful handling of collection, processing and storage of forest produce to avoid wastage. A compatible market structure should be developed by eliminating series of middlemen for maximum return to the tribals.
- There is a need to assess the export potentials.
- There is a need to develop cost effective strategy for large-scale plantation of non-wood forest product species.
- There is a need for increasing the private sector participation in NWFP sector.
- There is a need to initiate training and extension activities for increasing production, collection and processing and marketing of important forest produce.
- There is a great need to review rights and concessions in the light of shrinking forest resources and decreasing carrying capacity of forests.
- There is a need to develop institution and mechanisms for equitable distribution of usufructs.

Social and Economic Dimensions of NWFP Production

The range of management inputs to augment non-wood forest products may complicate the management process of the whole forests. This may decrease the revenue outturn from timber sale but could make the practice more environmentally efficient. But, sustainably managed forests for non-wood forest products provide a range of environmental services as well as goods. Some of the best known of these are soil and water conservation and other life support services. Apart from this, other social benefits like income generation, livelihood security, increased food security and enhanced well being accrue. Such social benefits nullify the increased cost of managing such forests or forgone benefits out of intensive timber management.

Forests contribute to achieving social benefits like sustainable livelihood, alleviating poverty, improved food security and enhanced well beings. More immortally, the NWFPs provide the maximum of these social benefits. These benefits are discussed below:

Sustainable Livelihood: A livelihood comprises the capabilities, assets and activities required for a means of living. A livelihood is sustainable when it can cope with and recover from stresses and shocks, and maintain or enhance its capabilities and assets both now and in future, while no undermining the natural base (Carney, 1998). The ability to move out of poverty is critically dependent on access to assets. Food insecurity arises when people lack access to sufficient amounts of food and therefore they are not able to consume food required for normal growth and development. This may be because of lack of access to food. Considered things in this backdrop, forest provides a range of income generation activities. More immortally, conservation, development, collection, marketing and processing and value addition of NWFPs generates livelihood and income opportunities in the rural sector. This resultantly provides poor people access to food.

A total contribution of forests and trees to livelihoods is difficult to quantify. Significant proportions of forest produces are consumed by those who collect them. Increased income alone is insufficient as a means of removing poverty. But it is clearly relevant to the economic sustainability of the household. Earnings from sale of forest products are often important as a complement to other income. Very large number of households generate some of their income from selling forest products, often on a part-time basis when farm production is not enough to provide food self-sufficiency round the year. Income from forest products is often used to obtain inputs for other activities that contribute to livelihoods: to purchase seeds, hire labour for cultivation or generate working capital for trading activities (*e.g.* Leach and Fairhead, 1994, cited in Byron and Arnold, 1999).

Improved Food Security: Food security is the key element of sustainable livelihood. Forests are the source of a variety of foods that supplement and complement what is obtained from agriculture. Probably the majority of rural households in developing countries, and a large proportion of urban households, depend on plant and animal products of forests to meet some part of their nutritional, cooking and/or health needs (Byron and Arnold, 1999). Therefore, forests play an important role in improving food security for the rural poor.

Reduced Vulnerability: Poor people often live precariously, with no cushion against adversity. Non-wood forest resources have an important role as a reserve or safety net, providing both subsistence and income in times of crop failure, shortfalls during particular seasons in the year. Energy-rich forest foods such as roots, tubers, rhizomes and nuts are especially important in emergencies such as floods, famine and droughts.

Increased Well-being: Forestry initiatives that supports access to non-wood forest resources, participatory decision-making and equity assist in increasing the well being, especially that of the poor. Forests provide non-material goods that contribute to livelihoods by enhancing social and human capital. Sense of well-being is affected by numerous factors including sense of involvement and control, access to resources and political enfranchisement. Forest management initiatives which devolves power to people enhance the sense of well-being among people.

SFM for Biodiversity Management

The ever increasing impact on the environment makes the conservation of natural resources, including biological diversity, an urgent and critical task. Two recently released publications add to the many warnings that the future of the world's biological diversity is severely threatened. The 2000 IUCN Red List of Threatened Species indicates that the number of critically endangered species has increased since the publication of the last report four years ago. Habitat degradation is the major threat.

Forests, the biological diversity they contain and the ecological functions they perform help maintain our heritages. Forest and woodlands contain a large range of species of actual or potential socio-economic importance globally, nationally and locally, including wildlife species, wild relatives of important crops and trees producing wood and timber, fodder, fruits, latex and other products (FAO, 1988). Among the other conventions in Earth Summit in Rio de Janeiro, Brazil in 1992, the Biological Diversity Convention generated much heat. It is because of the fact that biodiversity is being projected as developing futuristic economic resource over the last few years.

Defining Biodiversity

There is a lot of talk on conservation of biological diversity. Therefore, it is necessary to know exactly what is biological diversity. The WRI, IUCN and UNEP (Anon, 1992) in Global Biodiversity Strategy mentioned that 'Biodiversity is the totality of genes, species and ecosystems in the region'. It can be divided into three hierarchical categories—genes, species and ecosystems. Conserving biodiversity in a broader sense means conserving the integrity, productivity and diversity of nature. Integrity in the context of conservation means functional integrity. In other words, integrity means the proper working of ecosystems and of the whole biosphere. Through the conservation of functional integrity, the cycle of the elements is sustained; climates remain within reasonably predictable limits; and the needs of all components of the living system are met. (Holdgate, M., *et al.*, 1994). Productivity is the capacity of organism to fix carbon and energy and pass the products on through various food chains. We all depend on that productivity for meeting our daily food, feed and fibre needs, and we are all aware of what happens when we undermine productivity through pollution, overuse, desertification and a number of other destructive processes. (Holdgate, M., *et al.*, 1994).

Diversity is the sum of genetic, species and ecosystem richness on the planet. It is the fundamental basis for evolution and continuing adaptation to changing circumstances. The present diversity of life on earth is a response to the planetary range of conditions, to what we used to recall ecological niches, available for organism. The diversity of nature is itself a spur to more diversity, and diversification is a fundamental attribute of life. Tomorrow's diversity will be the result of process that builds on what we have today, replacing some species by others and producing quite few forms. Diversity is thus foundation of the future, and is critically important to both integrity and productivity (Holdgate, M., *et al.*, 1994).

In simple words, biodiversity could be defined as the great variety that exists in living organisms, plants, animals and microbes on earth. Broadly it is of three kinds:

- *Ecosystem Diversity*: Mainly it consists of all different kinds of ecosystems that exist on earth.
- *Species Diversity*: The different species of plants and animals in a given area, *i.e.*, flora and fauna of an area.
- *Genetic Diversity*: Genetic or other variations with in a species such as ecotypes, land races, horticultural varieties, etc.

Biodiversity Strategy

Biodiversity strategy consists of overarching direction for conservation, sustainable use, and equity in use/benefit sharing. While formulating the strategy many aspects have to be looked at. Some of the aspects are proposed below:

- Conservation of biodiversity at ecosystem, species and genetic levels (through in-situ, ex-situ, in-vitro and other measures) and of the associated ecological functions, with a special focus on endemic, threatened, and otherwise critical elements;
- Sustainable use of biological resources, implying their use in such a manner as will not imperil their long-term existence, or will not in other ways threaten biodiversity;
- Social, economic, political and intergenerational equity, including in decision making with regard to conservation and use, in sharing of benefits, in access to protection of knowledge and information relevant to biodiversity, and so on.
- Ethical, cultural, scientific and economic dimensions, including: (1) the right of species and ecosystem to survive, and (2) the primacy of survival and likelihood based on biodiversity, and of creating a stake for people in conservation and sustainable use.

Though the strategy consists of many aspects, it is out of scope of this chapter to deal with all. Therefore, we shall be discussing about factors responsible for loss of biodiversity and conservation aspects in Protected forests (PAs) and non PA areas *i.e.* managed forests.

The major threats faced by the forest ecosystems in world are: commercial clear felling and selective clear felling, conversion for agriculture, settlements, road construction; inundation for development projects like multipurpose river valley projects; shifting cultivation; conversion to monoculture; army operations; grazing; mining; firewood collection; introduction of exotics; fire and pollution. The major factors threatening the species and genetic diversity are common in every country. Threats to species and genetic diversity are linked to threats to the ecosystem. In addition, habitat destruction, over exploitation, poisoning by pollutants, introduction of exotics, imbalances in community structure, epidemics, floods, droughts and cyclones affect species and genetic diversity. The diversity of indigenous varieties of livestock, crops and other cultivated plants face many threats from introduction of exotic and high yielding hybrid varieties.

Protected Areas for Biodiversity

The World Conservation Strategy suggests that the initial efforts of biodiversity conservation should aim at establishment and maintenance of a network of Protected Area (PA) system involving local people in PA management and mobilising resources for their conservation and protection. The commission of National Parks and Protected Areas of IUCN, in its steering committee meeting held in 1993, decided to have six categories of Protected Areas (PA). These are given in Table 10.3.

Expanding Protected Area Networks

FAO's Global Forest Resources Assessment 2000 estimates that 10 per cent of the world's forests are located within protected areas. While this is a large area, for various reasons it is still generally not considered to be enough. The representation of different forest ecosystem types in the global protected area network and effectiveness of different areas in conserving biological diversity vary widely (Miller, 1999). To enhance the conservation value of protected areas, there is a need not only to increase the area of land in protected area systems and but also to make more strategic choices concerning the protection of additional areas. A major emphasis is also required to be placed on improving the effectiveness of conservation within existing protected areas, improving the conservation of biological diversity outside protected areas, and managing the two in an integrated way.

Table 10.3: Set of Categories for Protected Areas (PA)

Category	*Name of PAs*	*Functions*	*Comments (Practice in India)*	*Objectives*
Category I	Strict nature Reserve/ Wilderness areas	Protected areas managed mainly for science or wilderness protection.	Sanctum sanctorum of PAs	Ecosystem and genetic conservation
Category II	National Park	Protected areas managed mainly for conservation and recreation.	Managed PAs	Ecosystem conservation and recreation
Category III	Natural monument	Protected areas managed mainly for conservation of specific natural features.	Outside Conventional PA areas	Conservation of special feature
Category IV	Habitat/ Species Management Areas	Protected areas mainly for conservation through management intervention	Sanctuaries Managed PAs	Habitat and species conservation through management intervention
Category V	Protected landscape/ Seascape	Protected areas managed for landscape/ seascapes conservation and recreation	Managed PAs	Protection of catchment areas, sea coast and for recreation
Category VI	Managed Resources/ Protected Area	Protected areas mainly for other sustainable use of natural ecosystem	Biosphere Reserve Managed PAs	Ecosystem conservation and sustainable use of other wood and non-wood forest products.

Sustainability Dimensions

Managing forest for exclusive biodiversity conservation has distinct and unique sustainability dimensions. It constitutes the foundation for environmental sustainability of the ecosystem. Environmental sustainability constitutes the bedrock for the rest of two dimensions *i.e.* economic and social. If we analyse the sustainability value of this strategy, it is found that it has different values for different dimensions of sustainability. It has high value of environmental dimensions. Socially such management strategies are also sustainable, but only on long-term basis. On short-term front, it is weak. It is same with the economic sustainability also. However considered from a wider perspective, biodiversity management assumes utmost significance because it has high value of environmental sustainability which holds key to other dimensions of sustainability.

Genetic Diversity and Factors Affecting it

Genes are fundamental unit of biodiversity. They constitute the raw material for evolution of life forms in the earth. They are the ultimate source of all variations. Genetic difference exists at many levels like individuals, population, ecotypes, local strains, species, genera, families and so on. Genetic-diversity refers to genetic variation that exits within species *i.e.* the gene pool. They control individual characteristics of organism. Genes have distinct effects on individuals, population and species. There is an intimate relationship between changes in gene pool diversity and species declines. A change in species composition and variability which leads to loss of ecosystem productivity indicates how important is the role of genetic diversity in promoting goals of forest conservation.

Genetic diversity in forest ecosystems and variation among different communities is the basis for their adaptation to environmental stress, including the future, and possibly more extreme, effects of global climate change and the emergence or introduction of new pests or disease (FAO, 1994). Therefore, genetic diversity is the fundamental base for developing and improving the forest resources for human use on sustainable basis. Expansion of human population and higher aspiration for economic development presupposes an efficient use of the finite land resource and the conservation of the resources base.

There are many forces that influence the composition and structure in forest gene pool. The important category of such forces is natural. Successions, predation, natural disturbance, climatic changes on account of increased impact constitute some of the natural forces for genetic change. Such forces influence natural evolution process. Mutation taking place on account of natural processes is the prime source of all new genetic variations in nature. Few of such mutation may be beneficial and few may be detrimental to the organism. Once new alleles arise by the process of mutation, they are assorted and distributed among individuals. This process continues and it produces enormous degree of genetic variations among individuals. Again, in the process of selection, individuals whose genetic characteristics provide an edge over other in riding over difficult situations like extreme weather keep on multiplying. Apart from this, on account of natural selection, individuals are adapted to local environment. When gene flow among groups is diminished because of reason like geographical isolation, natural selection leads to evolution of ecotypes, land races and sub-species.

Apart from the natural causes, human activities act as the causative agent of mutation and influence the process of evolution of gene pool. There are certain activities of man, which have the potential to change the direction and rate of natural selection and gene flow significantly. In other words, certain human activities, few among may be management initiatives in the course of furtherance of silvicultural manipulation, lead to significant genetic effects that take place at gene pool level. Few of such activities are presented in Table 10.4.

The genetic consequence of forestry activities on the species genome depends on how the activities are conducted. For an example, in case of timber management as one of the objective of forest management, the intensity of felling, species preferences, the phenotype and age of trees and season of harvest have different genetic effect on the forest gene pool. Again with a proper and appropriate silvicultural regime with an objective to promote or maintain biodiversity, it can be managed in such a fashion that it will have less deleterious impacts on the genetic diversity of the species.

In the past, economic forces and market demands regulated the evolution of management systems which affected the natural complexity and successional development of forest ecosystems. But over the years, with the growing recognition of the potential value of biological diversity including genetic diversity, the prospect of harmonising biodiversity conservation with other economic and social needs has improved.

Table 10.4: Forestry Activities and their Effects on Gene Pool

Activities	*Effect on Gene Pool*
Timber harvest	• Adding or removing significant number of individuals from natural population. • Alter the sex ratios of the breeding individuals significantly. • Affects the reproductive capacity, fecundity, and viability of individuals, survival and motility of certain age classes. • Disrupt or significantly alter meta-population structure and other geographical patterns and related processes.
Livestock grazing, land clearing, biological control	• Changes population size of natural species significantly. • Eliminates the palatable species from the population slowly.
Tree planting or introducing non-local germplasm	• Significantly increase the potential for hybridization over what would occur naturally.
Introduction of access points into native population	• Introduce disease vectors or insects, especially those that are non-native.
Road and dam construction	• Fragment the population size such that gene flow is drastically reduced. • Alter population structure such that formerly isolated populations regularly inter-breed. • Decrease the population size and genetic variability. • Eliminate populations, especially systematically from portions of a species range.

Managing Genetic Diversity

Every country has some forests, which are unique in terms of its genetic resources. So there is always a need to have as appropriate strategy for their management. Each area should contribute to the national objectives of conservation of genetic diversity. The degree of genetic resources may vary from one location to another. It is because of the fact that it depends on environmental conditions, species composition, size and shape; and many such factors. However, sustainable forest management should, by definition, always include provisions for protecting site condition, seed trees, seedling regeneration and advance growth of desirable species (FAO, 1994).

Managing genetic diversity of a forest gene pool includes maintaining diversity of genes within and among population, ecotypes and sub-types, transfer of genes between them and changes in gene pool composition over time. The most vital need in conservation is the adequate control and continuity of management to meet specified aims and to be carried out within consistent land-use plans and national forest policies. Based on sufficient knowledge of forest composition and dynamics, management system aimed primarily at producing timber and other forest products and services can contribute substantially to conserving a forest resource (FAO, 1994).

Managing genetic diversity necessitates two things. They are in-situ and ex-situ conservation. In in-situ conservation practices natural populations are managed to achieve genetic conservation goals. Management requirement may ranges from establishing genetic conservation areas to developing prescription for genetic conservation. The principles applied are: (1) designing and developing natural resources; biosphere reserve, natural areas, (2) protecting populations of rare and endangered species, (3) restoring species, habitat, and communities, and (4) controlling activities that manipulate native populations. In ex-situ conservation practices germplasm (seeds, pollens, whole plant and animals, sperms and other genetic propagules) is removed from native habitat and preserved in storage.

In summary, the challenges for genetic resource conservation is not to select, set aside and guard protected areas containing genetic resources, nor to preserve seed, pollen or tissue in a seed bank. It is to maintain the genetic variability of target species with in a mosaic of economically socially acceptable land use options, including protected areas and managed forest reserves (FAO, 1994). Such in-situ conservation should, wherever feasible, be complemented by ex-situ conservation of genetic resources of priority species.

Managing Species Diversity

The predicament of sustainable forest management lies in the fact that concerns for biodiversity focuses on less conspicuous texa, but management for commodities from which the society benefits immediately, emphasises on trees and tree products. These two are linked separately. In order to increase the potentiality of marketable forest products like timber and non-timber forest products, it is necessary to affect changes in overwood competition, but such alternatives have important consequences for biodiversity, because of the linkages between trees and micro floras. Trees affect the texa and the ecosystem processes such as nutrient cycle, water retention, and temperature regime, under-story productivity. Different tree texa provide structural, biodiversity and resource richness. Consequently, it affects the ecosystem processes in different ways. When we change the composition of the stand in a forest to meet specific management objectives, the linkage between overwood and/or middle-story and other texa is also changed. Therefore, while targeting an objective in forest management, there is a need to understand such linkages. This helps in developing a trade-off that occurs while managing forest resources for multiple management objectives.

Therefore, it is a daunting task to manage ecosystem in a way that minimises negative impacts of forestry on tree composition. Again, the task is compounded when we aim at minimising negative impacts of forestry on the ecosystem as such. However, the task can be addressed successfully, if we resort to innovative silvicultural and management tools.

Conserving Genetic Diversity in Production Forests

In some areas of production forest, prevailing needs and management prescriptions may lead to the extreme refinement of the stand composition to favour one or a few species in an ecosystem which, in its nature state, consists of a large number of species. If conservation practices are undertaken with full understanding of forest dynamics and the effects on the long-term functioning of the ecosystem, this action may contribute to conserving the genetic resources of those species targeted for use, at an acceptable cost to the total genetic diversity in the specific forest area concerned (FAO, 1984; FAO, 1993 a; Kemp, 1992). The conservation of genetic resources in-situ within natural forest ecosystems may be the only possible strategy for the great majority of species in the more complex tropical moist deciduous forests. However, provision for ex-situ conservation practices may also be required to complement such a strategy. Therefore, in-situ conservation in natural forest ecosystem deserves the most urgent attention particularly to take advantage of the conservation contribution of the production forests and to seek opportunities for combining the conservation of genetic resources for economically important target tree species with the protection of gene pools associated species, for example those providing non-timber products and benefits important to rural people (FAO, 1994).

There is a need to establish a network of stands of each of the economically most important tree species representing the principal ecological areas through out the country. Such original wild populations, left to evolve and adapt to changing conditions, constitute a standard against which different provenance or result of selection may be judged. Therefore, such selected stands should be average for the area and large enough to yield good supply of seed. The minimum stand size normally chosen for species should be 5 to 10 hectares in area.

Natural regeneration is the best form of in-situ conservation. Hence it is always preferable in forest practices. Besides, it is also the economy method compatible for sustainable management of production forests. However, in practice, non-occurrence of natural regeneration is the greatest challenge to sustainable forest practices. Over the years, it has been proved to be the most daunting task the forest management has ever faced all over world. Apart from this, increased demand and wider acceptability of less known species, leading to more intensive felling operations, have tended to favour pioneer or near pioneer species including some lesser important marketable timber and fuelwood, at the expense of slower growing heavier hardwoods. Again repetition of frequent felling and short felling cycle harms severely the breeding population and genetic resources of these slow growing hardwoods. Longer felling cycle helps in conserving a broader spectrum of genetic resources in terms of species composition. However selective felling has its own demerits. It removes the fastest growing and most desirable individuals. This, as a consequence may leave dysgenic effects within populations of harvested species, leaving less vigorous and perhaps defective stems to regenerate. Likewise, improvement felling and thinning operation carried out to favour certain economic species and individuals strongly discriminates and affects the genetic diversity at the species level. This leads to decrease in overall diversity in the forest ecosystem.

Therefore, timber harvesting based on sufficient understanding of ecosystem and ecological processes can be used to assist in the conservation of genetic resources of principal species. Selective logging can be planned to maintain a balance between the areas of forest allotted to different stages of ecological succession in the region. As a result, it allows the maximum total genetic diversity to be conserved of both pioneer species and those characteristics of latter successional stages. Towards this end, the following methods can be resorted.

- Full opening of small gaps through the removal of individual trees or by various possible intermediate patterns and harvesting intensities.
- Effects of interventions should be closely monitored. Shorter felling cycle with low intensity harvesting in a forest or longer felling cycle with high intensity harvesting may have an adverse impact of the breeding population of their slower growing species by altering the number and distribution of mature reproductive individuals in such species.
- The retention of enough seeds trees of good phenotype well distributed through the stand is important for future sustainable productivity and genetic conservation.
- Some time harvesting aggravates the forest conditions by opening the canopy extensively and suddenly initiates the process of alteration of the environmental conditions preferred by fast growing pioneers. Hence this aspect should be taken care of.
- Sometime the climax or the dominant species depends on animals for seed dispersal. Disruption of animal population caused by logging may have further adverse impact on these species. Therefore, continuity of animal population is a necessary requisite for natural regeneration on sustainable basis.
- Impact of selective logging on already rare species is severe because it reduces the future breeding population. Therefore, while selecting the individuals for harvesting, we should ensure that there is a trade off between the need of future breeding population and present timber yield. No timber yield should be carried at the cost of future potentiality of the forest to produce benefits.
- When market demand is very selective, exclusive emphasis is laid on removal of existing best phenotypes of the most desirable species from the forest. This is likely to result in progressive deterioration in the overall genetic quality of the stand. Here also there is a need to err on the side of caution and retain sufficient number of phenotypes.

Therefore a comprehensive study is required to evolve a combination of harvesting and silvicultural treatments to develop and maintain a mosaic of different stages of ecological succession as well as of different tree populations in conservation and production areas.

Economic Perspective of Biodiversity

Biodiversity provides valuable benefits to society. It is the basis of economic value of forests. Sustainable flow of all benefits depends on the biological diversity of the forests. However, managing the biodiversity involves cost and benefits. Study of such cost and benefits provides an economic perspective of biodiversity management.

Production and consumption of goods and services in the present system generally involve a negative impact on environment in the form of depletion of natural capital. Market generally fails to capture the environmental costs of production and consumption. It is because nature provides many resources free of cost. Degradation or depletion of natural resources does not attract the public attention. However, with the change in economic growth and increasing sensitisation of public about the priceless values of environment, it has become imperative to take adequate steps to prevent degradation of environment. Any strategy to address this requires comprehensive understanding of economic linkages between market and natural resources. Therefore, it is necessary to study the market forces, which are broadly responsible for depletion and degradation of such forest. Furthermore, it is also required to evolve a trade off between cost of sustaining or conserving biodiversity and benefits of obtaining goods and services.

Market generally fails to account fully for environmental costs and benefits. Market prices of forest produce do not reflect the cost of protecting or using natural capital. While pricing an environmental product, the loss of biodiversity is not charged to the producer and consumers of forest products. As a result, prices of these products tend to be lower and consumers develop a tendency to consume more. Hence price of the product acts as a facilitator rather than a regulator. Had it be the case where the loss of biodiversity is reflected or cost of restoration of biodiversity is internalised in the price of the forest product or services, there would have been less consumption because of the fact that in such situation price may act as deterrence. As a result, there emerges a situation where there will be efficient allocation of resources between competing uses of forest. This will lead to sustainable production and use of forest goods and services.

Establishing property regime along with a strong enforcement system is central to any such initiative to internalise the environmental costs. When property rights which are generally supported by well-defined laws, are not sufficiently strong enough to enforce, then degradation of resources takes place. In many developing countries, there is public ownership of forest resources. Such resources are considered as public property. Public has unregulated access to such resources. The institutional checks and balances have eroded over the years. As a result "the tragedy of commons" has already struck in such forests. Consequently, either little forests or vestiges of forests remain.

Biodiversity Conservation: Essential Elements

Strategy for biodiversity conservation must focus on the maintenance of integrity, productivity and diversity of our forests. Therefore, there is a need to develop strategies for conservation and sustainable use of biological diversity and their integration into relevant sectoral or cross-sectoral plans/programmes and policies. Essential elements of biodiversity conservation strategy are:

- Extensive knowledge of our bio-physical system.
- Inventorisation of floristic and faunatic wealth.
- Knowledge and documentation of traditional use of forest resources, mainly by indigenous people.
- Conserving diversity within species
- Multispecies and multitier composition in forests.
- Methods and procedure for conservation.
- Management of protected areas.
- Integration of forestry programme into other relevant sectors of natural resource management.

It is not necessary, nor usually possible to conserve all levels of genetic diversity in all areas. Some areas of forests may be devoted to ecosystem conservation while others may be managed to conserve intra-specific variation while others may be managed to conserve inter-specific variation as part of a network of conservation areas containing selected target species or populations (FAO, 1993). However there is inadequate information today on variation patterns of the majority of forests species. In the absence of reliable information, the best possible conservation strategy must be to conserve as wide a range of provenance as possible, after doing the sampling of the environmental conditions of the species habitat. In such conditions, the population of the target species is likely to be genetically distinct, on account of adaptation to the local environment. But, in the other hand, such populations are vulnerable to changes in stand structures and ecosystem disturbance because of logging and non-wood forest produce collection. Therefore, a conservation strategy aimed at capturing intra-specific variation thus requires a number of conservation areas scattered over entire range of species, many of which will also have other objectives, such as timber production or soil and water conservation (FAO, 1994).

Components of Management Strategy

The important components of the strategy are listed below:

- Intensification of surveys and inventorisation of floristic and faunatic wealth of all ecosystems. The survey should include information on distribution pattern of particular species/ population/communities and the status of ethnobiologically important groups;
- Conservation of biodiversity through a network of Protected Areas including Biosphere Reserves, Marine Reserves, National Parks, Sanctuaries, Gene conservation centers, Wetlands, Coral reefs and such other natural habitats of biodiversity. This should include taxonomic and ecological studies on the flora and fauna with adequate emphasis placed on the lower vertebrate, invertebrate and micro flora which are important in contributing to the healthy maintenance of ecosystems;
- Full and correct rehabilitation of rural poor/tribals displaced due to creation of national parks/ biosphere reserves/ tiger reserves;
- Protection and sustainable use of plants and animals genetic resources through appropriate laws and practices;
- Protection of domesticated species/varieties of plant and animal in order to conserve indigenous genetic diversity;
- Maintenance of corridors between national parks, sanctuaries, forests and other protected areas;
- Documenting the knowledge of traditional usage of forest resources mainly by indigenous people;
- Emulating, supporting and protecting traditional skills and knowledge for conservation;
- Development of methodology to multiply, breed and conserve the threatened and endangered species through modern techniques of tissue culture and biotechnology;
- Discouragement of monoculture and plantation of dominating

and exotic species, in areas unsuitable for them and without sufficient experimentation;

- Restriction on introduction of exotic species of animals without adequate investigations;
- Preparation of detailed biodiversity map, based on existing data, to facilitate further action;
- Involvement of various departments, such as agriculture, forestry, irrigation, village industries, rural development, etc. for drawing up a village level programmeme pertaining to conservation and sustainable use of biodiversity for enhanced well-being of the people;
- Encouragement of identified institutions and organisations involved in biodiversity studies, to compile and develop data base including on-going researches;
- Encouragement of private and public sectors for tissue culture of rare and economically important plants and development of full-fledged research centers for local genetic resources and biotechnology at appropriate levels;
- Evaluation of existing methods/procedures and facilities of in-situ and ex-situ conservation of critically endangered species and identification of more such species for conservation, captive breeding and gene propagation;
- Maintenance of a National Register to regulate inflow-outflow of genetic resources by a National Authority; and
- Integration of forestry programme into other relevant sectors of natural resource management.

SFM for Ecosystem Management

In the past, the silvicultural systems followed in forestry focused on maximisation of goods like timber, and few commercially important non-wood forest products. It did not aim at maintaining the structural and functional integrity of the forest ecosystem. If it cared for such objective, then it was only for a short-term basis. It lacked the ecosystem dimensions in its trué sense. As a result of this, the structural and functional integrity of forests eroded. The quality and quantity of goods and services derived from forests drastically declined. It affected all sections of the society, and more specifically poor people living near the forests. However, recently, there have been many changes in the silviculture front. But a total focus on ecosystem sustainability is yet to come. Therefore, it is imperative to draw a strategy totally focussed on ecosystem and landscape management approach.

The Convention on Biological Diversity describes the ecosystem approach as follows:

> "The ecosystem approach is a strategy for the integrated management of land, water and living resources that promote conservation and sustainable use in an equitable way. An ecosystem approach is based on application of appropriate scientific methodologies focussed on levels of biological organisation, which encompasses the essential structures, processes, functions and interactions among organisms and their environment. It recognises that humans, with their cultural diversity, are an integral part of many ecosystems."

Ecosystem approach heralds a new beginning in forest management. It marks a shift from major to minor forest produces, from crown to multi-tier forestry and from flagship species to smaller denizens of the forests. The principles and operational guidelines for the ecosystem approach better known as "The Malawi Principles" are presented in Box 10.2.

Sustainable forest management from the point of ecosystem is an evolving option in the forestry front. Approaches to forest management such, as "ecosystem and landscape" management are becoming more widely accepted in many countries. These approaches recognise the dynamism of ecological and social systems, the necessity of adaptive management and the importance of collaborative decision-making.

Ecosystem management approaches are basically based on critical elements like recognition of ecological, social systems, ecologically derived boundaries, consideration of different time scale, adaptive management to deal with change and uncertainties and collaborative decision-making. Some people views the maintenance or restoration of ecosystem integrity or health as the overall goal of management, where as other considers human needs to be equally or more important (Yaffee, 1999). Many countries are increasingly using an ecosystem approach for planning and managing natural resources. In addition, Parties to the Convention on Biological Diversity agreed in the fifth Conference on May 2000 to apply the principles of the ecosystem approach in managing their natural resources.

Objective of Managing Forest Ecosystem

The objectives of managing forest ecosystem are various. Generally they involve the maximisation of desirable outputs that the system is capable of producing as efficiently as possible and minimisation of inputs and undesirable outputs. Timber, biodiversity, non-wood forest produce, and biodiversity may be some of the desired outputs of which peoples value today. The cost of management may be the unwanted outputs like disease, negative externalities.

This system of management treats the forests as an ecosystem. It respects the structural and functional imperatives of the ecosystem. It involves application of the desired inputs to influence the processes in the ecosystems to maximise desired output and minimise undesirable outputs and inputs, without impairing the ecological integrity of the ecosystem. It treats the ecosystem as a part of the landscape. It also takes care of anthropogenic need of people living in and around such ecosystem.

Sustainability Value of Ecosystem Management

Managing forests with this strategy has distinct and unique sustainability dimensions. It constitutes the foundation for all other forms of forest management strategies/practices like SFM for wood and non-wood forest products. If we analyse the sustainability value of this strategy, it is found to have different values for different dimensions of sustainability. It has high value of environmental dimension. Socially such management strategies are also acceptable, but only on long-term basis. On short-term front, it is weak. It is same with the economic sustainability also. The best example of such an approach is the management of Protected Areas (PAs).

Essentialities of Ecosystem Management

The moot point in ecosystem management is how to maintain the structural as well as functional integrity of the managed forests *i.e.* out side Protected Areas (PAs). A natural forest ecosystem always tries to conserve structural and functional integrity. Human intervention in the form of silvicultural regimes symbolises a compromise between ecological integrity and societal demand for forest products and services. It is always difficult to balance these two conflicting demands in forest management practices. With the fast changes in political, social and economic milieu of the society, the balancing act is becoming more difficult. Now it is clear that no single approach in forest management can satisfy the society's needs without impairing the potentiality of the forest to provide benefits in the future. Therefore, it is necessary to adopt different approach in different part of the forests to achieve different objectives. When the objective of management is to maintain the ecosystem in its true sense, then the strategy must focus on this approach. (See also Box 10.2) This approach may not be necessarily adopted to the whole of the forests, but to a significant part of the forests or forest management unit (FMU).

BOX 10.2: PRINCIPLES AND OPERATIONAL GUIDELINES FOR THE ECOSYSTEM APPROACH: THE MALAWI PRINCIPLES

Principle 1: The objectives of management of land, water and living resources are a matter of societal choice.

Principle 2: Management should be decentralised to the lowest appropriate level.

Principle 3: Ecosystem managers should consider the effects (actual or potential) of their activities on adjacent and other ecosystems.

Principle 4: Recognising potential gains from management, there is a need to understand and manage the ecosystem in an economic context. Any such ecosystem management should:

(a) Reduce those market distortions that adversely affect biological diversity;
(b) Align incentives to promote biological diversity conservation and sustainable use;
(c) Internalise costs and benefits in the given ecosystem to the extent feasible.

Principle 5: A key feature of the ecosystem approach includes conservation of ecosystem structure and functioning.

Principle 6: Ecosystem must be managed within the limits of their functioning.

Principle 7: The ecosystem approach should be undertaken at the appropriate temporal scales.

Principle 8: Recognising the varying temporal scales and lag-effects that characterise ecosystem processes, objectives for ecosystem management should be set for the long-term.

Principle 9: Management must recognise that change is inevitable.

Principle 10: The ecosystem approach should seek the appropriate balance between conservation and use of biological diversity.

Principle 11: The ecosystem approach should consider all forms of relevant information, including scientific and indigenous and local knowledge, innovations and practices.

Principle 12: The ecosystem approach should involve all relevant sectors of society and scientific disciplines.

Operational Guidelines

1. Focus on the functions of biodiversity in ecosystems.
2. Promote the fair and equitable sharing of the benefits derived form the functions of biological diversity in ecosystems.
3. Use adaptive management practices.
4. Carry out management actions at the scale appropriate for the issue being addressed, with decentralisation to the lowest level, as appropriate.
5. Ensure inter-sectoral co-operation

Managing the whole of forests only from the standpoint of ecosystem approach will not solve the problems. Different strategies should be adopted in different areas. This approach makes it possible to set aside a chunk of forests for ecosystem management. But it does not preclude the option to manage forests for producing commodities which society values. However, allocating a sizable chunk of forest for ecosystem management may reduce the prospect of timber production. But this approach of management generally promotes sustainable production of non-wood forest products (NWFPs). In such scenario, more secondary forests should be created for timber production.

Management Needs

Social, economic and political aspects of the management are being dealt separately. In order to focus on technical aspects of ecosystem management, we shall be discussing the management needs of this approach. Management needs encompass four major elements. These elements or factors are described below.

1. Recasting the Objectives of Forest Management
2. Adopting a New Management Process.

3. Revamping the Traditional Management Methods.
4. Establishing a strong Monitoring and Evaluation System.

Recasting the Objectives of Forest Management

The objectives of management are a matter of societal choice. This apart, there is also a need to understand and manage the ecosystem in an economic context. These principles have already been established and accepted in the form of Malawi Principles.

In the past the general objectives of management were more of the reflection of what man required, rather than what forests required. Such objectives were aimed at improving the forest crop. Again the forest crop implied the timber part and not the enrichment of ecosystem. Contrary to this, in the context of ecosystem approach to forest management, the general objectives of management should be decided on the basis of factors like societal needs, national forest policy/state forest policy imperatives and ecosystem requirement. Some of the general objectives of forest management may be:

- Maintaining environmental sustainability and ecosystem services.
- Social and economic security through forestry.
- Energy security.
- Production of timber and other forest goods.
- Pursuing the aforesaid objectives with people's participation.

Adopting a New Management Process

An emerging challenge is to maintain ecosystem integrity in the face of changing paradigm of forest management, increasing anthropogenic pressure, diversion of forest land to non-forestry use, over extraction of commodity from forests and legacy of silvicultural errors. Now forest management is concerned with maintaining those values, which help to sustain the potentiality of the ecosystem for the present as well as for the future. In one hand, the complexity of forests from individual organism to the global scale makes the task of managing forest ecosystem a daunting one. In the other, the society cannot have the choice of not managing the forest ecosystem for maximum production of goods because it reduces the opportunities for human welfare.

Therefore, managing forests with an ecosystem approach is a challenge to all professional foresters and policy makers. It necessitates co-ordination of an array of interventions at many spatial and temporal scales—from individual organisms to the global scale. Such interventions include the initiatives and coordination at the local level. They should be very effective, so that it can deliver the goods and services from forests to society in response to its needs. Forestry over the last century, to a great extent, has undergone a change to meet such challenges.

The management processes applied to forests in the past are mostly based on silvicultural systems and regimes which promote timber content in the growing stock of the forests. Over the years, a lot of change has taken place in silvicultural regime. But the management process still contains certain important elements responsible for promotion of timber content in the growing stock. In the ensuing paragraph, basic elements of management process, which need to be addressed, are described.

Adopting a new management process consists of taking many new initiatives and excluding certain elements and amending old methods or techniques. Important steps towards establishing a new management process are:

I. Understanding the ecosystem hierarchy.
II. Understanding disturbance regime.
III. Managing disturbance regime.
IV. Deciding regeneration process .

Understanding the Ecosystem Hierarchy

Ecosystem Hierarchy

Forest management has been historically organised in a hierachial system. Such hierarchical system of management ensures smooth flow of goods and services from forests. This task is again accompanied by coordinating different operations in the ecosystems. Such operations are varied but they can be organised as a hierachial system - from individual level to policy level. The ecosystem hierarchy is managed by coordinating different components of management process at different spatial and temporal levels as well as scales. This aims to achieve desired goals by scientific methodologies, which are applied to execute the management process.

Ecosystem hierarchy, from the point of present study, can be separated into three levels like strategic, tactical and operational levels. In order to co-ordinate these three levels, forestry is again grouped into three disciplines:

- *Silviculture*: It co-ordinates management activities within each stand in the ecosystem.
- *Forest Management*: It co-ordinates management among generally congruous stands within an area with the help of management plan, tactical plan and operational plan.
- *Policy and Administration*: They co-ordinate forest management within a political and social unit with inputs from policy, legislation, strategic planning, administration, etc.

In contrast to this, forest ecosystem can be put in a different hierarchy based on spatial scale. The rationale behind this hierarchy is that forests provide many values at different spatial scales. This basically facilitates the smooth process of management. They help to evolve proper task at each level and scale. Apart from this, it also helps to focus on the objectives, which can be determined at each such spatial level. There are mainly four sub-divisions organised in the ecosystem hierarchy. These sub-divisions are:

- Silvicultural operation.
- Silvicultural regime.
- Landscape level or forest management unit (FMU).
- Policies.

Silvicultural Operation

Silvicultural operation lies in the bottom level of the management hierarchy. It focuses on individual plants and animals within a stand and is concerned with changing their abilities to survive and grow at a given time and space through various activities. Examples of such operations are harvesting, planting, weeding, thinning, controlled burning, pruning, cleaning and collecting of non-timber forest produce (NTFP). Various operations are developed by studying "natural" process of crop growth. Different silvicultural operations are evolved for different objectives. But, no silvicultural operation should aim at changing the character of the stand. Rather the silvicultural operations shall be so tailored that they help to maintain the ability of the ecosystem to produce goods and services at a sustained level.

Silvicultural Regime

Silvicultural regime level focuses on the individual stand level. It is concerned with co-ordinating the various silvicultural operations to achieve the desired stand structure and other outputs over a temporal scale. A "silvicultural regime" is defined as series of operations applied to a specific stand at specific time to try to achieve the target changes in structures and other outputs, such as timber and other goods and services like habitat for certain services (Oliver, *et al.*, 1999). Silvicultural regimes are based on silvicultural systems. Silvicultural systems are broad management approaches based on different methods of regenerating forests (Smith, *et al.*, 1997). Silvicultural regime is generally used not only to describe but also to prescribe a stand specific set of operations like regeneration, thinning, pruning, harvesting suitable for specific times to a specific stand. It also helps to change one type of stand structure to another. Different regime creates different stand structure, which adds diversity to the crop. Therefore, evolving the right kind of silvicultural regime is the key to success in stand management.

Landscape Level

Landscape constitutes the next level in the ecosystem hierarchy. It generally consists of a large tract of forests having composite stand structures. Management of forests at this level requires coordination of the spatial and temporal considerations. Managing the forests from a landscape level or perspective is a recent phenomenon. This approach has been adopted because it has been felt that to deal with the range of essential needs, to integrate economic, environmental and social aspects of development, we need a form of management that takes into account all aspects of the landscape in its totality.

A landscape constitutes a forest area delineated as an area having relatively uniform range of soils, climate, vegetation, demographic conditions and non-commodity values. Multiple values can be derived from such landscapes by coordinating the changes in commodity and non-commodity values among the micro-landscapes within that area. Management at this level aims at coordinating changes in landscape patterns including forestry activities, and other values among the landscapes to achieve the desired values of the forests as a whole. A landscape can be managed to provide different benefits not only for the present generation but also for future generation also. There may be many wildlife habitats in a single landscape. A watershed area can be taken as a landscape. There may be more than one forest types in one landscape. Multiple values are attached to such landscapes. Such multiple values can be managed efficiently so that they cater to the increasing need of the society.

Policies

Policies constitute the top level of the ecosystem hierarchy. This level of the management hierarchy can again be divided into three spatial levels. The first is local or regional, the second is national and third is global level. It aims at coordinating the commodity and non-commodity values of a unit or region or nation. It may consist of many levels, beginning from stand level to global level. It balances the commodity value and non-commodity values of forests and develops a policy, which constitutes a trade-of between the two. The national level evolves a national policy and global level develops an international policy for forest management.

The concept of zonation is an outcome of policy approach towards forest management. Zones differentiate different forest areas for managing it for different objectives or values. This concept has been in vogue in wildlife management since a long time. Biosphere reserves have been developed in many countries as a part of UNESCO's "man and biosphere" programme. These reserves are zoned for different commodity and non-commodity values. Likewise delineating a chunk of forest as wildlife sanctuary or National Park from the landscape and managing them as biodiversity reserve is testimony to this concept of zonation. Another approach is called as integrated approach. It attempts to manage a large tract of forest area jointly for many commodity and non-commodity values. This approach is also called as integrated management or landscape management. This helps to provides many of commodity as well as non-commodity values by maintaining a mixture of stand structures across the landscapes and maintaining different patterns on different landscapes within a region. Presently this approach is being adopted in many countries.

Understanding Disturbance Regime

Ecosystem management aims at managing the forests within the threshold of natural disturbance patterns. Ecological forestry is that manipulation of a forest ecosystem should work within the limits established by the natural disturbance patterns prior to extensive human alternation of the landscape (Seymore and Hunter, 1999). Disturbances are normal ecological events. Ecologists define disturbances as any relatively discrete event in time that disrupts ecosystem, community or population structure and changes resources, substrate availability or the physical environment' (Picket and White, 1985).

Understanding disturbance regime is key to ecosystem management. This helps in assessing the effects of disturbance on plant and animal communities. It is necessary to understand natural as well as man-made disturbance regime because it helps to determine the impact of any new forestry programmes or operation on the ecosystem.

The forest operations constitute disturbance to the ecosystem, but, generally since such disturbance are within the threshed of natural disturbance, they don't have large scale impact on the ecosystem. However, if such disturbances are more severe because of certain drastic silvicultural decisions, they can impair the structural and functional integrity of forest ecosystem. Under 'ecosystem and landscape management' approach, it is imperative to keep various forest operations within the threshold of natural disturbance.

Managing Disturbance Regime

Some of the important management tools or principles required for manipulating the disturbance regime, while perusing the goal of producing goods and services from forest are presented below:

- Felling cycle
- Severity of disturbance
- Crop age
- Harvesting time
- Wood harvest level

Felling Cycle

Felling cycle is the time interval between two successive felling operations in a given forest. In the context of forest crop whose rotation has been fixed at 100 years, if the felling cycle is determined at 25 years, then 4 per cent of the total area will be disturbed every year in the given forest. If the felling cycle is fixed at 50 years, then 2 per cent of the area is put to disturbance every year. This can also be explained in different ways also. In a forest, with felling cycle of 25 years, there will be four disturbances in the form of felling and if it is 50 years, then there will be two disturbance in the forest in the span of 100 years.

Severity of Disturbance

Severity of disturbance indicates the degree or intensity of disturbance to the ecosystem. It is attributed to reasons like area of felling operation, felling intensity, method of felling and period of felling. Amount of vegetation or tree removed or felled and the type of growing space, which is made available in the forest for the new emerging plants or already exiting and upcoming crop, determine the severity of disturbance.

Crop Age

Management objectives determine the crop age. There are two types of stand with respect to crop age; firstly, it is even-aged and secondly, it is uneven-aged or irregular crop. In even-aged crop, trees are more or less of same age. Where as in uneven-aged crop there are at least three or more age classes.

Management objectives determine silvicultural decisions, which influence the crop age of the forest. More importantly, silvicultural systems are chosen according to the objectives of the management with respect to crop age. A un-evenaged forest crop symbolises diversity in a stand level. Therefore, management of diversity with respect to crop age helps the forest stand to cope with the disturbance that occurs during the felling operation. In this context, the selection system of silviculture is more in consonance with natural operation of disturbance that emanates from felling operations. The merits of the system lie in the fact that it advocates removal of large trees. Besides, it reduces density uniformly through out the stand to a level that promotes natural regeneration.

It is important to retain dead trees as part of the biological legacy as are living one. A very important reason for reserving mature individuals is to ensure that during the next generation of crops, there will be a continual supply of large dead trees for cavities and other habitats. This promotes diversity in the forests.

Rotation/Harvesting Time

It is required to decide the rotation of the crop in an even-aged crop.

Apart from this, it is also necessary to decide the exploitable girth of target species in the un-evenaged crop. With the closure of option for clear felling in tropical forests, there is an increased emphasis on deciding the proper stage of the tree when it will be felled. Under the system of sustained timber yield, rotations or exploitable girths are decided on the basis of economic criterion rather then on biophysical conditions. Economic criteria is used to find out the period that maximises commodity (merchantable) outputs or present networth (Davis and Johnson, 1986). But, choice of harvesting time or exploitable girth plays an important role in creating disturbance in the ecosystem.

Managing the Regime

Managing the disturbance regime holds the key to the success of ecosystem approach. However the intensity of management will very with the change in degree of severity of disturbance. If disturbance regime is attributed to one factor, then it is easy to manage. When it is attributed to a host of agents, then the management will be very complex and difficult.

An uneven stand in a mixed forest is always subject to a complex regime of disturbance. Managing stand structure in such situation is the most daunting one. There cannot be a single exploitable girth applicable to all species. There will be different exploitable girths for different species. It is because in mixed species forests, there are different species having different growth patterns, physiological process and stages of life span. The stage of maturity of one species differs from others. But, succession patterns in such forest indicates a commonality. Therefore, foresters, over the years have discovered different stages for different species. Stand management practices revolve around manipulating such succession principles.

Setting a large rotation in mixed forests of a higher exploitable girth would emulate natural disturbance pattern well, but would sacrifice substantial economic production of timber of shorter rotation species. Therefore, a reasonable compromise in such stands is to use multiple rotations in the form of multiple exploitable girths (species-specific) with an optimum felling cycle. Such a system ensures in maintaining species diversity in mixed forest. Therefore, in mixed forest primarily dominated by multi-storied stand community, there is no rotation *per se*. Here periodic harvest is undertaken to perpetuate the process of regeneration. In other words, the harvesting operation is so managed that it not only follows the natural pattern of death of trees but also encourages natural regeneration process.

The aforesaid discussion indicates that there is an imperative need to study the disturbance regime of the forest and decides the management prescriptions. If a stand takes more time to establish because of increase in disturbance regime, there is a necessity to increase the felling cycle. Holding the felling cycle and disturbance rate at harmony to each other promotes a perfectly balanced age structure within the stand. Off course nature is almost never so perfect and the cutting cycle and disturbance frequency could be varied to produce a more irregular structure of stands that occupies different special entities. Therefore, legacy tree of long life species should be preserved well beyond average rotational length to replenish large cavities. It is because such practice promotes species diversity.

Deciding Regeneration Process

Regeneration of the forest on a sustained basis is the *sin qua non* of the ecosystem. It is always obtained by the system of stand management supported with a natural regeneration. The basic objective of stand management of forest is to maintain structural and functional integrity of the ecosystem. Resorting to different silvicultural systems and regimes can fulfil this objective. Every silvicultural system aims at:

- regenerating the forests.
- maintaining and improving the stand.
- harvesting.

The volume of wood harvested annually from a unit of forests is the single most important decision affecting the forests. Foresters adopt two types of regulatory methods. First is volume control generally associated with un-evenaged forests and second is area control associated with normal or regular forests. Forest regulation under sustained yield timber management has always attempted to maximise wood volumes over times. The best way to determine an ecologically sustained wood harvest level is that method which aims at maintaining a normal or harmonised age structure in the forest stands. The key issues in forest harvesting are: (1) making temporal and spatial pattern of harvest; and (2) keeping the level of harvest below the threshold limit of natural disturbance.

Revamping the Traditional Management Pattern/Methods

(i). Inventorisation of Forest Ecosystem

Inventorisation of forests is an important aspect in ecosystem management approach. It helps to assess the resource status of the forests. It also helps to monitor and evaluate the ecological impact of management on forest ecosystem. It helps to evolve adaptive management practices too. Presently, inventories are not prepared on the basis of ecosystem. Rather they are prepared on the basis of forest management types (Teak Forests, Sal Forests, and Miscellaneous Forests) and working circles. Mapping of forest types based on ecosystem classification and habitat is required.

Inventorisation of ground flora and NWFP along with overwood and underwood species in forest inventory is also necessary. Presently, inventorisation of overwood and underwood species is generally done. The underground flora is not taken into consideration in the inventory. A balanced presence of all the strata in the forests indicates the structural and functional integrity of the ecosystem. Therefore, survey of MFP should be taken, either combinedly or separately, with the inventory.

(ii). Establishing Multi-tiers and Multiple Use Management System

Silvicultural systems adopted in most of the countries are more oriented towards timber management. In the tropical countries, the silvicultural systems adopted presently are selection system, coppice-with-reserve, coppice-with-standards, selection cum-improvement, and other special silvicultural system like gap planting, RDF, etc. There is a need to have a fresh look at the silvicultural system at work.

In an ecosystem approach, it is necessary to aim at minimum interventions in the forest. It is necessary to derive wood and other goods. So we cannot afford to stop at interventions in the form of silvicultural system. Some of the management objectives like sustainable wood management and non-wood forest products are slightly conflicting. However, we can synchronise such conflicting objectives to a great extent. To do this, we have to choose the silvicultural system and the regime, which cause minimum changes in the ecological processes of the forests.

(iii). Adopting Selection System for Managing the Primary Tropical Forests

Selection-cum-improvement system, coppice-with-reserve system and coppice-with-standard should be sparsely adopted. Selection-cum-improvement system (SCI) does not fully aim at regenerating the crop. Apart from the selection part, it heavily tilts towards improvement felling. Trever (1946) has suggested that improvement felling should be adopted to prepare the forests for eventual management under a more intensive system. Improvement felling aims at bringing these forests to the normal state. In other words, it is a method of treatment, which involves essentially the removal of inferior growing stock in the interest of better growth of the more valuable species and individuals. In good productive sites, selection felling is carried out with pronounced treatment of improvement felling. In this hybrid silvicultural system, the operation comprises two distinct components. They are as: (1) selection felling operation, and (2) improvement felling operation.

Selection system is the most environmentally friendly silvicultural system. Therefore, this system should be followed with local variation based on the management need. This system follows ecosystem approach in forest stand management. Other systems like coppice-with-standard (CWS) and coppice-with-reserve (CWR) are also widely applied to many forest areas of tropical region. It is difficult to effectively put this system into practice. It requires great skill in maintaining correct balance between standard and coppice. Above all, it is difficult to effect proper distribution of standards or reserves in the whole of the forests. It has been found that after three coppices, the trees normally lose their coppice vigour. Besides, owing to repeated coppice working there occurs an erosion of structural and functional diversity in such forests. Considered from this perspective, it is an ecological necessity to shift from SCI and CWR/CWS to selection system.

(iv) Marking Trees on the Basis of Physical Condition and not on Timber Value

Presently, the system of classifying the trees during the marking operation is generally on the basis of condition of the crop and timber worthiness of the tree. This smacks of more of timber primacy and less of ecosystem approach in our management. This needs a change. For an example, the trees like dead, dying, diseased, stumps/coppice, over selection and selection girth should be marked for removal on priority basis. No marking should be done on the basis of timber content of the tree.

Therefore, a change is required to facilitate adoption of ecosystem management approach. Classification of trees during the marking in the main felling should be done strictly on the basis of physical condition of the trees and not the timber worthiness. This helps to produce ecologically sound sustainable yield from the forests. This type of management helps to maintain the structural and functional integrity of the forest ecosystem.

(v) Revamping the 'Working Circle' and 'Treatment Type' System of Working

Presently the system of managing forests through working circles is in vogue. The whole area of the forest division or forest management unit (FMU) is divided into different zones to meet different objective of management. Again, to meet the special ecological, social and management need, each compartment is again divided into 'treatment types'. Such system of zonation and sub-zonation is a healthy management practice conducive to ecosystem approach. But it needs some improvement.

Firstly, few but focussed working circles should be proposed for management. All suggested working circle should aim at regenerative activity in the forests and development of the habitat/site and multi-layered forest crop. Use of forests should not guide the formation of working circles. In other words, regeneration and development of the forests should be the basis of working circle formation, and not the usage of the forests. Therefore, for managing the forests of central belt of India a list of prospective working circles with objectives are presented in Table 10.5.

Table 10.5: Management Objectives in Different Working Circles

Sl. No.	*Working Circles*	*Management Objective*
1.	Selection W/C	Selection forests & high forests and micro-habitat (treatment subtype) development
2.	SCI W/C	Selection forests, high forests and crop improvement
3.	Improvement W/C	High forests and crop improvement micro-habitat (treatment subtype) development.
4.	Bamboo (Overlapping) W/C	Development of bamboo forests and micro-habitat (treatment sub-type) development
5.	Rehabilitation of Bamboo forests W/C	Rehabilitation of degraded bamboo forests
6.	RDF W/C	Rehabilitation of degraded forests
7.	Plantation management W/C	Management of old plantations

Secondly, there is a need to revamp the 'treatment type' system. Presently, all the "treatment type" mentioned in the working circles are not taken up for treatment. Only treatment types like 'Areas suitable for Main Felling' and 'old plantation' are taken up for working under selection-cum-improvement/improvement felling working circle and "plantation management (overlapping) working circle" respectively. Other treatment types like protection, seed stand, and worshipping place or wildlife resource patches are not attended. Apart from this, there are very scanty management prescriptions for treatment of such management- type areas. Therefore, there is a need to improve upon this system of management type areas within the compartment. Operation to treat every 'management types' should be prescribed and necessary details should be worked out for implementation. The standard Treatment Types in working circles along with their objectives are presented in Table 10.6.

Table 10.6: Prospective Treatment Types in a Working Circle

Sl No.	*Treatment Type*	*Objective*	*Operation*
1.	Protection 'Type A'	Protection	Soil and water conservation
2.	Old Plantation 'type B1'	Plantation management	Cleaning and thinning
	Old Plantation 'type B2'	Plantation Restoration	Restorative operation
3.	Worshipping place 'type C'	Social and cultural service	Preservation and conservation
4.	Wildlife habitat 'type D'	Wildlife management	Wildlife management practices
5.	Research plots, Preservation plot and seed production areas 'type E'	Forestry research Biodiversity conservation	Research and preservation plot management and seed production measures
6.	Medicinal plant resource rich areas 'type F'	Medicinal plants conservation	In-situ conservation
7.	Areas suitable for RDF 'type G'	Regeneration	Restorative operation
	Areas suitable for plantation	Regeneration	Plantation
8.	Areas suitable for main felling 'type H'	Regeneration felling	• Marking • Low impact harvesting • Restorative measures after logging

Thirdly, a treatment map along with stock mapping during the working plan exercise should be prepared. Stock map aims to indicate the forest stocking and the treatment map shall show different treatment types in the map. At present, treatment maps are required to be drawn during the time of marking of trees. But in practice, such maps are not properly drawn. Drawing such treatment maps at the management planning stage shall help to focus on regeneration/development/rehabilitation of each treatment types. On the basis of such planning, operational plans for natural regeneration, artificial regeneration, protection, and rehabilitation of treatment types in each compartment can be prepared for every year and appended along with felling sequence.

Establishing a Strong Monitoring and Evaluation System

Monitoring and evaluation of the results of management activities and interventions into the forest ecosystem hold key to success in sustainable forest management (SFM). The Forest Principle in the Rio Summit required every state to develop mechanism to monitor and evaluate forest management practices on a periodic interval. Towards this end, the process of evolving Criteria and Indicators (C&I) for sustainable forest management has already been initiated in international arena. Considered in this context, it is now imperative to evolve certain pragmatic C&I for monitoring ecosystem management.

Therefore, it is necessary to develop methods and frameworks for measuring, monitoring and evaluating the ecological and social impacts of management on ecosystem. Such processes have been useful in catalyzing efforts and commitment towards sustainable forest management. The criterion for monitoring should relate to the conditions of forest and the healthy biological functioning of forest ecosystems. Forest condition and health can be affected by a variety of human actions and natural occurrences, *i.e.* from air pollution, fire, flooding, storms, pests and disease. The indicators for monitoring and evaluation can be of following types:

- Composition of forest crop with respect to tree categories like dead, diseased, dying and wolf trees.
- Area of forest damaged by human activities and degree of damage. The various human activities like encroachment,

agriculture, roads, mining, dams fire, grazing, illicit felling, should be enumerated and the extent of damage should be determined.

- Area of forest damaged by natural causes. The various natural causes like wild fire, drought, flood, cyclone, pest and diseases.
- Conservation and protection procedures relating to eliminating the human activities or to minimising the effect of damage due to natural cause.
- Biodiversity levels like ecosystem diversity, species diversity and genetic diversity.
- Anthropogenic pressure.
- Areas allotted to different management objectives.
- Soil and water quality of the forests.
- Impact of forest management on social and economic security of the people living near forests.

GLOSSARY

Afforestation: The establishment of a tree crop on an area from which it has always been or for very long been absent.

Agro-foresty: Land-use system in which tree crops are planted on the same land for raising agricultural crop.

Annual allowable cut or AAC: The amount of timber that is permitted to be cut annually from a particular area. It is used to ensure a sustainable supply of timber. It averages roughly the amount of new growth each year minus deductions for losses due to fire, insect or diseases.

Biodiversity: Biological diversity, which includes the diversity of species, genes and ecosystem and the evolutionary and functional process which link them.

Carbon sequestration: The removal and storage of carbon from the atmosphere by green plants through the process of photosynthesis, in which carbon dioxide is combined with water to form carbohydrates that, can be stored in plant tissues.

Carbon sink: An area where the rate of carbon uptake by living organisms exceeds the rate of carbon release, so that carbon is sequestered in organic or inorganic form.

Climate change: An alteration to measured quantities (*e.g.* precipitation, temperature, radiation, wind and cloudiness) within the climate system that departs significantly from previous average conditions and is seen to endure, bringing about corresponding changes to ecosystems and socio-economic activity. Associated with greenhouse gas, of which fossil fuel combustion and forest are contributors.

Closed Forest: Formation where trees in the various stories and the undergrowth cover a high proportion (> 40 per cent) of the ground and do not have a continuous dense grass layer. Typical examples of tropical closed forests includes tropical rainforest and mangrove forest.

Community forests: A forest area primarily designated to serve community needs.

Customary rights: Rights which result from a long series of habitat or customary actions, constantly repeated, which have, by such repetition and uninterrupted acquiescence, acquired the force of a law within a geographical or sociological unit.

Deforestation: Clearing an area of forest for another long-term use. Technically, a semi-permanent depletion of tree crown cover to less than 10 percent.

Desertification : Degradation of land that ultimately leads to desert-like land features.

Ecosystem: A dynamic and inter-related community of biological organisms and the surrounding environment linked through nutrient cycling and energy flows.

El Nino: It is also called the Southern Oscillation, or ENSO (El Nino Southern Oscillation) which is the largest climatic fluctuation observed on earth. It occurs sporadically with a period between 2 and 10 years and is accompanied by unusually high sea surface temperatures, air pressure and rainfall in eastern pacific near the equator. ENSO influences both the atmospheric climate and the ocean conditions.

Endemism: Endemic species are those whose distribution is restricted to a particular area or region.

Environmental impact assessment (EIA): A process designed to identify actual and potential environmental effects of operations in order to plan how to minimise or avoid adverse effects and maximise positive effects.

Forest: Communities characterised by a predominance of woody vegetation growing more or less closely together, whether 'closed' or 'open' in canopy, and whether fully intact ecologically or modified, fragmented or planted by humankind. Technically forests are defined as ecosystems with a minimum of 10 per cent tree canopy cover.

Forest capital: A weighted measure of the extent and integrity of forest resources in a given region (say a country). Primary forests may be deemed to have greater integrity than other types of forests, and therefore, be given more weight than modified fragmented or planted forests.

Forest decline: A blanket term encompassing deforestation (conversion of forests into other uses) and forest degradation (deterioration in health and quality).

Forest degradation: A reduction in the biomass, productivity or biodiversity of a forest, and alterations in ecological functions such as habitat, climate regulation and soil and water protection. Some times also refereed to as a lowering in the quality or integrity of a forest ecosystem. One example is a change in forest composition, which negatively affects the growing stock.

Forest management unit (FMU): An area of forest under a single or common system of forest management.

Forest services: Protection (against soil erosion by air or water, avalanches, mud and rock slides, flooding, air pollution, noise, etc). Social and economic values (*e.g* hunting and fishing, other leisure activities, including recreation, sport and tourism). Aesthetic, cultural, historical, spiritual or scientific values (including landscape and amenity). (FAO-FRA-Terms & definitions).

Global warming: Predicted increase in temperature worldwide due to increasing levels of 'greenhouse gases' in the atmosphere, especially carbon dioxide.

Habitat: The locality, site and particular type of local environment occupied by an organism.

Indigenous peoples: The existing descendants of the peoples who inhabited the present territory of a country wholly or partially at the time when persons of a different culture or ethnic origin arrived there from other parts of the world, overcame them and by conquest, settlement, or other means reduced them to a non-dominant or colonial situation; who today live more in conformity with their particular social, economic and cultural customs and traditions than with the institutions of the country of which incorporates mainly the national, social and cultural characteristics of their segments of the population which are predominant' .(Working definition adopted by the UN Working Group on Indigenous Peoples).

Landscape: The geographical and ecological integrity and resilience of a particular land areas, not mainly its aesthetic qualities. Landscape is not just a geographical concept, but includes human, cultural, and traditional values that are associated with the land.

Landscape management: Involves managing an area or region by integrating a variety of values associated with land that may be ecological, social, cultural or economic.

Natural forest: Natural forests are forests composed of indigenous trees, not planted by man. Or in other words forests excluding plantations. Natural forests are further classified using the following criteria: forest formation or type (closed or open), degree of human disturbance or modification and species composition. (FAO-FRA-Terms & definitions).

Non-wood forest products: Products for human consumption: food, beverages, medicinal plants, and extracts (*e.g.* fruits, berries, nuts, honey, game meats, mushrooms, etc.), and fodder and forage (grazing, range). Other non-wood products (*e.g.* cork, resins, tannins, industrial extracts, wool and skins, hunting trophies, Christmas trees, decorative foliage, mosses and ferns, essential and cosmetic oils, etc.) (FAO-FRA-Terms & definitions).

Open forest: Formations with discontinuous trees layer but with a coverage of at least 10 per cent and less than 40 per cent. Generally there is a continuous grass layer allowing grazing and spreading of fires. (FAO-FRA-Terms & definitions).

Other wooded land: Land either with a crown cover (or equivalent stocking level) of 5-10 per cent of trees able to reach a height of 5 m at maturity in-situ; or a crown cover 9 or equivalent stocking level) or more than 10 per cent of trees not able to reach a height of 5 m at maturity in situ (*e.g.* dwarf or stunted trees); or with shrubs or bush cover of more than 10 per cent (FAO-FRA-Terms & definitions).

Plantations: Forest stands established by planting or/and seeding in the process of afforestation or reforestation. They are either:

- Of introduced species (all planted stands) or
- Intensively managed stands or indigenous species, which meet all the following criteria; one or two species at plantation, even age class, regular spacing. (FAO-FRA-Terms & definitions).

Policy: A rule or norm usually prescribed by governments to help behaviour or decision-making.

Precautionary principle: The maxim that prevention is better than cure-where there are threats of serious or irreversible damage, lack of full scientific certainty shall not be used as a reason to postpone action.

Regeneration: Regrowth of the forest following harvesting, either through natural process of seed dispersal and germination of artificially by planting.

Shifting cultivation: Farming system in which land is periodically cleared, burned, farmed and then returned to fallow.

Silviculture : The science and practice of cultivating forest crops.

Stakeholders: People who are interested in, or affected by, forest management and operations: for example, government agencies, local communities, employees, investors, environmental interest groups, non-governmental organizations (NGO) and general public.

Sustainable development: Development that meets the needs of the present without compromising the ability of future generations to meet their own needs. It implies integrating traditional economic concerns with often –ignores social and environmental considerations.

Sustainable forest management (SFM): Sustainable forest management is a process of managing forest to achieve one or more clearly specified objectives of management with regard to the production of a continuous flows of desired forest products and services without undue reduction of its inherent values and future productivity and without undue undesirable effects on the physical and social environment. A process, rather than a fixed state. As such, universal prescriptions are oversimplistic. Elements may include participatory and equitable approaches to decision-making geared towards maintaining ecosystem and landscape functions while also meeting broad economic, social and cultural needs. The management context is all-important.

Sustained yield: Production of forest products on a perpetual basis, ensuring that the rate of removal of forest products does not exceed the rate of replacement over the long-term.

Use rights: Rights for the use of forest resources that can be defined by local custom, mutual agreements, or prescribed by other entities holding access rights. These rights may restrict the use of particular resources to specific levels of consumption or particular harvesting technique.

Yield regulation: A technique for calculating and controlling the harvest level to ensure that sustained yield is implemented.

Criterion: An aspect that is considered important by which sustainable forest management may be assessed. A criterion is accompanied by a set of indicators.

Indicators: A quantitative, qualitative or descriptive attribute that, when periodically measured or monitored, indicates the direction of change.

Synergy: The concept of synergy can be expressed simply as a situation in which 2 plus 2 becomes equal to five, or in which the whole is greater than the sum of the parts.

BIBLIOGRAPHY

Adam, W.M. (1990), *Green Development, Environment and Sustainability in the Third World,* London, Routledg.

Allan, M.J.R. (1987), *Impact of Afghan Refugees in the Vegetation Resources of Pakistan's Hindukush-Himalaya.* Mountain Research and Development, 7: 200-4

Allen, J.C. and Barnes, D.F. (1985), The Causes of Deforestation in Developing Countries; *Annals. Association of American Geographers*, 75: 163-84.

Annon (1999) National Forestry Action Programme – India; Ministry of Environment and Forests, GOI, New Delhi.

Anon (1953), Glossary of Technical Terms. British Commonwealth Forest Terminology (BCFT) (modif); Empire Forestry Research Association. England.

Anon (1983), Guidelines for Preparation of Working Plan and Felling in Forests. Ministry of Environment and Forests. Govternment of India.

Anon (1983), Abridged Glossary of Technical Terms.. Forest Research Institute. Dehradun, India.

Anon (1988), National Forest Policy -1988. Ministry of Environment and Forests. Government of India.

Anon. (1995). INDIA 1995: Publication Division; Ministry of Information and Broadcasting. Government of India.

Anon. (1994). Global Biodiversity Strategy. WRI, IUCN, and UNEP.

Aronoff, S. (1989). *Geographical Information System: A Management Perspective.* WDL Publications. Ottawa. Canada.

Ashley, C. & Carney D. (1999), Sustainable livelihoods: Lessons from early experience, London UK, Department for International Development.

Ayres, Robert U. (Edit) (1998); Eco-restructuring; Implications for sustainable development. United Nations University. Tokyo. Japan.

Babcock, G.D. (1927), The Taylor System in Franklin Management, 2nd Ed. New York: Engineering Magazine Company.

Barr. B. M. (1988), Perspective on Deformation in the USSR, in Richards, J.F., and Tucker, R. P. (eds). *World Deformation in the Twentieth Century*, Duke University Press, Deharadun, pp. 230-261.

Bartelmus, P. (1994). *Environment, Growth, and Development: The Concepts and strategies of sustainability.* London & New York. Routledge.

Bebarta, Kailash, Ch., (1999) *Teak: Ecology, Silviculture, Management and Profitability:* International Book Publishers and Distributors, Dehradun.

Bebarta, Kailash, Ch., (1999). Working Plan for Rajnandgaon Forest Division. M.P. Forest Department. Bhopal.

Brenner, Y.S. (1966), *Theories of Economic Development and Growth,* London, George Allen and Union.

Brigalke, R.C. & William, K.(1984) Effects of Fire Regime on Faunal Composition and Dynamics. In P. de Boosyen and N.M. Tainton. Eds., *Ecological Effects of Fire in South African Ecosystems,* pp.255-271, Berlin, Germany, Springlr 426pp.

Burrough, P.A. (1986). Principles of Geographical System for Land Resources Assessment. Clarendon, Oxford.

Burton, Gene, Thakur, Manab. (1995), *Management Today: Principles and Practices.* Tata McGraw Hill Publication Company Ltd. New Delhi.

Byron, N. & Arnold JEM (1999), What features for the people of the tropical forests? *World Development* 27(5): 789-805.

Carlsson, Jerkier; Kohlin, Gunnar and Ekbom, Anders. (1994). *The Political Economy of Evaluation: International Aid Agencies and Effectiveness of Aid*; New York: St Martin's Press.

Carney, D. (1998), Implementing the sustainable livelihood approach. In D. Carney, (ed). *Sustainable Rural Livelihoods: What contribution can we make*? London, UK Department for International Development.

Chambers, Robert (1994), "Participatory Rural Appraisal. (PRA) Analysis of Experience". *World Development,* Vol. 22. No. 9, pp. 1253-1268.

Champion, G. Harry and Seth, S.K. (1968). *General Silviculture for India.* Forest Research Institute. Dehradun.

Champion, J.L and Reiss, M.J. (1995), *Ecology: Principles and Application,* Cambridge University Press, U.K.

Connor, E.F. and E.D. McCoy (1979). The Statistics and Biology of the Species - Area Relationship. *American Nationalists,* Volume 13. 791-833.

Cowen, D.J. (1988). GIS *versus* CAD *versus* DBMS: What are the differences ? *Photogrametric Engineering and Remote Sensing* 54:155 1-4.

D'Arcy, W.E. (1910), Forest Working Plan, Government Press.

Dale, Earnst, (1976). Organisation. American Management Association. New York.

Dale, Reider; (1998), *Evaluation Framework for Development Programme*; Sage Publication, New Delhi.

Daly, H. E. and J.B. Cobb Jr (1990) For the common good: Redirecting the economy towards community, the environment and a sustainable Future. London Green Print.

David, Reid (1996), Sustainable Development International Guide, DFID.

DBB (1994), Evaluating Sustainable Forest Management: Report of the Working group of experts on Sustainable Forest Management, Den Haag, The Netharlands.

Department of Environment (DOE). (1987). Handling of Geographical Information. HMSO. London.

DFID (2000) (Department for International Development) Strategies for achieving International Developments Targets: Environmental Sustainability eliminating poverty, Consultation Documents, London, U.K. Department for International Development.

DFID, (1999): Sustainable guidance sheets Framed, London U.K. Department for International Development.

Diamond, J. M. (1987), Human Use of World Resources, *Nature*, 328:479-80.

Dobson Andrew (1998), *Justice and the Environment: Conceptions of Environmental Sustainability and Dimensions of Social Justice,* Oxford, Oxford University Press.

Dueker, K. J. (1979). Land Resource Information Systems: A review of fifteen years experience. *Geo-processing* 3. 105-28.

Dunster, J.A. (1988), Land Use Planning in Canada: An Overview of the Forestry aspects. *Land Use Policy*. 6:83-93.

Dwivedi, A.P., (1980), *Forestry in India*, Jugal Kishore and Company, Dehradun.

Earth Council (1996), Subsidizing unsustainable development; San Juse, Casta Rica, Earth council.

EC-UN/ECE (European Commission – United Nations/Economic Commissions for Europe) (1995, 96, 97). Forest Conditions in Europe Published under the auspices of the convention on long Range Transboundry Air Pollution, Brussels/Geneva EC-UN/ECE.

F.A.O. (1994); Reading in Sustainable Forest Management; FAO Forestry paper No. 122.

FAO (1963), World Forest Inventory. FAO Rome.

FAO (1971), Planning a Forest Inventory. FAO Rome.
FAO (1984), A Guide to in-situ conservation of Genetic Resources of Tropical woody species. FORGEN/MISC/84/2, Rome.
FAO (1990), The Major Significance of "Minor" Forest Products. The local use and value of forests in the West African Humid Zone. Community Forestry Note No. 6 Rome.
FAO (1991), Sustainable Management of Tropical Forests. Anex F. In rep. Committee on Forest Development in the Tropics. Tenth Sessions, 10-13. December. 1991, Rome.
FAO (1993a) Conservation of genetic resources in tropical forest management: Principles and Concepts. FAO, Forestry Paper No. 107, Rome.
FAO (1993), The challenge of sustainable forest management: What future for the Worlds' forest? Rome.
FAO (1995), Forest Resources Assessment 1990: Global Systems. FAO Forestry Paper. Food and Agricultural Regeneration of the United Nations, Rome.
FAO (1996), Forestry Resources, Assessment 1990, FAO, Rome.
FAO (1996), Sydney of tropical forest cover and Study of chąnge process. FAO Forestry Paper 130 Rome, FAO.
FAO (1997), State of World's Forest, 1997 Rome.
FAO (1997), State of Worlds Forests 1997 Rome, FAO.
FAO (1998), State of World's Forests, 1997, Rome.
FAO (1999), State of World's Forests, (1999), Rome.
FAO (2000), FAO Strategic plans for Forestry Resources.
FAO (2001), State of World's Forests, (1999), Rome.
FAO (2002), State of World's Forests (2001), Rome.
FAO (1987), (annual) Production Year Book FAO, Rome.
FAO, (1966) Wood: World Trends and Prospects. *Unasylva*, 20; 1-135.
Finnis Forest Research Institute, 1996; FAO, 1998.
Flavin Chris, Rennor Michael, Sheehan Molly O (2000) Resources on Real Audio Clips from the May 25th 2000 Press Conference (in the net access: Website World Watch Institute)
Forest Research Institute, Dehradun (1972), GOI, 100 years of Indian Forestry (Volume I & II).
Forest Resource Assessment (Global) (2000), FAO, Rome.
Forest Survey of India. (1999) State of Forest Report - (1999). Ministry of Environment and Forest. Dehradun.
Gale, R. P. and Cordray, S.M. (1991). What should forests sustain? Eight answers. *Journal of Forestry* 89(5), 31-36.

Gandhi, M.K. (1927), *An Autobiography or the story of my experiments with truth*, Navjivan Publishing House, Ahemedabad, India.

Glaeser, B. and Vyasulu, 1984. The obsolescence of Eco-Development: Concepts, Projects, Strategy, B-Glaeser.ed.Oxford: Programme Press pp., 22-36.

Goodland, R. (1995), The Concept of Environmental Sustainability, *Annual Revision of Ecological Systems*, 1995:26:1-24.

Goodlands, Robert, Asibey, E.O., Post J.C. and Dyson, N.D. (1990). *Tropical Moist Forest Management: The urgent transition to Sustainability.* Washington, DC: World Bank.

Government of India (GOI) (1984) Conservation of Biological Diversity in India. An Appraisal. Ministry of Environment and Forests. p.13.

Gow, D.D. (1998), Development Anthropology in quest of practical vision. *Development Anthropology Network*, 6(2): 13-17.

Grandin, Barbara. (1988). *Wealth ranking in small holders' communities: A field manual.* Intermediate Technology Publications, London.

Griffin, Ricky (1990). *Management.* 3rd Edition. Houghton Mifflin Company, Boston.

Gupta, Tirath and Guleri, Amar. (1982). Potential Production of Minor Forest produce—An overview. *Indian Forester*. Vol. 94(1).

Hamilton, A.C., (1984). *Deforestation in Uganda.* Oxford University Press. Nairobi.

Hardin, G. (1991). Paramount positions in ecological economics, in R. Constanza (ed) *Ecological Economics: The Science and Management of Sustainability*. New York: Columbia.

Heuveldop, J. (1994), Assessment of sustainable tropical forest management. Mitteilungen der Bundesforschungsanstalt fur Forst- und Holzwirtschaft, Hamburg, No.178

Holdgate Martin, Giovannini Bernard (1994). Biodiversity Conservation: Foundation for the 21st Centuary: Widening perspective on Biodiversity. IUCN and The International Academy of the Environment, Geneva.

Holt, David (1990), *Management Principles and Practices*, 22nd Ed. (Englewood Cliffs, N J.: Prentice Halls, 1990).

Hummel, F.C. (ed) (1984), Forest Policy: A Contribution to Resource Development, Martinus Nijhoft/Dr. W. Junk, The Hague.

IFF (1999), Role of planted forests in sustainable forest management. Report of the International expert consolation sponsored by the Governments of Chile, Denmark, India, New Zealand and Portugal. Secretariat. IFF division of Sustainable Development, United Nations, New York.

IFF (1999), Role of planted forests in sustainable forest management. Report of the international expert consolation sponsored by the Governments of Chile, Denmark, India, New Zealand and Portugal. Secretariat. IFF Division of Sustainable Development, United Nations, New York.

International Tropical Timber Organization (ITTO) (1998), Criteria and Indicators for Sustainable Forest Management of Natural Tropical Forests. Yokahama. Japan.

ITTO (1992), Criteria for the measurement of sustainable tropical forest management. Policy Development series No.3, ITTO, Yokohama. Japan.

IUCN *et al.* (1990), Conserving the world's Biodiversity. IUCN/ WRI/CI/ WWF-US/ World Bank.

IUCN with UNEP and WWF (1980), World Conversation Strategy.Gland: IUCN.

IUCN, UNEP, WWF (1991), Caring for the earth, a strategy for Sustainable Living, Earth Scan; London.

Jacob M. (1991), The tropical rain forest. pp. 12; 256 – 258. Berlin-Heidelbury. Germany.

Jain, S.K. (1994), Some perspectives in study and conservation Keynote address, Regional Consultations on Convention on Biological Diversity, 19-20 Jan., Regional Office Ministry of Environment and Forests, Lucknow.

Janzen, D.H. (1975). *Ecology of plants in the tropics*. Arnold Press. London.

Johns, A.D. (1992), Species Conservation in Managed Tropical Forests, In *Tropical Deforestation and species extinction*, Edited by T.C. Whitmore and J.A. Sayer, pp. 50-54. Chapman and Hall, London.

Jones, G.(1979), *Vegetation Productivity,* Longman, London.

Jordan, C.F. (UNESCO) Ed. (1989), An American forests: the structure and function of nutrient stressed systems and the impact of Slash-and-burn agriculture. In man and the Biosphere Series Vol. 2, Carnforth, UK The Parthenon Publicity Group.

Joshi, S (1999). *Times of India* (07-11-99), New Delhi.

Kemp, R.H. (1992). The Conservation of Genetic Resources in Managed Tropical Forests. *Unalsylva*. U3 (169): 34-40.

Khanna, L.S. and Ram Prakash (1979). *Principles and Practice of Silviculture.* Khanna Bandhu. Dehradun.

Khoso, T.N. (1995), *Mahatma Gandhi, An Apostle of Applied Human Ecology*, Tata Energy Research Institute, New Delhi.

King, K.F.S. (1975), It is Time to make Papers in the Tropics, *Unasylva* 109: 2-5.

Kirkby John; Keefe O' Phill; Timberlake Lloyd; (1995), *Sustainable Development*, Earth Scan Publication, London.

Kiss, A.C. (1983), Selected Multilateral Treaties in the field of Environment. UNEP.

Koontz, Harold and Weihrich, Heinz; (1998), *Essentials of Management*, Tata McGraw-Hill Publishing Company Ltd, New-Delhi.

Kotwal, P.C. and Benerje, Sujoy (1998); Biodiversity Conservation in Managed forests and protected areas; Agro-botanica, Bikaner, Rajasthan.

Kulshrestha, S.L. (1993), World Water Resources and Regional Vulnerability: Impact of Future changes, Luxembough: HASA, RR-93-10.

Kuznets, S. (1955) Economic Growth and Income Inequality, *American Economic Review*, XLV (1) March: 1-24.

Kuznets, S. (1965), *Economic growth and structure*: *Selected Essays*, London: Heinemann Educ. Books Ltd.

Lal, J.B. (1989), *India's forests: Myth and Reality*; Natraj Publication; Dehradun.

Lal, J.B. (1992), *Forest Ecology*, Natraj Publishers, Dehradun.

Lamb, D. Unesco (1990), Exploiting the tropical Rainforests. *Man and the Biosphere,* Series Vol. 3 Carnfarth UK, The Parthenon Publishing Press.

Lanly, J.P. (1982), Tropical Forest Resources, FAO Forestry Paper 30. Rome.

Lanly, J.P. (1985), Defining and measuring shifting cultivation, *Unasylva*, 37 (147), 17-21.

Leith, H. (1975), Primary Production of the Major Vegetation Units of the World, In Leith, H. and Whittaker, R. H. (eds), *Primary Productivity of the Biosphere*, Springer Verlag, New York, pp. 202-15.

Leslie, A.J. (1996), Sustainable Management of tropical most forest for wood. Reading in sustainable forest management, FAO Forestry Paper No. 122, FAO, Rome.

Mackinon John; Cathey, Child G. and Thorseli J. (1986). Managing Protected Areas in the Tropics. IUCN.

Maini (1991) Modinos, M. and Tsekouras G., (1987) *Forestry: Greece European Environmental Yearbook*, Doctor, London, p. 262.

Maini, J.S. (1989), Sustainable Development and the Canadian Forest Sector. Dissuasion Paper printed to the Canadian Council of Forestry Ministers on 6 October 1989 at Niagara Falls Forestry Canada, Ottawa.

Maini, J.S. (1991), Guiding Principles towards a global concerns for the conservation and sustainable development of all types of forests worldwide, Ottawa, Forestry Canada.

Margalef, Raman (1968), *Perspectives in Ecological Theory*. University of Chicago Press. Chicago. 112 pp.

Mather, Alexender S. (1990), *Global Forest Resources*. Belhaven Press. 25 Floral Street. London.

Mathews, A.S. (1990), *Global Forests Resources*, Belhaven Press London.

Mathews, J.D. (1989), *Silvicultural Systems*, Clarendon Press, Oxford.

Mathews, E. (1983), Global Vegetation and land use: New high resolution database for climatic studies *Journal of Climatic and Applied Metrology*, 22: 474-87.

Mathur, V.P., (1981), *Forest Management*. Jugal Kishore and Company, Dehradun.

Messerli B. & Ives J.D., eds, (1997). *Mounts of the World. A Global Priority*, New York, NY USA, Parthenon Publishing Groups, Inc.

Mikesell, Raymond, F. (1992), Economic Development and the Environment: A comparison of sustainable development with Conventional Development Economics. Mansell Publishing Limited. New York. (USA).

Miller D. and Rose R. (1985), Changes in the garden land base and the consequences for the future of forestry, in Sego, R.A. (ed.) *Environment in Forestry Resources, and use and public policy*, Westview, Boulder, pp. 73-119.

Miller D. and Rose, R. (1985), Changes in the urban land base and the consequences for the future of forestry in Sedjo, R.A. (ed) *Investments in Forestry Resources land use and public policy*. Westview, Boulder, pp.73-119.

Ministry of Environment and Forest (MOEF) (1994). Conservation of Biological Diversity in India. An Approach. Government of India. New Delhi.

Ministry of Environment and Forests, (MOEF) (1992). Government of India; National Conservation Strategy and Policy Statement on Environment and Development (NCSPED), New Delhi.

Mukerjee Amitava & Agnihotri, V.K. (1993), *Environment and Development; Views from the East and West*, Concept Publishing Company, New Delhi.

Mukherjee, Neela (1993). *Participatory Rural Appraisal. Methodology and Application*. Concept Publishing Company, New Delhi.

Mukherjee, Neela (1997). *Participatory Appraisal of Natural Resources*. Concept Publishing Company, New Delhi.

Myers, N. (1988). "Threatened Biota: Hot-spots' in Tropical Forests." *The Environmentalists*, Volume 8: 187-208.

Myers, N. (1990). 'The Biodiversity Challenge: Expanded Hot-spots analyses. *The Environmentalists*, Volume. 10 243-256.

Myers, N., (1981), The hamburger connection; how central America's forests become North America's Hamburgers, *Annie*, 10: 3-8.

Noss, R.F. (1990), 'Indicators for monitoring Biodiversity: A Hierarchical Approach.' *Conservation Biology,* Vol. 4:355-364.

Odum, Eugene, P. (1971), *Fundamentals of Ecology*. (Third edition). W.B Saunders Company USA.

Odum, Eugene, P. (1996), *Fundamentals of Ecology*; Natraj Publication, Dehradun.

Odum, Howard T; Cantlon, J.E.; Kornicker, L.S. (1960). An organizational hierarchy postulate for the interpretation of species individuals distribution, species entropy and ecosystem evolution and the meaning of a species variety index. *Ecology*, 41: 395-399.

OECD (1975), The Polluter Pay Principles—Definition, Analyzed, Implemented. Pairs. OECD (Organization for Economic Cooperation and Development).

OECD (1975), The Polluter Pay's Principle—Definitions, Analysis, Implementation: Paris, OECD (Organization for Economic Cooperation and Development).

OECD (1975), The Polluter Pays Principle—Definition, Analysis, Implementation, Paris. OECD (Organization for Economic Cooperation and Development).

OECD (Organization for Economic Cooperation and Development). (1975) The Polluter Pays Principle—Definitions, Analysis, Implementation, Paris.

Opschoor, J.B. (1992), Sustainable Development—The Economic Process and Economic Analysis' in Opschoor, J.B. Ed, *Environment, Economy and Sustainable Development*. Wolters Noardhoft, Groningin.

Ossting, H.J. (1958). *The Study of Plant Communities*. W.H Freeman & and Co, San Francisco, Oxford University Press.

Ozemoy, V.M., Smith, D.R. and Sicharman, A. (1981). Evaluating computerized geographic information systems using decision analysis. *Interfaces* 11: 92-8.

Pabla, H.S; Pandey, Sanjeeva; Badola, Ruchi. (1995) *Guidelines for ecodevelopment planning*. Wildlife Institute of India.

Pachuri, R.K. *et al.* (1998), *Green India 2047*, Paterson, SS (1956), The Forest Area of the world and its potential productivity, Regal University of Gothenburg.

Packham J.R., Harding D.J.L., Hilton G.M. and Stuttard R.A. (1992), *Functional Ecology of woodlands and forests,* Chapman and Hall, London.

Panwar, H.S. (1992), Eco-development: An Integrated Approach to sustainable development for people and Protected Areas in India. Paper presented in the IV World Congress on National Parks and Protected Areas. Carcus. Venezuela.

Pant, M.M. (1977), Sustained Yield—Some Views, *Indian Forester*, Vol. 103/3; Dehradun.

Parikh, J. *et al.* (1991), *Consumption Patterns: the driving force of Environmental Stress*, Bombay, Indira Gandhi Institute of Development Research.

Parker, H.D. (1988), The Unique qualities of a Geographical Information System: A Commentary: Photogrametric Engineering and Remote sensing 54(ii): 1547-49. Part I, Empire Forestry Association, London.

Paul R. Ehrlich, Anne H. Ehrlich and John P. Hodren (1977), Eco-science: Population, Resources Environment (W.H. Freeman, Sanfransisco), World Resource Institute and International Institute for Environment and Development, World Resources 1986 (Basic Books, New York, 1986) p. 5.

Persson, R. (1974), World Forest Resources in the Early 1970s. Research note 17, Royal College of Forestry, Stockholm.

Phillips, E.A. (1959), *Methods of Vegetational Study*. Henry Holt & Co. Inc.

Piearce, G.D., (1986), How to save the Zambezi teak forests, *Unasylva* 38 (152): 29-36/Allan N.J.R., 1987 Impact of Afghan refugees in the vegetation resources of Pakistan's Hindukush-Himalaya, Mountain Research and Development 7:200-4.

Poore D. & Sayer J. (1991), The Management of Tropical Moist Forests Lands: Ecological Guidelines. 2nd ed. Gland, Switzerland, IUCN.

Poore, D. (1993), Criteria for sustainable development for forests. *CSCE Technical Bulletin* No. 1, 71-84.

Prakash, Ram, and Khanna, L.S. (1979), Theory and Practice of Silvicultural Systems, Periodical Expert Book Agency, Delhi.

Price, M.F. (1998), Mountains: Globally important ecosystems, *Unasylva*, 49 (195): 3-12.

Rao, P.K. (2000), *Sustainable Development, Economics and Policy*, Blackwell Publishers Inc. USA.

Rapport, D.J.; Regier, H.A. & Huchinson, T.C. (1985), Eco-system behaviour under stress, *Am Nat*, 125: 429-433.

Raunikiar, C. (1934), The life forms of plants and statistical Geography. Clarendon Press. Oxford.Reference Series 3. Nairobi: United Nations Environment Programme.

Reed, D. (1995), *Edited Structural Adjustment, the environment and sustainable Development,* Earth Scan Publication Ltd., London.

Reid, V. Walter; McNeelay, Jeffrey, A. Tunstall, Daniel, B; Bryant, A. Dirk; Winograd, Manuel. (1993) *Biodiversity Indicators for Policy Makers*. WRI. New York.

Reid, David (1995), *Sustainable development: An Introductory Guide.* Earth Scan publication Ltd., London.

Richards, J.F. (1986), World Environment Forestry and Economic Development, in Clark W.C. and Munn, R.E. (eds.) *Sustainable Development of the Biosphere*, Cambridge University Press, Cambridge, pp. 53-71.

Rostow, W.W. (1956), The Take off into Self-sustained Growth'. *E J*, 66: 25-48.

Sach I. (1979), Gleaser and Vyasulu (1984), Eco-development A Defination *Ambio* 8(2/23)113.

Sagreiya, K.P. (1967), *Forest and Forestry*. National Book Trust. India, New Delhi.

Saleth, M. (1994), Sustainable Livelihood Security Index in M.S. Swaminathan (ed). *Eco-technology and Rural Employment. A dialogue*. Madras. Macmillan.

Sandler T (1997), *Global challenges: An approach to Environmental, Political and Economic problems*, Cambridge University Press, Cambridge.

Sandnes, Hilde (1993), Calculated Budgets for Airborne Acidifying Components in Europe, 1985,1987,1989,1990,1991, and 1992, EMEP/ MSC-W Report 1/93 (Oslo: Norske Meterologiske Institute).

Sawarkar, V.B. (1995). A Manual for planning wildlife planning in the protected areas and managed forests. Wildlife Institute of India, Dehradun.

Sawarkar, V.B. (1995), A manual for planning wildlife management in protected area and managed forests. Wildlife Institute of India.

Shagriya, K.P. (1967), *Forest and Forestry*; National Book Trust, New Delhi.

Shannon, C.E. and Weaver, W. (1963). *The Mathematics Theory of Communication*. University of Illinois Press, Urbana, p. 117.

Sharma Narendra P. (ed) (1992), Managing the worlds forests; Looking for balance between conservation and development; Kendel/Hunt Publishing Company, USA.

Simberloff, D. (1986), 'Are we in the verge of a Mass Extinction', ed. D. K. Elliot, pp. 165-180, New York, NY: John Wiley and Sons.

Simmons, I.G. (1997), *Humanity and Environment: A Cultural Ecology*. Addisson Weslay Longman Ltd. England.

Simpson, E.H. (1934), Measurement of Diversity. *Nature*, 163-688.

Smith, D.M. (1986), The Practice of Silviculture 8th Edition John Wiley and Sons, New York.

Smith, T.R., Menon, S., Star, J.L. and Estes, J.E. (1987), Requirement and principles for the implementation and constructions of large-scale geographical information systems. *International Journal of Geographical information systems* 1: 13-31.

Spellerberg, Ian F. (1992): Evaluation and Assessment for Conservation, Ecological guidelines for determining priorities for nature conservation. Chaplen and Hall, London

Spurr, S.H. and Vaux, H.J. (1976), Timber, Biological and Economic Potential *Science*, 191: 752-6.

Stebbing, E.P. (1921), *The Forest of India*, London.

Sutton, W.R.J. (1975), Forest Resources of the USSR: Their Exploitation and Potential, *Commonwealth Forestry Review*, 54: 110-38.

Taylor, Frederick (1911), *The Principles of Scientific Management*, New York: Harper.

Thomas, C. (1992), *The Environment in International Relation*. London: Royal Institute of International Affairs.

Tinbergen, J. (1965), The Edition 1967, *Economic Policy Principles and Design*. North Holland, Amsterdam.

Trevor, C.G. and Smithies, E.A. (1923). *Practical Forest Management*. Government Press, U.P.

Ullstin, O. (1991) Keynote Speech in D. Hewlett & C. Sargent eds. Prac. Tech. Workshops to Explore options for Forestry Management, Bangkok. Office of the National Environment Board, Ministry of Science, Technology and Energy.

UNDP (1994), United Nations Development Programme 1994, Human Development Report1994, New York, Oxford University Press.

UNDP (1995), Human Development Report 1995 Oxford: Oxford University Press.

UNDP (1995), Human Development Report 1995, Oxford: Oxford University Press.

UNECE/FAO. (1985), The Forest Resources of ECE Region, ECE/FAO, Geneva.

UNEP (1991), Register of International Treaties and Other Arrangement In The Field Of Environment. Nairobi: United Nations Environment Programme.UNEP/GC16/Inf.4

United Nations (1993), Report of the United Nations Conference of Environment and Development, Rio de Janirio, 3-14 June 1992 Vol.1, New York: United Nations.

United Nations Population Fund (1994), The state of World Population 1994: Choices and Responsibilities (New York: UN Population Fund).

United Nations. (1993), Report of the United Nations Conference on Environment and Development, Rio de Janeiro, 3-14, June 1992 volume 1, New York; United Nations.

Upton C. and Bass S. (1995), *The Forest Certification Handbook.* Earth Scan Publication, London.

Wackernagel Mathis and Ress Willium (1996), Our ecological footprint; reducing human impact on the earth; New Society Publishers, Canada.

WCED (World Commission on Environment and Development – The Brundtland Commission.) (1987). Our Common Future. Report of the WCED, Oxford. Oxford University Press.

WCMC/IUCN/WWF, World Conservation Monitoring Center/IUCN – The World Conservation Union / World Wide Fund for Nature, 1998.

Westboy, J. (1989), Introduction to World forestry, Basil Blackwell, Oxford.

Wickens, G.E. (1994), Sustainable management for non-wood forest products in the tropics and sub-tropics. Research in sustainable forest management, FAO Forestry paper No. 122 Rome.

Wickramanauake, Ebel. (1994), How to check the feasibility of projects. Bangkok: Asian Institute of Technology.

William, M. (1989b), Deforestation: past and present paragon in *Human Geography*, 13: 176-208.

William, M. (1989), American forestry and historical geography. Cambridge University Press Cambridge and New York.

Wittaker, R.H. (1965), Dominance and Diversity in land Plant communities. *Science*, 147: 250-260.

Woodwell, G.M. (1970), *Effect of Pollution on the Structure and Physiology of ecosystems science*, 168: 429-433.

World Bank (1992), Development and the Environment: World Development Report 1992 Oxford/New York: Oxford University Press, p. 308.

World Bank, (1998), No Forest without Management, Paper issued by consultation arranged by the World Bank, 2-7 October, 1998 at Graves Mountain Lodge, Suriya, Virginia, USA.

World Bank, World Development Indicators 2000 (Washington DC: 2000) 10-12.

World Commission on Forests and Sustainable Development (WCFSD) (1999), Our Forests Our Future: Cambridge University Press.

World Commissions on Environment and Development (WCED) (1987), Our common future, London: Oxford University Press.

World Health Organization (1999), Annual Report: Washington.

World Resources Institute (1994), World Resources 1992-95 (New York: Oxford University Press).

World Resources, 1990-91, Water V. Reid and Kenton R. Miller keeping option alive (World Resources Institute, Washington DC, 1989)

World Watch Institute (1997), Alens Realeas, 23rd April 1997, Washington DC, World Watch Institute.

World Watch Institute (1999), New releases: April –1999, Washington DC Woodwel (1970).

World Watch Institute (2001), State of the World – 2001, USA.

WRI (1986), World resources 1986, Basic Books, New York.

WRI (1992), World Resources, 1992-93.

WRI (1994), World Resources, 1994: A report by the World Resource Institute, Oxford.

WRI (1995), World Resources, 1994-95: A report by the World Resource Institute, Oxford.

WRI (1996), World Resources, 1996-97: A Guide to the Global Environment, Oxford: Oxford University Press.

Index